Contents

COMMITTED TO MEMORY

To Mark —
Thanks for all your
encouragement and
support.
Wear the yellow
star with pride!

— Dovid

OREN BARUCH STIER

Committed to Memory

CULTURAL MEDIATIONS OF
THE HOLOCAUST

University of Massachusetts Press
AMHERST AND BOSTON

LC 2003005062
ISBN 978-1-55849-795-5

Designed by Dennis Anderson
Set in Trump Mediaeval by Graphic Composition, Inc.
Printed and bound by The Maple-Vail Book Manufacturing Group

Library of Congress Cataloging-in-Publication Data

Stier, Oren Baruch, 1966–
Committed to memory : cultural mediations of the Holocaust /
Oren Baruch Stier.— 1st ed.
p. cm.
ISBN 1-55849-408-1 (Cloth : alk. paper)
1. Holocaust, Jewish (1939–1945)—Influence. 2. Memory.
3. Holocaust, Jewish (1939–1945)—Historiography.
4. Holocaust, Jewish (1939–1945), in literature.
5. Holocaust, Jewish (1939–1945), in motion pictures. 6. Holocaust memorials.
I. Title.
D804.3 .S79 2003
940.53'18—dc21
2003005062

British Library Cataloguing in Publication data are available.

This book is published with the assistance of a generous grant from the
Lucius N. Littauer Foundation.

TO ALL MY TEACHERS

We feast to keep our promise of never again.

—MICHEAL O'SIADHAIL, "Never"

Illustrations

Preface

IN THIS BOOK I look at the ways the Holocaust is remembered through some of the media employed in and committed to its remembrance. The manner in which the Holocaust has been committed to memory is tangled up with the commitment and dedication of a variety of individuals, groups, and institutions to that memory. Although I take issue with some of the modes and methods of this memorialization process—and some of those individuals and institutions may certainly disagree with my assessments—I want to be clear about my own commitment to Holocaust memory. Indeed, my fascination with this material has long been fueled by an interest in the importance of remembering and commemorating the Holocaust. My interest has been marked by a desire for a critically informed public memory of the Holocaust, one that nonetheless remains sensitive to the power and reality of the mythic and mystic forces undergirding that remembrance. That interest parallels the dedication of those countless individuals—survivors and others—who are themselves absolutely committed to furthering the memorial quest. I hold them all in high regard, and I respect their commitment. Every institution discussed in these pages is one of great integrity; nothing I say in this book should be construed to mean otherwise. And yet, because the Holocaust is a sacred reality and because its memory is concomitantly volatile, the close and critical analyses that I pursue here may ruffle some feathers. This is good. For although an unexamined memory may feel more comfortable to many of the committed, only an examined one can and will continue to develop. As Holocaust memory moves into the twenty-first century, as the commitments it engenders become the possessions and responsibilities of new generations unconnected through life experience to the events of World War II, it is imperative that the mechanisms and media of such memory and such commitment be clearly understood.

This book has evolved over several years. For early support and guidance I am grateful to Richard Hecht, W. Richard Comstock, Sidra DeKoven Ezrahi, Roger Friedland, and Charles H. Long. As I worked on early drafts of the manuscript, I was greatly assisted by the opportunities to present various parts of the work in progress at scholarly gatherings. These include national meetings of the American Academy of Religion and Association for Jewish Studies, as well as the Conference on Media,

Religion, and Culture; the Judaism and Postmodern Culture Colloquium at the Berman Center for Jewish Studies at Lehigh University; and the Remembering for the Future 2000 international conference at Oxford. In addition, I offer warm thanks to the colleagues who invited me to present papers at more select gatherings: Erin Addison at Hollins College and Laurence Silberstein at Lehigh University. In all these cases, I benefited from the lively atmosphere of scholarly exchange and mutual interest. I am also grateful for the support of my colleagues at the University of Cape Town (UCT) and at Florida International University, and I thank the members of my UCT postgraduate seminar, "Representing the Holocaust: A Multimedia Inquiry," with whom I tested many of the ideas contained herein.

The research and fieldwork for this book could not have been completed without the access granted me by the following institutions and organizations and the frank and open exchange of information and ideas offered me by many individuals associated with the institutions at the time: the Florida Holocaust Museum: Noreen Brand and Steve Goldman; the Fortunoff Video Archive for Holocaust Testimonies at Yale University: Geoffrey Hartman, Dori Laub, and Joanne Rudof; the Survivors of the Shoah Visual History Foundation: Michael Berenbaum, Matthew Chuck, Lisa Goodgame, Janet Keller, Daisy Miller, Michael Nutkiewicz, and Ari Zev; the United States Holocaust Memorial Museum: Stephen Luckert; the Simon Wiesenthal Center's Beit Hashoah-Museum of Tolerance: Abraham Cooper, Michele Eisman, Janet Garfinkle, Liebe Geft, Paul Hamburg, Gerald Margolis, Elana Samuels, and Avra Shapiro; and the March of the Living: Michael Berl, Miles Bunder, Gene Greenzweig, and Zwi Weiss. I also acknowledge, with deepest respect, the survivors and those who perished, whose memories and stories have, regrettably, made this book possible.

Through the long period of this book's evolution I received advice and support from many friends and colleagues who read parts of the manuscript, responded to my queries, offered intellectual or psychological encouragement, and all the possible permutations of these. I thank the following people: Jonathan Boyarin, David Chidester, Shifra Epstein, Shoshanah Feher, Jackie Feldman, Lisa Firer, Michelle Friedman, Heidi Grunebaum, Shelley Hornstein, Gary Laderman, Laura Levitt, Deborah Malmud, Michael Nutkiewicz, Miriam Peskowitz, Daniel Schwartz, Naomi Seidman, Arthur and Barbara Seltzer, Jeffrey Shandler, Larry Silberstein, and others whose names I cannot recall; I remain grateful to them all nonetheless.

Many thanks as well to the colleagues and friends who devoted time and effort to reading and commenting on the final drafts of the entire manuscript: Edward T. Linenthal and Sara R. Horowitz for the press; Richard Hecht; Michael Berenbaum; and my father-in-law, Jonathan Weiss.

The manuscript was completed with the assistance of a Provost's Summer Research Grant from Florida International University (FIU), for which I am grateful. Preparation of the figures was supported by a grant from FIU's College of Arts and Sciences Office of Research and facilitated by Blanca Perez and George Valcarce of FIU's Instructional Photography and Graphics department. I thank Curt Millay and Leslie Swift at the United States Holocaust Memorial Museum Photo Archives and Marcial Laviña at the Museum of Tolerance for their generous assistance in locating and securing photographs used as illustrations in this volume. I am especially grateful to James E. Young, not only for reading the entire manuscript and offering feedback and encouragement but also for steering me toward the University of Massachusetts Press. I am thankful as well for Nancy J. Raynor's expert copyediting and managing editor Carol Betsch's careful attention to the manuscript's preparation for publication, and especially for the support of the press's director and mensch, Bruce Wilcox: working with him has been a happy privilege.

Many thanks to my extended family, my in-laws, Wahoos everywhere, and the Young Israel of Miami Beach congregation. A special word of thanks to my parents, Jochanan and Rina Stier, who have waited a long time for this moment and who have encouraged me every step of the way. They were my first teachers, and I hope they see their own efforts and influence reflected in these pages. And to my wife, life partner, and best friend, Danielle Dvora, I offer an endless supply of gratitude; without her unflagging support and confidence in my work, this book could not have been completed.

Figure 6 is from *Maus: A Survivor's Tale: My Father Bleeds History* by Art Spiegelman, copyright © 1973, 1980, 1981, 1982, 1984, 1985, 1986 by Art Spiegelman. Used by permission of Pantheon Books, a division of Random House, Inc.

Figure 7 is from *Maus II: A Survivor's Tale: And Here My Troubles Began* by Art Spiegelman, copyright © 1986, 1989, 1990, 1991 by Art Spiegelman. Used by permission of Pantheon Books, a division of Random House, Inc.

A revised and condensed version of chapter 2 of this book will be published in *Impossible Images: Contemporary Art after the Holocaust,* edited by Shelley Hornstein, Laura Levitt, and Laurence J. Silberstein, published by New York University Press.

Chapter 3 is a revised and expanded version of "Framing the Witness: The Memorial Role of Holocaust Videotestimonies," in *Memory,* vol. 3 of *Remembering for the Future: The Holocaust in an Age of Genocide,* edited by John K. Roth and Elisabeth Maxwell (London: Palgrave, 2001). Reprinted with permission of Palgrave Macmillan.

An earlier version of part of chapter 4 was published as "Virtual Memories: Mediating the Holocaust at the Simon Wiesenthal Center's Beit Hashoah-Museum of Tolerance," *Journal of the American Academy of Religion* 64, no. 4 (1996): 831–51. Used by permission of Oxford University Press.

An earlier version of part of chapter 5 was published as "Lunch at Majdanek: The March of the Living as a Contemporary Pilgrimage of Memory," *Pilgrimage,* edited by Shifra Epstein, special issue of *Jewish Folklore and Ethnology Review* 17, nos. 1–2 (1995): 57–66. Copyright © 1995 Jewish Folklore and Ethnology Section of the American Folklore Society. Used with permission.

COMMITTED TO MEMORY

CHAPTER ONE

Remembering Memory

CULTURE, TRADITION, AND
THE MEMORY PROBLEM

History is not the past, but a map of the past drawn from a particular point of view to be useful to the modern traveler. . . . Reality is not in the present but between the past and the future.

—HENRY GLASSIE, *Passing the Time in Ballymenone:*
Culture and History of an Ulster Community

The historical cogito is a cogito whose horizon and intentionality may be defined as memory—a mode of perception that anchors our life in prereflective experience. It is this horizon and its intentionality which has been overlooked by those who portray the subject as an ego isolated in contemporaneity.

—CHARLES H. LONG, *Significations: Signs, Symbols, and*
Images in the Interpretation of Religion

DESIRING MEMORY

MEMORY MATTERS. Turn on the television, open a newspaper or magazine, and you will likely find, before too long, some mention of the impact the past has made and continues to make on the present. And, even though the events of World War II have long passed their jubilee anniversary, it is likely that the mention of memory one finds in the contemporary media relates in some way to those events. In many cases, they relate specifically to the Holocaust. So Holocaust memory matters. It matters to an ever diverse array of groups and individuals for whom it functions as reference point. It matters to the generation that was "there": survivors, liberators, perpetrators, bystanders. It matters to generations who were not there: children of survivors and others who had direct contact with and involvement in the events of the Holocaust, others who trace their relationship to the past through communal and religious identification, and those for whom the Holocaust bears no distinct legacy at all, though it matters nonetheless. For all these groups and individuals, Holocaust memory matters because it is made to matter by and through the cultural forms and institutions that mediate the Holocaust in the present day. This book is about those processes of memorial mediation.

The book is therefore about some of the media through which we come to know about the Holocaust. I discuss the ways those media embody and transmit the material of the Holocaust—what matters—for the sake of memory. As such, the ways memory is made to matter intersect with the matter—the material—of memory. Thus I call attention to the constructed nature of memory as a social phenomenon built out of material bequeathed by history. This sets up memory in opposition to history, though that opposition should not be construed as polar or particularly rigid. Simplistically, history is concerned with events in the past and their meaning *for* the present, while memory involves the impact of the events of the past and their meaning *in* the present—the ways the past becomes a present reality, how it is made to matter. Let me add another gross simplification: history is what we need, memory is what we desire.

The desire for memory comes in a variety of forms. In some cases, it is an intensely personal quest for narrative, for the ability to tell a story and thereby alleviate a burden. This occurs oftentimes when survivors recount their wartime experiences, but it also can be found in the search by survivors' children for their place in the present, a place not always guaranteed by their parents' stories. Another form related to desire is identity. Identity is a concern not only of the second generation but also for anyone who seeks to establish a claim to memory as an inheritance, as a legacy. Identity relates to the issue of embodiment: memory as desire is embodied by the people desiring it and the media designed to encompass and transmit it. Memory also takes the form of myth, understood as a sacred narrative that authorizes identity in the present, and of ritual, understood as sacred behavior that similarly authorizes one's connection to the past and "tradition." Both myth and ritual, taken as memorial constructs, highlight the religious aspects of the desire for memory. Nostalgia is another form engendered by the desire for memory, a style marked especially by longing for a past one may or may not have had any knowledge of in the first place.[1] Finally, the desire for memory takes the form of art and artifice—the creative construction of a relationship to the past built out of the intensely felt desire for that relationship. Such creativity calls attention to the crucial fact that memory is about the presentation and representation of past events, not the events themselves.

Indeed, representation is a central concern in this book. How is the Holocaust represented, and thereby mediated, in contemporary culture? In considering this issue, we may distinguish between *metonymic* and *metaphoric* styles of representation. Jack Kugelmass, at the conclusion of his analysis of the "icon" of the Hasid in Jewish American folk culture, uses the distinction between the two terms as a fulcrum for the discussion of the Hasid's simultaneous difference from and identity with American Jewry: "Metonymy acts as *pars pro toto*—one part stands for the whole. Metaphor joins together two otherwise discrete domains of experience."[2] For Kugelmass, this invites an assessment of the image of the "other" as both similar to and different from the "self" of the American Jew. Here, the distinction between metaphor and metonymy can highlight the difference between two kinds of Holocaust representation. One, metaphoric representation, turns on the struggle for likeness via comparison in depicting the Holocaust and its effects in the present (the situating of *difference*), and the other, metonymic representation, relies on elements drawn in some way from the Holocaust and the Holocaust's remnants or residues in the present (the situating of *identity*). For example, a child's shoe, rescued from the ashes of the Holocaust, could be the basis for a metonymic representation of the Holocaust (as a part standing in for the whole), while a poem utilizing the image of that shoe to suggest the experience of a child in the Holocaust could be a metaphoric representation linking the two together. While these two styles of representation surely intertwine and interact, in this book I focus on the more metonymic forms of memorial representation. Indeed, because memory is constituted of and by the past, it is more suited to the metonymic than to the metaphoric style.

COLLECTIVE MEMORY

What do I mean by memory? Clearly, I am not talking about individual, personal memory. As the late historian Amos Funkenstein observed in an article in the inaugural issue of the journal *History and Memory*, "Memory can only be realized by an individual who acts, is aware, and remembers. Just as a nation cannot eat or dance, neither can it speak or remember. Remembering is a mental act, and therefore it is absolutely and completely personal."[3] Indeed, "memory," stemming from the Latin *memor*, connotes an individual being "mindful," and it can be traced back to the Sanskrit root *smar-*, "to remember."[4] "Remember" itself stems from *re* plus *memor*, suggesting that the act of remembering is simply the process of being mindful again, of recalling to mind a past event or thing. Thus "memory," the result of an act of remembering, is a wholly individual construct.

Or so we would think. In the 1920s, the French scholar Maurice Halbwachs was probably the first to turn scholarly attention to what he called "collective memory."[5] Halbwachs was particularly concerned with how the past is made known through symbol and ritual in the context of social groups, and argued that all memory, even "individual" memory, is thoroughly social and discursive.[6] Halbwachs's main thesis is simple: "It is in society that people normally acquire their memories. It is also in society that they recall, recognize, and localize their memories." On the individual level, then, people remember only when they think in social frameworks, but those social frameworks themselves are not only the sum, result, or combination of individual recollections of members of the same society but also have a characteristic that leads to the formation of collective memory. "Collective frameworks are . . . precisely the instruments used by the collective memory to reconstruct an image of the past which is in accord . . . with the predominant thoughts of the society." For Halbwachs, the most basic (and stable) of these collective frameworks is language.[7] It is through this conception of language that Halbwachs argues that individual memories are located in "the totality of thoughts common to a group"—whether or not the group is even aware of them—because those memories depend on discourse for their perception, and discourse is already social.[8]

Halbwachs argues that, because all memories therefore depend on the present social milieu, the collective memory of the past is actually a reconstruction of the past in light of the constraints of the present, particularly as enforced by the authority of social institutions. Such institutions coerce members of society to abide by various collective representations. But Halbwachs sees a certain "incongruity in many respects between the constraints of yesterday and those of today, from which it follows that we can only imagine those of the past incompletely and imperfectly."[9] The extreme case of this incongruity is breakdown: if we cannot encompass all the constraints into one coherent framework, the framework of the present predominates, and in the most radical case, the past is forgotten. But usually there is a compromise between the two frameworks of the past and of the present, so that collective memory emerges as a dialectical negotiation between the two.

In a subsequent discussion, Halbwachs turns his attention to "religious collective memory," something of great relevance to my discussion. He largely considers Christianity, "entirely oriented toward the past as is the case with all religion," in order to examine whether religious collective memory is comparable with the general concept of collective memory he develops, that is, whether religion reproduces the past in the context of the present. On a very basic level, Christianity certainly does this in the way it builds on Judaism and its mythology, appropriating and modifying the past. Beyond this, religion, in the eyes of its believers, creates collective memory in its depiction of divine or sacred entities; thus "people have preserved the remembrance of gods or heroes, telling their story and commemorating them in the form of a cult."[10] But a question arises: how can collective memory account for the way Christianity (and religion in general) presents itself as a permanent institution—outside of time, as it were? Religious collective memory, Halbwachs argues, needs to set itself apart from the collective memory of other social frameworks, which feeds off of the continuous existence of the society that supports it. He contends that "soon religious society begins to realize that the groups that it progressively attracts preserve their own interests and their own memory, and that a mass of new remembrances bearing no relation to its own refuses to be located within the frameworks of its thought. It is at this point that religious society retreats and establishes its tradition, that it determines its doctrine and imposes on the laity the authority of a hierarchy of clerics who are no longer simply functionaries and administrators of the Christian community but who constitute instead a closed group separated from the world and entirely turned toward the past, which they are solely occupied with commemorating." This description of the crystallization of tradition is intriguing, because it accounts for the very real way in which religious tradition attempts to ward off change and appear outside of history. Of course, tradition always changes; it is only that religious institutions would have it appear that it does not. Thus, "although religious memory attempts to isolate itself from temporal society, it obeys the same laws as every collective memory: it does not preserve the past but reconstructs it with the aid of the material traces, rites, texts, and traditions left behind by that past, and with the aid moreover of recent psychological and social data, that is to say, with the present."[11]

Halbwachs's conclusions to "The Social Frameworks of Memory" suggest that the kind of dialectical give-and-take described by the relationship between the past and the present in his analyses is duplicated in other pairs such as individual/collective and remembering/forgetting.[12] "We might perhaps be led to distinguish two kinds of activities within social thought: on the one hand a memory, that is, a framework made out of notions that serve as landmarks for us and that refer exclusively to the past; on the other hand a rational activity that takes its point of departure in the conditions in which the society at the moment finds itself, in other words, in the present." For Halbwachs, all these are synthesized in the overarching collective representations of social thought, which consist of collective recollections.[13] These collective representations/recollections thus maintain the presence of collective memory in society, from which one potential criticism of Halbwachs's argument arises. For though he recognizes that this memory is largely made up of trace structures, effacements, and forgetfulness covered up by creative reconstruction—though he admits that the past is never fully present but exists only as those in the present reconstruct it—he is not particularly self-critical about this, unwilling to focus much attention on society's countermemories. Halbwachs's preference for and insistence on memory's presence over its absence invites a deconstructive critique of his overreliance on and reification of that presence. Though such a critique stretches beyond the bounds of this book, some aspects of it will emerge in the following pages, hence the need to bear its more fully developed possibility in mind.

Halbwachs's groundbreaking 1941 study, "The Legendary Topography of the Gospels in the Holy Land," provides an excellent and highly relevant example of an application of Halbwachs's theses concerning the formation and development of collective memory.[14] The essence of his argument is that, over the course of history, different Christian groups have emphasized varying aspects of the life and death of Jesus, which is reflected in the "physiognomy" of the Holy Land itself and in these groups' (varying) collective religious memories. Thus, Halbwachs discusses not only collective memory but also its association with sacred space and the evolving sanctification of space, as well as its dependence more on dogma than on actual testimony. In this way, Halbwachs argues that, at or before the time of the Gospels, the early Christian collective memory was mostly concerned with building on Jewish collective memory, to strengthen its own case. "The Christian collective memory could annex a part of the Jewish collective memory only by appropriating part of the latter's local remembrance while at the same time transforming its entire perspective of historical space." At the same time, Christian memory needed to distinguish itself from Jewish memory, especially where the elements of the Christian drama contradicted Jewish memory. In this way, the new Christian community both transformed and appropriated Jewish traditions and rewrote them by changing their position in time and space.[15]

As time wore on, those distinctive aspects of the Christian faith demanded more attention in the collective memory; thus, Jerusalem as the center of Jesus' Passion was emphasized over the Galilee as the place of his teachings and most of his life. The development of rites commemorating the Passion helped solidify this collective memory. With the conversion of Constantine and the creed formulated at the Council of Nicea, Jerusalem's centrality was confirmed, even though the sites of Jesus's Passion were by now hidden and unknown. "None of them appeared in the visible framework of Jerusalem. But, since the dogma had been formulated in such a way as to imply a site, it was necessary that this site be found." By the time of the Crusaders, the collective memory was so well formulated that Jerusalem, never seen in reality, was the holy city par excellence in their imagination and was rebuilt according to that image. Halbwachs argues that the periods of Constantine and the Crusaders marked two moments when the Christian collective memory was reorganized according to contemporary images and conceptions of the localizations of those memories as well as according to the contemporary needs and aspirations of Christianity. By examining this, Halbwachs posits, we can trace "the course of time. Whatever epoch is examined, attention is not directed toward the first events, or perhaps the origin of these events, but rather toward the group of believers and toward their commemorative work. When one looks at the physiognomy of the holy places in successive times, one finds the character of these groups inscribed."[16] Halbwachs's attention to the inscription of collective memory on the physiognomy of commemorative sites is enormously instructive for my book. Furthermore, as he resists tendencies toward both archaism and nostalgia (understood as more negative memorial forms), we sense the profound relevance of commemoration. He also offers a model for the skillful interweaving of scholarly attention to time and space, myth and history, providing a useful context for analyzing the production of collective memory in any era and for any significant event.

REFINING MEMORY

Halbwachs left a significant intellectual legacy, though it appears he has been rediscovered only more recently in scholarly literature. Many of his recent interpreters attempt to refine his observations and rename or reposition his object of study. For example, James Fentress and Chris Wickham suggest that Halbwachs's investigations resulted in "a concept of collective consciousness curiously disconnected from the actual thought processes of any particular person." Anyone wishing to follow these investigations would, they argue, need to resist the impulse to "render the individual [as] a sort of automaton, passively obeying the interiorized collective will."[17] Fentress and Wickham therefore prefer the term *social memory* over *collective memory* and concern themselves more with active, embodied responses to the mediations of the past in the present. This view represents a critical and relevant revision of Halbwachs's theory.

Amos Funkenstein also reconsiders Halbwachs's research. While Funkenstein agrees that all memory has a social context, he reconfigures the relationship between individual and collective memory to account better for that relationship. Funkenstein suggests, therefore, an analogy based on the linguistic distinction between "language" (*langue*) and "speech" (*parole*): language is the system of symbols and its rules of functioning that are realized in every act of speech, which is always different and thus always changes the language. Collective memory, then, corresponds to "language"—it is the basic system—while individual remembering is like "speech"—the actualization of these symbols.[18] This instructive analogy suggests a relatively stable formal framework within which one can perceive and trace variations of expression. The argument, echoed by Fentress and Wickham, also highlights the tension between the individual and the collective embodiments of memory.

But the notion of collective memory still bothers Funkenstein as a historian, because it does not account for the relationship between collective memory and historiography. To what extent does the historian rely on collective memory? Funkenstein proposes the concept of "historical consciousness" as a "dynamic heuristic construct" to help describe "the degree of creative freedom in the use and interpretation of the contents of collective memory." Historical consciousness differs from collective memory in that its "essence lies not only in the reminder of the past for the purpose of creating collective identity and cohesiveness, but in the attempt to understand the past and to give it meaning." Historical consciousness also becomes the locus of myths and historical fictions for Funkenstein, placing these items at the movable midpoint between memory and history. For Funkenstein, what he calls "Western historical consciousness" becomes a "developed and organized form" of its collective memory.[19] This view is another useful modification of Halbwachs's position.[20]

Peter Novick would disagree with Funkenstein's assessment, preferring a sharper distinction between history and memory. He resists the term *collective memory* because it is an oversimplification, too committed to its own unambiguous version of the past, reducing "events to mythic archetypes." Novick's version of historical consciousness is ultimately concerned with the "*historicity* of events," the difference between then and now. "Memory," he argues "has no sense of the passage of time; it denies the "pastness" of its objects and insists on their continuing presence."[21] I side with Funkenstein: memory does bear within it an appreciation of time and history, and it is certainly concerned with the past's "continuing presence," though it is less concerned with the details of historical research.

Novick's views are more useful where he examines the root analogy at the heart of Halbwachs's thesis:

When we speak of collective memory, we often forget that we're employing a metaphor—an organic metaphor—that makes an analogy between the memory of an individual and that of a community. The metaphor works best when we're speaking of an organic (traditional, stable, homogenous) community in which consciousness, like social reality, changes slowly. When Maurice Halbwachs first advanced the idea of collective memory in the 1920s, the great French medievalist Marc Bloch, who was suspicious of organic metaphors for society, nevertheless thought it might be usefully applied to such things as a peasant grandparent, grandchild on knee, passing on rural traditions. A very organic image. How appropriate the metaphor is for the very inorganic societies of the late twentieth century (fragmented rather than homogenous, rapidly changing rather than stable, the principal modes of communication electronic rather than face to face) seems to me questionable.[22]

Novick has a point, similar to one raised by Pierre Nora in an article about his massive editorial project tracing the contours of French collective memory in the contemporary era. Nora argues that that there "are *lieux de mémoire*, sites of memory, because there are no longer *milieux de mémoire*, real environments of memory."[23] But rather than lament this fact, Nora explores an interest in uncovering the remnants and reconstructions of memory in a wide variety of cultural "sites" that have emerged in the modern age. What is of most interest for me here—and what I find most applicable—is Nora's sensitivity to and insistence on the eruption of memory at points of *discontinuity* with the past. In the contemporary milieu, sites of memory emerge at points of rupture in order to counteract forgetfulness.

In this book I explore such "sites" of memory's construction (though I try not to fall into the trap of nostalgia Nora sometimes slips into). Against Novick, it is my contention that the metaphor of organic memory *is* applicable in this postmodern age. The sites of memory's inscription, framing, mediation, and performance in contemporary society are loci for the transmission of memorial sensibilities, though they may expose a greater degree of appropriation and construction than in more "organic," traditional eras. Indeed, it is particularly in the media of memory, however fragmented, changeable, and electronic they may be, that we can perceive the continuing effects of the past on the present.

Memory, history, and society are therefore entangled, and nowhere is this more evident than in the cultural realm.[24] Because memory must be shared for it to have more than personal relevance, it is the cultural forms that mediate the process of sharing which interest me. As Iwona Irwin-Zarecka argues, making sense of the past "is motivated by our personal experience but facilitated (or impeded) by public offerings, and . . . such public offerings are a mixture of presences and absences. A 'collective memory'—as a set of ideas, images, feelings about the past—is best located not in the minds of individuals, but in the resources they share." She focuses her attention on the "infrastructure" of collective memory, understood as "all the different spaces, objects, 'texts' that make an engagement with the past possible."[25] In this way culture mediates memorial engagement, and "cultural memory" becomes a refinement of "collective memory," exposing the fault lines of agreement and disagreement as they emerge through competing narratives about the meaning of the past. In the case of the production of more recent American memory, for example, Marita Sturken suggests that cultural memory "is a field of contested meanings in which Americans interact with cultural elements to produce concepts of the nation, particularly in events of trauma, where both the structures and the fractures of a culture are exposed."[26] Sturken's definition highlights the prominence of traumatic experience in the continual renegotiation of narratives of nationhood and identity. This idea will be crucial for my considerations of the production of Holocaust memory.

Sturken's attention to cultural memory accentuates the interrelationships between memory and identity as they are refracted in cultural representation and negotiation, resulting in an entanglement of the two concepts. John Gillis points to this entanglement and the resultant reification of its intertwined terms in "Memory and Identity: The History of a Relationship," the introductory essay to his edited collection *Commemorations: The Politics of National Identity:*

The parallel lives of these two terms alert us to the fact that the notion of identity depends on the idea of memory, and vice versa. The core meaning of any individual or group identity, namely, a sense of sameness over time and space, is sustained by remembering; and what is remembered is defined by the assumed identity. That identities and memories change over time tends to be obscured by the fact that we too often refer to both as if they had the status of material objects—memory as something to be retrieved; identity as something that can be lost as well as found. We need to be reminded that memories and identities are not fixed things, but representations or constructions of reality, subjective rather than objective phenomena.[27]

Gillis's attention to the constructedness of memory and identity highlights their culturally relative positions. This relativism might lead some to think that memory is arbitrary and artificial, subject to the passing fancy of impermanent cultural conventions and political expediencies. Such a "postmodern" threat is particularly bothersome to historians, which might explain why many have difficulty with the very idea of cultural or social memory.

But the critics forget Halbwachs's observations regarding the constraints under which memory labors. Yael Zerubavel writes, for example: "In spite of its dynamic character, collective memory is not an entirely fluid knowledge nor is it totally detached from historical memory. . . . Collective memory continuously negotiates between available historical records and current social and political agendas. And in the process of referring back to these records, it shifts its interpretation, selectively emphasizing, suppressing and elaborating different aspects of that record."[28] In this view, memory is constrained by *historical* constructions of the past, while for Irwin-Zarecka, it is *experience* that determines the basis for the construction of memory: "This close connection to experience, whether real or imaginary, bounds collective memory in a number of ways. Certain stories are judged as plausible, others are not. And certain ways of remembering (and forgetting) are seen as appropriate and others as not. A narrative of victimization can serve to bolster group identity or to support political claims, it cannot be the basis for joyous celebration. Yes, we do use the past to various ends, and yes, we often liberally mix facts and fiction, if not inventing altogether. But no, collective memory is not a terrain where anything goes."[29] For both these authors, memory construction is memory negotiation, and the negotiation process depends, as one would expect, on a limited selection of available options, each of which expresses its viability within certain constraints.

This issue of negotiation within constraints leads to the recognition of memory's nature as a kind of representation. The "re-" is pivotal here, for memory is always "after the fact," constructed as the result of some form of narrativization. It is not, as Sturken points out, a "replica of an experience that can be retrieved and relived. . . . What we remember is highly selective, and how we retrieve it says as much about desire and denial as it does about remembrance."[30] Sturken's comments bring me back to the issue of desire, now as it is illuminated by attention to the difference between memory and what is being remembered. The desire for memory here highlights the gap between memory as representation and its referent in history and experience—the gap between signifier and signified.

Memory's representative qualities are also complicated by the acts of mediation that produce memory and the (often reified) matter on which it depends. These both tend to erase the gap between signifier and signified and present memory as more coexistent with the temporal and spatial contexts of the events being remembered. (Indeed, for survivors of the Holocaust, the memory of their trauma is often experienced as cotemporal and cospatial with the trauma itself.) The gap between signifier and signified is also disrupted, in the contemporary scene, by the forms of production of those media of memory. George Lipsitz explains that "time, history, and memory become qualitatively different concepts in a world where electronic mass communication is possible. Instead of relating to the past through a shared sense of place or ancestry, consumers of electronic mass media can experience a common heritage with people they have never seen; they can acquire memories of a past to which they have no geographical or biological connection. This capacity of electronic mass communication to transcend time and space creates instability by disconnecting people from past traditions, but it also liberates people by making the past less determinate of experiences in the present."[31] I will return to the issue of technological mediation below. For now, let me focus on unraveling the tangled skein of memory's presentation and representation in order to understand the "pastness" of memory in its production and reproduction.[32]

PAST PRESENTS

How can collective/cultural/social memory be theorized so as to keep the issues of negotiation and representation in mind? In more recent years, several writers have sought further ways to talk about memory which attend to its constructed nature while also addressing its belatedness. Some of the most important reconsiderations of memory also address the specifics of Holocaust memorialization. James Young, the most influential commentator on the arts of Holocaust memory, has continually assessed both the ways in which memorials represent the past and the ways they interact with the present in the context of what may be called a performance-based understanding of memory. In the preface to *The Texture of Memory,* Young, like others, resists the term "collective memory" in favor of the more social, aggregate, and multiple "'collected memory,' the many discrete memories that are gathered into common memorial spaces and assigned common meaning. . . . If societies remember, it is only insofar as their institutions and rituals organize, shape, even inspire their constituents' memories."[33] Such attention to "collected" rather than "collective" memory not only calls attention to the continually (re)negotiated qualities of memory's construction and embodiment in society but also reminds us of the "pastness" of memory's representation. For "collected" implies interactions and engagements that have *already* occurred—that have already been gathered—so that the resulting memory here is *re*-collected.

Young further refines his understanding of memory's belatedness in *At Memory's Edge* (2000), in which he discusses the vicariousness of memory in the experience of a postwar generation whose knowledge of the Holocaust arises through cultural productions. "It is necessarily mediated experience, the afterlife of memory, represented in history's afterimages: the impressions retained in the mind's eye of a vivid sensation long after the original, external cause has been removed."[34] The processes of mediation cited by Young as critical to contemporary society's sense of the presence of the past are one of the central foci of my book.

Another significant reconsideration of terminology comes from Marianne Hirsch, who coins the term *postmemory* to signify the gap marked by memory as representation:

I propose the term "postmemory" with some hesitation, conscious that the prefix "post" could imply that we are beyond memory and therefore perhaps, as Nora fears, purely in history. In my reading, postmemory is distinguished from memory by generational distance and from history by deep personal connection. Postmemory is a powerful and very particular form of memory precisely because its connection to its object or source is mediated not through recollection but through an imaginative investment and creation. This is not to say that memory itself is unmediated, but that it is more directly connected to the past. Postmemory characterizes the experience of those who grow up dominated by narratives that preceded their birth, whose own belated stories are evacuated by the stories of the previous generation shaped by traumatic events that can be neither understood nor recreated.[35]

Of course, the current generation of postmemorialists *does* continually attempt to understand and re-create the "memory" of the past under whose shadow they labor, and thus, though I applaud the utility of Hirsch's distinction, I find it too neatly separates "authentic" rememberers from less authentic postmemory artists, voyeurs, and tourists. What she would call an act of postmemory does relate to its referents through a form of recollection: that it is a contrived recollection does not take away from its perceived and lived immediacy. Similarly, "real" memory also depends on "imaginative investment and creation," though I do not mean to deny the "real" at the heart of memory. The relationship between post-memory and memory is similar to that between postmodernism and modernism, in that the "post" implies a critique and complication of what it precedes, so that renewed attention is paid to the complications inherent in the term being modified.[36]

The distinctions between these refinements and qualifications of the term *memory* are critical and important to bear in mind. Some memories are collective, some collected. Some are social, some more cultural. Some relate more to actual experiences of past events, and others more to the experience of their mediation in the present. But all memories, at least when expressed outside the mind, are constructed and mediated in some way. Therefore, my choice not to use any one of these nuanced terms in particular in the course of this book is deliberate (and not just avoidance of choosing). For I wish to call attention to the slipperiness of all these distinctions and the mediation present in every kind of memory. As I will discuss in these pages, the desire for memory more often than not crosses boundary lines (whether they be generational or generic) and engenders such a great deal of appropriation and disruption (especially in the temporal and spatial realms) that any sharp distinction made between then and now, there and here, authentic and inauthentic, memory, rememory, and postmemory, detracts from the constructed and mediated nature of memory as a mechanism for representing the impact of the past in the present.

JEWISH MEMORIES

I have not yet addressed the Jewish context for memory and specifically Jewish modes for theorizing it. The seminal work in this area is Yosef Hayim Yerushalmi's *Zakhor: Jewish History and Jewish Memory*, which remains the most comprehensive treatment of this topic. Yerushalmi's attention is unabashedly textual, appropriate for a historian discussing the relationship between Jewish memory and history. Beginning with the biblical period and moving on through each successive period of Jewish history into the modern, Yerushalmi charts a sustained Jewish interest in the meanings of the past first felt in biblical writings as sacred and covenantal. "Only in Israel and nowhere else is the injunction to remember felt as a religious imperative to an entire people. Its reverberations are everywhere, but they reach a crescendo in the Deuteronomic history and in the prophets."[37] Often configured with the reminder against forgetting, biblical remembrance is doubly intensified. Perhaps the best example of this re-

doubled intensification is the following configuration, the memorial injunction regarding the perennial Jewish enemy: "Remember what Amalek
did to you. . . . You shall blot out the memory of Amalek from under
heaven. Do not forget."[38]

Jewish memory thus begins in the context of a theological paradigm
dedicated to recounting foundational, mythic moments in a sacred history. Configured in covenantal terms, memory exists in continual "recip-
rocal" tension with any early attempts at historiography.[39] In postbiblical
Judaism, after the destruction of the second Temple, an interpretive tradition of memory was cultivated at the "'Vineyard at Yabneh' . . . the
fortress against oblivion."[40] This inaugurated a new, more diffuse and
democratic era for memory's ongoing reflection on history: the rabbis
"were engrossed in an ongoing exploration of the meaning of the history
bequeathed to them, striving to interpret it in living terms for their own
and later generations."[41] Concepts of temporality and history, according
to David Roskies, one of the most significant interpreters of Yerushalmi's
work, "were restructured to fit a new liturgical mold. Henceforth, the
contexts of memory were all to emanate from Scripture, study house, and
synagogue. Multiple copies of the Temple key were reentrusted to the
synagogue wardens for safe-keeping."[42]

The results of this shift toward textual interpretation also shifted the
spatial locus for memorial reflection toward its preservation in the textual. The Mishnah, for example, as described by Jacob Neusner, marks out
the territory of memory by positing a utopian system of organization cen-
tered on an absent center. In this way the Mishnah stands in for that center, making it accessible to all and keeping the memory of the Temple
alive. "In the world of disaster and cataclysmic change, Mishnah stands
as a statement of how the old is to be retained. It defines and effects the
permanence amid the change." In a certain sense, then, Mishnah transforms space into time: "Mishnah permits the people, Israel, to carry [the
world of the cosmic center] along through time until the center once more
will be regained."[43] As time wore on, historical and mythical events were
also "programmed" into the ritual fabric of memory by the rabbis.[44] Part
of the ongoing interpretation of texts and events was also "reminding"
God, as it were, of God's covenantal responsibility.[45]

In the medieval period, the ritual and liturgical engagements with history through the text became the primary channels through which Jewish memory flowed and survived.[46] But according to Yerushalmi, this rit-
ual-liturgical memorial process was "not a matter of intellection, but
of evocation and identification." The example he brings is that of the

Passover seder: "Here, in the course of a meal around the family table, ritual, liturgy, and even culinary elements are orchestrated to transmit a vital past from one generation to the next. The entire seder is a symbolic enactment of an historical scenario whose three great acts structure the Haggadah that is read aloud: slavery—deliverance—ultimate redemption. . . . Memory here is no longer recollection, which still preserves a sense of distance, but reactualization."[47] In this and other ritual-textual "vessels and vehicles of Jewish memory" in the medieval period, Yerushalmi examines the increasingly self-reflexive and active conflations of time and space, myth and history, that signal the emerging breakdown of Jewish historical consciousness, culminating in the Kabbalah, particularly that based on the teachings of R. Isaac Luria. On the verge of modernity, Jewish memory is poised to break free of its history and become a more vibrant force for embodying and enacting the past.

While Yerushalmi appears to lament this development, I find it exciting. Whereas he traces the decline of memory in the modern period to the concomitant decline in the "continuity of Jewish living," I find that newer and more variegated forms for reconciling the past with the present have emerged within that gap. Anticipating Novick's "organic" critique of Halbwachs, Yerushalmi argues that the "decline of Jewish collective memory in modern times is only a symptom of the unraveling of that common network of belief and praxis through whose mechanisms . . . the past was once made present."[48] But it is the reconstitution of Jewish memorial sensibilities, linked to but not bound by the threads of memory's past glories, that most interests me here. Both with and against the ever present threat of forgetfulness, memory (especially in the postmodern, post-Holocaust era) thrives in the gaps left by social and cultural fragmentation and diffusion.

In some sense, Yerushalmi would support this view. He suggests that Jewish memory has not suffered a total decline but has been recast, exceeding the bounds of Jewish tradition. "Hardly any Jew today is without some Jewish past. Total amnesia is still relatively rare. The choice for Jews as for non-Jews is not whether or not to have a past, but rather—what kind of past shall one have." That choice, Yerushalmi argues, has been based on perceptions more "mythical than real."[49] Perhaps he should have said "more memorial than historical." Indeed, Jewish memory's reality is not in question. Rather, we ask how, under what conditions and circumstances, and through what media it is constructed and reconstructed, produced and reproduced. As David Roskies has more recently argued, "Once the search for a usable past was being waged through new venues and institutions . . . the structure of remembrance began to change as well. It became ever more contrapuntal, as choosing one set of memories entailed actively opposing another set." Approaching the eve of the Holocaust, "Henceforth and in perpetuity, the only usable past was an isolated, segregated, repackageable past."[50]

HOLOCAUST MEMORY

Jewish memory has, in many respects, based itself on the historical experience of trauma and catastrophe. The ruptures and discontinuities in the Jewish experience have fueled in large part the desire for remembrance.

Catastrophe, in fact, has always been a part of the process of rethinking the past. Like the rabbis of old who worked with any and all available materials . . . so long as they could bridge the abyss left in the wake of the Great Catastrophe, the writers and artists of the nineteenth and twentieth centuries mixed symbol systems, juxtaposed sacred and profane, borrowed ferociously in order to face their ever-greater losses. Just as the Temple destructions were consciously fashioned into archetypes by the exiles in Babylonia and by the Tannaim and Amoraim, so the new destruction, the Holocaust, was lifted from the straight line of allusions back to the old archetypes and inaugurated into its own archetypal nature.[51]

That artistic and literary responses to the Holocaust have built on the structures and paradigms of past creativity in the face of catastrophe is well documented. Memory here is very often a strategy for reconstruction fed on the experience of destruction; loss becomes the "precondition of renewal."[52] Ideally, such memory would be aware of its dependence on loss and rupture as a bulwark against a too facile repair of historical continuity and covenantal connectivity.

But what of the more socially and technologically mediated forms of memory's reconstruction, often negotiated outside high religious and cultural paradigms? What of memory's competition in the public sphere, in the arena of popular culture? One result of the modern and postmodern democratization and fragmentation of memory is its increased volatility and negotiability, leading to a loss of stability in the construction of memory. In this context, one might say that the ideal form of Holocaust memory bears within it a sense of its own deconstructive potential. A self-consciousness about how memory might easily unravel is an excellent check on the impulse to knit the threads of continuity too tightly in an age lacking easy answers and final solutions. But how can one encourage such self-consciousness? I aim to do so in this book by discussing and analyzing the tensions within four distinct strategies of Holocaust remembrance in order to expose the workings of memory in its construction and reconstruction.

The volatility of which I write is particularly evident on the Jewish front, as Roskies points out. "Jews do not want to share the same past anymore," he argues. "Every denomination has carved out a different piece of it, and thank God, there's enough to go around. Only when one or more groups lay claim to the same past does it start getting dicey. The Holocaust is an obvious case in point, because within Judaism, destruction is always fraught with covenantal meaning."[53] This is a crucial point, and some sense of the Jewish competition for memory and meaning in the context of Holocaust remembrance will arise in the course of these pages.

But my overall task really lies elsewhere, at the intersection of Jewish and cultural studies. For if one of the legacies of the disruption and diffusion of traditional memory's authority is the decline of specifically parochial, communal memory, then an analysis of the contemporary contours of Holocaust remembrance will have to go beyond the specifically Jewish case. I have begun to move in this direction here, within certain limitations. For one thing, the production of Holocaust memory is still largely limited to Jewish culture, even if that culture is itself informed by broader social influences. Produced *by* Jews, it is still largely produced *to remember* Jews as well (this is appropriate: the "Holocaust" denotes the Jewish experience of and in World War II). Nonetheless, the consumers of Holocaust memorial culture are, in many cases, not exclusively or even primarily Jewish. And how that more broadly defined society understands the Holocaust and its legacy as a result is of paramount importance for the future of its memory.

Thus, the issues surrounding the propriety of memory are central to my discussions here. Propriety is taken in a dual sense: as the notion of what is "proper" (what is *appropriate* in the realm of representation) and what is "property" (what is *appropriated* in the course of representation). Attention to the various ways Holocaust memory is constructed and negotiated engages this double-edged issue of propriety and takes the discussion across the (arbitrary) line separating specifically Jewish concerns (such as the reconsideration of covenantal paradigms of representation and response) from more generally cultural ones (such as the ways techniques of representation impact how the Holocaust is remembered in society). My hope is that this book will straddle that line, so that insights relating to Jewish issues will inform those relating to broader cultural ones, and vice versa.

Let me move, then, to an overview of my subject. How can we better understand the production of contemporary Holocaust memorial culture? I maintain that it is only through careful attention to some of the most significant media involved and invoked in producing that culture that we gain a clearer sense of what that culture is and what it means today. Because Holocaust memory faces specific challenges in the twenty-first century—most significant, the imminent passing of the "survivor" generation—such attention to how Holocaust memorial culture is produced is urgently needed. The emptiness of some of the most prevalent manifestations of that culture necessitates the investigation and uncovering of the manners in which those manifestations are created and continue to evolve. As the anthropologist Jonathan Webber puts it, "The slogans, stereotypes, and generalizations Jews conventionally use to comprehend the Holocaust—or, as I should prefer to say, to mythologize the Holocaust—these slogans converge today on the duty to remember. Indeed, the single Hebrew word *zakhor!* ('remember!') is the principal slogan used by Jewish congregations, student bodies, youth groups, and the like, the motto that appears on banners at marches or demonstrations, on leaflets at commemorative meetings."[54] It is the blanket injunction to "remember" that must be examined and unpacked.

Often it is the felt duty to remember—memory itself—which is remembered in contemporary Holocaust memorial culture. Without denying the importance of this memorial activity, I wish to examine and deconstruct the forces and processes that converge in such a slogan or felt duty or in many other condensed memorial strategies for representing the past and conveying its important reality in the present. I am therefore interested in how the "mythologized" versions of the Holocaust are generated and how, with critical attention to the production of these memories, vicarious memorialists (and the readers of this book) might turn their own attention to these constructions (and their own roles within them) and thereby think a bit differently about the nature of memory. They may (and will) go ahead and continue to remember the Holocaust, but perhaps they will do so with more awareness of the pitfalls and processes of memory itself. By "vicarious" here I do not mean to imply any inauthentic or exploitative behavior; rather, I wish to highlight the ways in which Holocaust memory is adopted and appropriated through complex and serious strategies of embodiment by those who engage in and produce that memory.

I focus primarily on contemporary popular cultural forms of memory, for several reasons. One has to do with issues of prevalence and presence.

As Peter Novick observes, the Holocaust's general presence in American culture has, since the 1970s, been perceived as "contemporary," as either a cause or an effect of its continual presence in the news.[55] I leave to Novick the challenge of proving his historical thesis; if he is even partially correct concerning the assessment of the Holocaust's contemporary presence, then he is also pointing to the role popular culture plays in authorizing and sustaining that presence. And while excellent scholarly work has addressed specific cultural mediations of the Holocaust in literature, art, architecture, photography, film, and television,[56] much less has been concerned with the institutions devoted to Holocaust memory and their role (in concert with visitors and voyeurs) in constructing and mediating that memory. This multimedia, interdisciplinary analysis goes beyond those largely single-genre case studies to paint a more synthetic picture of the process of memorial mediation itself.

I focus, therefore, on a highly active and engaged series of memorial strategies as gleaned from attention to the structures of memory's mediation. By examining the modes and media of memorialization and by looking at the symbols on which these strategies depend, we gain a clearer sense of the mechanisms of Holocaust memory. Each of the four modes mapped in this book—the iconic, the videotestimonial, the museological, and the ritual-ceremonial—contributes unique qualities to the production and reproduction of Holocaust memory in general.

In the next chapter, I begin with what I call the *iconic* mode of memorialization as it is *inscribed* in contemporary culture, for this is where some of the most essential strategies of mediation and commitment are established. As against the more idolatrous mode, I argue that Holocaust icons, in a variety of expressions, embody the ideals of Holocaust remembrance as a transmissible phenomenon by which the past can be made to matter in the present and with which vicarious memory artists can effectively relate to that past. The iconic tendency outlined in this chapter serves to enhance the religious and cultural engagement with Holocaust history and establishes the basic symbolism and vocabulary of remembrance.

In chapter 3 I examine the *videotestimonial* mode in the context of the *framing* of remembrance. Through this trope I consider the frames of remembrance created and invoked via the medium of video recording and the role played by that medium in the shaping of Holocaust memory. These frames contextualize a series of relationships engendered by the testimonies: witness to interviewer, witness to camera, witness to viewer, witness to society. Here I address the issue of transmissibility more precisely by assessing how videotestimonies, particularly as they are viewed and institutionalized, act as media of memory between those giving testimony (usually survivors) and those viewing it. How different institutions are capitalizing on the race to record these testimonies and how they act to produce versions of Holocaust memory as a result are also concerns in this chapter. I argue that it is only through careful attention to the unique qualities of the video frames and the forms of mediation they engender that we can assess the impact of this important new memorial form.

Chapter 4 focuses on what kinds of vicarious memorial experiences are created in the museum environment and how a museum narrative contributes to an ideology of remembrance. In the context of the *mediation* of memory, I examine this *museological* strategy for memorialization. While this strategy is often played out, as at the United States Holocaust Memorial Museum, through a series of well-placed artifacts and their implied power of mediation, I ask what the impact on memory is in museums such as the Simon Wiesenthal Center's Museum of Tolerance. Here, where technology and virtual reality replace traditional object-driven narrative, I argue that what are often constructed in these museums are at best virtual memories, imagined contexts for memorial engagement.

In chapter 5 I assess the ultimate result of vicarious memorialization in the *ritual-ceremonial* strategy. In the context of the *performance* of memory, I wonder what happens when people put themselves in the Holocaust's historical environment and enact its memorial strategies there. This chapter focuses on the vibrant creativity of the March of the Living, the contemporary paradigmatic Holocaust pilgrimage to Poland and Israel. I examine how march participants create new memorial relationships driven by ideological agendas and play out the Jewish narrative theme of "destruction and redemption" on their highly symbolic (and highly mediated) trip.

My attention to mediation serves as an overarching and unifying perspective. Through it run two thematic progressions in the material I study. In the temporal progression, each mode (with the exception of the iconic, which serves as a pretemporal anchor for considering symbolic appropriations of Holocaust imagery outside of time, as it were) has as its central orientation one zone of temporality. For the videotestimonial mode it is the preservation of the images and language of the past (for the sake of the present and future). For the museological mode it is the mediation of the Holocaust in the present (while nonetheless preserving the evidence of the past and the lessons for the future). And for the ritual-

ceremonial mode it is in establishing a trajectory for the future of memory (while respecting the memory of the past and engaging the needs of
those in the present). The second progression is physical: through attention to mediation it becomes clear how engagement and, especially, embodiment figure in the construction of Holocaust memory. Thus, the
iconic mode of remembrance embodies memory in the most abstract and
theoretical manner. This engagement is intensified in the videotestimonial mode, which involves the bodies of testifiers relating, across a barrier,
to the bodies of voyeur-auditors. The museological strategy for remembrance further embodies memory, as narrative simulations of and interactive engagements with both the material and the legacy of the Holocaust bring people into museum environments in order to produce
memory. Finally, in the ritual mode of memorialization, the bodies of vicarious memorialists are brought into the landscape of Holocaust memory's own history in Europe to embody that memory through physical activity. This process further shrinks the distance between experience and
reproduction made progressively less distinct in the media analyzed in
the central chapters of this book.

My attention to mediation also necessarily invites my concern with
technology. The technological aspect of the media I study is not, however,
limited only to new forms of mediation (such as videotapes, interactive
computer simulations, CD-ROMs, Internet sites, and the like). Rather, a
focus on technology further exposes the centrality of mediation to my
work. As Sturken observes, "Cultural memory is produced through objects, images, and representations. These are technologies of memory, not
vessels of memory in which memory passively resides so much as objects
through which memories are shared, produced, and given meaning."[57] In
this way, attention to the technologies of the production and reproduction of memory highlights the importance of memory as a shared and
mediated social and cultural phenomenon, exactly what Halbwachs was
concerned with. Focusing on the broadly defined technologies of memory
also reveals how "they embody and generate memory and are thus implicated in the power dynamics of memory's production," an understanding
that returns memory's construction to the activity of individuals engaged
in self-transformation and identity building through their variously imagined relationships with the past and its personification in the present.[58] At
the same time, this concern with technology and mediation—understood
more as modes of engagement than as terms identifying the scope of the
material being discussed—delimits a range of material chosen and scrutinized not because it is a representative sample of Holocaust "media"

but because it represents a range of strategies employed in mediating the Holocaust. I do not examine Holocaust film, television, or photography (except where cases of these media serve as examples of mediation), not only because fine and comprehensive work has been done already but also because my primary concerns lie elsewhere.

Memorialization is conceived here as a process, something of continual concern and emphasis in this book. The process of memorialization, an outgrowth of negotiation and mediation, ideally walks a precarious line in its quest to apprehend the Holocaust. Cultural critic Andreas Huyssen offers both a methodological suggestion and a warning: "No matter how fractured by media, by geography, and by subject position representations of the Holocaust are, ultimately it all comes down to this core: unimaginable, unspeakable, and unrepresentable horror. Post-Holocaust generations can only approach that core by mimetic approximation, a mnemonic strategy which recognizes the event in its otherness and beyond identification or therapeutic empathy, but which physically innervates some of the horror and the pain in a slow and persistent labor of remembrance."[59] The struggles for remembrance discussed in this book—mediated and embodied memory-work undertaken in a range of religious and cultural contexts—must certainly be read to reveal the inherent tensions of the mnemonic strategies of which Huyssen speaks.[60] We cannot forget the "otherness" to which such labors of remembrance must always point. But Huyssen also overstates his case. The Holocaust has been and will continue to be imaginable, speakable, representable; people do indeed struggle to identify and empathize with its effects, however difficult and approximate the results. To state otherwise is to avoid the very real impact the Holocaust has had and continues to have on and in contemporary culture. In tracing the modes of this impact, we see more clearly the ways in which individuals and institutions are committed to memory.

CHAPTER TWO

Inscribing Memory

ICONIC PARADIGMS FOR
HOLOCAUST REMEMBRANCE

I want to submit that the positioning of both the writer and the audience in relation to this mountain or this defiled center [the image of the Holocaust] functions much as does the positioning of the pilgrim vis-à-vis the holy mountain or the sacred center; in what closely approximates a theological quest at the postmodern end of our millennium, a new aesthetics and ethics of representation are being forged with Auschwitz as the ultimate point of reference.

— SIDRA DEKOVEN EZRAHI, "Representing Auschwitz"

"Thou shalt not make unto thee any graven image or likeness." It is possible to draw another Guernica, to sing the songs of the Partisans, to present "Ghetto," but the Holocaust itself cannot be represented. No artistic or literary representation can succeed. Whoever tries to peek through the furnace of revelation and describe what he saw with his own eyes, or in his mind's eye, is destined to fail. . . . What was then real is beyond the capabilities of poetry, art and dramatic reconstruction. Exactly as it is impossible to understand the transcendental in the framework of a scientific theory, it is equally impossible to capture it in the realms of the imagination. The outcome of every such analytical or artistic attempt is distortion rather than representation, camouflage rather than reconstruction, forgetting rather than remembering.

— ADI OPHIR, "On Sanctifying the Holocaust: An Anti-Theological Treatise"

ICONS

THAT THE Holocaust is the ultimate reference point for any contemporary discussion of ethics, violence, totalitarianism, and so forth—the "master moral paradigm" as one scholar has put it—is increasingly commonplace.[1] What is equally well known is that the terrible truths which occupy that "defiled center" and point of reference are becoming increasingly "unknowable." That unknowability arises not only because many argue that the Holocaust itself is unrepresentable (it is not) but also because, as representations proliferate, the real-life referents for those representations grow old, die, or otherwise become increasingly tangential to the representations themselves. There is a disconnection between Auschwitz as an absolute, an (un)holy mountain, and many of the specific representational vehicles that would take us there. What we are left with as our main access points to the Holocaust are these representations, all straining toward the truths to which they refer, truths that nonetheless continually evade our grasp.

The struggle to represent the Holocaust is therefore a struggle for adequate and appropriate modes of representation. What kind of language, what vocabulary, suits the task? To begin our journey into Holocaust mediation and commitment, we must first consider the symbolic language established and utilized in various memorial contexts to convey a sense of both the horrors experienced and their meaning in the present. As I have suggested in chapter 1, one could classify Holocaust representations in two general categories: metaphoric and metonymic. While metaphoric language maintains its important place in Holocaust representation ("the Holocaust is now among the most scrutinized—and contested—subjects of metaphor in American public culture"),[2] metonymic modes of engagement are claiming an ever greater share of the representational pie. In these variegated metonymic cases the Holocaust is represented by way of symbolic, often visual, pointers that are themselves derived directly from the events to which they refer. As parts of the whole, these pointers act as mediators for Holocaust awareness and memory, in that they refer metonymically to the events of which they somehow once took and still take part, and present in condensed form images of what is deemed most essential to the process of remembrance.

I will call certain uses of these metonymic images "icons" so as to initiate a discussion of the role such images play in Holocaust representation and memory. These Holocaust icons act as cultural reminders, vehicles (literally) for the construction of memory and the public sense of the past. As in the case of the Holocaust-era railway cars I will discuss, certain images and artifacts, when utilized iconically, are transformed into bearers of memory that can transport those who engage in their symbolic presentations to a deeper understanding of the Holocaust. I choose *icon* as the central term of my argument because it captures the sense of an image put to a religious use and thus conveying meaning in a symbolic context. The term immediately raises the issues of the propriety of such religious applications of metonymic imagery. As the first foray into the modes of commitment to Holocaust memory, I examine a cluster of theoretical appropriations and representational strategies associated with the notion of the "iconic" in the broader enterprise of Holocaust mediation.

The second edition of the *Oxford English Dictionary* (*OED*) defines "icon" (from the Greek: "likeness," "image," "portrait," "semblance," "similitude," "simile") as "an image, figure, or representation; a portrait; a picture, 'cut,' or illustration in a book" and "an image in the solid; a monumental figure; a statue." Of course, it also notes the religious meaning of the term: *"Eastern Church.* A representation of some sacred personage, in painting, bas-relief, or mosaic, itself regarded as sacred, and honored with a relative worship or adoration." In the contemporary literature on Holocaust representation, the term is used frequently, sometimes carelessly, sometimes more critically, but in all cases as a common linguistic indication of the representative, even paradigmatic, status of a particular object, image, or personality. Generally, such icons are deemed capable of standing in for the events of the Holocaust and conveying their enormity in some way, while nonetheless reminding viewers and readers that what is being symbolized remains more complex than the icon itself.

Let us consider several examples of the use of "icon" in the critical literature. One is Tim Cole's somewhat sensationalistic discussion of the making of the "myth of the Holocaust" in the representation of three central figures and three central sites of remembrance. Cole considers the "Holocaust" itself a "dominant icon at the end of the twentieth century."[3] By this he seems to mean its centrality to contemporary consciousness, what Yehuda Bauer calls a "ruling symbol."[4] In this context Cole assesses the roles played by such personalities as Anne Frank (a "contemporary cultural icon"),[5] Adolf Eichmann (who "assumed a key role in the iconography of 'Holocaust' perpetrators, which in many ways stood unchallenged until Spielberg's 'Holocaust' villain Amon Goeth graced our screens"),[6] and Oskar Schindler. For all three, Cole evaluates what he considers the packaging of the Holocaust for consumer consumption, but this would be more critically understood as the transformation of Holocaust personalities into memorial referents. Consider, for example, his reading of Schindler. "In re-writing the past, Spielberg has created a Schindler who is not simply a liberal icon, but also a humanist icon. The effect of this screen redemption is to transform Schindler into not just a hero, but something of a saint, whose tomb on Mount Zion is shown to be a site of pilgrimage. . . . If the 'Holocaust' has gained such an iconic status that it can be seen as acquiring almost a religious aura, then surely Oskar Schindler has emerged in the aftermath of *Schindler's List* as a contemporary Holocaust saint (if not a new Holocaust 'Christ')." Thus, though Cole sees the Holocaust and its icons as "contested brandname[s]," it is clear that "icon" refers simply to these characters' (and the Holocaust's) referentiality and prominence in the representational landscape.[7]

More relevant and critical appropriations of "icon" and of the phenomenon of Holocaust representation are found in Barbie Zelizer's and Jeffrey Shandler's work. In her detailed study of the use of "atrocity photos" from World War II as part of the ongoing construction of collective memory of the Holocaust, for example, Zelizer argues that "the images of the concentration camps . . . have become a lasting iconic representation of war atrocity and human evil." What is more, these icons transcend the merely symbolic to produce far-ranging impacts: "Photographs turn somewhat magically into iconic representations that stand for a system of beliefs, a theme, an epoch."[8] In this way, Zelizer pays close attention to the role played by the photographic image in metonymically representing the Holocaust and signaling to viewers its horrors.

As testament to their iconic qualities, she notes how, after the war, some of the most memorable photographs "turned up as reality markers in other modes of Holocaust representation" such as painting and fiction. In these and other ways atrocity photos serve as vehicles for the symbolization and generalization of the once specific and contingent stories of World War II. In many cases, this has led to more "formulaic" and less nuanced revisions of Holocaust representation that focus almost exclusively on images of survivors and the "accoutrements of atrocity." If at times overused, this positioning of a photographic vocabulary nonetheless initiates an agenda of representation: "The predictable arrival of iconic images of barbarism adds new residents to already populated categories of visual representation: as soon as we see the agonized collectives of survivors and victims, gaunt faces behind barbed wire, vacant stares of the tortured, and accoutrements of torture, we recognize the atrocity aesthetic." As we recognize it, Zelizer warns, we are also liable to "forget" what is ultimately being referred to, a process that, among other things, can neutralize our potential responses to present-day atrocities. On the contemporary scene, it often appears as if photographers (and newspaper editors) frame and present images of latter-day horror according to the iconographic vocabulary established in the Holocaust. In the extreme case, "Holocaust photos actually replace the depictions of contemporary atrocities" so that "memory crowd[s] out the ability to attend to the event," effacing the temporal distance between then and now.[9] Here, Holocaust icons in their photographic mode continue to have a powerful impact on contemporary consciousness.

Shandler's reading of the role played by television in shaping Holocaust consciousness also pertains critically to the issue of visual icons. Considering moving rather than still images dating from World War II, he credits television with "transforming [them] into widely and swiftly recognized icons of the Nazi era . . . [and] reaffirm[ing] their value as virtual witnesses of the Holocaust." But it is also clear that the establishment of an early iconic "canon" distorts the historical representation of the icons' subjects: survivors, for example, who are portrayed as "ghosts, creatures beyond the resumption of normal life routines." As the representation of the Holocaust on television entered the 1960s (as a "guest" in episodic series), it demonstrated the "codification of a Holocaust iconography in American popular culture. This association of various signs with the Holocaust enabled both its easy identification as a discrete subject and its ready application as a paradigm." In this way, the visual lexicon associated with atrocity is transformed into a representational vocabulary. In the late 1970s, according to Shandler, survivors began to show up on American television as "distinctive voices of authority" and "metonyms of the past" (thus enlivening, or at least supplementing, their earlier, ghostly representations).[10] This further complicated, I think, the iconic canon by lending visual form to greater embodiment. Indeed, Shandler marks the ascendance of the survivor in the Holocaust's representational pantheon with the rise in prominence of Elie Wiesel, marking as well a generational and representational shift and supplanting Anne Frank in archetypal status. "This development also constitutes a shift from a dead figure, who is the posthumous object of memory, to a living person who has played an active role in molding his iconic stature."[11] But Shandler also notes that in recent years Wiesel himself is perhaps being eclipsed by the prominence of Steven Spielberg, evidence for another shift in remembrance to the "creators of Holocaust mediations."[12] True or not, the suggestion points to the proliferation of iconic representations of and representatives for the Holocaust in contemporary society. In this way, the range of iconic representations continues to expand.

Writers such as Zelizer and Shandler point to the complexities in the production and reproduction of the Holocaust's visual icons. One example discussed by both authors will illustrate some of the important issues (see figure 1): a well-known photograph, first published in German general Jurgen Stroop's report on the 1943 liquidation of the Warsaw Ghetto, features a young boy in cap, coat, and short pants with his hands raised. The broader frame shows, on the left and in the background of the street scene, other Jews with hands raised, some carrying bags, and on the right, a German soldier pointing his rifle at the boy. Shandler discusses a television documentary made in 1990 which "examines the claim of Holocaust survivor Tsvi Nussbaum" that he is the boy in the photo: "As *A Boy from Warsaw* reminds viewers, this photograph has achieved iconic status as a representation of the Holocaust," as supported by scholars such as historian Lucy Davidowicz.[13] Continually reproduced as *the* pho-

Figure 1. The iconic photograph dating from the liquidation of the Warsaw Ghetto in 1943.
Main Commission for the Prosecution of War Crimes against the Polish Nation.
Courtesy of USHMM Photo Archives.

tograph representative of the Holocaust experience, the picture has also
appeared as the basis for memorial reflections and artistic works at various degrees of remove from the Holocaust: Yala Korwin's poem "The Little Boy with His Hands Up"; Ingmar Bergman's film *Persona*; Judy
Chicago's *Holocaust Project*; and a cartoon by Antonio Attunes Moreira,
"who in 1982 turned the famous boy from the Warsaw Ghetto into a kaf-
fiyehed Palestinian" in Lebanon.[14] Marianne Hirsch, who in an important essay uses the photo (and the image of Anne Frank's face) as a spring-
board for a meditation on the roles such iconic images, especially of
children, play in the public construction of Holocaust memory, adds that
"the boy from Warsaw . . . appears obsessively in advertising brochures
for Holocaust histories, teaching aids, and books."[15] While the television
documentary "neither endorses nor dismisses fully Nussbaum's claim,"
it does highlight the complicated afterlife of this image in Holocaust
memorial culture, "validat[ing] the meaning that attaching himself to
the image has given Nussbaum's sense of self as a survivor of the Holocaust."[16] It is this afterlife that is encompassed by the concept of the icon.
But the meaning of the image, along with the others imposed on and

served by the reproduction of the photograph, overlay but do not (or should not) erase the photograph's original intent: recording for posterity the German army's liquidation of the Jewish ghetto in Warsaw. This meaning reminds us of the ethical as well as representational complexity of the use and reuse of iconic imagery from and of the Holocaust. The notion that this image is "iconic" should include all its meanings and referents. Clearly, as this brief excursus has shown, referential images of the Holocaust have cultural afterlives that may never be exhausted. Sorting out these afterlives—their roles as mediators of and motivators for memory—will illuminate their cultural positions.

My interest in Holocaust icons is motivated by a concern for how the meanings of the Holocaust are determined, represented, and, especially, conveyed. How are specific representational distillations of such meanings created through the use and contextualization of Holocaust symbols? I want to investigate where our images and understandings of the Holocaust originate, how they are produced and reproduced, and toward what they ultimately point. What is it that stands in for, takes the place of, or otherwise symbolizes the Holocaust, and what does it tell us about how we remember? I nonetheless recognize that much discomfort can arise with the use and reuse of Holocaust imagery: there are enduring concerns about appropriation, voyeurism, commodification, pornography, and kitsch.[17] These are valid concerns. They can best be met not by the regulation of such imagery but rather by the careful examination of strategies of representation. How are Holocaust icons positioned in order to convey certain commemorative messages? In this chapter I want to subject the icon to critique and see not only how it is constructed but also how it shapes our perception of the Holocaust.

REMNANTS OF ATROCITY

The images that I call Holocaust icons are especially potent as conveyors of perceptions when built from authentic artifacts from World War II; we rely on such artifacts to communicate some aspect of the enormity of the events in which they somehow participated. They often speak in their multiplicity to the reality of devastating loss. Such discourse was already operative in the first journalistic accounts of liberation. Note, for example, this report in 1944 from Time-Life correspondent Richard Lauterbach on visiting a "shoe warehouse" at Majdanek: "I stepped up and went inside. It was full of shoes. A sea of shoes. I walked across them unsteadily. They were piled, like pieces of coal in a bin, halfway up the walls.

Not only shoes. Boots. Rubbers. Leggings. Slippers. Children's shoes, soldier's shoes, old shoes, new shoes. They were red and grey and black. Some
had once been white."[18] Such images of atrocity indicate, however indirectly, the destruction of which the shoes are, presumably, the only remnants. As metonyms of the Holocaust, they are already iconic because, in
their roles as artifacts, they are physical representations of the destruction
that produced them, subsequently regarded with a certain degree of veneration. Their roles as icons are further reinforced by their later incorporation into visual and oral narratives that are often dramatically reenacted. This effect can be seen in one Eichmann trial witness's recounting
of a visit to Treblinka after liberation, where he too found many shoes:
"As he spoke these words, he carefully unwrapped a tiny pair of shoes and
held them up for the whole courthouse to see. . . . This dramatic testimony . . . provided a potent image of the 'Holocaust,' later to be incorporated into the Historical Museum at Yad Vashem where a lone child's shoe
is displayed on a plinth bearing the number of child victims of the Holocaust."[19] The dramatic reproduction of these material icons raises their
potency in metonymically representing the entirety of the Holocaust.[20]

We rely a great deal on these types of representation in our "sacred" engagement with the Holocaust and its meanings. Our reliance on such
hypersymbolic representation bears within it a number of risks, all of
which circle around how remembrance is performed and what is remembered with and through these icons. At the extreme, we, as visitors to
contemporary constructed memorial environments, risk "forgetting" the
events referred to, the things we are asked to try to remember, and "remembering" only the representations of those events. In these cases the
icons cease both to mediate memory and to facilitate the referentiality
that is central to the memorialization process. I associate this potential
forgetfulness, this cessation of mediation, with the notion of idolatry.
Such idolatrous representation is problematic because it erases the voice
of the past in favor of the more audible noise of the present and the increasingly vicarious memories of contemporaneous visitor-voyeurs fash-
ioning their memories at the altar of these Holocaust idols.

In contrast, I define the Holocaust icon as a more successful appropriation of a memorial artifact that nonetheless does not elide the past in establishing a relationship to it. In embodying memory, icons act as true
mediators for memory's enactment, while idols serve as false gods in the
quest for memorial embodiment. The *OED* defines "idol," from the Latin
for "image, form, spectre, apparition," in several ways. In the Jewish and
Christian context it is an "image or similitude of a deity or divinity, used

as an object of worship" and, figuratively, "any thing or person that is the object of excessive or supreme devotion, or that usurps the place of God in human affection." In classical Greek (and Latin) use it is an "image, effigy, or figure of a person or thing; esp. a statue," "a counterpart, likeness, imitation" and a "mental fiction; a phantasy or fancy," among other meanings. Distinguished from the mediating function of and contextual, relative reverence paid to the icon, the idol demands absolute worship as the supreme object of such worship. Thus I draw a distinction between Holocaust icons—those representations which, though complex and inspiring a certain level of discomfort, nonetheless communicate something of the meaning of the past without overly distorting it—and Holocaust idols—those representations which offend not so much because they cross some line of propriety (though they often do) but because they demand allegiance more to the image itself and its own mode of presentation than to what it purports to represent. In the current age of representation and hypermediation, it is of utmost importance that this distinction be made.

The term for idolatry in the Jewish rabbinic tradition, *avodah zarah*, literally means "strange worship," which can be read in two ways: as the improper form of worship or in reference to the improper god being worshiped ("the strangeness of the ritual or the strangeness of the object of the ritual").[21] Jewish thought rejects the latter. But the former definition is more ambiguous, and understanding that allows for acceptable and effective iconization. A Jewish icon, as a memorial representation, would act as a reminder—of God, of catastrophe, of past redemptions and their long-awaited but ever deferred future recurrence. Icons thus call attention to the gap between then and now, there and here, to the necessary vicariousness of their (re)presentational strategies. Idols often erase that distinction, offering too much closure.[22] When the icon's memorial trajectory is turned in a different direction—inward or toward some contemporary, immediate form of redemption—idolatry rears its ugly head. Icons are dynamic; idols static. A religious icon is a medium for worship; an idol is itself the object of worship.

Holocaust icons operate according to the same structure. When the image points back to its own past, functioning as a mediator of memorial experience and as a model of sacred engagement and embodiment, then it is an effective icon. Icons become idols only when a mistake of interpretation is made: when the voyeur mistakes the part for the whole, the artifact for the events that generated it or the ideologies that have put it on display, when the icon replaces the discourse that produced it. In this way the icon becomes instrumentalized, idolized, made into a false god. Idol making shows a misplaced (or displaced) impatience for redemption, and easy redemption, especially in the case of the Holocaust, is an impossible desire, an ever deferred wish. But in this post-Holocaust age, it is not only that the medium is the message (and messenger as well) but that it is the totality of our experience of the Holocaust past. The symbolic media of Holocaust memory are, in many cases, all we have to work with. We can resist the temptation toward redemption and idolatry only through the critical apprehension of those media of representation and transmission. Only through attention to effects and contexts can those icons and the people who memorialize with them resist the seductive pull of idolatry. "You shall have no other gods before me" reads the biblical text. Perhaps this is also the cry out of the whirlwind of Holocaust memory we must increasingly find ways of hearing and seeing. But we must recognize nonetheless that we need those symbolic mediators of memory I call icons in order to carry out the project of remembrance.

This notion of the Holocaust icon, in all its complexity and multiplicity, is situated in the middle of a continuum of possible representational styles. At one extreme lies the Holocaust idol, the problematically embodied distortion of memory; on the other end lies the more disengaged Holocaust symbol. While there is nothing particularly troubling about the symbolic, I distinguish it from the more potent iconic mode of representation on the level of embodiment: icons here are embodied memorial representations, symbols are not. Symbols crop up everywhere and are not regulated or controlled in any way; icons, as I define them, are always presented in a performative and visual context, often in memorial-museological environments, and thus they are embodied, invested with a surfeit of signification. In this way, one could say that Holocaust symbols (the Jewish star, for example, or the swastika) constitute the *grammar* of Holocaust representation, while Holocaust icons, especially when taken in their museological or memorial contexts, participate in establishing the *narratives* of representation.

Holocaust icons, then, lie at the crux of a discussion regarding the nature and propriety of the visual and material representation of the Shoah. While some would deny the validity of any visual representation of the Holocaust, I argue for the necessity of both the iconic mode of representation in providing a link to the past that is being displayed and an analysis of this mode to better apprehend its memorial role. Situated at the center of the spectrum ranging from the nearly disengaged symbol to the overengaged idol, these icons (along with their strategies for emplacement and emplotment) model techniques for effective memorialization. Attention to the mechanics of symbolization, iconization, and idolization will therefore sharpen the critical assessment of those techniques. Let me now discuss the use of Holocaust-era railway cars in memorial contexts in order to provide an example on which to base such analysis. The incorporation of this potent symbol of the Holocaust into broader memorial narratives is particularly resonant here because, as a visual reminder of the deportation of Jews, the railway car is a literalization of the notion of the icon as a vehicle for the construction of memory.

BOXCARS

In the United States, authentic Holocaust-era railway cars tend to be housed *inside* museums and treated as artifacts. The first one ever displayed in the United States is at the Dallas Holocaust Memorial Center, which opened in 1984. The best-known boxcar in the United States is most likely the one housed at the United States Holocaust Memorial Museum (USHMM) in Washington, D.C. (see figure 2). The USHMM specimen fits within the overall narrative and collection philosophy of the museum's organizers, who sought to ground the validity of their project as well as the reality of the Holocaust and its narration in an impressive array of genuine artifacts. The railway car in the USHMM is thrust in the path of the museum-goer: the visitor is encouraged to go through the boxcar to get to the next section of the exhibit (though he walks through it on a metal grate installed over the car's floor and is prevented from exploring it by guardrails); those wishing to avoid this experience may discover the less-than-obvious way around the railcar.[23] In Dallas, the car forms the entrance to the exhibit space; a hidden panel installed to the side of the boxcar provides a way around for survivors (and others) wishing to avoid passing through the icon of their own suffering.

In another example, the Florida Holocaust Museum in St. Petersburg also features an authentic fifteen-ton freight car ("Auschwitz boxcar #113 0695-5," according to the museum's Web site), which, like many of these artifacts, actually dates back to World War I. Here, the railcar stands as the focal point of the main exhibit area in the central atrium of the museum; it can be touched but not entered. A narrative supplement to the boxcar's presentation is provided by museum founder Walter Loebenberg: while cleaning the car after its arrival in Florida, workers discovered a child's ring that had evidently been knocked loose by the force of the water hoses. After having it examined, museum officials confirmed that the

Figure 2. Installation of the railcar at the U.S. Holocaust Memorial Museum construction
site, Washington, D.C., February 1991. Courtesy of USHMM Photo Archives.

ring dated to the Holocaust era and speculated that it was hidden in the
floorboards by a girl en route to a camp (or perhaps trampled into the
wooden floor by the press of the crowd inside).[24] The ring is prominently
displayed like a religious relic next to the railway car. The museum also
advertises for sale an "artist's interpretation" of the boxcar (see figure 3);
as described in the Web site's virtual gift shop, as a *tzedaka*, or charity,
box, for $39.95, plus $4.00 shipping and handling.[25] As disturbing as this
miniaturization may seem, it nonetheless makes of the Holocaust-era
railway car a powerful and provocative memorial symbol. The tzedaka
box(car), through its curious mix of consumer kitsch and Jewish memori-
alism, offers a redemptive slant on the commemoration of deportation.[26]

In opposition to the domesticization of Holocaust-era railway cars
housed inside U.S. museums and centers, the example found outdoors in
Jerusalem is strikingly monumental. Walking around the sprawling memorial sculpture park that rings Yad Vashem, Israel's Holocaust Martyrs'
and Heroes' Remembrance Authority, a visitor discovers one as the
central element of Moshe Safdie's *Memorial to the Deportees*.[27] Safdie
(b. 1938), an Israeli architect, is perhaps best known for his Habitat '67
housing complex, built for the Montreal exposition in 1967 and made of
stacked modular prefabricated "boxes." He also designed the late Yitzhak

Rabin's tomb and Yad Vashem's children's memorial (itself a model of
iconic reflection in its seemingly infinite visual repetition of a single candle flame) and is currently working on the renovations for Yad Vashem's
historical museum.[28] Situated on a hillside overlooking one of the many
pine-filled valleys that ring Israel's memorial mountain, the *Memorial to
the Deportees* (1995) is visually arresting (see figure 4).[29] It features an authentic Deutsche Reichsbahn railway car (donated by Polish authorities)
perched precariously on an iron rail line jutting out from the steep slope.
The viewing platform restrains the visitor from approaching the boxcar,
which appears to have stopped abruptly, moments before it would have
tumbled off the edge of the track into the valley below. The broken track
is described on Safdie's Web site as the "replicated remains of a bridge after an explosion."[30] Together, railway car and track mark out an impossible journey, frozen and suspended in time and space over the steep hill.
This line ends, as it did for so many deportees, violently, a moment symbolized by the twisting and shearing of the rails. As a symbol of the Holo-

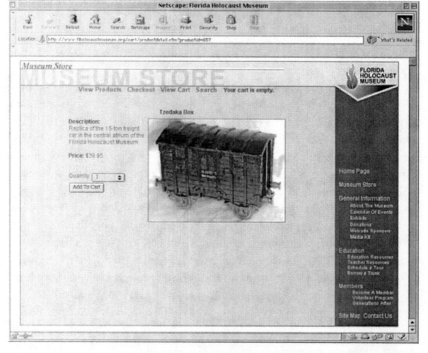

Figure 3. Web page from the Florida Holocaust Museum online store, advertising for sale a
tzedaka box replica of the museum's Holocaust-era railway car, © 2001 Florida Holocaust
Museum. Reproduced with permission of the Florida Holocaust Museum.

Figure 4. Moshe Safdie, *Memorial to the Deportees* (1995), Yad Vashem, Jerusalem, Israel.
Photograph by the author.

caust turned into a memorial icon, the *Memorial to the Deportees* literally stops us in our tracks.

Of the four examples cited, the *Memorial to the Deportees* at Yad
Vashem is the most self-consciously iconic. The context of its presentation reinforces this view. The Safdie memorial presents the railcar on its
track extending from a viewing platform inscribed with the famous short
poem by Dan Pagis, "Written in Pencil in the Sealed Railway Car":

> here in this carload
> i am eve
> with abel my son
> if you see my elder son
> cain son of man
> tell him that i[31]

One of the most widely anthologized poems of the Holocaust (and one of
the "most highly-crafted . . . in modern Hebrew"), "Written in Pencil"
has achieved "canonical status" through its inscription here, becoming
"embalmed in official Israeli memory."[32] This brief but searing distillation
of biblical myth and primal fratricide/genocide offers itself as an artifact
of the Shoah, as if it were actually written, and abruptly cut off, inside one

of those infamous railway cars. By itself the poem is a literary icon, a fictitious remnant, invoking the presence of its speaker through its form and mythic resonances. It symbolically enlarges the narrative of Nazi deportations through the retelling of the "family drama" of the West's religious origins (recall that when Cain killed Abel he murdered one-fourth of the current human population), even as it compresses the scope of genocidal history into a scant six lines.

As a *fictional* artifact, we can read the poem more as an example of Holocaust presentation than representation, suggesting a direct and unmediated link to the past. "Death is not *represented* in this truncated poem but *enacted*."[33] In breaking off so abruptly and evocatively, the poem becomes an urgent and direct message to readers to complete the transmission—finish the sentence, deliver the message, carry on the story.[34] We are thus implicated in Pagis's (re)writing of myth and history; we participate in it, we are drawn into the memorialization process. In the context of *Memorial to the Deportees*, the presentation is intensified; the railcar becomes the physical marker of the poem's possible embodiment, so that the visitor imagines it is *this* car that produced or contained *this* written message. Together, poem and artifact appear to etch into the Israeli landscape an iconic presentation of memory with a voice that speaks directly to the visitor. In juxtaposing verbal and visual imagery in this way, Safdie reenacts the scene of deportation by cattle car, bringing it out of the distant and disengaged past into the engaged present of memorialization.[35] The visitor is encouraged to imagine the deportation scenario even as it is transplanted and arrested in monumental form over a Judean valley. This transformation of memory presents a multilayered image of the railcar: as it may have been "then" and as it appears now, simultaneously.

This embodiment of memory presents both a challenge for interpretation and a model for Holocaust representation. How do we read these symbolic vehicles of Holocaust memorialization? How can we contextualize their strategies for embodying and thus transmitting memory? The other presentations of railway cars offer their own somewhat different strategies for embodiment and transmission. In Dallas and Washington, for example, the visitor becomes part of the (imagined) unfolding narrative of deportation and must supplement through imagination any literary or linguistic icon—any text—of the sort that Pagis has (unwittingly) provided for the Israeli memorial. This supplementation makes the narrativization of the icon more personal and individual, which is accentuated, if the visitor is particularly lucky, by the story of deportation told by a local survivor-docent. The work of reenactment through artistic presentation and juxtaposition performed by Safdie at Yad Vashem is done in Washington and Dallas by way of emplacement and emplotment. If in Jerusalem I would need to use Pagis's poem as a vehicle for imagining the space of deportation, in Washington and Dallas I can stand in that space myself—the story is literally more engaging.

The embodiment of memory in Florida works more indirectly. As in Israel, the car is closed to visitors, though its proximity to the voyeur can give rise to a more pronounced engagement with the car through imagination and touch: though closed, the railcar in St. Petersburg is accessible and may be tactilely explored. But the memory is best embodied here through the story of the child's ring and through the tzedaka box, both offering redemptive narratives that counterbalance the mute presentation of the boxcar itself. Each of these supplementary narratives, based on additional artifacts (authentic or not), provides an access point for the otherwise mysterious railway car.

Nonetheless, the overtly artistic and self-consciously iconic presentation of the boxcar at Yad Vashem will serve as the primary reference point for my discussion here. I argue that it offers a provocative and ultimately problematic example of a Holocaust icon: presenting a blend of representation, presentation, and embodiment, it challenges expectations concerning the proper use of artifacts and goes far beyond the largely symbolic and more disengaged modes of Holocaust representation. Because its narrative context is less personal and literally set in stone, because it is more public and monumental, the Safdie memorial raises issues concerning the memorial and ideological appropriation of Holocaust symbols and artifacts, their roles in referring to the "defiled center" that is the Shoah, and the potential for the co-option of those roles. As a monumental incorporation of the railway car, Safdie's memorial stands out as a powerful Holocaust icon and, possibly, an idol.

ICONOLOGY

I now return to the term *icon*, for its religious connotations naturally raise issues central to this discussion. My approach here echoes that of James Young, who hopes that by making "visible the activity of memory in [Holocaust] monuments . . . such a critique may save our *icons* of remembrance from hardening into *idols* of remembrance."[36] While "icon" invokes a certain degree of discomfort, particularly in the Jewish context, it also evokes powerful notions of sacralization that are attractive from a

theoretical standpoint and apropos of the "theological" styles of reference
and representation alluded to in the epigraphs to this chapter. Indeed, the
notion of sanctity in Holocaust symbols, whether it is derived from the
presumed sanctity of the Holocaust itself or from its "sacred" artifacts
and narratives, is a key subtext to this entire discussion. In this sense
Holocaust icons and Holocaust idols are competing versions of sanctification and sacralization. Turning a religious studies perspective on these
images, along with the processes that produce them, contributes to a
deeper understanding of those images and processes. In particular, I am interested here in exploring the interrelationships of literary and visual aesthetics through the lens of religious studies, a field whose natural inter-
disciplinarity, incidentally, enables me to engage in this discussion.

    W. J. T. Mitchell's typology of images in *Iconology* is helpful because
he outlines a view of the iconic mode of representation that, while respecting its religious orientations, also invites an interdisciplinary perspective. Mitchell identifies a "family tree" of different types of imagery,
ranging from the graphic (on the left side of his schema) to the optical,
the perceptual, the mental, and, finally, the verbal (on the right side) categories of images, each with its own disciplinary discourse. Over these is
the parent concept, the image "as such," whose institutional discourses,
incidentally, are philosophy and theology.[37] Mitchell's typology opens up
the concept of the icon as an image *of something* while "naturalizing"
the term so as not to engage the charge of the impropriety of such imagery (the *idol* presumably remains the term for the "improper" image or
representation).

    What attracts me to Mitchell's schema, besides the seductiveness of
the "logos" of the icon he develops, is the important correction he offers
for any theoretical consideration of visual imagery. Mitchell broadens the
range of imagery one may rightfully consider iconic while restoring to the
"icon" its role as the image "as such." His typology accepts as iconic
those classes of images on the right side of his spectrum—perceptual,
mental, and verbal images—against the idea that such icons are "improper," thereby engaging the debate over the propriety of images. Thus
he rightly suggests that the icon, in and of itself, is nothing to be feared.
Lest anyone set graphic and visual icons apart from mental and verbal
ones, Mitchell maintains that nothing is more or less proper in any class
of imagery, not only because of the fallacy of such charges of impropriety
regarding the perceptual, mental, and verbal classes of images but also because, according to Mitchell, the very root of the idea of the image—the
notion of "likeness" in the Bible—is resolutely nonpictorial, immaterial,

spiritual. This "spiritualization" of the concept of the icon allows it to continue to resonate aesthetically and religiously while further distinguishing it from idolatry. Moreover, in calling the "parent concept" of the image the "icon," Mitchell suggests a concept of imagery that is broadly inclusive as well as deeply engaging. Representation of any sort, then, relies on some form of imagery, and in calling the pivotal type of Holocaust imagery "iconic," I wish to reflect this argument and counter any misguided charges of impropriety. As I have suggested, it is more constructive to debate the effectiveness and form of different types of images than it is to legislate which images may not be permissible.

To reiterate, I use the term *icon* because of its religious connotations, which speaks to the issue of the presumed sanctity of Holocaust symbols and, especially, artifacts. When physical remnants are put on display—items that are actual artifacts from the time of the Holocaust, such as shoes or railway cars—the iconic mode of presentation is at its most visible. All these present themselves as unmediated effects of the Shoah, material witnesses, though mute, to the events that produced them. Attention to the contexts of their presentation—to the fact that they have been placed, arranged, naturalized, domesticated—makes clear that mediation is present nonetheless.[38] When they are displayed in memorial-museological environments, they carry, as vehicles of and for memory, an abundance of signification; these icons enact the past and offer a physical reminder of its weight and enormity.

They also highlight a problem of Holocaust representation. For close attention to the nature of these remnants on display shows a disturbing characteristic: their abundance of signification speaks a language of victimization and loss. Their sanctity is the product of two forces of objectification—that of the Nazis, who (sometimes) unwittingly but nonetheless disturbingly memorialized their victims by collecting their belongings in massive quantities, and that of museum curators, who memorialize those same victims by re-collecting (hence, *recollecting*) their belongings in display cases: "These remnants rise in a macabre dance of memorial ghosts. Armless sleeves, eyeless lenses, headless caps, footless shoes: victims are known only by their absence, by the moment of their destruction. In great loose piles, these remnants remind us not of the lives that once animated them, so much as the brokenness of lives."[39] The struggle represented by the Holocaust icon, then, is to transform this ghostliness and loss into life and presence, without violating the truth to which it refers in the service of the memory those employing it wish to create. I take this issue up again, in its broader museological context, in chapter 4.

Thus, I use the word "icon" to evoke the power and mystery of Holocaust symbols and remnants, to suggest the religious aura around them, and to call to mind the memorial roles they play in specific contexts. When the propriety of Holocaust symbols is invoked—specifically, the concern for protecting the sacred core of the Holocaust from abuse, as expressed by survivor-commentators such as Elie Wiesel—the symbolic easily becomes the iconic. The Holocaust, in this setting, is a sacred mystery held "over there" behind a carefully circumscribed fence that, presumably, protects it from abuse at the hands of all who would violate its memory and its symbols. But those symbols are not so easily controlled; they have a life of their own. It is that life to which I point in using "icon."

Let me clarify the representational problems invoked here with a digression into the display of women's hair shorn from camp inmates, arguably one of the most viscerally moving and ethically complex types of museum presentation. Once again one must pay attention to the complexities encompassed by the strategies of display and resist the urge to see the icon as self-evident (and self-presenting), as unmediated reenactment. At the Auschwitz museum, for example, nearly two tons of hair is displayed inside an enormous glass case—pure physical presence, unmediated "evidence of evil." The USHMM, in its quest to locate and display authentic artifacts as part of its museum narrative, had intended to display twenty pounds of the hair on loan from the Auschwitz museum. Though this amount would not have had the "weight" of the display at Auschwitz, it nonetheless would, one presumes, have created the desired effect. But two female survivors on the content committee objected to the presentation. "For all I know, my mother's hair might be in there," one said. "I don't want my mother's hair on display."[40]

Clearly, there was something about hair, as a literally (formerly) embodied remnant, that disturbed some survivors. Because of its connection to human life, its display was considered by some to be sacrilegious, a desecration of that life. So the museum decided to install a wall-length *photograph* of the nearly two tons of human hair exhibited in Auschwitz, instead of the "real thing" (see figure 5). But twenty pounds of that hair remain in a storage facility in Maryland, perhaps awaiting a time when no objections will be raised to its display. Had the hair been displayed, as it is at Auschwitz, the USHMM would have had to contend with the risk of fetishizing the hair and commemorating the perpetrators' acts of destruction. It also would have had to deal with claims of impropriety from survivors, of going too far in exhibiting victimization. But, in not displaying it, the Washington museum has chosen representation over presentation. It has reduced the icon to a disengaged symbol, one that may not have the authenticity and directness to carry the burden of memory adequately. The struggle of Holocaust representation, at least in the case of the display of objects I call iconic, is to overcome the victimization motif borne by the remnants themselves

Figure 5. Detail of a photo mural installed at the U.S. Holocaust Memorial Museum, Washington, D.C., depicting a pile of hair shorn from female Auschwitz prisoners as displayed at the National Museum of Auschwitz-Birkenau. Courtesy of USHMM Photo Archives.

without overcompensating and fetishizing, ultimately creating an idol in place of an icon.[41]

Holocaust icons, in their broadest sense, are thus "living," embodied distillations of Holocaust images, of the "Holocaust" itself. Better yet, they are enlivened embodiments of the Holocaust, whose life comes from a blend of their own inherent qualities and their emplacement in museological contexts and memorial narratives. They have a degree of presence (or presentness) that cannot be ignored, which marks them as different from other symbolic representations. This further refinement of the notion of the icon is partially informed by Ernst van Alphen's conceptualization of the Holocaust effect, though it differs from it in one important respect: "When I use the term *Holocaust effect*, therefore, I do so to emphasize a contrast with the term *Holocaust representation*. A representation is by definition mediated. It is an objectified account. The Holocaust is made present in the representation of it by means of *reference* to it. When I call something a Holocaust effect, I mean to say that we are not confronted with a representation of the Holocaust, but that we, as viewers or readers, experience directly a certain aspect of the Holocaust or of Nazism, of that which led to the Holocaust. In such moments the Holocaust is not re-presented, but rather presented or reenacted."[42] The notion of reenactment supports conceptualization of the enlivened quality of the Holocaust icon. I therefore find van Alphen's distinction supremely important and useful.

I differ with his argument with respect to mediation: for van Alphen, Holocaust "effects" are unmediated, whereas for me, Holocaust icons remain mediators of the memorial process. While the term *effects* strikes me as emphasizing the outcomes of memorial and representational processes, "icon" preserves the dual import of an object at once an artifact of that time and place and a present-day image standing in metonymically for the whole to which it refers. Direct experience of an aspect of the Holocaust is never completely unmediated, and mediation is crucial to the experience of Holocaust effects and Holocaust icons. One might distinguish between *external* mediation, what van Alphen calls Holocaust representation, because of its objectivized and referential qualities, and *internal* mediation, which occurs in any "reenactment" of an aspect of the Holocaust. In the latter case, the presence of the Holocaust is still invoked through the mediation of the reenactment, but because of the economy of presentation and its proximity to the subject, much of the work of mediation is transferred to that subject. As a result, a person "experiences" the Holocaust "directly," but mediation is still central to his experience, even if it is masked as subjectivity. I think van Alphen may ultimately agree with this assessment: "We are there; history is present—but not quite" he argues; we respond to the objects of van Alphen's study directly, but "in a different way."[43] That difference, I argue, is the all-important trace of mediation at the heart of what I call the Holocaust icon. Without it, we are lost; we become an indistinguishable part of the effect so that, in the case of Holocaust reenactments, the distinction between then and now, there and here, disappears.

The "re" of "reenactment" is therefore important, for no experience of a Holocaust representation or of a Holocaust effect is original.[44] Equally important is the enactment itself, as it is the performative quality of how an aspect of the Holocaust is contextualized that gives it its vibrancy and lends the illusion of immediacy. This performative aspect is better captured by the term *icon* in my estimation, especially in its religious connotations—ritual and ideological qualities that also highlight its simultaneous embodiment of past and present. As results of representational strategies, Holocaust icons share one key quality with Holocaust effects: both are necessarily "after the fact," and their study is to be seen in the context of the work of several scholars engaged with these issues, such as James Young, Marianne Hirsch, and Michelle Friedman, as I discussed in chapter 1. Despite their differences, these scholars share an interest in those who relate to and identify with the Holocaust through its memorialization—those who seek to articulate a *relationship* to the Shoah, in spite of the historical-temporal distance from the events being remembered. Holocaust icons as posthistorical reenactments engender the kinds of relationships these scholars find compelling.

What finally distinguishes Holocaust icons from Holocaust symbols is their rich discursive context: these particular symbols are overdetermined because they are formed by and through the discourses that have sprung up around them, which enhance their significance and provide narrative contexts for their memorial applications and social engagements. Such a discursive framework has made an icon of Auschwitz itself: the verbal image that partakes of the mystery of the whole, stands for it, represents it, and even presents it for memorial consumption. It is precisely this phenomenon Sidra DeKoven Ezrahi points to in the first epigraph to this chapter. Ezrahi situates her discussion against the background of sacred mystery and the language used in approaching it, which brings us back to our starting point.[45] To summarize, Holocaust icons are intensified forms of Holocaust symbols because they embody memory, model sacred engagement, mediate experience, and establish re-membered (re-memoried?) relationships to the past. Following Mitchell, they are complex images that challenge assumed proprieties of representation. Moreover, the most provocative icons are complex hybrids, intersections of two or more classes of imagery. These icons, like the *Memorial to the Deportees*, are what interest me the most.

But the very idea of a Holocaust icon—especially as sacred embodiment—may be viewed as problematic, particularly from the Jewish perspective, with respect to iconic representation. In the Jewish context there is a long history of religious and political debate over icons, largely because of the presumption that icons are idols. Jewish thought is commonly assumed to oppose visual representation. This proscription originates with the biblical prohibition against "graven images," generally taken to refer to the pictorial representation of the divine; such representation is a concern in the traditional view because it runs the risk of setting up alternative gods. But "why are linguistic representations of G-d apparently permitted while visual representations are forbidden? If it is permitted to describe G-d as possessing a hand, why is it forbidden to draw it?" ask Moshe Halbertal and Avishai Margalit.[46] Why indeed. It might seem that, as if based on the fallacy that linguistic images are not really images, Jewish thought has found a way to circumvent its own prohibitions against representation in order to imagine the divine linguistically, while maintaining that such imagination is not at all representative of the divine. This circumvention has the added advantage of maintaining an illusion of unmediated relation: the idea that through a linguistic mode of imagery a divine-human relation is engendered that is unsullied by graphic images (understood as illegal mediators).

Thus Judaism has long preferred the safety of seemingly aniconic verbal, rather than pictorial, language, and it has privileged word over (traditionally conceived) image; similar status is purportedly accorded to sound over sight, the ear over the eye. All these are conceived as political dichotomies, in that they preserve structures of power and preference for certain styles of communication and representation. In this light, is it any wonder that the Holocaust narrative still has primacy in discussions about appropriate memorial representations? It appears to offer a more politically and religiously acceptable strategy for approaching that "sacred mystery" without invoking the potential wrath of the memory police and their presumed charge of improper iconic representation.

But we need not accept the supposedly traditional dichotomy—not only because we learn from Mitchell that such hierarchies are essentially political at heart but also because the opposition within Jewish thought to graphic representation is itself neither long-standing nor particularly rigid (with the exception of the prohibition against representing G-d, which I uphold in this sentence). Kalman Bland, in his groundbreaking book *The Artless Jew* (2000), argues successfully that Jewish aniconism is an "unmistakably modern idea," dependent more on the "construction of modern Jewish identities" than on an actual history of aniconism.[47] Bland's observations suggest that resistance to the concept of the iconic within Jewish thought says more about Jewish struggles with modernity than about aesthetics. Thus one could conclude that Holocaust icons are properly Jewish icons; at the very least they are not, by nature, improper. Holocaust icons therefore play a crucial, necessary, and appropriate role in the construction of Holocaust memorial consciousness. Distinguishing them from their inappropriate relations, Holocaust idols, is a project that clarifies the contemporary production of that consciousness and its other possible outcomes.

Holocaust icons, as vehicles of Holocaust memory, have much to teach us about mediation and representation. As modes through which we approach the "sacred mystery" of the Holocaust, these icons are excellent models for memorial engagement. "Graven images" are both possible and appropriate for apprehending the "transcendental" experience Adi Ophir cynically calls the Holocaust in the second epigraph to this chapter. Representation must be endorsed, and Ophir's parody of a second Holocaust "commandment" is actually part of a larger argument *against* such a commandment and against the kind of "theological" representation that creates idols. Rather, Ophir favors more-engaged and embodied presentations which veer away from theological mystifications that make false (though unrepresentable) gods of the Holocaust and its effects. If there is anything "sacred" about the Holocaust it must be contained within the icons that serve as its mediators, its transmitters, if it is to be communicated to those who would appropriate its memory.

I return now to the issue of mediation, so crucial to the effectiveness of the icon and to its distinction from the idol. If Holocaust icons are to embody memory, they must nonetheless do so self-consciously, as it were, so as not to efface the very representational strategies that make them iconic. In other words, we as visitor-voyeurs must be able to trace a path *through* the icon *to* memory to discover our relationships to the past. Marking such a path is what the best of the Holocaust icons should embody.

ICONIC MEDIATION

Attention to the self-consciously mediative qualities inherent in and implied by Holocaust icons invites a broadening of the scope of discussion. For if we apply Mitchell's typology to the production of Holocaust representations, an entire range of images comes into view. What particularly interests me is how iconic imagery is appropriated for and applied to the development of Holocaust narratives: how the narrative qualities of the icon—how it tells, metonymically, a particular story—lead to further narrativization. Here, Holocaust icons are turned more directly into mediators for memory, suggesting as well further conceptualizations of the meaning of the Holocaust in the present.

In this regard I will discuss two examples of a more literary and graphic nature, whose strategies of embodiment are in many ways more interpretive and imaginative and less dependent on material metonymies than those mentioned above. In both cases complex Holocaust icons are created through a mix of suggested or actual visual imagery and verbal description; the mode of representation and its results are arresting and provocative. And in both cases, strategies for literal remembering offer models for engaging the "sacred mystery" of the Holocaust and mediating its effects for the reader-voyeur.

The first example derives from Art Spiegelman's remarkable graphic biography/autobiography *Maus*.[48] Though *Maus* relies on the artistic appropriation and transformation of numerous Holocaust symbols (such as swastikas and six-pointed stars) and images, I will focus specifically on Spiegelman's use of more-generic, even mythic, symbols in the depiction of different nationalities as different animal types, as represented by the use of animal heads and extremities for otherwise human characters.[49] Particularly interesting is that Spiegelman himself frequently reflects on the very strategy for graphic representation which he has adopted in his work. It is a bold and audacious representational technique, one that has met with some resistance. "Because *Maus* adopts a cartoon convention more usually associated with the happy-ever-after imaginings of Walt Disney, its critics accuse it of betraying the communal Jewish memory of the Holocaust, replacing fact with folklore," noted one reviewer. Going even further, Michael Rothberg states, "Spiegelman transgresses the sacredness of Auschwitz by depicting in comic strip images his survivor father's suffering and by refusing to sentimentalize the survivor."[50]

But from the perspective of iconic construction, this strategy can be read as a savvy way of further rehabilitating Nazi images, channeled through characterizations that resonate fabulistically, even mythically. Thus, by depicting Jews as mouse-folk, Germans as cat-people, Poles as literally pigheaded, and so on, Spiegelman takes the idea of framing survivor experience in the graphic context of a symbol such as a star or swastika steps further, so that real-life characters become mythological types (without losing their individuality). Some may find this cat-and-mouse game a bit disturbing and even offensive, as it casts Jew and German in the familiar and constricting eternal roles of victim and victimizer, offering no escape from the inevitable, recurring play of destruction and providing a literal and pictorial dehumanization.[51] Moreover, the representation of Poles as pig-people could be seen as an especially distasteful form of iconography—a deep-seated comic book revenge on years of Polish anti-Semitism that makes Poles boorish and *treyf* (nonkosher).[52] But I suggest that this representational strategy actually turns Nazi racial categorizations inside out, giving graphic shape to some of the very images and policies that motivated Nazi actions in the first place. This representational revisionism also serves to distill those complex policies into easily apprehended images, thereby offering a series of potent vehicles for the transmission of Holocaust memory and its impact on subsequent generations. Stereotypes they may be, but they nonetheless offer compact presentations of real historical relations in condensed forms, presentations that are remarkably effective.

Spiegelman's representational choices, incidentally, echo one well-known Jewish strategy for avoiding the representation of the human face. The idea is that the person, made in the "image" of God, should be depicted as missing or lacking an essential element, as in the Sarajevo Haggadah, with its famous birds' heads in place of human ones.[53] The missing piece of the iconic representation thus rejects totality and complete identification in favor of a broken kind of similitude, which in the case of Spiegelman is neither man nor mouse.[54] In this way we get a window onto the underlying sophistication of Spiegelman's strategy, which resists the kind of simplification his critics assume is present in his work. Adam Gopnik writes, "It's extremely important to understand that *Maus* is in no way an animal fable or an allegory like Aesop or *Animal Farm*. The Jews are Jews who just happen to be depicted as mice, in a peculiar, idiosyncratic convention. There isn't any allegorical dimension in *Maus*, just a convention of representation." That convention of representation, in other words, does not work indirectly, in which case the images would serve to convey something other than what they convey in and of themselves, but works directly to convey something essential about the events depicted. The simple sketches (Spiegelman has said that he wanted the finished product to have the look and feel of a manuscript or someone's personal diaries) succeed in doing "what all artists who have made the Holocaust their subject have tried to do: to stylize [I would say symbolize] the horror without aestheticizing it."[55]

What is fascinating about Spiegelman's open strategy of symbolization and iconic construction is how the artist continually undermines and subverts that strategy. "By adopting the mouse as allegorical image for Jews, Spiegelman is able to caricature—and thereby subvert—the Nazi image of Jews as vermin."[56] This strategy also adds to the reasons for rejecting the implications of allegory in *Maus*. Spiegelman himself notes, "Because I'm working with a metaphor that is absolutely flawed, the idea is to work against the metaphor as often as I work with it." At times, this subversion happens subtly, as when Vladek and Anja are hiding and a rat terrifies Anja (to which Vladek replies, "It's only a mouse"). More noteworthy is an episode when, pretending to be Poles, the couple walks the streets wearing pig masks over their mouse heads (see figure 6).[57]

Here Spiegelman graphically depicts both Nazi racial classification and the terror of its consequences, presented in the context of "passing" as a non-Jew in Nazi-occupied Poland; he addresses the connection between racial identity, physical appearance, and survival through the very convention of representation he has established in his books. In this panel, Anja is "clearly" more "Jewish-looking" than Vladek, who has discovered that he is generally more able to pass in non-Jewish society than is she; Spiegelman conveys Anja's physical vulnerability by the long mouse tail sticking out from under her coat, even as she and Vladek wear pig masks that are clearly invisible to those they pass on the street. Rothberg observes that "while Vladek is able confidently to feign Polishness, Anja's body leaks Jewishness, her mouse tail drags behind her and signals the limits of her *goyische* drag."[58] Later, at the end of the first volume of *Maus*, the couple is on a train, presumably on their way to safety in Hungary after having entrusted their fate to a dubious band of smugglers. They are suddenly surprised and captured by the Gestapo, who literally and figuratively unmask the Jews. In both cases, Spiegelman throws into sharp relief the problem of racial identity, refracted through the convention of animal-like representation he has honed to perfection.

The panels show Spiegelman playing with his own representational schema. As media for conveying Holocaust-era racial categories and relations, the animal-human hybrids are effective icons, while the panels depicting animal heads as masks undercut any easy assumptions one might make about those racial roles or their representation. The most severe, perhaps iconoclastic, self-critique of this strategy occurs in volume 2 of *Maus*, where one page sums up the entire range of representational complexity found in the work (see figure 7).[59]

Here Spiegelman draws himself at his worktable, wearing a mouse mask over his *human* head, reflecting on both personal and collective Jewish history on the first page of a chapter titled "Time Flies." The conflation of various historical events in time, both great and small, through their recitation, is reflected pictorially in the complete breakthrough of

Figure 6. Art Spiegelman, *Maus: A Survivor's Tale*, p. 136.

Time flies...

Figure 7. Art Spiegelman, *Maus II: A Survivor's Tale: And Here My Troubles Began*, p. 41.

the past into the present: as in the Auschwitz-style guard tower outside the window and the pile of mouse-head corpses (complete with flies— "*time* flies," perhaps?) under Art's desk. Another example of this technique, in which past and present mingle, occurs as Vladek is recounting the story of the Auschwitz camp rebellion. The legs of the women who struck back at the Nazis encroach into the frame of the story line, just as, one presumes, the memories of those times constantly invade Vladek's present.[60]

The intent of the technique seems clear: to indicate, by indirection, of course, both the quality of memory and its invasion on Art (and on his father) and the horrific nature of those memories, their nightmarish aspects, made all too real by our knowledge that they really did occur. The "distanced realism" of the iconic pile of corpses (so reminiscent of those horrific early films and photographs of the camps after liberation) protects us from blunt reality, as the corpses are "only" mice, not men in masks, even as the representational metaphor is subverted in Art's own mouse mask.[61] Art now adopts the very convention he has used for others, no longer keeping it at bay, like the memories he grapples with and struggles to represent. Furthermore, Art, depicting himself as fully human (elsewhere he too is a mouse-person), initiates two processes of representation and reflection. First, he distinguishes himself from his narrative creation, not now a character in his father's story but a creator trying to represent it. Thus he sets himself apart from his convention of representation just long enough to remind us (in case we forgot) of what is really at stake— the Holocaust as a real historical event involving real people, not a cat-and-mouse game. Art feels the burden of history here as literally subversive—not so much weighing down on him as piling up under him as he works; it is no wonder that he is depressed.

In the second process of representation and reflection, by adopting the mask of racial Jewish identity (within his schema), Spiegelman reminds us that he has taken upon himself the burden and the challenge, as one who comes after, to tell the tale and accept a responsibility to the past, to his father's memory, and to the future. Simply by adopting the mouse mask, he questions his own abilities to meet this challenge successfully, even in the midst of his commercial and critical success. Subsequent panels show him getting smaller and smaller, eventually crying for mommy, and remaining small into the next scene, where he talks about his work with his "shrink"—who, incidentally, has a home overrun with stray dogs and cats. This story is certainly no animal fable but rather the crisis of the Holocaust's iconic representation actualized: how does one

appropriate, transform, and embody Holocaust symbols to communicate
best a relationship to the past? It is as if Spiegelman has depicted the contemporary struggle to find a way *into* the narratives of the Shoah through
the symbols and stories that are, in many cases, the only inheritance
from that place and time. It is a delicate balance between appropriation
and imagination, embodiment and engagement, which is mediated by
Holocaust icons but not necessarily guaranteed by them. The danger is
that, in remembering the Holocaust through the distilled media of its expression, we risk becoming traumatized ourselves. Spiegelman's technique offers a way into a story of the Holocaust without eclipsing that
story through an overreliance on his particular medium of expression.
With the sign of the mask, he thus maintains that crucial balance.

   Maus is, after all, a memorial book, commemorating not only one
man's story of survival and another's quest for remembrance but also, in
winding the tales together and presenting them in an economy of words
and pictures, investing them with symbolic significance in the present.
For Spiegelman, the book fulfills a quasi-religious function, both because
of the link it creates with a sacred past (he has said that "the Holo-
caust/the Shoah/the Genocide has become one of the central Holy Sacra-
ments of secular Judaism, the primary bond that many of us have to
the Faith of our Fathers") and because of a real purpose it has filled.[62] In
one article, Spiegelman recounts how, near the time of the anniversary of
Vladek's death, Françoise suggested they get a *yahrzeit* (memorial) candle:
"And it made me real uncomfortable, and when we were getting to the
checkout counter, this thing was beginning to glow, you know, next to the
Rice Krispies. I just didn't want it there. And at the last minute, I just
couldn't do it; I just put it down next to the TV Guides and didn't get it.
And trying to think about it later, I figured that ultimately 'Maus' is sort
of like this incredibly long and arduous and intense yartzeit [*sic*] candle,
so what the hell did I need this flickering light for?"[63] The *Maus* volumes
themselves become iconic here, standing in, at least for Spiegelman, for
other mediators of memory and providing an important link to the Jewish experience of World War II, writ archetypally via the author's particular technique. This hypersymbolic level of meaning, like the others explored thus far, depends on the taut maintenance of representational
paradox and contradiction: "At the heart of our understanding (or lack of
understanding) of the Holocaust is our sense that this is both a human and
an inhuman experience. . . . In order to show that these events are in some
way sacred to us, we have to indicate, in art [pun intended?], that they are
at once part of human history and outside it. The overlay of the human

and the inhuman is exactly what *Maus*, with its odd form, is extraordinarily able to depict."[64] And through this overlaying strategy, Spiegelman succeeds in constructing a symbolic vocabulary for the mediation and appropriation of the Holocaust legacy.

INSCRIBING THE BODY OF MEMORY

I will continue to flesh out this mediation process through the discussion of another provocative example, Emily Prager's novel *Eve's Tattoo*, in which the author frames in interesting ways an essential element of the symbolic vocabulary of Nazism as it is specifically inscribed on victims' bodies: tattooing. The literal embodiment of Nazi ideology in the tattooed identification number itself reflects the notion of the icon as a form of memorial embodiment. When that potent remnant of Nazism's assault on European Jewry is itself appropriated in Prager's novel and made both the subject and, within the book, the object of fictional narrative, the literal embodiment becomes a literary embodiment. The novel thus brings together the literary and the visual, the real and the fictional, within a narrative that engages issues of propriety and sanctity. The ways Prager adapts what has up until now been viewed only as a largely static, museological-memorial model of iconic presentation, transforming it into a fictional version of performance art and filling out its narrative potential, shows how an icon such as the image of the tattoo can become a medium for Holocaust memory. But let me first frame this discussion with reference to an image borrowed from the U.S. Holocaust Memorial Museum.[65]

Here in one memorable room is a wall almost entirely covered with photographs of camp inmates' forearms—seventy-two of them, roughly life-sized—with the tattooed numbers clearly visible (see figure 8). In the center of the display is a posed photo of four men from Salonika, all heads and tattooed arms, taken at a survivors' reunion, showing that their bodily inscriptions have hardly faded with the passage of time. All this is set below a quotation from Primo Levi's remarkable memoir, *Survival in Auschwitz*: "My number is 174517; we have been baptized, we will carry the tattoo on our left arm until we die."[66] The image is arresting, and it speaks to the multiple and mass experiences of the Nazi language of domination as it is literally inscribed into human flesh. Yet the image is complicated by Levi's (borrowed) inscription, which speaks in a decidedly Christian idiom. Moreover, the disembodied arms make it more difficult to see any gender differences in these individuals, presenting instead the perspective of a unified Nazi "master" narrative that sought to strip gen-

Figure 8. Mural composed of photographs taken by Frédéric Brenner, part of the permanent exhibit at the U.S. Holocaust Memorial Museum, Washington, D.C. Photograph by Edward Owen, courtesy of USHMM Photo Archives.

der from its victims. As if to respond to this issue, on the opposite side of the same room at the USHMM, separated by a partition, is the glass case containing the photograph of women's hair discussed above: against the multiplicity of individual arms and their gender indeterminacy, the massive photo of the hair speaks specifically to women's experiences. Both images, incidentally, flesh out the narrative more indirectly represented by the boxcar in a previous room; these photographs show, we presume, what became of the people we imaginatively place in the railway car. The images thereby highlight issues concerning memorial embodiment, engagement, and narrativization explored more fully in Prager's novel.

Eve's Tattoo tells a fairly straightforward story whose narrative context tells us much about the Holocaust's iconic representation. The narrative begins with protagonist Eve Flick's trip to Big Dan's Tattoo Parlor ("a monument to male violence" and Nazi fetishism) to get herself a fortieth birthday present.[67] Her gift? A tattooed identification number copied precisely from a photograph of an anonymous female death camp victim who bears an uncanny resemblance to Eve (who is not Jewish): blond and blue-eyed, the "perfect Aryan specimen." Eve's goal is clear: "I want to remember her. I want to keep her alive. I'm wearing the tattoo like an MIA bracelet" (11).[68] Eve's project is nothing less than the memorialization of all women who lived and died during the Holocaust, the reinscription of women's stories into the flesh of the historical record and memorial discourse that have largely excluded them. It is also the quest for the expiation of a personal sense of guilt: "[The tattoo is] about the hearts and souls of women. About me. I'm of German ancestry. I'm a Christian. I'm a woman and I have to know—do I have mass murder in my blood or what?" (51).[69]

Thus, Eve's project is one of remembering women through her act of bodily inscription, an incorporation of women in history through memory. Within the novel, Eve's representations of "Eva" (the name she gives to the woman in the photograph) serve to refigure and recast as multiple individuals the generic woman of Holocaust discourse, commonly thought of (*if* she is thought of) as a nameless, faceless victim. Eve's embodiment of Holocaust memory through her tattoo engenders seven stories about seven different "Evas," returning gender to a discourse that has largely excluded it and also giving women multiple voices over an oppressive monologue. There is a double reinscription and rememorialization going on here, the reinscription of gender into the master narrative of the Holocaust and the reinscription of individuality.[70] But as Eve's women reenter history and memory under the tattooist's gun, the reinscription and remembering occur via a problematic reappropriation of the image of tattooing. Can that image be rehabilitated?

Eve's project of reinscription depends on her sense of the urgency of remembrance: "Well, in a very few years . . . the people who lived through the Third Reich will all be dead. And when the people who experienced an event are no longer walking the planet, it's as if that event never existed at all. There'll be books and museums and monuments, but things move so fast now, the only difference between fantasy and history is living people. I'm going to keep Eva alive. She'll go on living, here, with me" (11). But Eve is blind to her own confusion of fantasy and history: the fictional project of historical revision Eve attempts, conceived as an alternative to the museological mode of memorialization, depends on the fantasies she creates about her different Evas. Eve's mission of (re)memory turns, therefore, on the disturbing symbolic appropriation and embodiment of a copied tattoo, something many might call improper for a variety of reasons. But Eve's memorial (re)inscription also loses something "in translation." Consider, for example, her summary of Nazism: "a psychotic obsession with glory, a murderous mania for purity, and a visceral hatred of women" (28). Where are the Jews in this description?

Prager credits Claudia Koonz's noteworthy *Mothers in the Fatherland* as a key source for her novel. Without it, she notes, "Eva's tales could not have been imagined." Unlike the historian Koonz, who keeps the parallel discourses of Nazism distinct (Nazis versus women and Nazis versus Jews), the fictional character Eve seems to sacrifice the nature of the Jewish experience of the Shoah for that of women in her memorial tapestry. Thus only two of the seven tales Eve tells are about self-identified Jewish women: the first, for example, is about "Eva Klein," a Jewish yuppie "U-boat" hiding "underground" in Berlin for most of the war, posing as an Aryan.[71] If Prager, as the author, is reclaiming gender as a forgotten category for apprehending and representing the Holocaust, her protagonist may be accused of violating the propriety of Jewish memory in her own parallel project. Indeed, it is this aspect of the novel that makes it both provocative and problematic as a Holocaust "tale." The construction of an icon of remembrance here appears to involve some degree of forgetfulness in the interplay of representational agendas.

Or it may simply rest on a shaky foundation. In attempting to personalize the Holocaust in her fourth tale, told to her gay Uncle Jim who is dying of AIDS, Eve begins to slip. This story tells of "Eva Marks," a Red Cross nurse assigned to dole out water to troop transports at the Berlin *Bahnhof*. One day she sees a different sort of train pull in, made of cattle cars and guarded by SS men. As she tries to give water to those inside, she is shoved in and trapped by one of the guards. Eva Marks was "gassed by mistake at Auschwitz six months later" (92). Was it a mistake? Is there a difference between her death by gas and all the others?

Eve's fifth tale marks a further deterioration of the protagonist's qualities of discernment and the concomitant dangers of memorial embodiment. From the moment she got her tattoo, Eve's lover, Charles César, refused to have sex with her and eventually left her. "Now that Charles César was gone, Eve had begun to talk to Eva in her mind, their relationship had progressed from remembrance to cohabitation, from the past to the present. People, Eve thought, would think her mad if they knew. But they'd be wrong. It was keeping her sane" (93). Eve's Holocaust fantasies have become her reality; she has fully appropriated them, and they have taken up residence in her mind. When Eve picks up a young man at a club and takes him home for a one-night stand, he asks about her tattoo:

> "Oh," he said, examining it, "were you in a camp?"
> "What?" she asked.
> "Were you in a Nazi camp?" he asked again.
> Eve looked at him sharply. She had told him she was thirty-five. He was looking back at her, concerned, empathetic, sincere. Could it be that he didn't know that World War II ended in 1945?
> "Yes," she ventured. "Yes. I was at Auschwitz."
> He saw no contradiction there. He just felt rotten about it. (98)

Ignoring the implied critique of Americans' lack of historical awareness, in the context of the progression of the novel Eve's tattoo has become more than a vehicle of and for memory. It has become the embodiment and object of fantasy—new rather than mediated experience.

Eve proceeds to tell the young man about herself as the Jewish "Eva Flick" (Eve's "real" last name), who was arrested by the Gestapo during a roundup of Jews with police records—"Eva" had once received a speeding ticket. But this revelation serves only to arouse the young man. Has Eve's memorial representation veered off into kitsch eroticism and away from its purported goal?[72] In this fictional episode, the young man's fascination with Eve's tattoo highlights its symbolic potency as a vehicle for a variety of performative and representational agendas. At the same time, this episode makes a powerful statement regarding gender representation and women's sexuality, working against both male objectifying representations and radical feminist ones that make a victim of any woman who seeks out heterosexual relations.[73]

Issues of sexuality, gender representation, and propriety come to a head when Eve faints at a film screening and an old man, Jacob Schlaren, helps her. Schlaren, who bears an authentic tattooed number (and the authentic "memory of offense," to use Primo Levi's phrase), tells Eve his "real" Holocaust story.[74] He recounts how he, like her, looked "the perfect Aryan specimen" (150). And he tells how he survived for a while by posing as an Aryan girl, "becoming" a boy again only in the railway car on the way to the death camp, assuming the identity of a dead passenger and thus "qualifying" for work rather than gassing. Noting that "his sexuality was indeterminate" (147), Eve soon learns that Schlaren is in fact a renowned Yiddish transvestite. We would think that Schlaren's tale, which in the context of the novel is not "fantasy," would expose Eve's appropriations as improper, but he does not condemn Eve for her memorial activity and, therefore, neither does the reader. His "true" tale reflects both the story of gender indeterminacy of Holocaust victims—shaved heads, unisex uniforms, tattooed numbers instead of names, and starvation all served not only to dehumanize but also to strip away gender distinction—and the suggestion, made by several commentators, that women possessed certain skills (despite greater responsibilities) that better equipped them for survival.[75]

Immediately after this episode, Eve sets out to discover the "real identity" of the woman whose tattoo she wears. On the way she is in an accident, which serves as a convenient plot device: run over by a van, Eve's arm is shattered, the bone protruding right at the tattoo. After the arm is operated on, Eve wakes to realize that "the tattoo was gone—in its stead, a neat row of suturing staples. Eva's lifeline to earth had been severed, her memory imprisoned by a newfangled barbed-wire fence" (176). "Eva's" memory is once again made inaccessible, because its adopted icon has disappeared. As a result, however, she and her lover are able to reconcile, and they immediately have sex in the hospital bed. What can we make of this disturbing resolution? Sara Horowitz writes, "Pushed to its extreme, the idea of seeing the Holocaust solely in terms of eros and sexual violation (as in Emily Praeger's [sic] novel, Eve's Tattoo) domesticates the Holocaust, diminishing its horror to something more ordinary and sparing the reader a more disturbing confrontation."[76] Isn't the erasure or cover-up of Eve's tattoo much too easy a way out for the protagonist?[77] How many victims and survivors have tattoos and memories that are indelibly inscribed (represented by the wall of photographs at the USHMM)? How do we assess this attempt at iconic presentation and embodiment?

In the denouement of the novel, Eve learns "Eva's" "real" story, which is disturbing: "Eva" was Leni Essen, a good Nazi mother who took great pride in her twin sons, enrolling them in the Hitler Youth. But as the war progressed, Leni's sons rebelled and joined an anti-Nazi gang. Beside herself with worry, anger, and shame, Leni could do nothing until one day she learned they were being hanged for their activities; Leni ran with a butcher knife, screaming, and stabbed the first Nazi she saw. She was arrested, sent to Auschwitz, and "murdered by a capo a week before liberation" (193). Again, such a tale threatens to de-Judaize the story of the Holocaust (it does not help that Eve says Leni was "tattooed by mistake" [193]), confounding our expectations about Nazi tattooing. But it also makes a profound statement about the nature of the Nazi assault on women, illustrating the effect of the internal separation of the "folk organism" that Eve might call (in another context) a "self-disembowelment."[78] The layered, fictional narrative of one woman's appropriation of Holocaust memory through its reinscription in her own flesh and its exposure to various improprieties thus ends with a complex and provocative image. As a (fictional) vehicle for memory, the iconic tattoo has served as a medium for storytelling, but some of these stories complicate our expectations concerning what the Holocaust means.

Roz Kaveny, in a review of the novel, notes that "it is difficult for a non-jew [sic] to find a voice in which to talk about the Holocaust without being accused of insulting the memory of the dead."[79] Do we accuse Eve of this as well? If, in Prager's attempt to turn around an icon at the very core of Nazism's literal and symbolic vocabulary of violence to serve the project of memorialization, she pushes the bounds of propriety, shouldn't she nevertheless be commended? Clearly, a difference exists between Eve, the storytelling protagonist with a shaky grip on history and propriety, and Prager, who has created Eve as a fictional character. Prager is in the position of making Eve whomever she wants her to be, while Eve is constrained by her creator's wishes. But because Eve herself is an author of stories, a certain parallel structure and movement is initiated. Prager is to Eve what Eve is to Eva: creator and therefore mistress of iconic construction and memorial presentation. If we momentarily forget the differences between them, we see how Eve mirrors Prager's memorial acts and, moreover, surpasses them through her willing embodiment of the mark of memory's inscription and enactment. In this way, Eve's Tattoo resonates with remembrance, enacting through narration the process of internal mediation posited above.

Furthermore, by making Eve (and Eva's "real" embodiment in Leni Essen) such a "perfect Aryan specimen," who nonetheless is moved to embody Holocaust memory through her own, albeit adopted, tattooed icon of remembrance, the author challenges both those who would claim ownership of the Shoah and its symbols, as well the religious exclusivity that would make idols of icons. Against such notions of a "memory offended," Eve appropriates the fictional Leni's tattoo in order to engender a historical revision, reinscription, and remembering. Eve's physical embodiment of Holocaust memory in her tattoo initiates a quest for the lost presence of this memory. The narrative image thus created is one of Holocaust iconization and presentation merged, at least within Prager's narrative framework, to peak effect.

Thus, Eve's particular engagement with the past confronts as well the challenges faced by those with a pronounced distance—whether by gender, generation, or faith—from the Holocaust and its memorial discourses.[80] It is this distance that is increasingly commonplace, at the same time as it creates the "theological quest" Ezrahi refers to in the first epigraph to this chapter. Indeed, this distance also creates the need for Holocaust icons. Prager as the author works to preserve both the universal and the particular aspects of the Holocaust and its memory as she attempts to make it relevant for the contemporary era: despite their apparent impropriety, their unsuitability, Eve's seven tales are actually tailor-made, ideally suited for their audiences. As such, they jolt their listeners and readers to a certain historical awareness, even as they reclaim some of that history, in its fragmented multiplicity, for women. In this way, they accentuate the iconic potential, at least in fictional form, of the (appropriated) Holocaust tattoo, where a mark of suffering can be transformed into a vehicle for remembrance. Perhaps the reader should follow Schlaren, the Yiddish transvestite, who, as an "authentic" survivor, is *allowed* to permit Eve access to Holocaust symbols as she struggles to remember women, and find a place for herself, in Holocaust memory. Or perhaps one should follow James Young, who argues that "to remove the Holocaust from the realm of the imagination . . . to sanctify it and place it off-limits, is to risk excluding it altogether from public consciousness. And this seems to be too high a price to pay for saving it from those who would abuse its memory in inequitable metaphor. Better abused memory in this case, which might then be critically qualified, than no memory at all."[81] To the question of memorial propriety, then, Prager responds, in her novel, by arguing that any symbolic ownership must be shared by men and women, Jews and non-Jews; Holocaust icons are the proper possessions of no one, which, in a way, is part of what makes them iconic.

HOLOCAUST IDOLS?

Both Emily Prager and Art Spiegelman pay close attention to the difficulties encountered in the appropriation and construction of effective memorial icons of the Holocaust. Each represents these struggles in the context of his or her protagonist's own challenges of representation. Thus, in each case, the author's struggle to represent a Holocaust effect is mirrored by his or her alter ego's struggle at iconic presentation. In each case, author and character(s) offer ways *into* an engagement with the memory of the Holocaust. This internal reflexivity reveals a degree of complexity in each work that enriches our perception of it. But it also serves to initiate a kind of movement, a representational repetition or recurrence, that highlights the mediating effect of the icon as a whole, which I argue is so crucial to our apprehension of it as an icon.

It may seem that I have strayed quite far from my initial territory. Yet the discussion of *Maus* and *Eve's Tattoo* actually returns me to the debate over the nature and constitution of Holocaust icons and their distinction from Holocaust idols. The analysis of Spiegelman's and Prager's works reveals their resistance to idolatry, despite the complex engagements with memorial figures and the vocabulary of Nazism depicted therein. Neither author, in the end, makes of his or her material a false god; neither completely fetishizes his or her subject in the course of reproducing remembrance.

The discussion of these two cases posits two models, though creative and at least somewhat fictional, for iconic engagement with and transformation of Holocaust symbols that, however "improper," nonetheless display the mediative potential of such appropriations. Such icons, generative of so many meanings, allow the process of Holocaust signification to remain open and flexible, resistant to the closure of meaning generated by the idol. In *this* case, when the literalism of the icon is overpowering, or when it simply lacks the internal reflexivity that prevents a literal reading, the icon is overdetermined and veers into idolatrous territory. If the icon is bounded on one end of its spectrum by the disembodied symbol, its other extreme is the idol. While this version of idolatry is less a risk in the case of literary and graphic imagery, it is a greater concern in the case of artifactual presentation. Peter Novick is struck by how "'un-Jewish'—how *Christian*" Holocaust commemoration has become, as in the "fetishized objects on display like so many fragments of the True Cross or shin bones of saints. . . . Perhaps most significantly, there is the way that suffering is sacralized and portrayed as the path to wisdom—the cult of the survivor as the secular saint. These are themes that have some minor and peripheral precedent in Jewish tradition, but they resonate more powerfully with major themes in Christianity."[82] Clearly, the transposition of such objects to the American context has in many cases required a translation of their presentation and reception into the local religiocultural idiom. Such a process participates in the broader debate between universalistic and particularistic interpretations of the Holocaust's legacy, which extends beyond the boundaries of this discussion. Nevertheless, in terms of this analysis, idolatrous representations of the Holocaust would appear as transformations of Holocaust icons, redemptive closures to the complex, multivocal narratives icons initiate, intensified sacralizations of the images out of which they are constructed. As a way of engaging this distinction, I return now to the use of railway cars in memorial contexts.

How is the risk of idolatry played out in the case of the boxcars under consideration here? For the *Memorial to the Deportees*, the stability of the icon as a nonidolatrous symbol is threatened by its inaccessibility and inflexible narrative voice. But as long as the visitor understands this icon as only a *possibility* of reenactment and presentation, as long as we do not believe that it was *this* car that yielded this poem, as long as this memorial remains a vehicle for reminding visitors of the history that lies behind it, then the icon remains an icon, open in its memorial possibilities. But when the memorial is put in the service of a different historical-memorial narrative, when the overall image the icon presents is given closure in pointing toward a redemptive narrative, away from the Holocaust, the problem of idolatry arises. Precisely this kind of narrativization is expressed in Yad Vashem's Web site describing the *Memorial*: "Although symbolizing the journey towards annihilation and oblivion, facing as it does the hills of Jerusalem the memorial also conveys the hope and the gift of life to the State of Israel and Jerusalem, eternal capital of the Jewish people."[83] This alternative narrative voice calls our attention to the way in which this memorial is positioned ideologically, for it is a staple of contemporary Holocaust memorialization that the birth of the State of Israel be configured as coming out of the ashes of Jewish Europe. Even in the standard structure of commemoration, "Holocaust" is coupled with heroism, destruction with rebirth in the Promised Land, understood as the symbol of national redemption.[84] In the memorial strategy of displacement and replacement, Safdie's railcar has been transplanted from its original environment, brought "home" to perch precariously over a Judean valley. In this context the icon has been made into an idol of the state.

Idolatry is also a possibility in the implicit fetishization of the railcar instigated by the Florida Holocaust museum's tzedaka box miniaturization, which makes the vehicle of memory and historic suffering, through the artist's interpretation, into a vessel for charitable giving and, perhaps, religious reflection. Hopefully, those purchasing and using the tzedaka box(car) find ways to remember something of the Holocaust in the course of their charitable reflections, rather than merely remembering their visit to the museum in St. Petersburg through their kitsch souvenir. A good balance between fetishization and idolatry, on the one hand, and disengaged, disembodied symbolization, on the other, occurs at the USHMM. Here, as visitors walk through the railway car, memory is embodied and personalized without becoming commodified or theologized. Because they walk through and also emerge from the car, visitors can take away a sense of both victimization and loss, blended with the awareness of life and continuity in the present.[85] Perhaps this is the mix of memory and forgetfulness that is the hallmark of the effective Holocaust icon.

Sidra Ezrahi, concluding the introduction to her remarkable literary study *Booking Passage*, writes: "The ultimate challenge to the Israeli writer is how to keep images from becoming icons, archaeology from becoming eschatology, 'arrival' from becoming the terminus of a vengeful excess of memory, the eros of an unconsummated journey from being extinguished in the killing fields of exclusive visions—how to *reopen* the narrative so that narrative itself can continue and one can hear the suppressed, the silenced, the restless and unpatriated voices."[86] In the ongoing struggle to represent the Holocaust adequately and appropriately, I have argued that the icon actually plays a significant role in "reopening" Holocaust narratives, allowing us to hear those forgotten voices. In this way, I disagree with Ezrahi's dichotomy, or rather, I wish to refine it. For it is the icon, I contend, that offers the best hope for such symbolic integration and repatriation and the "idol" that embodies the "eschatological" transformation of memory. In this light, where Ezrahi writes of "icons," I would substitute "idols."

Holocaust icons are the media of Holocaust memory in the twenty-first century. Though they are often given homes in museums and memorials far from their birthplace or inscribed and adopted as appropriated images, they retain their connections to the events that spewed them out and convey the multiple meanings of those events through their roles as vehicles of and for memory. These meanings, embodied by the icons, are endlessly renewed and renewable, because the icons that convey them do not close off the routes to memory that continue to sustain and enliven their significatory roles. Were they to do so, memory would calcify, icons would become idols, and, in the extreme, the Holocaust itself would be forgotten. In the face of so much suffering, that would be the ultimate memorial impropriety.

The icons discussed here are a small sampling of many and variegated strategies for symbolically representing and engaging the Holocaust and its impact on the present. Each one offers a particular technique for embodying memory. The use of Holocaust-era railway cars, as at Yad Vashem and elsewhere, represents a more traditional (and museological) strategy for placing artifacts in the context of specific memorial narratives which are themselves embodied in that artifact. These icons serve memory tourists in their quest for memorial engagement, which I will further address in chapters 4 and 5.

The transformation and incorporation of aspects of the symbolic language of Nazi persecution, as represented in very different ways by Spiegelman and Prager, present more complex models for engagement. Prager's rehabilitation, through Eve, of the bodily inscription of tattooing (one of the more brutal discourses of Nazism), so as to re-member women into the discourse of remembrance, suggests at least the possibility for a careful appropriation of the language of atrocity and dehumanization in the service of the rehumanization of victims of Nazism. Though Eve's embodiment of memory is extreme, it is suggestive of the process whereby those removed from the events and the experiences of the Holocaust may draw closer to them. This kind of perspective recurs in all subsequent chapters of this book.

Finally, Spiegelman's translation of the Nazi image of the Jew as inhuman (and forever persecuted) into a serious cat-and-mouse game highlights the near mythological manner in which Nazi discourse, as well as subsequent, almost religious, commentary on the brutal consequences of that discourse, has figured and inscribed the memory of World War II, and continues to do so—both in survivors and those who come after. Spiegelman's continual deconstruction of his own symbolic language also serves to question that iconography and the status of the survivor and the child of survivors (and all the other "types") it represents in such economy of form. Within Maus, Art struggles as well with the representation of the Holocaust itself—a fitting model of questioning and difficulty we should bear in mind—and with his very relationship to what is being represented, particularly as embodied in his father. Thus, even as Art (and the author) frames Vladek and his experiences, he questions the process whereby those experiences are framed. This issue of framing memory is the subject of the next chapter.

CHAPTER THREE

Framing Memory

VIDEOTESTIMONIES AND THE TRANSMISSION
OF HOLOCAUST REMEMBRANCE

> The storyteller makes no choice
> Soon you will not hear his voice
> His job is to shed light
> And not to master.
>
> —ROBERT HUNTER, *Terrapin Station*

VIDEO FRAMES

THE VIDEO begins with familiar material: images from newsreels, old photographs, melancholy music, all evoking the difficult and disturbing history of the Holocaust. A disembodied voice comes over the images, sounding vaguely familiar. Soon, the images fade and are replaced by a distinguished-looking gentleman walking slowly through a high-tech media center. And then we recognize him: Ben Kingsley, well-known actor and costar of the Holocaust blockbuster *Schindler's List.* Though he looks "normal" in this setting, we cannot help but think of him in his movie persona, the paradigmatic Jew Yitzhak Stern, standing in then (and now?) for the impersonal mass of Jewish suffering of the Shoah. In his appearance, Kingsley represents, perhaps, the double (though in this case assumed) identity of the survivor, embodying two distinct strains of lived and remembered experience: life then, "over there," and life now, "over here." The blurring and confusion is intentional, I think; we are meant to conflate the two roles Kingsley plays and understand something about the frames of reference this video offers as a result.

This opening scene is the beginning of a Hollywood production slightly different from the one for which Spielberg won several academy awards: a short promotional video shot "behind the scenes" at the Survivors of the Shoah Visual History Foundation (the VHF or, as its own staff refers to it, the Shoah Foundation), a project reportedly inspired by the director's work on *Schindler's List* and funded with seed money from the film's proceeds.[1] As the tape depicts, while Spielberg was making his film in Poland, "'at least a dozen Holocaust survivors journeyed there, using the film as a cushion to find closure with their nightmare. They showed up, and often through tears, began telling us their stories. I kept saying to them, "Thank you for telling me, but I wish you could say this to a camera because this is important testimony." I asked them if they'd be willing to do this and they all said yes.'"[2] This is a potent "myth of origins," conjuring an image of filmmaking as catharsis—an epic artistic project that spawns a real-life correlate, which addresses the needs of survivors to bear witness and give testimony in unprecedented fashion, all this using the very latest technology.

But the film produced "behind the scenes" at the Shoah Foundation is also an example of a certain type of promotional tape. Like most videos of its genre, it stars a noted Hollywood personality with some recognition value, it is about twenty minutes long, and it offers the image of a busy, bustling, professional operation. It is used in presentations to business and community meetings around the globe to build interest and, if possible, raise funds for the massive costs of the project, by "taking you back" into what the foundation does and by portraying its enormity—this according to Kim Feinberg, South African coordinator for the VHF.[3] And the project *is* enormous: its original goal was to record, digitize, archive, and make accessible (via not-yet- but soon-to-be-developed technology) at least fifty thousand testimonies of Holocaust "survivors, rescuers, liberators, and witnesses so that the world will remember and learn from their legacy. This is a race against time."[4] The promotional video starring Ben Kingsley, with a cameo appearance by Spielberg himself, not only offers a window onto the efforts of one archiving project that seeks to record and manage the overflow of available testimonial data but reflects as well the broader movement in contemporary culture to capture, process, and render meaningful the unique, highly individualized stories of those who were "there." Reflecting the "privileged status" contemporary society accords the survivor and her testimony,[5] it also complicates that position by reminding us of the production at the heart of the reception and transmission of such testimony. The promotional video highlights the continuing demands for documentation of the events of the Holocaust initiated by survivors struggling to communicate their experiences, but mediated as well by scholars, archivists, and producers, all serving as midwives to the narration of trauma.[6] Finally, the video dramatizes the idea, briefly raised in the previous chapter, of the survivor as metonym or icon of the Holocaust, even while, with the appearances of Spielberg and Kingsley, it indicates as well the significant roles others play representing or standing in for those survivors. The Shoah Foundation promotional video, which incorporates clips of survivors' testimonies, is therefore engaged in a process that mediates those testimonies to a wider audience. I will call the broad, multileveled process of mediation indicated by the video "framing memory." In the context of this book, attention to framing sheds light on the role witnessing plays in the contemporary culture of Holocaust remembrance, especially the ways technology affects the structure of testimony.

On one level, I could describe my concerns here in terms already proposed by the media critic and cultural historian Andreas Huyssen, who asks in an essay published in the companion volume to the exhibit *The Art of Memory: Holocaust Memorials in History:* "How . . . do the technological media affect the structure of memory, the ways we perceive and live our temporality? As the visual media invade ever more aspects of political, cultural, and personal life, we may well want to ask what a postmodern memory would look like, memory at a time in which the basic parameters of an earlier self-confident Western modernity have increasingly come under attack, in which the question of tradition poses itself anew precisely because the tradition of modernity itself is lacking in answers for our predicament. What of the institutions and sites that organize our social memory in the age of television?'" In other words, what difference does a video archive of Holocaust testimonies make? This question has a particular urgency with respect to the social memory of the Holocaust, especially as the events of World War II recede beyond the half-century mark and the witnesses to the horrors grow old and die, but also because, like it or not, the Holocaust is being represented more and more often in the audiovisual media. For several reasons, therefore, a number of institutions have formed in recent years to attempt to capture the stories of survivors and others who had direct contact with the Holocaust, benefiting greatly from the timely availability of the medium of videotape recording, which they have made an asset. From the Fortunoff Video Archive for Holocaust Testimonies at Yale University to the Shoah Foundation, archivists, historians, videographers, interviewers, and computer technicians—all are "racing against time" to preserve the stories of thousands of witnesses.

But Huyssen's questions only point up the extent to which scholars are largely unprepared to consider the impact of new, technologically facilitated forms on the construction of memory and its institutional contexts. If we are to seriously engage the impact of projects such as the VHF's, we must necessarily examine the nature and style of the medium at the heart of such endeavors: videotaped Holocaust testimonies. In exploring this realm of mediation, I offer an analysis of the videotestimonial genre different from that of Lawrence Langer, whose *Holocaust Testimonies* remains the benchmark study of this type of memorial document. Langer's painstaking, years-long study resulted in the first extended consideration of Holocaust videotestimonies and their role in shaping our sense of the past. In his book he outlines five distinct types of memory represented in these tapes (deep, anguished, humiliated, tainted, and unheroic) and five corresponding versions of the survivor self (buried, divided, besieged, impromptu, and diminished). As a result, Langer's is an important and comprehensive examination of this material and what he perceives as its underlying, antiredemptive structure.

But Langer does not adequately address the uniqueness of the medium itself and the significant ways in which it frames Holocaust memory's mediation. According to Michael Rothberg, Langer "contributes to an appreciation of the particularities of the genre of oral testimony, although he refuses to treat it as a representational medium that is mediated and governed by conventions just as is written work—even if by *other*, not yet fully understood conventions."[8] Langer himself compares grappling with the textual mediation of written Holocaust literature and memoirs with watching and listening to witnesses on the screen or in the studio: "Nothing . . . distracts us from the immediacy and the intimacy of conducting interviews with former victims (which I have done) or watching them on a screen."[9] Similarly, Geoffrey Hartman, faculty adviser to the Yale archive, presses the case for a lack of mediation: "In video testimonies (or 'testimonial video' generally) there is nothing between us and the survivor; nor, when an interview really gets going, between the survivor and his/her recollections." Furthermore, Hartman links emotional impact to such immediacy: "The effect, therefore, can be extraordinarily intimate—it is hard not to cry."[10] No doubt videotestimonies are an intimate form of representation. But it is almost as if Langer and Hartman are somewhat hesitant to draw attention to the potential misinterpretations any attention to these testimonies' mediated aspects might invite. As otherwise sensitive and precise readers and critics of written documents, one would expect them to read these audiovisual "texts" with an equal precision. Of course, videotestimonies *are* subject to critique as to their mediatory and representative functions. Such a critique, as well as discussion of their role in the production of images of the Holocaust and its place in contemporary culture, is my aim in this chapter.

This analysis is best accomplished by breaking down the multilayered discourse engendered by and in these testimonies. We can do this by looking, in different ways, at the "frame" constructed around the witness to the horrors of the Holocaust or otherwise implied by her presence and role as the one giving testimony. I therefore propose the rubric of framing, considering critically the various strategies of framing in which the principal players involved in the production of Holocaust testimonials are engaged. I want to think carefully about the roles these actors play (for they are, in a certain sense, actors, even if they are "playing" themselves without artifice) and how they are involved in framing activities. How, for example, does a survivor frame her own testimony even as she is giving it? How is that testimony framed by the activities of interviewers or camera technicians or by the formal properties of the medium of video itself? How do *we* frame the witness by our own viewing strategies? And how does the institutional context (the Shoah Foundation, for example, or any particular screening setting) establish yet another frame of reference and analysis? What temporal frame is served by the production and screening of videotestimonies? What, finally, do all these different frames tell us about the process of testimony, about the making of witness, about the medium of video, and about the ways we apprehend and comprehend the Holocaust now, nearly sixty years later? The "frames of remembrance" I consider here ultimately constitute, in all their range and variety, a unique and compelling genre of memorial activity that plays a crucial role in establishing the propriety of memory and in shaping various commitments to Holocaust memory.[11]

Thus I seek to distinguish between the content of the survivor's testimony—the testimony as such—and its context or container—the testimony in the act of its being given, as it is framed. This distinction is crucial because people often seem to confuse one with the other; the most extreme form of this confusion sees the videotestimony as identical with the survivor giving it, which is certainly not the case. Avoiding this confusion is one of the aims of this chapter. And by taking a critical look at this very sensitive material, I do not intend to criticize the witness herself. What she experienced we can never fully share, never really appreciate. Therefore, I suggest we circumscribe an area around the witness, marking out a great respect. For while such circumscription is, for many, an automatic process (one that should itself be subject to scrutiny), it may nonetheless be demanded by the nature of witnessing itself. Indeed, this area of circumspection is itself a frame of remembrance constructed around the testifier, protecting her from inappropriate criticism but also screening the critical viewer from a fuller engagement with her testimony.

Furthermore, let me be equally clear about the nature of the truth told in these videotapes and framed by their contexts: my attention to the strategies and politics of framing here does not (and cannot) throw into question the historical realities to which the testifiers refer. While there is some valid debate over the usefulness to historiography of individual, personal, and fallible memories, the memories themselves are no less real because of such debate. The testifier's world is a real one, however mediated it may appear to be by technology or by the foibles and fallacies of individual remembrance. There is a great divide between attending to the ways Holocaust memory is constructed and the grossly inaccurate assumption that such construction equals artifice. Especially in the case of videotaped Holocaust testimonies, memory remembers the real, and that is one of the reasons why it matters.

THROUGH THE LOOKING GLASS

I will begin to zero in on the issue of framing and its utility by looking through the eyes of a "bystander" to the Shoah, himself a witness to the deportation of Jews. Father John S., born in 1922 in Kosice, Czechoslovakia, is dressed for his testimony in a black shirt with a priest's collar; he has thinning gray hair and large, plastic-framed, slightly tinted glasses. He speaks expressively, using his hands a great deal. Father S.'s testimony here is excerpted from an early tape recorded by the Fortunoff Video Archive for Holocaust Testimonies (FVAHT) at Yale University and available to the public in one of several self-produced composite videos designed for distribution to schools and community groups. The FVAHT, originating in a local New Haven videotaping initiative in 1979, is the oldest of the Holocaust videotestimony archiving projects. It is decidedly academic in intent, and it currently holds over forty-two hundred video-recordings of survivors and other witnesses to the Shoah.

Now, my personal encounter was with the railroad station. . . . They built a tall wooden fence there and. . . . nobody was permitted to approach the fence. The word was out that they had machine guns lined up alongside the fence in the street which paralleled [the] railroad tracks. But even then you see I was not so much afraid of the machine guns as, you know, my discipline, you know I did not have permission to sneak up on the railroad station, I had permission to go and get something from the city, buy something. But I sneaked up to the fence, and I was in my cassock, so I really stood out there because I looked left and right but I didn't see anybody, even soldiers, so and . . . [indicating with thumb and index finger, looking through them] I found a hole there, you know it was a raw wood fence. . . . And that was the day when I saw my train, my deportee train, and it just must have pulled into the station. That I see very . . . with great clarity, no difficulty to record at all, colors, everything, it was a cattle train and . . . right in front of me, just about two tracks from the . . . fence stood one of the wagons—I could see some more because the hole was large—and it was just opened, it was opened by an SS soldier, that I noticed, those were already German soldiers, I didn't see Hungarians there. And it was . . . the impression was terrible because it was terribly packed. I literally saw what you see in pictures, mothers with children and people and old people and little children and all . . . the impression was terrifying, it was really . . . packed, I mean compressed. And one man immediately jumped off, and I always remembered his face because he looked a little bit like my father, and he must have been something like midforties closing on fifty. I did not hear what he said to the German soldier, to that SS soldier, but his behavior was polite. He jumped off and—my feeling was, my instinct, or, what I made out is that he was asking for water, and immediately that SS soldier, with the club of his rifle, clubbed him down, and—several times [imitating a club with two fists], I—to insensitivity, whether he died or whether he was later put on the train—and then I ran away, I was so scared and I was so upset, I never saw anything like this in my life, I simply ran away. [The camera closes in on his head alone] and you know, this, I see it, personally, as the greatest tragedy of my life, that . . . there Jewish people were deported all around me, I didn't do anything, I panicked, I . . . not even panic, not even fear, I just didn't know what to do.[12]

Here, as in our opening scene, is another double role: not just "then" and "now" (a continuing characteristic, as in all the videotestimonies, of the tape's temporality) but also two kinds of witnessing. One shows Father S. reporting on what he saw, the other features him testifying as to what he did and its impact up to and including the time of videotaping. Father S. represents a testimonial model useful for the beginning of this discussion. Perhaps, like him, we too have a unique opportunity here to peer, as through the frame of a fence's knothole, into the narrated experiences of Holocaust victims. But also like him, we remain outside the atrocities, safe and secure in our voyeuristic posture. Thus we too must consider critically the moral, educational, and memorial implications of this position by thinking carefully about our frames of reference. Furthermore, attention to the trope of (literal) witnessing indicated here highlights the significance of vision and perspective in the context of the memories of witnesses, the narration of those memories, and our viewing of those narratives.

I wish to organize the frames of reference alluded to above in the following manner: envision, if you will, a television screen on which we may view a testimonial excerpt like that from Father S. Think of it as a literal frame for the testimony, and then consider it as a point of departure for two perspectival shifts, one that zooms in and one that zooms out from the TV screen as frame. As we move inward or outward from our initial frame of reference, we pick up other frames, even frames within frames, along the way. Moving inward, we can identify four distinct frame types consisting of the formal, visual frame created by the camera technician plus three others arising from the testimonial act: narrative self-framing, linguistic self-framing, and spatial-temporal distortions or disruptions created in the embodying of the memory of trauma. Moving outward, we identify two essential frames of reference: that of the auditor-voyeur, who is engaged in the testimonial act in the process of viewing and listening to it, and that of the institution which houses, sponsors, and organizes the testimony, thus framing its very existence. I will explore these different frames of reference and analysis as well as their relevance and importance with respect to the role of videotestimony in the construction and mediation of Holocaust memory.

To begin, consider the visual frame created by the camera technician, who generally focuses on the upper torso of the person giving testimony. Without this frame there would be no testimony, no mediation, nothing for us to watch. But this frame is also somewhat deceptive—it gives the illusion (partially true) that the witness is speaking directly to us, the viewers. This illusion is beneficial, for it lends a sense of immediacy to the testimonial proceedings. In actuality, the witness is speaking to us through intermediaries: in the Yale tapes, there are usually two specially trained interviewers, often psychotherapists, just off-camera but nevertheless present in their gentle questioning, their subtle guidance of the narrative of the testimony unfolding before our eyes. According to the FVAHT Web site, "The Archive's interviewing methodology stresses the leadership role of the witness in structuring and telling his or her own story. Questions are primarily used to ascertain time and place, or elicit additional information about topics already mentioned, with an emphasis on open-ended questions that give the initiative to the witness. The witnesses are the experts in their own life story, and the interviewers are there to listen, to learn, and to clarify."[13] For the VHF, which uses a similar formal framing device, off-screen interviewers are generally not psychotherapists. Here, too, the setting is important: for the Yale archive, testimony is usually given on neutral ground, in a sparsely decorated television studio, while for the Shoah Foundation, testimonies are generally recorded in the witness's own home.[14] Setting thus frames the context for the testimonial narrative, both for the person giving the testimony and for those viewing it, in each case affecting the production of that narrative.

Indeed, the testimonial narrative is the most salient frame of reference we must consider. It might seem that the witness is hardly being "framed" as she tells about her experiences before, during, and after the Shoah, over the course of the videotaped testimony (tapes can last anywhere from thirty minutes to over six hours, though most are one and a half to two hours long). Thus the confusion mentioned above: we are quick to assume that the testimony unfolds directly from the witness's experience, unmediated, certainly not "framed" except by the subtlest guidance from off-screen (and thus nearly invisible and surely forgotten) interviewers, who are hardly expected to advance anything but the most transparent of agendas in coaxing the testimony's unraveling. But such is hardly the case. So we must stop and consider the choices the survivor makes as she gives her testimony, choices dictated in part by the structural context, in part by the interviewers, and in part by her own internal mediation process. James Young, the foremost expert on Holocaust memorials, provides an idea of the complexity contained in the witness's narrative:

"Start at the beginning," suggests the interviewer, at which point the survivor must determine where this beginning came. Was it when the family moved to Germany from Russia after World War I, or when they heard on the radio that Hitler was appointed chancellor, or was it Kristallnacht? Was it when the community was deported to the ghetto, or when they arrived at Auschwitz? Or does one's personal memory of the Holocaust actually begin on a collective basis centuries before, in the Churban of the First and Second temples [sic] and subsequent pogroms? And where then does one's testimony end? At liberation from the camps, or on one's arrival in Israel? When the tape runs out, or when the interviewer grows tired? Can memory ever have closure? Depending on where the beginning and end of testimony come, particular premises, conclusions, and meanings are created for the whole of testimony.[15]

Young's attention to the collective locus for memory implies a tension between individual and collective that also contributes to the process of framing. Clearly, the simple "frame" of Holocaust testimony is complicated by the narrative poles of that testimony, however they are defined, and we must be sensitive to the ways such narratives are framed. What differences would be made if the witness began with her childhood, her expulsion from school, her deportation, or the last time she saw her parents on the ramp at Auschwitz?

Most of the time, survivors' stories begin with some words about their families and lives before the war, often moving soon thereafter to accounts of the circumstances under which the Nazi era first affected their

own lives. In many accounts, this is followed by descriptions of deportations, of ghetto life, of separating from family members, of entering the
camps. After descriptions of experiences in the camps, most tell of liberation, of journeys back to hometowns to try to find family members, of
leaving Europe. In almost all the videotapes I viewed at the Yale archive,
the survivors close by describing coming to America and, with a quick
jump to the present, by reflecting back on life in the United States, their
children, and the painful legacy of the past (this narrative structure is endorsed with even greater consistency by the VHF).[16] But the testimony is
rarely conveyed so smoothly or with such regularity. Rather, one witnesses a journey over a bumpy and textured terrain of memory that each
person traverses individually, an excursion that is anchored at both ends,
with assistance from interviewers, by images of life before and after the
war.[17]

Beginning and ending in "normalcy" thus frames the survivor's narrative in the familiar, setting "Auschwitz" (taken in its iconic sense) in the
midst of a zone of relative comfort that eases the witness, along with
those accompanying her on her memorial journey, into and out of the
more traumatic aspects of her experiences during the war. This narrative
frame is artificial, though, and it would be wise to remember that the
memory of trauma is likely not to be naturally couched and buffered in
this way. In addition, ending in the present can make the testimony relevant and vibrant for those of us who watch it, offering a continuous thread
from then to now, there to here. In many of the VHF tapes, such an ending is accentuated by the practice of inviting family members to join the
survivor for the conclusion of her testimony, while the camera pans back
to offer a sweeping visual panorama of life "here" and "now." These two
shifts in framing raise the issue of the construction of redemptive narratives of the Holocaust (something to which Langer is strongly opposed)
and of redeeming, via visual strategies, the narratives of trauma offered by
these witnesses.[18] I will pick up these threads again later in this chapter.

We recognize now that the narrative frame for testimony is itself subject to scrutiny. Ernst van Alphen, who has also considered the discursive
frames that authorize the testimonial transmission of experience, considers the ways in which discourse also closes off the possibility for such
transmission and how such possibility may have been closed off already
at the time the recounted experiences occurred. Van Alphen identifies
two representational problems related to the narrative frames provided
for experiencing the Holocaust discursively, and both add to the complexity of the notion of framing, seen now as a semiotic function. Narra-

tive framing here is the active production of meaning, but such activity is confounded by the unprecedented nature of Holocaust experience, so that there is an absence of a coherent narrative framework (the first "problem"). In other words, according to van Alphen, the very experience of trauma precludes its being registered narratively. Moreover, van Alphen suggests, in his second representational problem, that such coherent narrative frameworks may not only be lacking, in the context of the experience itself, but may also be inadequate, once they have been constructed or established. One reason he gives, referring to the tendency I noted for interviewers to frame the survivor's narrative temporally (before, during, and after the war), is that such frames offer a structure of continuity and unity that is unacceptable to survivors and incommensurate with their experiences.[19] Temporality is something that has largely been disrupted for those giving testimony, an issue to which I will return.

Each of the two internal frames discussed (the technical frame and the narrative frame) must therefore be viewed as delineating a distinct layer of presentation, actively producing meaning or actively disrupting the transmission of the witness's experience, or both, because of varying degrees of structural limitation. Because of these narrative layers—frames within frames—videotestimonies, on one level at least, are richly textured memorial artifacts. We need to become sensitive to this texture, learn to carefully unravel the warp and woof of testimonial fabric, and see how the overall garment of memory is stitched together (and unstitched). In so doing we become more attuned to the distinction between the body (the survivor) giving testimony and the garment (the frame) woven around it. This brings into sharper focus the nature of memory's embodiment and, in some cases, its disembodiment.

SEARCHING FOR LANGUAGE

The internal narrative—the survivor's own self-framing—is also shaped by a number of distinctive processes and characteristics. Most often, memory is converted into speech (and gesture, silence, and a host of subtle visual cues that must be viewed to be appreciated) for the first time, and it is thus profoundly self-reflexive. This conversion may involve a process of self-translation: events experienced and processed in European languages are now expressed in the vernacular, which is usually English for the major archiving projects based in the United States.[20] The process of self-framing is another example of the inadequacy of discursive frameworks, but it also goes beyond the problems outlined by van Alphen. Testimony unfolds into a narrative; we see how a survivor struggles to find the right language to express her memory, how testimony is figured. The very process of expressing experience in order to transmit memory yields another internal frame of reference for analysis, as the witness frames her narrative for reception and comprehension, for herself, for the interviewers, for us, for posterity. The process goes beyond the issue of simple narrative self-framing, involving shifting and selective linguistic and spatial-temporal reference points.

One particularly articulate woman, for example, finds herself as a medium or meeting point for a number of temporal, spatial, and linguistic frames of reference: "My sister—I have one who is in St. Louis and I was the youngest of the three sisters—whenever she sees me she still cries because I was growing and my spine was completely . . . curved out and I had no hair on my head and then one time there was . . . on a Sunday they were taking people . . . *links* and right and *links* and right and my sister found someplace a piece of red paper so she put it on my cheeks and she put some . . . two pieces of rags on my head so I won't look so devastating and . . . or devastated and she um . . . somehow I made it to my sister's."[21] Sally H. well expresses what many viewers and scholars have noted as the continuing presence of the past experience of trauma in survivor testimony. In this way memory disrupts the linear orderliness of time and space, often inserting itself into temporal and spatial gaps and making such categories subservient to its own purposes—inverting and subverting the expectations of narrative. In survivor testimony, time and space often distort and conflate, so that presence in *this temporal* frame can quickly become presence in *that spatial* frame, there rather than here.

One reason why this occurs is because, as van Alphen has noted, the survivor's experience does not directly translate, unmediated, into testimony: "Experience is not a *transposition* of the event to the realm of the subject; it is an interpretive *transformation* that depends on the symbolic order to occur."[22] The witness's experience of *experience itself* is thereby compromised. No wonder, then, that the testimonial act is so fraught with difficulty, subject to the revealing frame of self-figuration. Self-translation into testimony thus leaves gaps and eruptions behind that are themselves remarkably telling in their spontaneity, as in the example above where scraps of German intrude into the English-language narrative frame. Needless to say, the video medium is particularly well suited to convey such convergences.

But let me distinguish two aspects of the example cited above: that of linguistic self-framing, which I consider now, and that of spatial-temporal distortion, to which I will return. The search for adequate, appropriate language often relies on or incorporates metaphor and simile—figures of speech marked by the struggle to express what was frequently felt as otherworldly in a this-worldly context. Consider, in the following excerpt, Edith P., whose slightly perspiring face fills and even overflows the screen, so that her chin and forehead are cut off, while her voice and breathing are audibly labored: "Auschwitz, if I would like to describe it, I would say there is, there has not been, there has not been . . . [she struggles to speak] people did not invent an expression what Auschwitz was. It was hell on earth and . . . the silence of Auschwitz was hell. The nights were hell and the days . . . somehow. . . . We got up at three o'clock in the morning and at four o'clock summertime or four-thirty when the sun came up, it was not like the sun, I swear to you it was not bright, it was always red to me, it was always black to me, it never said . . . never was life to me, it was destruction. The sun was never beautiful."[23] The language is striking and darkly, viscerally poetic. Young observes the way it alludes to the famous first lines of Paul Celan's "Todesfugue" ("Black milk of daybreak we drink it at evening / we drink it at midday and morning we drink it at night"), even if the speaker remains unaware of the reference. "In these testimonies, the speakers necessarily figure their experiences as the images on the video screen inevitably figure the speakers themselves."[24] Young draws a connection between the technical frame and the linguistic one in the act of their production. Self-figuration is thus framed in the very process of its unfolding (and framed once more here in print, in a feeble attempt to render in this dimension and medium what was experienced and then conveyed in others).

The same woman, responding to her own reflections about Germans, conveys her feelings through recourse to a classical image of exile:

How should I feel towards these people, who have . . . the greatest tragedy that they have done to us is . . . that they have unrooted us, we are a people without a past [she clenches her fists]. And I have been one among the very lucky ones, because I have a *beautiful* family who understands me, but we have been *unrooted* of our past, we had to bring up children . . . without mothers, without grandmothers. When I came home with my first daughter from the hospital there was nobody to *wait* for me, I didn't know how to bring *up* a child, I didn't know that a child needs to be warm or cold or has to cough or has to cry. There was nobody there to tell me *relax;* there was nobody to share with when the child *smiled* her first time, or brought home a good report card. His mommy and daddy was the uncles and the . . . and the cousins and the grandmother. They uprooted us; we have been *exiled.*[25]

The collective Jewish experience of Galut, of dispersion from one's roots, is here twisted to express a feeling of being exiled from one's own past; this survivor's loneliness is expressed as the exile from personal history. Edith P.'s testimony highlights the sharp break caused in family continuity by her experiences, a break that is covered up by a facile acknowledgment of her position as a "survivor." In this age of diasporization, of continued dispersion and dislocation of peoples and cultures, Edith P.'s combined reflection on the present and memory of the past bears special relevance and poignancy.

In one more example of this unique metaphorization process through which witnesses frame their experiences, survivor Martin S. offers a provocative image of self-figuration and self-framing as he answers a question about a typical day in the labor camp: "I hate to say this, but periodically, when I see . . . I go to Houston a great deal, and you can't get away from the cockroaches there, in the plants, and I see one dodging, I see myself, I can't bring myself to kill it [he smiles]. And I . . . I see myself in that . . . when I see sometimes on television, they show rats, and the way they're treating them and the way they dodge, I see myself that way. That was the typical day [he smiles]; that's all I can remember, this constant looking over my shoulder."[26] What can we make of this difficult and disturbing description? Is Mr. S. aware that he is using the very same metaphor of dehumanization applied in actuality by the perpetrators themselves? What are the implications of this image? Is his language a rehabilitation of an externally imposed figuration (as in the case of the pink triangle in the gay/lesbian rights movement),[27] a successful and powerful moment of insight, an unwitting descent into self-victimization, a hackneyed cliché? In framing his experience in this way, in order to make it commensurable, Mr. S. is framing himself, offering a context in which he (and we) can understand his own experience. He thus incorporates his very being into the testimonial process, invoking what Young calls "the ontology of testimony, [when] witness is quite literally being made before our eyes."[28]

Let us briefly examine this "ontology." How do we understand what testimony is or who the witness is? Giorgio Agamben notes that Latin gives two words for "witness": "The first word, *testis*, from which our word 'testimony' derives, etymologically signifies the person who, in a trial or lawsuit between two rival parties, is in the position of a third party (*terstis*). The second word, *superstes*, designates a person who has lived through something, who has experienced an event from beginning to end and can therefore bear witness to it."[29] Here, the juridical sense of witness, "testis" is sharply set off from what may be called the experiential sense. In the latter case the bearing of witness stands outside the realm of judgment. What is important, as Agamben suggests, is that conflating the two senses of witness may confuse the juridical resolution of Holocaust testimonies with their continuing ethical impact. The former testimony is the type given in court cases, whose outcome leads us to believe that "the problem of Auschwitz ha[s] been overcome" because the case is literally closed,[30] while the latter, ethical type remains unresolved and, as I have noted, continues to live in the experience of the witness. Agamben then adds a third term to his discussion of the meaning of "witness," the Latin *auctor*, which we recognize in "author" and "authorize": "*auctor* signifies the witness insofar as his testimony always presupposes something— a fact, a thing, or a word—that preexists him and whose reality must be validated or certified. . . . Testimony is thus always the act of an 'author': it always implies an essential duality in which an insufficiency or incapacity is completed or made valid."[31] In light of my analysis of the process of self-figuration and self-framing, this discussion is significant: it calls attention to the process of giving testimony not just as the expression of ongoing experience but as the shaping of that experience in the act of bringing it forth from a preexisting state of being. This understanding of testimony raises the issue of mediation again.

The figures and images I have mentioned—language choices and ruptures, metaphors and similes, metahistorical and even mythic constructs, all examples of the inward-moving frame of the entire testimonial process—not only reveal the distinctive nature of videotestimonies but also mark them with what we might call a vernacular poetics, an immediate, spontaneous, perhaps naïve kind of figuration that renders the testimonies so truthful and worthy of close analysis. And if this figuring in language of Holocaust experience emerges through what in a literary analysis would be considered cliché at times (rats and cockroaches, black suns, "hell on earth"), one must nonetheless consider carefully the source and basis for such facile metaphors. Is it because such figures are already operative as verbal icons in general culture? Is it because the survivor has no other words, because she does not and did not live in a figurative vacuum, then or now? Or is it because viewers pay particular attention to the appropriateness of Holocaust language, to the modes and manner of its expression?

Consider, for example, the possibility of tension between different testimonial styles and frames of reference, the wide range of possible outcomes in the search for language. One dapper-looking gentleman, a medical scientist by trade, has been reflecting on issues surrounding the transmitting of the "lessons" of the Holocaust to the next generation (an essential component of the testimonial framework), when an interviewer asks whether he responds to people such as Elie Wiesel: "Very much so. . . . I don't quite agree with him because I think he, he does his job so well and so effective that he almost, I may be using the wrong word, romanticizes the experience to a certain degree. It's overpowering, but it just wasn't so, I mean it was, it wasn't at that intellectual level that he's trying to portray it as. It was much cruder, much more violent, and much more—I'm not saying that he's underdoing it, I don't know whether I am expressing myself, but I mean it's sort of—"[32]

Here an interviewer cuts him off to ask whether there are any representations that he *does* find more moving or closer to his own experiences. The survivor's critique is not to be taken harshly; rather, it indicates a concern for the propriety of language and for the variety of survivor experiences and the manners in which they are conveyed. The comment really calls attention to the distinctions between literary and videotaped testimonies and the different kinds of languages used there, each with its own rules and stylistic order (or disorder). It therefore calls to mind the crucial difference between the more spontaneous, vernacular expression of memory in the tapes and the more highly crafted style of literary memoirs, with their inherent temporal buffer. Each presents its own style of mediation.

Consider in this light Lawrence Langer's argument that these testimonies are marked by what can be called an *anesthetics.* By this suggestive term he refers to a certain distorted sensitivity required for one to be aware of the "an-aesthetics" and "non-sense" of Holocaust testimonies and the stories they embody.

If we cannot find an aesthetics for Auschwitz, we must be content with what [Jean-François] Lyotard calls an "anesthetics." . . . As anesthesia is the medical means for making one insensible, anesthetics deals with the art of the insensible (and in a related way, with the non-sensible), plunges us into the non-sense (not the nonsense) of the disaster, reminds us that no ordinary feelings will make us sensitive to the appeal of such an unprecedented catastrophe. If art is concerned with the creation of beautiful forms, Holocaust testimony, and perhaps Holocaust art as well, deals with the creation of "malforms," though we may not yet have arrived at recognizing the legitimacy of this undertaking—to say nothing of the word itself.[33]

Part of the anesthetics of memory, then, involves the non-sense of the temporal layers and frameworks of the survivors' testimonies, captured on video in all their fullness. Such anesthetics points both to the clichéd style of figuration in the testimonies and to the possibly banal nature of their telling. For Hartman, one is struck immediately by the difference in expression characteristic of these tapes. He notes that "the survivor's language has an uncalculated poetry that won't fit in with most poetry as we know it, let alone most prose."[34] But this non-sensical figuration is also anesthetic in that it numbs those watching and listening. Langer's anesthetics thus reminds one as well of the ways viewers are implicated in the non-sense of Holocaust testimony.

Such "non-sense" also points to the ultimately contingent and inconclusive nature of Holocaust testimonies, especially as framed in and by videotape. Part of this inconclusivity stems from the very impossibility of testimony itself: the thing about which survivors struggle to give testimony—what we call Holocaust, Shoah, Churban—always eludes, at some critical stage, description and containment, so that, paradoxically, the events to which survivors are witnesses black out the witnesses' memory of them because of their traumatic impact. The result is a "black hole" at exactly the site of the trauma's recollection: "The impossibility of speaking and, in fact of listening, otherwise than through this silence, otherwise than through this black hole both of knowledge and of words, corresponds to the impossibility of remembering and of forgetting, otherwise than through the genocide, otherwise than through this 'hole of memory.'"[35]

This "impossibility" is illustrated in Dr. Fred O.'s testimony, given in 1987. Dr. O. was born in Poland in 1909; he speaks very expressively, using his hands often to accentuate his points:

I still feel that, no matter what I said here, these episodes and things like that, these are only words that try to describe emotions, feelings, situations, whatnot. But these are only words that are too feeble expressions of what really they should mean. You can't, you can't . . . you can't exteriorate from your deep well, deep hidden emotions, you can't exteriorate them and show them in words. It's impossible. There are things that will never be told, because they cannot be told. Like, like the other day, somebody said it's—here's a photograph of . . . let's say five hundred bodies, right in a concentration camp. You can see them, in one frame you can still, from far away you can see those piles of bodies. You have seen the pictures. But to say the 6 million perished in a similar way. There's no words. Six million . . . billion [sic] becomes a . . . two words: "Six, million." But what does it mean? Because you cannot multiply, in your mind, those five hundred by . . . what is it, twenty thousand. [I don't know] how many times it is, to have a conception of what it is 6 million. . . . I don't know, maybe a poet can do better justice.[36]

This struggle for the proper language in which to express these memories, for a container to hold them, a framework in which one may express them, beyond the issues of figuration already addressed, emerges in countless versions in these tapes.

Its emergence illustrates the intriguing concept of "traumatic realism" articulated by Rothberg. The primary tension in representation, according to Rothberg, is between realist and antirealist positions: the former, often more scholarly approach embodies "both an epistemological claim that the Holocaust is knowable and a representational claim that this knowledge can be translated into a familiar mimetic universe." The latter, often more popular, literary, aesthetic, or philosophical reading refers to "both a claim that the Holocaust is not knowable or would be knowable only under radically new regimes of knowledge and that it cannot be captured in traditional representational schemata." What is important is the recognition that videotestimonies embody both approaches simultaneously, a position I would align with Rothberg's reading of the mediating stance of "traumatic realism." While Rothberg deals primarily with written testimonies that reflect this coincidence of approaches, clearly audiovisual "texts" of Holocaust remembrance also respond to the double-edged demand of documentation: "On the one hand . . . call[ing] for an archive of facts or details referring to the event [and o]n the other hand . . . indicat[ing] the need for the construction of a realistic narrative that would shape those details into a coherent story."[37] Assisted by the medium of video, these testimonies accomplish precisely this, as perceived through their various frames.

We return, therefore, to the issue of mediation. Clearly, the one giving testimony attempts to overcome the "memory gap" between trauma and its narration by volunteering to mediate the trauma rather than control its outflowing: what makes the witness an "innovative figure" is his "readiness to become himself a *medium of the testimony*."[38] The initial trauma becomes something akin to what astrophysicists call a "singularity," an all-consuming point of origin from which the testimony ensues, a point before spatiality and temporality, outside of which nothing exists. The return to the point of origin occurs not only because survivors often narrate their experiences for the first time in these tapes but also because this particular framework makes of their testimonial performance an entirely new event, even if they have told their stories before. As the testimony coaxes the narration of trauma from its silence, which always threatens to engulf it once more, a remarkable performance is created, with a unique presence and presentness, a space-time all its own: language itself is "in trial" (note that it is not "on trial"), in practice, real and not abstract or theoretical, tentatively articulating a singular temporal and spatial realm from which few escape to tell their tales.[39] Thus, testimony arises from an originary disruption, a "Big Bang" for the person offering the testimony. In this context, Dori Laub suggests that the

> listener to trauma . . . needs to know that the trauma survivor who is bearing witness has no prior knowledge, no comprehension and no memory of what happened. That he or she profoundly fears such knowledge, shrinks away from it and is apt to close off at any moment, when facing it. He needs to know that such knowledge dissolves all barriers, breaks all boundaries of time and place, of self and subjectivity. That the speakers about trauma on some level prefer silence so as to protect themselves from the fear of being listened to—and of listening to themselves. That while silence is defeat, it serves them both as a sanctuary and as a place of bondage. Silence is for them a fated exile, yet also a home, a destination, and a binding oath. To *not* return from this silence is rule rather than exception.[40]

Before the articulation of memory, there is no memory; its time and space have not yet been created. The silence that stands in its place is home and exile at one and the same time.

SPACE-TIME

A more critical engagement with the witness's search for proper language highlights the consequent disruption of the spatial-temporal frame of reference. For Langer, a certain amount of sense can be made of the narrative's space-time by considering two testimonial clocks: "a time clock (ticking from then to now) and a space clock (ticking from there to here). They seek to sensitize our imaginations to twin currents of remembered experience. One flows uninterruptedly from source to mouth, or in more familiar historical terms, from past to present. The other meanders, coils back on itself, contains rocks and rapids, and requires strenuous efforts to follow its twists and turns." This explanation is akin to what Mikhail Bhaktin, in Michael Rothberg's reading, calls a "'chronotope'—a form of literary expression in which the spatial and temporal axes are intertwined." One can perceive the production of such chronotopes in videotestimonies in the course of the witness's embodiment of memory. In this way, the tapes reflect Bhaktin's observation concerning the articulation of the chronotope: "time, as it were, thickens, takes on flesh, becomes artistically visible; likewise, space becomes charged and responsive to the movements of time, plot, and history."[41] Listen to Edith P. again (the camera has now pulled back to reveal a woman with dark, medium-length hair in a long-sleeved plaid blouse) as she describes the experience of being deported in a cattle car holding ninety people,[42] reflecting on and merging past and present, there and here: "It was hot, there was no air, I still see my mother sitting there in the corner [indicates off to her left] with my sister, going [reaches with both hands to her neck and chest, miming an opening motion, and opening her blouse slightly] . . . 'I'm so warm, I'm so hot, I have no air.' And today, I couldn't understand it [lowers hands, which have been frozen at the opening of her blouse until now], maybe I wasn't that warm, but I, today I understand what she went through, not only because there was no air but the anguish, what has happened to her six children, maybe that's what made her choke. Today as a mother I can understand it."[43]

Langer goes on to suggest that this dual narrative movement can also be characterized in literary terms as the twin progression of story and plot: the former, the story, being the chronological narrative, whereas the latter, plot, "reveals the witness seized by instead of selecting incidents, memory's confrontation with details embedded in moments of trauma. . . . 'Arrival at Auschwitz' is . . . tellable and told as both story *and* plot: Auschwitz as story enables us to pass through and beyond the place . . . while Auschwitz as plot stops the chronological clock and fixes the moments permanently in memory and imagination, immune to the vicissitudes of time."[44] "Plot" here bears a structural similarity to the "black hole" "singularity" of memory discussed previously. As the twinned narrative told as story and plot folds in on itself, the result is the fractured testimonial style of these tapes. The memory of trauma, when emplotted, freezes time and space and resists integration into narrative.

If we nonetheless identify the "story" of Auschwitz as the conventional narrative frame of reference and remembrance, Auschwitz as "plot" becomes an alternative (but coterminous) frame, one that continually threatens to engulf the entire testimonial narrative. Listen to Sally H.: "I have like a panorama in front of me, constantly. I could be in a room full of people. And . . . there was a time when I was, let's say in Skarzysko, where I didn't, I didn't talk at all. And . . . I just couldn't believe it, I just didn't talk. And then I was constantly talking after the war. Because then I realized I was afraid if I won't talk I'll see everything. . . . And even now, when . . . I vacuum or do some tedious household thing I always cry. I always see . . . I could be with a hundred people and if I sit quiet, it's just like a panorama with all that stuff coming through my head."[45] This constant threat, this palpable presence of the past (Langer calls this persistence of memory "durational time," distinct from chronological time), not only disrupts the space-time of the survivor and her testimony but draws us in as well.[46] This disruption also works in the other direction, so that, as Hartman suggests, "stories converge, but voices remain individualized, haunted by the present as well as the past, by ricochet thoughts about life now (many years later) rather than then, and often distinguished by . . . a directness that turns the testimonies collectively into wisdom literature."[47] Though Hartman's statement, which implies an archetypal timelessness to these testimonies, may smack of hyperbole, the point is that in the course of temporal-spatial disruption, the perceived mediatory effect of videotestimony is elided, thereby heightening its power and impact. Watching such accounts, we are no longer simply voyeur-auditors (as if voyeurism were ever simple) but are ourselves implicated in the unfolding narrative. As participant observers to the remembering process, we cannot help but be drawn in.

The interviewers themselves are not immune to the almost seductive chronotopical pull resulting from the performative tension between durational and chronological time. Consider this long excerpt from the testimony of Jolly Z., her second interview for the Fortunoff archive, with Dr. Dori Laub and Professor Lawrence Langer as interlocutors:

Jolly Z.: You know what? [She leans forward, as if telling a secret.] Sometimes I don't believe it anymore. I . . . I sometimes ask myself, was it possible, how can anybody believe it, if I question it anymore, by now.

Dori Laub (interviewer): Now, when you tell it, do you believe it?

Jolly: I'm there.

Laub: Yah.

Jolly: It . . . it doesn't require me to believe it; I'm there.

Lawrence Langer (interviewer): Now, could you talk a little bit more, because that's an important issue too, about what you mean when you say, "I'm there." Internally, does your mind go back, do the images flood up from the past . . . ?

Jolly: I . . . I feel myself to be there. I see the mud around me; I smell it. Smell is very important . . .

Langer [while Jolly speaks]: I was just about to ask you that.

Jolly: . . . I smell it. I see the bodies [she looks up and around] the . . . dead and alive. I'm there. I see . . . all details. I'm there. I'm very visual. I'm there. . . . I see [she looks up and around] the sun or the rain. I feel [she touches her chest with open hands] the wet clothes, I'm there. . . .

Laub [while she speaks]: What age are you?

Jolly: Pardon me? [Her focus returns to the interviewers.]

Laub: What age are you?

Jolly: Seventeen, eighteen.

Laub: When you tell . . .

Jolly: Oh, I'm there. I'm not here [Laub: mm-hmm]. I'm there.

Laub: At that age?

Jolly: Yes . . . yes. I'm . . . I don't even know about myself now. I'm there. It's like being . . . you know, when you say that I just said before that as if I . . . somebody else talks out of me. You see, it's not me, it's that person who experienced it who's talking about those experiences, and maybe that's what I'm referring to, because I'm there, it's that part of me, not now.[48]

We see here the extent to which the conflated temporal and spatial frames of trauma dominate memory and disrupt the entire testimonial framework, even implicating the interviewers. This expands the frame of Holocaust remembrance created by the videotaped testimonial narrative outward to frame us as well. If for Laub the frames of witnessing to the horrors of the Holocaust might be distinctly delineated, here the dividing lines are blurred (Laub "recognize[s] three separate, distinct levels of witnessing in relation to the Holocaust experience: the level of being a witness to oneself within the experience; the level of being a witness to the testimonies of others; and the level of being a witness to the process of witnessing itself").[49] Not only are the time and space of memory and the frames of testimony determined by and negotiated in the give and take between the survivor and her memories and between the survivor and her interviewers, but the video medium also ends up mediating a commemorative narrative negotiated between the survivor on one side of the screen and the viewer(s) on the other. Thus the testimonies become public documents and "public acts of witness" that help to construct "ad hoc communities" of the videotestimonies' reception. In this way, "testimonies evoke a transgenerational recipient through the survivor's willingness to record and the ad hoc community's readiness to listen. The testimony project is based on the hope of finding a witness for the witness."[50] According to Laub, "The listener (or the interviewer) becomes the Holocaust witness *before* the narrator does," which makes sense in light of the earlier discussion of testimony's temporal distortions and disruptions.[51]

It is important to consider such disruption carefully, for it appears to depend on three characteristics of the testimonial process: its contingent and inconclusive nature, its performative qualities, and its noncognitive aspects. Together, these come to mark testimony as something always in process, never finished, something that emerges in a negotiated space often without prior thought—testimony, in its "pure" form (if there ever were such a thing), appears to grow directly out of the survivor's trauma from which the memories "speak themselves," with little intervention from the conscious intellect. To elaborate on Laub's statement in the preceding paragraph, the knowledge generated within the broad testimonial framework is also continually in process.[52] Van Alphen posits that one of the reasons for this disjunction in knowledge relates to the difference between memory (as a constructive representation of the past) and trauma (which one might call the deconstructive presentation of the past). Memory, as memory of something, is distinct from the event it recalls, while trauma, because it defers the very experience of an event, makes that experience cotemporal with its recollection and representation.[53] Holocaust videotestimonies, in the scene of their reception, offer the viewer the desired epistemological content in their framework for the repetition of trauma and in the performance of memory as it is being constructed. In this way they are critical components of an evolving memorial culture.

Testimony, in this context, both deeply informs and involves the one who is witness to the *making* of testimony, the one who "takes on the responsibility for bearing witness that previously the narrator felt he bore alone." As Laub argues, it is this joint responsibility for the act of witnessing that produces knowledge and meaning.[54] This testimonial repossession is a literal re-collection, which also serves to gather together all the people invoked by the act of testimony into a kind of dialogic community (played out visually in the VHF tapes where family members join the testifier for the conclusion of the testimony). As a result, the nearly predatory presence of memory stalks those of us privy to the unfolding memorial narrative, which literally and figuratively breaks the testimonial frame.

ZOOMING OUT

The frame of the survivor's testimony is "broken" in a variety of ways. One might suggest that the very act of giving testimony is already a breaking free of the trauma of survival, that the performative act of witnessing necessarily exceeds its own framework. Even survival itself can be construed as breaking the framework of the Nazi death world, where the survivor's testimony is a record of that eruption. This eruption itself may break the bonds of historical accuracy: one woman's testimony, for example, includes a description of the famous Auschwitz uprising, in which she inaccurately describes *four* crematorium chimneys being blown up, not just the one that really was destroyed in the rebellion.

Does this render her testimony invalid? No, but it does speak to a truth different from the one historians generally seek out, notes Laub: "The woman's testimony . . . is breaking the frame of the concentration camp by and through her very testimony: she is breaking out of Auschwitz even by her very talking."[55] Laub also pays close and critical attention to the negative spaces of testimony: both to the silence that (almost) engulfs speech and to the inaccuracies in the repossession of speech.

Breaking out of the frame of death in this way is essentially a distortion; testimonies necessarily feature the few who survived, narrating the improbability of survival. Hartman frames this turn toward the "others" as a facing toward the dead whose ghostly presence haunts the testimonial framework; the survivors' testimonial dialogue is not only with "us" but with those who died. Such testimony is often more than facing or speaking *to*; in many cases it is also a speaking *for*.[56] That survivors frame themselves in this way is appropriate (though, one must assume, terribly burdensome). But, on our side of the TV screen, Vivian Patraka warns us not to "make [survivors] stand in for the dead."[57] To do so would be to fetishize the survivors unfairly and actively perform yet another temporal and spatial distortion.

Nevertheless, the ghosts of those who did not survive remain present, even (and especially) in the negative spaces of testimony. For Agamben, this realization engenders a long philosophical meditation on the internal paradox of testimony: the incongruity between the testifying survivor and the dead who are incapable of speaking for themselves. He plays off Primo Levi's haunting assertion that "we, the survivors, are not the true witnesses," that the "complete witnesses" are the *Muselmänner*, the "submerged," those walking corpses of the camps who were already dead, who already touched bottom, the "ones whose disposition would have a general significance. They are the rule, we are the exception."[58] Thus, Agamben notes that the "true witnesses" cannot and did not bear witness, while those who survived and speak for them, as it were, bear witness to a "missing testimony." It is as if "Levi's paradox" reveals a fundamental impossibility at the heart of the testimonial act, as if those who do speak are impossible witnesses, like sparks of light attesting to their escape from the black hole that by nature engulfs all light.[59] Rothberg, also commenting on Levi's claim, argues that this "experiential hole in our knowledge of the camps is the one that works of testimony seek to fill, but it also represents the limit where they fail." This "failure" is incorporated into the nature and structure of testimony, built as it is on a fundamental betrayal (to name its theoretical extreme) of "true" victimhood.

We are reminded that "survival is a precondition of narration, but that for that very reason narrative traduces the time and space of the narrated events."[60] Such a reconsideration of the basis for testimony leads Agamben to argue that "testimony takes place where the speechless one makes the speaking one speak" in such a way so as to distort the propriety of speech and complicate the position of witnessing.[61] What is crucial is not so much the philosophical paradox or the ambiguity of subject positions but rather the evidence for the radical alterity of the one giving testimony. Ultimately, any strategy of self-framing cannot adequately contain the experience simplistically referred to as "survival."

Indeed, it is crucial to consider the very name we give these witnesses. What is contained by the word "survivor?" Alvin Rosenfeld, among others, notes that, until the late 1960s, no construct called "survivor" had yet taken hold in postwar American society. When this changed, as a result of various factors including the Eichmann trial and the 1967 Israeli-Arab war as well as the political repositioning of American Jewry, the "survivor" emerged and continues to exist as "a much-honored figure and, in some instances, enjoys something close to celebrity status," even displaying "an aura that elicits honor, respect, fascination, and no small degree of awe."[62] In fact, according to Peter Novick, survivorship became a "lifelong attribute."[63] The shift in attention and identification has served to transform victims into "survivors," but in doing so it may have contributed to the further elision of the memories of the "true witnesses," those who did not survive the war. The position of the survivor is also complicated by the death of survivors, represented paradigmatically by the suicide of writers such as Primo Levi but also by the "natural" passing of many others with time. What is the status of the survivor after she has died? Is there such a thing as a "dead survivor?" How does one survive survival?

Therefore the initial, internal frame of testimony hardly contains, on closer scrutiny, the excesses of memory. Contrary to what we see in ever repeated yet endlessly original forms, these narratives represent a gross imbalance with respect to the great majority of those who did not survive and thus are not able to give their testimony: video archives preserve, therefore, a rarefied, select fraction of the total potential Holocaust memorial narratives that would be accessible were this a world beyond death. Though the majority of such narratives remain inaccessible, the testimonies that do exist function as memorial pointers gesturing in the general direction of those who cannot speak for themselves; thus the void of silence, which surrounds the testimony and out of which (or into

which) the witness speaks, is also this distortion, this narrative imbalance.[64] As testimonies pile up (recall Spiegelman's image of mouse corpses
underneath his writing table), it is possible to see them as ever greater in-
dicators toward the black hole of testimony out of which most did not
escape, like a ring of fire around an impenetrably dark core. Excess, in
testimony, and in the excesses to which testimony points, can thus
illuminate.

I return now to the image with which I began, zooming out from the
television screen rather than zooming in. If we envision that TV frame
once more, we can consider the implications of frames of reference on its
other side, frames that might be more social or intellectual in nature, such
as the historical and philosophical frames to which I referred. Most interesting here are two perspectives on our side of the TV screen: the viewer's
frame and the institutional frame. Consider, for example, our position
watching these tapes. Are we simply passive observers, looking through
the knothole in the fence of history, safely separated in time and space
from these events, untouched and untouchable? The testimony of Father
John S. would already suggest otherwise, as would the preceding observations about the testimonial performance as it is enacted in the presence
of a listener/voyeur. What are our own frames of reference? What do we
expect from these witnesses? What are our presuppositions? Can we even
relate to them?

For Dori Laub, as I have suggested, the very nature of the testimonial
process demands the eruption of the witness's narrative into the viewer's
frame of reference, because it is the viewer who actually serves as the address for the testimonial transmission. It is the listener-voyeur, in fact,
who authorizes and mediates the "cognizance" of the events being narrated. "The testimony to the trauma thus includes its hearer, who is, so
to speak, the blank screen on which the event comes to be inscribed for
the first time." Testimonies of the Holocaust therefore *require* the presence of a viewer to whom the witness becomes bonded because of her role
as other.[65] The otherness of the viewer is crucial, for the goal of generational transmission proposed by these archiving projects posits the existence of such an "untainted" auditor, the blank screen or clean slate on
which and for which the survivor gives testimony.[66] But such an auditor
is hardly and rarely untainted, for she brings to her side of the television
screen her own interests and agenda and her own preconceptions of the
Holocaust. She becomes the coauthor of the testimony. Memory can
never make a "first" impression here; memory's writing pad is never
blank (and never erasable) in this context.

Martin S., the survivor who periodically goes to Houston and is reminded of his experiences when he sees cockroaches there, offers a suggestion in this regard, of which writers such as myself must take heed: "I would hate to think that my sitting here is just an academic exercise, because someone may be given a grant so that he may do additional research and thereby make a living. This is too painful. We *must* do something to change man [his voice breaks] because I'm a very bitter man [his voice almost gone, an almost pleading look on his face] [the tape ends here]."[67] If we are merely voyeurs, therefore, we may be taking advantage of the witnesses and not responding sufficiently to the privilege of our position and our frame of reference. If we expect the survivor simply to remain passive, on his side of the television screen, then we are not being sensitive enough to our own roles in the memorial-testimonial process, roles that are invoked in the very act of testimony.

Indeed, our implication in the testimonial act makes of us more than merely voyeurs or auditors to the narration of trauma. The structure of testimonial transmission turns us into vicarious witnesses, though not, we hope, willful and eager ones. That is, as we watch and listen to those "impossible witnesses" who speak to us out of the darkness of their as-yet-unknown experience, we do more than simply coax, by our presence (implied or actual, from the perspective of the testifier), that narrative to come forth. We participate in the testimonial act as partners in a dialogue and as imaginative listeners and viewers who choose to engage the testimony in its unfolding as bearers of our own need to testify. We become what Langer (according to Dominick LaCapra) calls "secondary witnesses in a specific sense": listeners exposed to and empathizing with trauma while resisting the compulsion to inhabit that trauma, "to become a surrogate victim."[68] This is no small risk; Hartman contends that "the media have turned all of us into involuntary bystanders of atrocities" subject to potential "secondary trauma."[69] Despite this risk, we bear witness to our *need* to bear witness to the events of the Holocaust, to which we ourselves have no direct access except through those witnesses on the other side of the television screen. We each want and need the other to advance our own memorial agendas.

EXCESSIVE MEMORY

These agendas are fulfilled, ultimately, in broader contexts. We therefore have to think responsibly about institutional frames of reference. While I recognize the necessity of making these tapes available to the public in some form, I wonder about the effect on Holocaust memory of the dissemination and distribution of such testimonies. To what do they testify? Is the viewer's imagination sufficiently malleable to accommodate the extreme horrors narrated at the core of the large majority of these tapes? One can assume that most of the publicly available edited tapes distributed by the Yale archive are used in an educational setting, with the requisite contextual frame provided by the teacher or other authority figure in a responsible capacity.

But this frame has its own problems: consider Shoshana Felman's experiences using videotestimonies in her classroom. Her essay "Education and Crisis, or the Vicissitudes of Teaching," narrates the story—her own "life-testimony"—of the genesis of her graduate seminar Literature and Testimony.[70] She describes a process whereby the analysis of testimony leads to its enactment, taking testimony beyond the bounds of expected classroom discourse. Felman's course concluded with the screening of two tapes borrowed from the Yale archive, effecting a shift from the "literary to the real," as she understands it (we should be skeptical concerning this dichotomy; as we have seen, testimonies have their own internal process of mediation and construction, and literary accounts are no less real for appearing to be more deliberately crafted). One tape in particular, the second one, was chosen "to conclude the course with the very eloquence of life, with a striking, vivid and extreme *real example* of the *liberating, vital function of the testimony.*"[71]

But the direction of expected "liberation" took it beyond the realm of expectation into crisis following the screening of the first tape, in Felman's living room. Felman understands this class crisis not as an outbreak of emotion (which did occur) or as immediate silence (which also occurred) but as an outbreak of relentless discussion that "could not take place, however, within the confines of the classroom but which somehow had to break the very framework of the class (and thus emerge outside it)." It turned out that the students in the seminar were obsessed with communicating with others and each other (even as they felt themselves a distinct group, set apart for having seen the video) about their experience of the video and could talk of nothing else, though they often could not express exactly what they wanted to say. They were "disoriented and uprooted" (recall Edith P.'s reflections). At the same time, Felman also realized "that the unpredicted outcome of the screening was itself a psychoanalytic enhancement of the way in which the class felt actively *addressed* not only by the videotape but by the intensity and intimacy of the testimonial encounter throughout the course."[72] She responded, therefore, by contextualizing that sense of being addressed by the video-testimony in the course as a whole and by bringing the students back to a sense of their own significance with respect to the subject matter. The overflow of the witnessed testimony thus was channeled back into pedagogy, as the students were given the opportunity to articulate their responses to the crisis in writing, in formulating their own testimonies to the testimonial event. Felman arrived at her own conclusions regarding the nature of testimony and its role in the classroom. For her, testifying means making something happen; it is a transmission that exceeds its own limits and the limits of classroom expectations. It is thus more performative than merely cognitive, and in its participants it results in a certain necessary transformation, which by nature breaks its initial frame of reference while also possibly leaving its participants broken. Although I have some difficulty with the ultimately self-referential nature of Felman's project, it nonetheless points up the performativity of videotestimonies and the dialogic qualities of the testimonial process.

But even Felman's experience in "breaking the frame" of Holocaust testimony is still itself framed within an academic context, delineated by her university classroom and by the Fortunoff Video Archive for Holocaust Testimonies at Yale University, both providing containers of different sorts for the constructive work of enacting testimonial performance. What do we do, however, with the excess presented by the Survivors of the Shoah Visual History Foundation? I return, now, to the frame of reference with which I began. In light of the foregoing discussion, how do we now respond to the Hollywood-influenced framing of survivor testimony that appears to be part of the VHF program, with its seemingly massive budget, high visibility, and over fifty-one thousand recorded testimonies since 1991? Let me be clear: I do not wish to offer some simplistic, academic-elitist critique of the project initially sponsored by Spielberg, but I do want to carefully and critically consider its operational framework and agenda.[73] Moreover, because the VHF is just now beginning to operate as a fully accessible archive, I can hardly discuss a presentational framework that is only in its first stages of dissemination. Therefore I limit my analysis to the VHF's framework for collection and categorization and for existing and future presentation and dissemination, as evidenced in foundation literature and in individual discussions with some of the VHF's principals over the past few years.

Simply put, the VHF is involved in a project of setting the agenda for future Holocaust education and memorialization which stands to have a far-reaching impact on the position of the survivor and the status of

testimony in Holocaust memory culture. In size and scope alone, it is
poised to dominate the field of Holocaust videotestimonies. According to
statistics updated in May 2001, the foundation holds over 116,277 hours
of testimony comprising 180 terabytes (1 terabyte = 1,024 gigabytes) in a
robotic archive.[74] (Shortly thereafter, the VHF announced it was shifting
its focus from interviewing to cataloguing, and in late 2001 it declared,
"In order to concentrate resources on the educational mission, the Shoah
Foundation has concluded its interviewing activities.")[75] This mass of
data is useless without a mechanism for dissemination. How can they get
the "message" of the archive across to an intended mass public audience?
For Matthew Chuck, the VHF's former manager of technologies, the trick
is to "personalize" the data, to devise a system whereby the VHF can
speak directly to the personal interests and questions of those who search
the archive via one of five initial "repositories."[76] At these sites (the Simon Wiesenthal Center in Los Angeles; the U.S. Holocaust Memorial
Museum in Washington, D.C.; New York's Museum of Jewish Heritage;
the Fortunoff Video Archive for Holocaust Testimonies at Yale; and Israel's Yad Vashem), a local "cache" will provide instant access to about
three hundred testimonies, selected to respond to the expected issues and
concerns facing the particular visitor to that repository.[77]

Though Chuck, as well as the VHF as a whole, is reluctant to identify
any particular "agenda" at the heart of their project, he does say that the
main thrust of the VHF is to amass a particular kind of evidence:

The goal of the foundation [is] to get as much information to as many people, to
learn, not just of the Holocaust, but about tolerance, and about how we envision ourselves in the future by how we think of the past. And where we make that step and
we change what has been done in the past is [that] we are no longer telling history
through hearsay, it will no longer be, "My mother told me this story about my grandmother, about something called the Holocaust." It's easy to deny hearsay; it's not
easy to deny fifty thousand people looking you in the face and saying, "This did happen to my grandmother, this did happen to someone I know, this happened to me."
And when we eliminate hearsay from history, it's firsthand, and what we're doing,
it's not just firsthand for our generation, it's firsthand for generations and generations and generations to come. When there are no survivors, we still have the ability to ask firsthand accounts. . . . If you want to look at it this way, fifty years from
now, my grandkids can look in the eyes of the survivor and say, "How did that feel?"

This conceptualization of the role and function of the VHF archive sees
it as thoroughly future-oriented (Michael Berenbaum, former president
and chief executive officer of the VHF, has said that the archive has been

"created for the age that is going to be"), as a form of "time travel" that will harness technology for the purpose of bringing a present-day version of the past into dialogue with the future.[78] But, from the perspective of the videotestimonies, it is also a strategy for making the Holocaust eternally present, offering survivors a way to survive survival. This view continues the disrupted temporality central to this genre of representation, and it capitalizes on the profoundly interactive nature and possibility of the medium.

Chuck's understanding of the difference between "firsthand" history and hearsay, beyond indicating the VHF's interest in offering an archive of evidence of Holocaust atrocities, also points to a populist bent at the heart of the Shoah Foundation's philosophy. The VHF seeks to liberate the stories of the survivors from certain frames of reference and constraint that restrict their access and facilitate the passing on of these stories to anyone and everyone who might be interested in hearing them. In this manner history, which is presented as something based on someone else's off-screen testimony, as it were, and therefore neither as compelling nor as reliable as something based on an on-screen account (hearsay versus firsthand), is made popular and desirable to all members of postmodern society at large. By means of technology, the evidence contained in survivor testimonies becomes present, accessible, and hence incontrovertible, buttressed in no small part by the proposed ubiquity of the videotestimonies recorded by the VHF. Berenbaum, when he was president of the foundation, would have liked to see this material in all major cities, in universities—a vast, searchable, profoundly effective framework (he has called it a "skeleton") by which all can participate in constructing a history of the Holocaust.

Thus, as Berenbaum sees it, the VHF is involved in creating a "people's history," in which the "quantity solves the problem of quality." In this respect the VHF is driven by a broad, almost totalizing vision to establish the very agenda for "values education" in the twenty-first century. More than merely setting the tone for future discussion and analysis, in a few years it is very possible that the VHF will have succeeded in dominating entirely the realm of Holocaust (and tolerance) education. In this light, the Shoah Foundation's shift in the summer of 2001 to embrace a new mission statement that makes no mention of the Holocaust is significant: "To overcome prejudice, intolerance, bigotry—and the suffering they cause—through the educational use of the Foundation's visual history testimonies."[79] What will the landscape of Holocaust memory look like if thousands of videotestimonies are available at the touch of a button, far overshadowing the current availability of written memoirs?

I suggest that a new balance will emerge, effecting a shift from a text-based sense of historical consciousness dependent on more deliberately crafted images and representations to an audiovisual-based awareness of the past that relies on what appear to be more spontaneously generated accounts but which remain highly mediated and framed, by and through the videotape medium. For example, the VHF policy of recording testimonies in survivors' homes, following intensive preinterview discussions in which the basic outline of the survivor's narrative is determined, establishes a domestic space for the narration of experience (Alan Mintz calls this a "softening and harmonizing of memory") that is framed off-screen through the prior intake of information.[80] In addition, the policy of inviting interviewees to bring photographs and memorabilia and even other family members (at the very end) into the recording session reveals a high attention to context, setting, and the impact on the viewer. Much attention is paid to framing the presentation for a current and future audience.[81] These policies set the stage for a more immediate transmission of history that undercuts its distance from the voyeur-auditor, even though that distance remains intact and, with the passage of time and the passing of the last survivors, actually may intensify.

The VHF will therefore have the ability to determine for many years to come the medium by which most members of the next generation learn about the Shoah. It is for this reason that Berenbaum saw a crucial aspect of the VHF agenda as rescuing the narratives of the last survivors, before it was too late, even as the format for processing and transmitting these narratives is only now being developed. He suggests that the full impact of the videotestimonial medium may not be known for another hundred years but that the opportunity to preserve these stories in this manner must nevertheless be seized. Their potential impact further transforms victims into witnesses, not only to their own past but also to a future that has yet to be determined. Consider the linguistic context of this transformation's significance: victims appear to be passive and perhaps anonymous actors—people to whom something has been done—while witnesses are envisioned as active authors of their testimonies (however mediated), transmitting what they have seen. The chance to participate in this transmission also establishes a crucial entry point for voyeurs to engage the narrative.

The VHF is thus, in Berenbaum's language, more involved in "marketing" the Holocaust than in "promoting" it, which is not necessarily meant to commodify the Shoah. Rather this approach recognizes that the former strategy aims to create a "product" and then get people to "buy it" (believing they need it), whereas the latter is more concerned with first defining the need for a certain product and then responding. The "witness" is therefore one "product" of the VHF's archiving project. For Berenbaum, the VHF and the U.S. Holocaust Memorial Museum are both examples of marketing rather than promotional strategies, and both take the Holocaust beyond its "instrumentality for the reparochialization of Holocaust memory as Jewish memory." Here Berenbaum presents an image of expansion over contraction. Rather than refocus the witness's testimony inward, toward a limited Jewish communal context and sense of almost peripheral value, a marketing strategy moves (indeed, practically explodes) outward, setting the videotestimony in the center of a new universe of values education and refocusing its memorial relevance. Again, such an approach clearly sets a new agenda for Holocaust education and memory, though the implications of this strategy are as yet unclear.[82]

Because of these issues of size, scope, and agenda, a crucial difference exists between the VHF and the Yale archive, one that is instructive with respect to the future of Holocaust memory as mediated through the genre of videotestimony. In Matthew Chuck's opinion, the Fortunoff archive at Yale, because it is not designed to be fully computerized and searchable, is already quite large in terms of its own agenda (currently about forty-two hundred testimonies). The archive satisfies a primarily academic audience ready and willing to view whole tapes and thus, I would argue, "digest" complete accounts. This approach, however, also preserves the integrity of each testimony as a self-contained audiovisual "document." Yale's own rules regarding access treat the archive, according to Berenbaum, like a "rare-book room," a restricted place to which the researcher must come and at which she must spend significant time, thus requiring a seriousness of commitment in the engagement with the material. As argued by Michael Nutkiewicz, formerly the VHF's senior historian and educational programs and grants associate, archives generally exist to protect the material housed there (its "valuable artifacts"), whereas the VHF exists to put out the material and thus will (eventually) become a more egalitarian resource.[83]

In the meantime, the Shoah Foundation archive is now beginning to come "online," though not in the ways initially envisioned. Although the mechanics of dissemination at the repositories are still being worked out, the VHF has recently, in somewhat retrograde fashion, begun delivering searchable analog regional collections to locations such as Amsterdam and Charleston, South Carolina. More significant, the foundation has changed its academic access policies: scholars can now borrow VHS copies of testimonies central to their research agendas for a nominal fee. At this stage, about fifteen thousand testimonies have been fully catalogued for such access, while forty-four thousand testimonies are currently searchable according to their preinterview questionnaires (PIQs), and a search tool is being tested.[84] The VHF has also developed and released products that incorporate and edit the testimonies into (re)mediated outcomes. Yale's archive displays a more protective impulse, but there is as well a strong sense of the primacy of the testimony and a resistance to subjecting it to further mediation or production except of the most rudimentary sort. This difference can be traced back to the Fortunoff archive's inception (long before Spielberg came on the scene). Shandler notes how accounts of its "approach to mediating the Holocaust have repeatedly conceptualized it as a corrective response to the misbegotten genre of Holocaust television" (especially against the NBC miniseries *Holocaust* and "Hollywood" in general), which can be read as a concerted effort against any potential commodification, fetishization, or trivialization of the testimonies.[85] Despite this approach, the Fortunoff archive has itself recently become more easily accessible, at least for initial exploration, through its Web site and the Yale University library's online resources.[86]

As Berenbaum argues, the Shoah Foundation is much more like the "other side of a museum," in that a museum (and by analogy the Yale archive) brings people to a place, while the VHF, in theory at least, "brings experience to a people." But what experience is brought? There is a risk here of overindulging the desire for vicarious witnessing, overmediating the testimonies and ending up with too little context and referentiality. For Berenbaum, the ultimate goal of the Shoah Foundation is to be spaceless, an archive whose spatial limitations are only those of the available technology for dissemination. Curiously, this despatialization is the extreme version of the temporal-spatial distortion prevalent in the tapes themselves. The VHF positions itself as more "public" than Yale's collection, which is understood in this context as a more private archive. The "public" the VHF will serve also comes with a different agenda and different expectations, driven by a sound bite–based, technologically saturated environment in which virtually all information is available on demand. The VHF will therefore offer Shoah-on-demand to a new age of cyber-surfing data samplers, a full technological generation beyond the intended audience of the Yale archive. The danger is that these new "witnesses" will be less committed to the cocreative processes of watching and listening to videotestimonies and less well versed in the necessary context for their own witnessing.

And, for this new generation, size is always a priority, perhaps one of the reasons why the VHF is so vast in scope. Clearly the archive wishes to capture and preserve as many testimonies as time and money will allow. Is this excessive? Yes, but that may be the point: to meet the excesses of the Shoah, an event that already exceeds its own bounds and its own representation, with excess, to meet the specter of total annihilation with another kind of totality, to answer any charge of impropriety with an onslaught of data in all its multiplicity. Also, to rush to rescue, before it is too late, the stories of those whom no one rushed to save years ago.

The VHF thus carries the inherent excessiveness of testimony to an institutional extreme. As such, it also stretches the notion of what constitutes an archive, which is by nature a legal institution: archives literally "lay down the law" in their role as repositories for the various records of human memory. Traditionally, archives existed as dry, stale places to which only those sufficiently energetic and qualified could gain access. But now, especially with the work of the Shoah Foundation, the archive of the memory of the Holocaust will be more widely and easily accessible than any archive before it. In this manner, the project of the VHF exposes the dual character of the archive, which is, according to Jacques Derrida, "at once *institutive* and *conservative*. Revolutionary and traditional."[87] The archive thus moves in two simultaneous directions: toward the past and toward the future, even as it sits in the temporal juncture between these two poles. And when we come to that space, burning with the feverish desire for knowledge, for the authority and the authorization that the archive grants, we express our own need for the archive:

We are *en mal d'archive:* in need of archives. Listening to the French idiom, and in it the attribute *en mal de,* to be *en mal d'archive* can mean something else than to suffer from a sickness, from a trouble or from what the noun *mal* might name. It is to burn with a passion. It is never to rest, interminably, from searching for the archive right where it slips away. It is to run after the archive, even if there's too much of it, right where something in it anarchives itself. It is to have a compulsive, repetitive, and nostalgic desire for the archive, an irrepressible desire to return to the origin, a homesickness, a nostalgia for the return to the most archaic place of absolute commencement. No desire, no passion, no drive, no compulsion, indeed no repetition compulsion, no *"mal de"* can arise for a person who is not already, in one way or another, *en mal d'archive.*[88]

Holocaust videotestimonies, in all their frames, well depict this "passion," this "sickness," this need to "return to the origin" in memory, a return that is represented in the physical movement of the videotape, toward an origin that in many ways is unknown prior to its telling. And they also contain within them the desire of the voyeur, herself in search of this place of commencement. Not only are she and the witness bound together in the testimonial enterprise, but their joining also points to the archive's other gesture toward the future:

> The question of the archive is not . . . a question of the past. It is not the question of a concept dealing with the past that might *already* be at our disposal or not at our disposal, *an archivable concept of the archive.* It is a question of the future, the question of the future itself, the question of a response, of a promise and of a responsibility for tomorrow. The archive: if we want to know what that will have meant, we will only know in times to come. Perhaps. Not tomorrow but in times to come, later on or perhaps never. A spectral messianicity is at work in the concept of the archive and ties it, like religion, like history, like science itself, to a very singular experience of the promise.[89]

That is, an archive is always about some future purpose and goal that are promised but not yet realized, a messianic dream endlessly deferred. The archive is thus a redemptive institution that by nature exceeds the bounds of the past conserved within it. An archive of Holocaust video-testimonies only makes this messianic promise acute.

But this reading may be too positive. We may be succumbing here to what Langer would see as the danger of imposing a redemptive meaning on the testimonial narrative and its performance (and, in this case, on its institutional frame). Perhaps we can better express archival space as emerging between two dichotomous poles, as Derrida does, without invoking any redemptive presence. Giorgio Agamben, who follows Foucault in articulating a different sense of the archival dimension, expresses such an approach: "How are we to conceive of this dimension, if it corresponds neither to the archive in the strict sense—that is, the storehouse that catalogs the traces of what has been said, to consign them to future memory—nor to the Babelic library that gathers the dust of statements and allows for their resurrection under the historian's gaze?" Agamben's idea of the archive situates it between "the obsessive memory of tradition, which knows only what has been said, and the exaggerated thoughtlessness of oblivion, which cares only for what was never said."[90] Here the archive is what is left behind; it is less a container for testimonies than the substrate of potential testimonies out of which any one particular testimony temporarily bursts forth. If Derrida focuses more on the messianic promise of the archive, Agamben reminds us of the impossibility of realizing that promise in its totality. What he calls its "dark margin" is the black hole of the forgotten, hanging in the background of any singular testimonial performance—not just those thousands of testimonies recorded but remaining "unsaid" until they are retrieved and engaged and listened to, but also those millions of testimonies that remain wholly irretrievable, completely swallowed up by the void. However comprehensive, an archive of Holocaust videotestimonies thus remains incomprehensible, an impossible memory.

Nevertheless, between the past and the future, the longing for origins and the promise of redemption, the archive of Holocaust videotestimonies in its audiovisual enactment brings survivor and witness together in an eternal present. Where technology once limited the eternal present of catastrophe to the confines of liturgy and commemoration, these new technological advances have enriched and enhanced the fabric of communal memory, offering as well a medium for the construction of a sense of the past and its meaning in the future in the form of videotestimony.

PRODUCING THE HOLOCAUST

That medium remains largely inaccessible to the general public, however. The vast bulk of these Holocaust videotestimonies cannot yet be accessed in the manner envisioned by the principals at the Shoah Foundation, largely because of the high cost of and time involved in indexing their massive holdings but also, it would seem, because of unresolved issues concerning the nature and details of the broad accessibility touted by the foundation. It would seem, then, that making sense of this body of testimony is itself constrained by logistical limitations.[91] What have become available more recently are specific products that distill a fraction of this material into mass-produced forms and thus mediate the testimonies themselves. This additional level of mediation and framing deserves scrutiny.

Such productions have their modest beginning in the early years of the Yale archive through its predecessor, the Holocaust Survivors Film Project, founded in 1979 in New Haven. In conjunction with WNEW-TV, the project produced an Emmy Award–winning hour-long documentary, *Forever Yesterday.* Over the years the Fortunoff Video Archive for Holocaust Testimonies has produced several short documentaries and programs for use by schools and community organizations. These modest undertakings focus on introducing the subject of the Holocaust through the videotaped testimonies of its witnesses and establishing the videotestimony as one document among several resources for engaging with the legacy of

World War II. Its most recent product is *Witness: Voices from the Holocaust*, a documentary that first aired on many PBS stations on May 1, 2000, along with a book of the same name. Incorporating testimonies from the late 1970s and early 1980s, *Witness* preserves the raw, rough feel of the complete tapes at the archive. Nothing is domesticated here, and little artifice (none beyond the formal techniques of framing discussed already) intervenes in the testimonial tapestry: we watch and listen only to the images and voices contained in and bounded by the videotestimonies themselves, interspersed with archival footage. And not one of the testimonies screened as sources for this product "celebrate[s] the act of survival."[92]

Not surprisingly, a more extensive array of products has been released by the Shoah Foundation. Founded by a noted Hollywood director and based in a set of trailers on the back lot of Universal Studios ("the only Holocaust-studies center, it seems safe to say, ever situated on a Hollywood studio lot"), the VHF is naturally suited to such production.[93] Along with its commitment to provide (one day) fully navigable digital accessibility to its holdings, the VHF has also been at the forefront in developing spin-offs from its sizable archive. The first significant product is a CD-ROM, *Survivors: Testimonies of the Holocaust*, presented by Spielberg and the Shoah Foundation and produced, conceptualized, and artistically directed by Stephanie Barish.[94] Narrated by Leonardo DiCaprio and Winona Ryder (who donated their time and voices to the project) and intended for high school–aged audiences, the product allows users to navigate their way through excerpts from four survivors' videotestimonies framed in a series of stylized interactive screens. For example, after selecting a survivor by clicking on a visual icon in the main menu, viewers are presented with a muted photograph against a textured background (perhaps meant to suggest the page of an old book). In the upper right corner of the screen is the time frame (before or after the war or any year from 1939 to 1945); the upper left offers navigation buttons; and in the center appear clips of highlighted archival photographs or films while the narrator introduces the segment (DiCaprio for the men, Ryder for the women) and sets the historical and geographic context. A separate band across the bottom of the screen offers the menu and various options for navigating out of the segment into others, including links to historical overviews (interlaced with facts about the four survivors' history), an interactive map of Europe, a timeline, and index. One can change reference years by returning to the homepage.

A picture of the survivor appears in the lower left corner in a space created as if the "page" of the background screen has been torn back. Each digitized segment is about one to two minutes long, excerpted from each witness's testimony for the VHF, always fading in and out of view, respectively, at the beginning and end of the segment. Following each segment, options appear in the upper left-hand corner for following links to the photos displayed in the segment or for topics related to those discussed in the segment. For the photos, one can click on the thumbnail image and the larger photo appears in the center of the screen, while a caption describes what is depicted. Similarly, clicking on a topic will open a narration box on the screen. Moving the mouse over the text highlights individual words or phrases whose definitions appear below in the menu box; some of these can also be clicked to reveal new windows and new narrative links. A sidebar registers the list of topics viewed and offers options to navigate one's way between them. When finished with this detour, one can return to the testimonial segment and its accompanying music. As one delves further into the narratives, one encounters a small technological barrier: for events from 1943 on, one must change discs; a short teaser invites viewers to keep watching.

Survivors is a rich document. Topics are cross-referenced with multiple media, creating a many-layered labyrinth of documentation. Testimonial excerpts are incorporated and transformed into hypertexts. In this way, the chronotope of testimony is further disrupted, beyond what has already been observed concerning the relatively linear movement of the unedited videos. Rothberg, though writing in this case about the *Complete Maus* CD-ROM, finds that such a story "now takes place in the nonlinear sequential space of contemporary computer technology and poses challenges to the singular place of narration that anchors the traditional act of witness."[95] His comment about nonlinearity applies as well to *Survivors*. Here, a computer-generated environment further complicates the temporality of the testimonies, making of their stories absorbing, interactive landscapes of play and exploration.[96] Thus, the testimonies become both more and less than what they were before.

Producing the Holocaust in this manner presents a variety of risks. Risks always accompany any kind of framing: no one wishes to be "framed," objectified like a painting on the wall. But the risk becomes more acute as technology progresses. On the one hand, the VHF is attempting to find innovative ways to integrate largely indigestible testimonies into the narrative skein of contemporary culture. According to Stephanie Barish, the CD-ROM interactive format invites a high level of investment and involvement from its viewers in what would otherwise be too raw and unnavigable a medium.[97] The Shoah Foundation thus seeks to make the memories of the witnesses who have given their testimony matter to the general public. But in integrating excerpts of testimonies in this way, the VHF both locates them within a wider narrative framework and reduces their overall narrative continuity. In reproducing the "Holocaust" on CD-ROM, the VHF is producing a certain image of survivors as Hollywood products, further editing, limiting, and ultimately containing the complexity of their stories beyond what has already been contained in and through the very act of giving testimony. The narration (indeed, the discovery and experience) of trauma has been domesticated, made into a commodity, a product absorbed into the technological web all around us. In giving the viewer choice and almost endless navigability, the VHF may be detracting from the (already complicated) temporal and spatial reference points of testimony. If nothing else, the viewer should be aware of this significant act of framing.[98]

Similarly, the Academy Award–winning documentary *The Last Days*, as engaging and emotionally wrenching as it is, also manipulates and frames the testimonies, though not without remarkable effect.[99] Weaving excerpts from the videotestimonies of five survivors from Hungary, it tells at least two stories. The first is the historical narrative of Hungarian Jewry, the large majority ghettoized, deported, and, in most cases, gassed at Auschwitz with astonishing speed and efficiency in 1944. The story is told metonymically, through the voices of these five survivors, generally speaking from what appear to be their current homes in the United States (where they were recorded by the VHF) but also, in several scenes, while visiting their former homes in Europe, presumably through the orchestration of the film's producers and director. The second narrative is a memorial one: it includes scenes of the survivors visiting sites of their former incarceration and looking for information about family members. In a chilling but ultimately unsatisfying section, this narrative incorporates a meeting between one survivor, Renée Firestone, and Dr. Hans Münch, a former medical officer at Auschwitz who experimented on inmates, including (the film suggests) Renée's sister.[100] This second, staged narrative complicates the original testimonial story lines (already edited but still chronologically linear). In this second version, the survivors are not only recalling their earlier lives but supplementing them with activity in the contemporary time frame. This allows them to break free of the framework of the Holocaust while still keeping them in a memorial context. Interestingly, present-day teenagers (and others) find in this process the most visceral, bodily entry point to the horrors these survivors would, presumably, prefer to find ways out of (see chapter 5). But for those who were there then, the visit "now" appears to offer some opportunity for mourning but no real exit. We are left at the end of the film with an unredeemed sense of sorrow, despite attempts visually and narratively to come to some closure (as in the placing of memorial candles and the reciting of Kaddish). Following the filmic narrative only tempts one to see a form of resolution to the survivors' testimonies, overlaid as they are by scenes staged in the present via a trope of return. Listening instead to the undigested chronotopic undercurrent (which the film tries to smooth over), one hears the undying keening that is the true and irreconcilable mark of videotestimony.

Michael Rothberg argues that the "traumatic realist project is an attempt not to reflect the traumatic event mimetically but to *produce* it as an object of knowledge and to *transform* its readers so that they are forced to acknowledge their relationship to posttraumatic culture." He later adds, "Traumatic realism produces knowledge, but not consolation."[101] Every videotestimony, as well as every product incorporating such testimony, certainly produces the trauma of survival or witnessing as an object of knowledge. The raw, unedited (though largely inaccessible) tapes also, as I have suggested, come closest to inducing the transformation of which Rothberg speaks. The various reproductions of the videotestimonies, including the as-yet-unrealized strategies for dissemination, are more problematic. In some cases, as in the documentary *Witness*, the shift from production to transformation is more secure. In others, as in the *Survivors* CD-ROM, it is complicated by the free play of hypertextual exploration. This complication also faces the proposed computerized accessibility of the Shoah Foundation's holdings, and it extends to any case where the frame of testimony offers an alternate (and possibly redemptive) narrative orientation to that intended by the witness. But as long as the "secondary witness" is sufficiently sensitive to the primary voice and her testimonial bond to it, false consolation may be kept at bay.

Holocaust videotestimonies are thus situated at an important juncture in the time and space of the memory of the Shoah. This position is exposed by attention to the various frames of reference through which such testimonies are contextualized and from which they burst forth. What I want to suggest, ultimately, is that attention to these various frames of reference reveals the highly mediated nature of Holocaust memory as it is constructed in and through the use of videotaped survivor testimonies. These audiovisual memorials stand directly between the past and the future and serve as the media through which such memory is negotiated between witness and audience. Because they show us "live" images of the survivors in the "present," they restore to presence, life, and wholeness the "canonical" images of skeletal survivors in striped uniforms barely alive, rehumanizing the static, lifeless images from the past that continue to haunt us.[102] "The video-visual medium does not exist for the sake of the narrative but to re-embody the survivor and replace demeaning and sometimes injurious Nazi photos which, till recently, were a staple of Holocaust museums. We cannot allow only images made by the perpetrators to inhabit memory."[103] But more than simply altering the "canon" of Holocaust representation, these testimonies, along with the institutions that frame them and preserve them for posterity, establish a new agenda for Holocaust memorialization. Let me be clear: this agenda is important and necessary. But we must also be sensitive to its constituent components.

Thus on several simultaneous levels, the survivor, as framed by the videotape, becomes a conduit for the ebb and flow and at times flood of memory. The medium of the video screen and the video narrative literally mediate our engagement, as the audience, with the survivor's story, itself so "immediate" (in its purest, albeit inaccessible form), so much a complete and complex memorial package, that without such mediation entry into the memorial process would not be possible. And this mediation, in turn, provides the context for the ultimate goal and purpose of such video archives as Yale's and the VHF: the transmission of Holocaust memory from survivor to viewer along the mediated conduit of videotestimony. Therefore, rather than suspect the video medium for leading us away from memory and tradition (Huyssen's question), we must realize that testimonies like these may actually lead us back to a more solid and grounded sense of the presence of the past and to a clearer feeling for the importance and relevance of Holocaust memory. We cannot forget, however, that such ground is never established outside particular linguistic, narrative, and institutional frameworks.

Ultimately, we see how the television-screen frame, the borderline separating, as I described in the beginning, inside from outside, one general frame of reference from another, is really an artificial dividing line. What must happen, what I have argued does happen, is that, from both sides, that frame is broken, violated, disrupted. The survivor speaks across it, directly to us, and asks us to remember her story, to fold it into some aspect of our own historical, social, and cultural awareness. And, equally important, we, in watching the testimony, enter her frame of reference and, in some small way, attempt to understand, apprehend, even embody the horrors she witnessed. The mediating process of Holocaust videotestimonies thus continues: the making of memory is an ongoing collective, communal, and cultural process that, like the memory of the survivors, never really comes to closure. In that continuing process, we ultimately create our own frames of reference and remembrance for viewing, understanding, and empathizing with the witnesses framed by the testimonial process, even as that process takes them, and us, beyond the bounds of time and space into a genuine engagement. Such engagement must ultimately be constructive of and for memory, though I hesitate to call it redemptive in any way that would take away from the witness her unenviable testimony. Perhaps this memorial commitment is what Geoffrey Hartman refers to when he calls such testimonies a "homeopathic form of representation," as each one, by offering up a minuscule sample of the excesses of the Shoah, begins to provide in the process a cure for the human ailment of which the Holocaust may be the most virulent strain.[104] Indeed, the homeopathic model may be highly instructive as I proceed further, in the next chapter, into the realm of the Holocaust's cultural mediation in museum settings. There I discuss how ideological and symbolic aspects of and artifacts from World War II, merged with the latest technology, are incorporated into broad representative narratives with their own mediating agendas.

CHAPTER FOUR

Mediating Memory

HOLOCAUST MUSEUMS AND THE DISPLAY OF REMEMBRANCE

Historians . . . will no doubt see the unparalleled effort and passion which created the greatest of the Holocaust memorials in the United States on the Mall in Washington as the contemporary version of the building of a "national Jewish cathedral." It enshrines the Holocaust as the via dolorosa and crucifixion of the Jewish people. Those who come to remember are transformed in this shrine into participants in the great sacrifice. They are confirmed in their Jewishness, leaving with "never again" on their lips. It is their prayer, even as they remember that "Hear O Israel, the Lord, Thy God, the Lord is one" was the holiest of all verses for their ancestors.

ARTHUR HERTZBERG, "How Jews Use Antisemitism"

TECHNOLOGY

IN THE COURSE of a visit to the permanent exhibit of the United States Holocaust Memorial Museum (USHMM), one encounters the large Hollerith machine, an early punch-card device, ancestor of the contemporary computer and a primitive example of IBM technology (see figure 9). The Hollerith machine was used by the Nazis to organize and process census data and information on conscript labor, and it may have been used to compile deportation rolls, the infamous lists that located and identified Jews and were instrumental in their murder.[1] Though the machine itself is not intrinsically sinister, its inclusion at this point in the narrative of the exhibit reminds us of the gravity of the relationship between modern technology and the Holocaust—a force that bears down on the museum visitor and contributes to his awareness that the Holocaust was a quintessentially modern, technological phenomenon.

As but one sample of an almost overwhelming array of artifacts, many of which convey an overarching concern for the power of technology, this relic of computing history joins with the museum's own architecture, which incorporates industrial forms and mechanical techniques, to elicit a certain sense of unease with impersonal, anonymous control. The glass-bottomed walkways leading visitors between sections, for example, through which other museum-goers are ominously visible, "call into question what [architect James Ingo] Freed understood as a misplaced

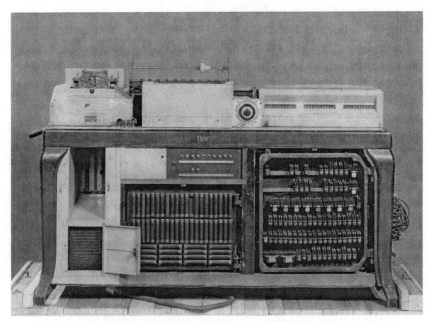

Figure 9. DEHOMAG D11 tabulator machine (ca. 1930–39) manufactured by the
German Hollerith Machine Company, an early data-processing device of the type
used in Nazi Germany to tabulate census information with punched cards.
Technisches Museum Dresden. Courtesy of USHMM Photo Archives.

confidence in the beneficence of technology. 'It failed us once,' he said,
'yet we have more faith in it than anything else.'"[2] But more than simply
conveying an ambivalence toward technology, the museum may be
viewed as "a useful antidote to America's infatuation with technology, so
predominant in other museums and memorials on the Mall," so that the
"dark side of technology" is presented to visitors. At the Treblinka death
camp, for example, technology facilitated the gassing of between 700,000
and 900,000 people by a staff of 120 (30 of them SS) over eighteen months
at the cost of five cents per person.[3] Together, the architectural design and
the design of the permanent exhibition create for the visitor a "feel" of the
Holocaust, much of which depends on incorporating into the museum, as
Edward Linenthal has observed, "the material reality of the Holocaust . . .
remov[ing] visitors . . . from American space and creat[ing] vestiges of the
world of the Holocaust in the suspended space of the museum," largely
via the inclusion of a great number of large and small artifacts collected
from the rubble of the European past. The Hollerith machine serves as
material witness to the Shoah, bringing the "visceral power of material

remnants" of the Holocaust to the visitor and enlivening the museum's narrative through physical presence.[4] While the U.S. Holocaust Memorial Museum relies as well on the power of multimedia displays incorporating film, video, photographs, and texts, the solidity of its presentation as a whole comes from its almost overwhelming array of material evidence.

But such a clear, if complex, program that articulates social ambivalence about the impact of technology while presenting an object-driven narrative of the events of the Holocaust—a narrative that at times makes one quite aware of the role of technology in those events—does not emerge in a visit to another important museum that purports to tell a similar story. A visitor's experience at the Simon Wiesenthal Center's Beit Hashoah-Museum of Tolerance in Los Angeles would be much different. As one commentator has noted, "The Simon Wiesenthal Center has created an experiential exhibit where emotions and images, not objects, become the driving and powerful artifacts."[5] What kind of museum is this, and what do visitors experience here? How does a comparison of the ideologies and impacts of these two important museums reflect on the problem of Holocaust memory? As memories of the Shoah recede further into the past, such museums as the USHMM and the Simon Wiesenthal Center's Beit Hashoah-Museum of Tolerance (MOT) play increasingly crucial roles in the mediation of memories and the construction of an accessible Holocaust past for the public at large. In this chapter I seek to unravel some of the forces at work in such mediation.

I also discuss issues that are situated at a more intensified level of what I call the progressive embodiment of Holocaust mediation. In chapter 2 I argued that certain modes of representation, utilizing material from the Holocaust or incorporating styles of imagery tied to the symbolic language of Nazism, were particularly potent in conveying the sense of the impact of the past on the present, without recourse to fetishization or idolatry. I called this the iconic mode of representation. In chapter 3 I addressed the role and position of the survivor, himself a central "icon" in the further construction, production, and reproduction of Holocaust memory. I argued that the videotestimonial mode of representation ultimately offers a conduit for the transmission of memory from those for whom it is a literal embodiment to those for whom it is an adopted or appropriated re-memory. This process, though necessary for the future of memory, is not without its risks. In this chapter I take the issues of embodiment and mediation one step further, assessing not only the embodiment of Holocaust memory in the Holocaust museum but also considering the potential impact on visitors (vicarious memory tourists) of different strategies of museological embodiment. I engage once more the issue of icons, this time as they are emplaced and emplotted in museum narratives, contexts, and environments. For as we move from the iconic mode of remembrance and engagement, through the videotestimonial mode, to the museological mode, we encounter a more intensified site of memory with its own conditions for constructing memorial relationships.

I return, therefore, to remarks made by Andreas Huyssen, cited in the previous chapter and published in the companion volume to the exhibit *The Art of Memory: Holocaust Memorials in History*, curated by James Young. Recall that Huyssen asks about the impact of the technological media on memory and the experience of temporality, particularly in light of the increasing criticism of the nature of tradition and its institutions in the age of television. He argues that "if we look at memory in the postmodern 1980s, we are immediately struck not by signs of amnesia but, rather, by a veritable obsession with the past. Indeed, one might even speak of a memorial, or *museal,* sensibility that seems to occupy ever larger parts of everyday culture and experience. . . . [T]he museum, in a broad sense, can be said to function as the key paradigm in contemporary postmodern culture."[6]

The suggestion is provocative: contemporary memory culture, rather than endorse the purportedly amnesiac timelessness of our technological age, actually accords greater centrality to the museum model. Thus, to perceive the museum as paradigmatic for our present cultural predicament accords no small role to such an institution in the formation not only of contemporary collective memory but also of the entire sense of the past and of tradition we continually construct for ourselves, a sense of the past that is more "museal" than we might unreflectively assume. Indeed, according to Huyssen, such centrality has been the museum's classical role, standing "in the dead eye of the storm of progress serving as catalyst for the articulation of tradition and nation, heritage and canon, and . . . provid[ing] the master maps for the construction of cultural legitimacy in both a national and a universalist sense."[7] As a legitimating institution, the museum affirms the continuity of past and present and stands firmly in the space of tradition.

But Huyssen's word choice also provokes critical reflection on the darker side of the museum's role in contemporary culture, recalling an argument articulated by Theodor Adorno at the opening of a discussion on museums: "The German word, *'museal' ['museumlike'],* has unpleasant overtones. It describes objects to which the observer no longer has a vital relationship and which are in the process of dying. They owe their preservation more to historical respect than to the needs of the present. Museum and mausoleum are connected by more than phonetic association. Museums are like the family sepulchres of works of art. They testify to the neutralization of culture."[8] Though this criticism is leveled mainly at the classic ideal of the art museum, it has relevance here as well, as it provides something of a warning to the critic to be aware of the distinct *separation* from lived experience and social memory engendered by the placement of artifacts in the family crypt of the museum. If museums "testify to the neutralization of culture," then they bear witness as well to the death of tradition. In this view, museums serve as repositories for a past that has been left behind, places to put things society no longer cares about, and a museum of the Holocaust would testify to an almost desperate need to freeze time and establish memory of the past "before it is too late." In this sense, the proliferation of Holocaust museums would be read as evidence of the increasing need to seize memory in order to ensure its generational transmission.

But Huyssen would have us balance these apparently contradictory processes as they are read into the museological project, most especially because the burgeoning interest in building Holocaust museums and memorials should not be seen only as a bulwark against forgetfulness.[9] No, such interest is evidence of a trend in contemporary culture which makes of the museum a site of crucial cultural negotiations, not a place of death at all: "One might even see the museum as our own memento mori, and as such, a life-enhancing rather than mummifying institution in an age bent on the destructive denial of death: the museum thus as a site and testing ground for reflections on temporality and subjectivity, identity and alterity." The museum is here a site of both death and rebirth, both a "burial chamber of the past—with all that entails in terms of decay, erosion, forgetting—and [a] site of possible resurrections, however mediated and contaminated, in the eyes of the beholder."[10]

Thus, the museum is located at the intersection of the twin dialectical currents of memory and forgetting; as a result it is the site of considerable tension in the articulation of our attitudes toward the past. How a museum expresses that tension is consequentially a crucial expression of cultural attitudes toward memory, and an understanding of the ideology behind any museum's organization and presentation becomes crucial, therefore, for an assessment of its memorial role and the relationship to the past it purports to depict and narrate. How and through what media a particular museum tells its story become essential components of its place (the place it creates for itself) in contemporary culture and community.

Most often, the role a museum plays and the place it occupies revolve around the objects that constitute its collection. And yet, if a traditional museum begins with the notion of *collecting*, organizing its artifacts into a literal re-collection (re-placing and re-contextualizing those artifacts in a new environment, one that, incidentally, is not their "natural" home), then I suggest that it is involved as well in a process of *recollection*—that as a museum purports to contextualize a series of objects it is also engaged in a discursive process that produces a discourse of cultural remembrance (remembering those objects into a historical and cultural narrative). This discourse creates a strong link between the museum's artifacts (material culture) and the social memory (i.e., tradition) the museum helps establish. But what happens to such recollection if a new museum comes along in which nothing is collected in the permanent exhibit beyond a series of concepts and emotions, reflections and representations? Is such a museum the cultural repository for nothing more than virtual memories? How can we understand its strategy of emplacement, the logic of its contextualization? As the institutionalized locus for what may be fairly called our (often material) obsession with the past, the museum that incorporates visual media into its memorial strategy, perhaps even substituting such nonmaterial representations for a collection of artifacts, may present something new on which society and social memory can feed.

ARTIFACTS

Before addressing these issues directly, I first want to consider the traditional, object-driven, collection-based museum, whose origins date to the nineteenth century, in a more critical and general theoretical perspective. I follow Irit Rogoff here, who attempts "to view the concept of 'museum' as a twentieth-century critical discourse, a theorization of the cultural practices of collecting, classifying, displaying, entertaining, and legitimating *various* histories through *selected* objects within *staged* environments." Rogoff perceives the museum "as a site of the production of knowledge and cultural sensibilities."[11] By paying attention to the modes of the production of knowledge within a museum context, we can better apprehend its cultural role and significance. One central aspect of this cultural role is the practice Ariella Azoulay identifies as "an act of petrification, taxidermy, or freezing," which purports to preserve the way things appeared in the past. This practice Azoulay continues, produces an "authentic" value.[12]

Such authenticity, I would argue, emerges from the traditional museum's significatory structure. Essentially, museums support a metonymic system of signification, creating what Eugenio Donato calls a "fiction that [the objects] somehow constitute a coherent representational universe." The fiction of "metonymic displacement" arises from the belief that the "spatial juxtaposition of fragments . . . can produce a representational understanding of the world." Without this fiction, he argues, the resultant disordered "heap" of fragments would not succeed in "substituting themselves either metonymically for the original objects or metaphorically for their representations."[13] In a traditional object-driven museum, then, the fictional coherence of metonymic displacement turns taxonomy into meaningful representation. Thus the nineteenth-century museum's project was to replace the heterogeneity of its artifacts with a coherent homogeneity, which we might call "tradition."[14] Indeed, one might argue that the museum's fiction of artifactual representation may be partially responsible for the construction of the very notion of cultural tradition, which is in some sense merely another fiction of coherence, a narrative representation of wholeness rendering the past accessible and comprehensible.

Yet, we cannot at the same time deny the meaningful content of museum objects, however fragmentary and fictional their metonymic coherence may be. The narratives in which museum objects participate, the homogenized story lines, are constructed with a purpose: to communicate information, to teach.

All museums are, at the most fundamental level, concerned with information: its generation, its perpetuation, its organization, and its dissemination. Implicit in this premise is the idea that museums' principal resource—their collections of material remnants of the past—are of value, and are worth preserving, primarily for the information embodied in them. The information may be intellectual, aesthetic, sensory, or emotional in nature (or more likely some combination), depending on the object and its associations. The same value is also applicable to the newer, non-material resource collections museums are building, such as oral histories, photographs, audiovisual materials, replicas, and reenacted processes.[15]

Here, George MacDonald represents a somewhat uncritical view of objects infused with an information content that almost naturally presents itself in a museum narrative. Moreover, MacDonald sees similar content embodied even in the "disembodied," nonmaterial collections of nontraditional museums. We need not accept this characterization at face value. Nevertheless, the premise on which it is based—that museums communicate information through their displays—is itself a crucial one.

Thus the complex array of relationships that one may call "museum culture" coalesces around the not unproblematic issue of museum objects. These objects have a complex connection to the culture that develops around them because the fictional coherence they participate in has social ramifications. As Richard Cohen demonstrates, the museum's artifacts *themselves* become public and social, establishing a sense of and relationship with the past. These objects, Cohen continues, even allow "for the interaction of diverse elements of society that were not likely to encounter each other."[16] In this way, the museum participates, according to Ivan Karp, in the articulation of social ideas, which, organized into hierarchical pairs (good/bad, superior/inferior, and so forth), "provide the unwritten, ever-changing constitution of civil society."[17] I will discuss just how the Simon Wiesenthal Center's museum approaches this process.

Museum artifacts mediate culture, standing as they do between present and past societies. The museum also participates in the construction of a certain loose notion of community, through the mediation of the objects on display and via the fiction of coherence they constitute. Of course, this community is not vibrant, active, "real," but rather a passing and passive forum for social interaction.[18] Recalling Adorno here, we see how that collective viewer is actually a voyeur to a funeral for a past that has only now become accessible and coherent. This complex process is a doubled movement that both establishes a connection to the past and immediately effects a break in that connection, constructing culture through homogenous narratives even as, because of an inherent heterogeneity, the museum remains distinct from its constructed public.

The process is made more complicated by the dual role played by the museum objects, which exist simultaneously in the past and in the present.[19] Rather than act as a stable, mediating filter or lens through which tradition is articulated in the linking of past and present, the artifacts appear to be both "here" and "there" at the same time, making for a highly charged atmosphere of mediation. And that mediation is further colored by narrative interpretation; as David Lowenthal notes, the construction of tradition and of the remembering community constituted around the museum's artifacts does not happen by itself but depends on amplification through accounts and reminiscences. Otherwise, whatever knowledge the visitor gets about tradition, attitudes, and beliefs from the museum is only conjecture. "Unlike history and memory, whose sheer existence betoken the past, the tangible past cannot stand on its own. Relics are mute; they require interpretation to voice their reliquary role."[20] This interpretation—the narrative framework of the museum exhibit—thus mediates between the mute series of artifacts (themselves construed as mediating the past) and the social community constructed around them, seeking to bridge the gap between the visitor and the "other" being represented, between the present and the past. The traditional museum, then, is a house for a number of mediating artifacts and narratives.

DISPLACEMENTS

Yet a problematic side exists to the processes of metonymy and mediation outlined above, especially with respect to the construction of cultural memory. Considering again the logic of displacement operating in the construction of a museum's narrative (the re-placing of objects in an institutional context to create a fictional coherence), we become more skeptical of the success of the museum's culturally mediating role and more critical of the image of tradition it fosters. James Young articulates these concerns well:

At least part of our veneration of ruins and artifacts stems from the nineteenth-century belief that such objects embody the spirit of the people who made and used them. In this view, museum objects are not only remnants of the people they once belonged to, but also traces of the values, ideas, and character of the time. In the subsequent fetishization of artifacts by curators, . . . however, we risk mistaking the piece for the whole, the implied whole for unmediated history. . . . As a result, museums, archives, and ruins may not house our memory-work so much as displace it with claims of material evidence and proof. Memory-work becomes unnecessary as long as the material fragment of events continues to function as witness-memorial.[21]

As long as we perceive museum objects as embodying memory, such memory may not get transmitted to the spectator. Rather than accept the muteness of artifacts, then, it is more likely that we attribute to the museum's objects the voice of the past, which we naturally regard as more of a legal "material witness" than as focus for our own efforts to remember. Of course, one way to overcome this displacement is to find ways to re-infuse objects with life, often through the very memorial activities created around those objects in the first place.

Museums thus end up displacing the objects on display in several ways: through their fictions of metonymic coherence, through their historical otherness, and through our own assumptions about their witnessing functions. These displacements can be organized into two stages: those arising from the artifacts' detachment from their original environments, and those arising from the artifacts' reorganization into representational series in museum settings.[22] In this view, the museum (unlike the library and, by analogy, the archive) renders the past inaccessible except through artificial construction: displacement is complete and inherent to the museological enterprise. And, in this way, museums are utopian sites "with no real places, supposedly representing society itself in perfected form" but actually establishing idealized narratives wholly removed from lived environments. For Rogoff, this removal from lived reality is the ultimate extension of Adorno's "museal," where "strategies of display actually make the museum the funerary site of uncomfortable or inconvenient historical narratives."[23] Museum artifacts on display are, literally, nowhere.

Of course, this "memory-work" may not necessarily have grave social implications. The memory-work in a natural history museum, for example, may be nothing more than the efforts of the visitor to piece together for himself a personal understanding of the grand developmental narrative of the natural world. But this work, too, may be displaced by the profusion of stuffed animals on display, silently presenting a narrative of the past. And in the case of the social memory of the Holocaust, such issues as narratives of coherence, metonymic representation, and artifactual displacement in a museum can become controversial and highly politicized. With respect to the U.S. Holocaust Memorial Museum, for example, one becomes aware of its strange program of contextualization, as objects, displaced from "over there," are re-placed over "here" in order to impress their American, largely non-Jewish public with their relevance. In this way, from the perspective of museum officials at Auschwitz and Majdanek, who lent the Washington museum some key artifacts, the U.S. Holocaust Memorial Museum was "an extension of the fabric of the center" of Holocaust memory: the "original sites." In Washington, "Americans could 'touch' the reality of the Holocaust through a museum whose use of artifacts would shrink the geographical distance between Poland and America and make permeable the boundaries between Holocaust and American space."[24] The USHMM's artifacts mediate geography as well as history, physically standing in for the very places from which they were taken. Such is the power of metonymic representation, where the artifact's authenticity is presumably not diminished by its displacement.[25] The very architecture, design, and structure of the museum in Washington echo this displacement, reproducing what Linenthal calls the "tectonics of the camps" and leading architecture critic Herbert Muschamp to observe that the museum "is a place quarried from the memory of other places."[26]

The collection and re-placing of distant memories and artifacts in an American context also raise issues surrounding the ownership of the Holocaust and its symbols, particularly Jewish claims on memory and debates over the bounds of narrative representation. The issue of displacement, then, touches the raw nerve of memorial propriety in its dual sense: "propriety" in terms of symbolic ownership of Holocaust *property*, and "propriety" in terms of the *proper* display of artifacts and images. Linenthal outlines some of the stakes involved in the debates over propriety in a discussion about the arithmetic of Holocaust victimization at the USHMM, debates that occurred "on a fundamentally religious level. Invoked were sacred promises made to the dead, blasphemy, and accusations of anti-Semitism expressed in the guise of inclusive memory. Certainly part of the survivors' enthusiasm for the project was their belief that a memorial would fulfill their heartfelt commitment that the dead never be forgotten, a commitment perceived to be at risk as Holocaust memory became public property, as Jewish victims were mixed with others."[27] Memorial propriety, as Linenthal describes it, is inextricably tied to the now public quality imparted to the "property" on display at the museum. This revisits some of the issues raised in chapter 2 concerning iconic versus idolatrous (re)presentations of the Holocaust.

SACRALITY

The debates around the display of displaced Holocaust artifacts at the USHMM point to the crucial issue of sanctity. Intimations of the sacral hover around the artifacts themselves, around their emplacement, even around their viewers. The aura of sacredness permeates Holocaust museology (not to mention other genres of Holocaust representation). On one level, this aura is certainly a result of the perceived memorial "embodiment" of artifacts; as David Lowenthal suggests, "The shiver of contact with ancient sites brings to life their lingering barbarity or sanctity, and merely touching original documents vivifies the thoughts and events they described." But it has also been suggested that, beyond the issue of communicating information, museums actually satisfy a *need* the visitor has for the sacral, which goes beyond the need for mere information. George MacDonald, for example, citing Robert Kelley, argues that museum-goers require sacred and social satisfaction: "Sacred needs are tied to the role of museums as pilgrimage sites, where visitors are linked with their ancestral pasts, as well as to rites of passages conferring social status." These functions speak to the ritualistic role museum-going plays, a view supported by Daniel Sherman and Irit Rogoff.[28]

But the image of the museum as pilgrimage site also points to the construction of museum space as sacred space, one of the most central issues in the orchestration of sacrality and an especially important one in a museum of the Holocaust. Consider the aging benchmark of all Holocaust museums, Yad Vashem, Israel's official Holocaust Martyrs' and Heroes' Remembrance Authority, established in August 1953, in which one recognizes immediately the museum's position in the Jewish state's ritual-memorial landscape (tied, as discussed in chapter 2, to nationalistic goals). First, the very idea that there can be a remembrance "authority" lends an air of solemnity and canonicity to the site which embodies that authority, allowing for its sacralization. But, as Saul Friedländer has shown, the very siting of Yad Vashem, on the far side of Jerusalem's Remembrance Hill (Har ha-Zikkaron), ties it in with the sacred nature of the military cemetery on the hillside facing the city, whose eternal inhabitants include Theodor Herzl as well as Hannah Senesh. Built on the hillside facing the outside world, Yad Vashem has come to stand in as a national shrine, similar to other countries' Tombs of the Unknown Soldier, whose "monuments are the hallowed places where foreign dignitaries express their respect for the country they visit and where the group ritually reaffirms its own identity."[29] Indeed, Yad Vashem's position in the Israeli landscape, spread out (and continually expanding) on the hill, among the trees, encompassing a museum and sculpture garden, tree-lined avenue honoring the "righteous among the nations" and hall of remembrance, and other points for reflection and contemplation—this complex defines a multilayered sacred space with a variety of entry points for the museum visitor as pilgrim, who is literally surrounded by sacred memory. As Tim Cole recalls, "Walking into the Hall of Remembrance, I was given a black paper *yamuka* [sic] similar to the one I had taken from a box at the Western Wall. I was obviously walking on holy ground."[30]

Even the Hall of Names, the archive in which records of those who perished during the Shoah are deposited by family members, is set up more as a memorial than anything else: the on-site literature suggests as much, warning visitors not to see it as a place for research, and the shelves of alphabetized files, in dark wood paneling, are cordoned off in somber lighting. In a display by the entrance, itself serving to encourage visitors with family members lost to the maelstrom to submit records, the pages of this memorial registry are described as symbolic tombstones, intended to "serve as a lasting memorial for the victims of the Holocaust. The details beyond names and places provide a 'personality' for an identity which would otherwise be lost in the coming generations." The simple display also encourages visitors to "FULFILL YOUR OBLIGATION by registering your dear ones." Furthermore, all of the approximately 2 million persons registered here have been granted certificates of commemorative citizenship. Clearly, this archive has been transformed into a passageway to national martyrdom, further reflecting Yad Vashem's sacred role as described by Friedländer.

But the U.S. Holocaust Memorial Museum also fulfills such a role, and the transposition of museum space into sacred space is more pronounced here, especially in its initiatory quality. In evaluating Elie Wiesel's early contributions to the planning and design of the museum, Linenthal suggests that, in Wiesel's view, the museum existed "not to provide proof to counter Holocaust deniers, or as an agent of civic revitalization, or as institutional prescription for the pathology of modern culture, but as an initiatory center. Here the sacred mystery that was the Holocaust would stamp itself on individual psyches, and visitors would, ideally, emerge with a renewed appreciation of its mystery. For Wiesel, the museum needed to be a place where the impossibility of knowing existed alongside the traditional ways of 'knowing' in a museum." This approach is not surprising: in bringing the otherworldly artifacts of the Holocaust over into the this-worldly environment of the Mall at the memorial heart of the nation's capital, the USHMM was importing remnants of a universe that is radically other in time and space.[31] To make it work, visitors would *have* to be initiated into this new, albeit temporary, reality. The strategies employed to bring museum-goers across this threshold create a zone of sacrality in the process, a carefully negotiated place of mystery where both speech and silence have their place.[32] But Linenthal also observes that, for some involved in the planning of the museum, the entire building was a "sacred environment," and any perceived encroachment of the profane into such an environment (as in the possibility of naming parts of the museum for prominent donors) would be viewed as a "form of defilement."[33] More than merely an initiatory center, therefore, the museum was seen by some as holistically holy, following a trend in Holocaust studies in general that marks out a sanctified zone around the Holocaust in its entirety.[34]

This attitude is most apparent in the reflections of the founding director of the museum Jeshajahu Weinberg. Again and again in his book, coau-
thored with museum consultant Rina Elieli, issues of sacrality arise.
Commenting on the USHMM's opening, the authors note, "Thousands of
people who, walking in silence together through the exhibition galleries,
are confronted with the images of extreme human tragedy, undergo an experience similar to that of pilgrims walking together to a sacred place."[35]
People "speak of feelings of fear, loneliness, helplessness, almost of panic,
but also of holiness," on entering the Hall of Witness, which "affords visitors an experience similar to that experienced by a believer in a holy
place," much like a "cathedral." The authors even note that no cafeteria
was planned for the museum itself (though one now exists in an adjacent
building) "for fear of desecrating the holiness of the place."[36] Clearly, the
founding director of the museum sees the museum as sacred space.

The sacral does not emerge only in reflection on the museum building
itself as a sacred container and as initiatory center but comes out as well
in the particularly memorial-oriented positioning of the USHMM. Of
course, this sense is evident in the very name of the institution (calling attention, as in other Holocaust museums, to the dual function of the institution: museum and memorial), a curious hybrid to be sure.[37] Nowhere
is the sacred memorial role of the USHMM more evident than in the Hall
of Remembrance, the hexagonal, skylit space, meant for contemplation
at the end of a visitor's encounter with the museum (see figure 10).
The space contains an eternal flame (similar to the *ner tamid*, the eternal
flame that burned in the ancient Jewish Temple in Jerusalem, itself often
represented symbolically in contemporary synagogues by a continuously
lit electric lamp, usually placed over or in front of the ark containing the
scrolls of the Torah) "under which is buried soil from Holocaust sites and
American military cemeteries." An act of sacralization, the blending of
soil ties the Hall of Remembrance not only to Holocaust spaces but to
"secular" military graveyards as well. This burial reinforces a memorial
link between the three and strengthens the somewhat artificial connection the museum makes between Americans and the Holocaust (first introduced in the initiatory threshold crossing represented by the elevator
ride at the beginning of the museum tour, with voice-overs from American servicemen on discovering the camps at their liberation). Linenthal
adds that this space, by virtue of its hexagonal structure, could be read "as
a Star of David, thereby consecrating the area as Jewish memorial space,"
a reading reinforced by quotations from the Books of Genesis and Deu-
teronomy etched in the walls.[38]

Figure 10. Hall of Remembrance, United States Holocaust Memorial Museum, Washington, D.C. Photograph by Max Reid, courtesy of USHMM Photo Archives.

For Michael Nutkiewicz, however, the merging of the public institutional role of the museum with its more specific function as memorial is problematic. The curious dual identity actually stands in the way of the museum's communicative, teaching function, for the sacred space created in the desire to memorialize is at odds with the museum's general social role; Nutkiewicz calls it "secular sacred space" because the specific memorial symbols culled from tradition are not seen by museum founders as adequate to convey the "pain and tragedy of the Holocaust" to general audiences. In this way, according to Nutkiewicz, the memorial voice of the institution is pitched to and for Jews, while the museum voice is largely intended for non-Jews; the former is more religious, the latter is more secular. Thus, if we follow Nutkiewicz, there is an internal contradiction at the heart of the issue of the museum's sacred function.[39]

Even if we do not agree with his characterization of the museum's identity, we recognize that museum objects lie at the center of the discussion, which brings us back to the sacral nature of artifacts. Certainly, their iconic role (in the sense established in chapter 2) plays a part in establishing a sense of the sacred in a museum collection: shoes, caps, eyeglasses—all are emblematic, all point toward something just out of reach, beyond vision, on the other side of death. These great piles of artifacts—along with those large, unique items (the boxcar, barracks, a casting of the Warsaw Ghetto wall, a Danish rescue boat, a replica of the Arbeit Macht Frei gate in Auschwitz) which represent enormity in a different way—all fill up the void, the yawning abyss of memory the museum struggles to express. This abundance of items is the "Grand Canyon of memory" that Weinberg agreed would have to be found in the USHMM.[40]

It is via this wrenching, twisted kind of sacralization that, as I noted in chapter 2, visitors can walk through a genuine railway car, similar to the ones used to transport Jews to their deaths,[41] even as they know that they are not "there" themselves—certainly not "there" (in Europe) then, at the time those train cars were used, but also not there now, where the artifacts might be more "at home." Attention to the placement of artifacts reveals a doubled displacement: the aim of the museum in Washington is first to remove visitors from American space and then to wrench them out of "normal" museum space, even as they must be reminded of the relevance of the exhibit narrative to their American lives. The doubled displacement is also evident in the museum officials' understanding that even "original" artifacts re-placed in a museum context do not re-create the original environment of the artifact (a notion recalling Walter Benjamin's thinking).[42] Rather, what is presented is ideationally akin to the

snapshot (in three visceral dimensions), preserved against the ravages of
time and space. As Cole argues, "For all the claims to 'past' authenticity
that filling museums with 'authentic' items—box-cars, suitcases, hair,
bones—makes, the heritage industry does not recover an authentic past,
but creates something new out of the past."[43] This new creation is memory, caught in the act of its mediation.

For Linenthal, displaying these objects is domestication, a process that
also impacts their status; he comments here on seeing and smelling the
same shoes in the third-floor tower room of the USHMM as he had seen
earlier in Poland at Majdanek:

It was easier somehow to view these [shoes] in the museum. The shoes were "visitors," and there was the sanctuary of recognizable space just outside. Even though
they—and other artifacts—were skillfully woven into the fabric of an intense Holocaust narrative, their raw power and seemingly unmediated presence in the barracks at Majdanek was moderated. In both places, of course, the shoes served as
props in a larger story. In Majdanek, however, the story was told within the total environment of the camp, an environment that seemed to collapse the distance between event and recollection of event, an environment in which the shoes were actually worn, taken off, left behind, collected. They were less selected artifact—by
definition something out of place, put on display—than remnant, at home in the
camp. In Washington, the shoes clearly had the status of artifact, and for me, at
least, their presence as part of a narrative in the controlled environment of the museum domesticated them, made them "safer" to view.[44]

The mediatory function of the museum domesticates and protects the
visitor from the "unmediated" horror of artifacts in their "home" environments; the latter appear to be remnants of traumatic experience, the
former representations of that experience.[45] Thus museum space is constructed as both domesticated and estranged, a process that is tied to its
objects' heterogeneity. In estranging the objects from their "natural" environment, museum officials therefore call attention to their roles as memorial mediators while digesting and mitigating the impact of those
objects. Such housing of Holocaust artifacts becomes part of a logic of
distancing, where the object, de- and recontextualized, is set off in a narrative we are asked to consider from a spatial and temporal distance, even
as, simultaneously, we are asked to reflect on and identify with the story
the objects purport to embody.

Yet, the domesticated replacement of displaced artifacts in the safe
context of the museum can also be seen as a misplacement, which is
also tied to the issue of sanctity. Recall, for example, the debate over the

display of women's hair (see pages 42–43). For museum planners, the hair
was an essential part of the story of dehumanization and commodification of Jewish bodies and had to be included in the permanent exhibit,
but they faced stiff opposition from members of staff and survivors. Museum consultant Alice Greenwald and former curator Susan Morgen-
stern wrote, for example, that they could not "endorse a wall of human
hair. . . . These fragments of human life have an innate sanctity, if
you will; they are relics of once vital individuals, which do not belong
in a museum setting but rather in a memorial setting. You run the very
real risk of creating a cabinet of horrible curiosities by choosing to use
them . . . and encourag[ing] . . . a more ghoulish than emotionally sym-
pathetic response or painful memorial response." They continued to argue that had the hair remained "at home," that is, in a museum at the
site of its removal from victims, then its display would be valid. But re-
moving it to Washington and displaying it out of context, as it were,
would perpetuate its commodification and continue the violence done
to the dead (Linenthal calls it "human 'matter' out of place").[46] The
argument for sacrality and propriety was also made by museum staff
member Alvin Rosenfeld: "Many visitors, myself among them—and I
am totally non-religious—will consider such displays sacrilegious, a
desecration."[47] Interestingly, the museum's content committee listened
to the objections yet still voted in favor of displaying the hair, but the
decision was overturned after a final plea on the behalf of two female
survivors, whose sensibilities might be offended, leaving the hair itself
in limbo, in a storage facility outside Washington, displaced by a photograph, but not (yet) re-placed.[48]

Ultimately, the negotiation of the place of artifacts, especially in light
of their perceived sacrality, makes their memorial emplacement highly
contested. We might therefore follow Young in attending to an even
deeper sense of misplacement caused by the display of Holocaust artifacts
in museums, one that goes beyond mere festishization: "What precisely
does the sight of concentration-camp artifacts awaken in viewers? Historical knowledge? A sense of evidence? Revulsion, grief, pity, fear? . . .
For, by themselves, these remnants rise in a macabre dance of memorial
ghosts. Armless sleeves, eyeless lenses, headless caps, footless shoes: victims are known only by their absence, by the moment of their destruction. In great loose piles, these remnants remind us not of the lives that
once animated them, so much as of the brokenness of lives."[49] There is a
danger that, by highlighting and sacralizing the relics of World War II
atrocities, a museum might encourage a misplaced focus on those objects

as embodying all there is to know about the past, the people who once used them, and the lives that inhabited them.

The issue of misplaced sacrality arises as well in the consideration of the position in the museum accorded to artifacts associated more with the perpetrators than with the victims. How does this impact the museum's commemorative role, and what kinds of narratives might these objects participate in? Linenthal suggests that, "given the boundaries of the commemorative voice at work, this idea [of allowing perpetrators to 'speak' in the exhibition] threatened to contaminate what for many was commemorative space." Moreover, concern arose that a too effective portrayal of the Nazi "industry of murder would be worse than appalling to visitors—it might be perversely fascinating as well."[50] Recall, for instance, the Hollerith machine. We might call this concern one of misplaced reverence, something closely allied to the problem of kitsch representation of the Nazi worldview. This concern is no small problem when we consider the mystical and mythical aura, albeit of a radically negative kind, that surrounds Nazi paraphernalia and artifacts of Nazi atrocities; yet, without these objects, perpetrators nearly disappear behind the lack of material evidence of their actions on display.[51] How does one navigate the terrain occupied by artifacts of atrocity that, in many respects, may only disturbingly entertain and fascinate?

Clearly, the issues surrounding the perceived sacrality of museum space and, especially, the artifacts on display raise a host of concerns involving the potential misplacing of representational and memorial attitudes that might be at odds with the purported aims of the museum itself. "The risk of aestheticizing here," argues Andrea Liss, "is directly linked to the project of historicizing to the point that artifactual display can become dangerously equated with inevitable cultural extinction. In this sense the United States Holocaust Memorial Museum in Washington, D.C., obliquely stands in as the silent other to the Nazi's Central Jewish Museum in Prague."[52] Recalling that the Nazis themselves sought to establish in Prague a collection of artifacts by which their anticipated destruction of European Jewry would be commemorated, we should be aware of the potential problems associated with object-driven museum displays and wary of any overdependence on Holocaust artifacts in constructing museum narratives. As Young suggests: "That a murdered people remains known in Holocaust museums anywhere by their scattered belongings, and not by their spiritual works, that their lives should be recalled primarily through the images of their death, may be the ultimate travesty. These lives and the relationships between them are lost to the memory of ruins alone—and will be lost to subsequent generations who seek memory only in the rubble of the past. Indeed, by adopting such artifacts for their own memorial presentations, even the new museums in America and Europe risk perpetuating the very figures by which the killers themselves would have memorialized their Jewish victims."[53] These artifacts, here understood as contextualized icons, invite further reconsideration of the museological mission.

ALTERNATIVES

While the classic object-driven museum may play a great role in the formation of contemporary culture and its image of tradition and the past, it remains flawed. Moreover, the enormous task of representing the Holocaust only accentuates the more subtle imperfections of the traditional museum project. Therefore, aside from simply using available technologies, newer museums may be consciously attempting to address and solve some of these crucial representational issues, seeking to mediate the past in a novel way. Certainly, the Simon Wiesenthal Center's Beit Hashoah-Museum of Tolerance is one of these. Whether consciously or not, its designers have responded to a number of the concerns outlined here, subsumed under the polarities of displacement and replacement, sacred and profane: the muteness of artifacts and embodied memory, the simultaneous distinction and confusion of temporal contexts, the evocation of death in the mausoleum-like traditional museum, the fiction of metonymic representation, the homogenizing effect of the museum narrative, the diversity of the museum's public, and the distinct cultural gap separating the artifact in its display from the visitor. For all these, the ways a museum exhibit mediates the past it is presenting and the tradition it is representing for its public become important. What is the nature of the alternative offered by the museum in Los Angeles?

First, consider its name. Above the entrance to the reddish-brown building on busy Pico Boulevard in West Los Angeles, the visitor can read, against the stone, "Beit Hashoah-Museum of Tolerance," the double title split and linked by a hyphen. In the museum's literature, a bullet often used to take the place of the hyphen (over the past few years, "Beit Hashoah" has ceased to appear in museum documents). What do we think when we see the name of this institution? Do we think that "Beit Hashoah" means "Museum of Tolerance," the former an unknown foreign term for the latter? We might, though this would be incorrect. "Beit Hashoah" literally means "house of the Holocaust," and I would argue that using such a title intentionally calls to mind, for those who are familiar with the terms, other Hebrew titles using the construct form *beit: beit hamidrash*, "house of study," and *beit haknesset*, "house of prayer" (literally, "house of gathering") among them. Is the Simon Wiesenthal Center suggesting a religious context in the name of the museum? Perhaps, but for most such an allusion is hidden, and in any case it remains untranslated. "Beit Hashoah" is invoked as a largely meaningless term, which is perhaps why most people (including the city of Los Angeles, whose road signs direct travelers to the museum) refer to the place as simply the Museum of Tolerance, and why museum officials have stopped using the name. Once inside one realizes that the museum is actually split into two parts and that the doubled name of the museum refers to its two distinct sections. Thus, the museum has a certain split (and somewhat ambiguous) personality illustrated by its peculiar hyphenated title, which is no mere whim of appellation. I would argue that the split and the ambiguous personality is at the heart of the museum's noncommittal program, and that the hyphen in its original name performs the same function as that in another ambiguous hybrid, the "Judeo-Christian," an idea to which I will return.

My analysis here is complex. Over the past few years the Museum of Tolerance has undergone a number of significant renovations and revisions, particularly in its first section. Each time its narrative has been altered, it has not only affected the visitor's experience but also impacted the ways the Holocaust is contextualized and memory mediated. Therefore, rather than erase the museum's own internal history and past incarnations, I will offer three successive "tours" of the MOT based on my own visits to the museum and its evolving discourse. Thus, each of the descriptions of the museum (including the last, one would suspect) is already more a history of a soon-to-be-forgotten series of displays (apt, to be sure, considering the postmodern tone of the museum) than a representation of a museum space that can still be visited. In light of the increasing malleability of Holocaust spaces, this layered reading is important. Though it would be too much to say that the end result of my repeated tour is three different museums, I nonetheless hope that this Rashomon-like effect will suggest several layers of narrative that can highlight the processes of mediation I perceive in the museum's representational strategies.

In 1995–97, the standard tour at the museum begins with a descent down a four-story-high spiral ramp that circles around the Tower of Witness, a metal sculpture featuring an array of anonymous photos of Holocaust victims (periodically changed), during which a docent reminds us that there will be no bathrooms until the end of the tour, some three hours later. On one visit, when I accompanied a school group from Los Angeles's Arlington High School, students were told to keep their voices down and not to giggle, lest they offend any survivors who might be with them for the tour. Walking down a corridor lined with images of shining, happy American faces, we soon meet the "Manipulator" (also called the "Host Provocateur" in museum literature), our video screen host, whose "body" is made of video monitors roughly arranged in human form. He will pop up throughout the first section of the museum, challenging us to choose and think while assuring us, in his smarmy way, that we really have no need for a lesson in tolerance. At the conclusion of our virtual host's introduction, he invites us to enter the exhibit through one of two doors, labeled "Prejudiced" (red) and "Unprejudiced" (green). In several visits, I observed a number of teenagers trying to open the "Unprejudiced" door, only to retreat sheepishly when finding it locked. Indeed, this experience is meant to be the first of a series of jarring lessons inside the museum: no one is perfect, we are reminded, and we must always consider carefully the choices we make.

Inside the Tolerancenter we are greeted with a barrage of images and sounds, in an environment Jeffrey Shandler likens to a "videogame arcade."[54] Several interactive, multimedia displays address issues of stereotyping and prejudice, forcing visitors to respond, make choices, and consider their ingrained presuppositions with respect to their fellow human beings. Wandering among a total of thirty-five "hands-on" exhibits with titles such as "Images That Stay with Us," "It's So Easy to Misjudge," "Me . . . a Bigot?" and "What We Say, What We Think," we explore, at our own pace, the relationships between words, images, and intolerance, responding interactively to a series of colorful and even entertaining displays. Such relationships are also addressed in the Whisper Gallery, a dark, winding corridor where racial epithets and hateful slurs ("camel jockey," "jungle bunny," "greasy dago," "bulldyke bitch," "loudmouthed kike," and the like) assault us.

The centerpiece of the Tolerancenter is a handful of interactive computer-video stations labeled "Timeline: Understanding the Los Angeles Riots." Here visitors can view a short film on the riots that erupted in 1992 following the acquittal of four white police officers on trial for the beating of African American Rodney King. They may then explore the riots in detail via interactive video replay and by adopting a range of interviewed subjects' perspectives, choosing from several time line segments ranging from the King beating through Los Angeles's rebuilding efforts.[55]

Responses to various questions about justice and social behavior are tab-
ulated and compared with those of visitors before us. The tolerance section also features an interactive map display on "the other America," allowing the visitor to learn about the hundreds of hate groups throughout
the United States. And it offers a short film, *It Is Called Genocide*, which
states that the Holocaust was neither the first nor the last incident of attempted genocide this century: featured are the Armenians, the Cambo-
dians, and the indigenous peoples of Latin America.[56]

This section of the museum concludes with a graphic chronology of incidents of tolerance and intolerance in U.S. history; a film, *Ain't You
Gotta Right*, on the civil rights movement, shown on a sixteen-screen
video wall; and displays focusing on the immigrant experience and the
power of demagoguery. The progression of this last display moves from
the power of words to that of images and finally that of the media, so that
a subtle connection is made between the isolated influence of individual
speakers and the media's ability to spread their messages far and wide.
Here again are mixed signals concerning technology: on the one hand, it
is the medium through which the museum communicates its message,
while on the other, the message is that it should be treated with suspicion. Though the Manipulator returns for a brief parting shot, he soon disappears, replaced by the question "Who is responsible?" and the multi-
lingual answer: "You are." In the words of the exhibition catalogue: "The
Tolerancenter's parting words convey its ultimate message: though people
and the media can exert a great deal of power, we can *choose* not to
succumb. Otherwise, we risk repeating an era of extreme inhumanity,
such as the Holocaust, which is portrayed in the next section of the museum."[57] Without any material evidence, the museum, in this first section, appears to have succeeded in displaying and even enshrining an elusive sociocultural ideal such as "tolerance" through a series of mediated
images and (vicarious) experiences of intolerance. So primed, we wait for
the doors to the next section to admit us.

By 1999 the Tower of Witness had disappeared and the structure of
the standard tour has become less regulated. The MOT receives so many
visitors and groups with varying time frames that it is not always possible for each group to experience the museum narrative in its original
and intended sequence.[58] Thus, some see only the Holocaust section or
spend only a short amount of time in the Tolerancenter. The Manipulator still welcomes us, and the two doors to the Tolerancenter remain:
the "Unprejudiced" one is still locked. But inside much has changed;
some of the well-worn "arcade" exhibits remain, though one is covered

with a tattered poster and others are chipped. The main attraction now is the Point of View Diner, an interactive video exhibit created in the form of a 1950s-style diner, complete with red booth seats and a central counter. But the jukebox at each seat is an interactive video screen whose buttons allow the visitor to select scenes and respond to questions. The docent informs us, "It is called the Point of View Diner because we serve up food for thought rather than real food."

Two programs are on the menu at the diner: *Talk Radio: The Bostics* (screened most often for adults) and *Prom Night* (for teens). *Prom Night* opens as a "special report" local newscast about a terrible accident in which a vehicle with two teens in it has collided with another carrying a family: the driver of the first auto is dead, the little girl in the second car has been gravely injured. The "special report" is immediately supplemented with follow-up reports that reveal new information about the accident: the teenage driver of the first car, Charlie Aronow, had been drinking; his girlfriend, Deborah, riding with him, had used a fake identification card to get them liquor; Charlie's mother is suing Rayko, the liquor store owner, and Deborah for causing Charlie's death. At one point, we are informed that the little girl has died. At the end of the program, we are asked some questions about where responsibility lies for the accident and Charlie's death. We are then asked to vote at our individual jukebox stations: who is responsible? Charlie, Rayko, Deborah, or Charlie's mother? Finally, we get to ask questions (selected from an array of onscreen options) of Rayko, Deborah, and Charlie's mother (but not of Charlie) to ascertain responsibility further. When our time is up, we are asked to vote again. All this seems a fairly benign educational lesson on the dangers of drunk driving until the omniscient narrator, accompanied by atrocity images ranging from homelessness to child labor, suggests that not taking responsibility leads to unspeakable horror and the "only following orders" argument of the Nuremberg defendants. We learn that by our tacit support for what goes on around us, we are shirking our responsibilities to the world. In closing, a camera captures a panned image of the visitors in the Point of View Diner and projects it onto the big screen in front of us.

Talk Radio: The Bostics plays as a "day in the life" of Pete Bostic, incendiary talk radio host, and his citywide fans. The premise is that TV crews have fanned out in the city filming these "Bostics," raising free speech issues, and that the reports have been edited into a news documentary. The segment opens with Bostic talking about feminists while a couple listens over breakfast; he loves what he hears, she detests it, argu-

ing that Bostic is a bigot and should be fired. Later we see the same man
joining his friends at a diner where they sit and listen to the radio broadcast from their booth. Sam, the black owner of the diner, has recently
hired Earl for security. Earl, we soon see, is also bigoted, against whites.
When Bostic moves on to an "ebonics" joke, the tension in the diner rises,
and when one of the group of (white) men at the table comments about
the food, Earl confronts them. Tempers flare, there is a struggle, Earl's gun
is drawn, and a bystander is shot (dead, we presume). Now we get to ask
questions of Bostic, the breakfasting couple, and Sam about the power of
words and about taking responsibility for them, as well as issues of moral
obligation. Bostic, for example, denies any responsibility; he champions
free speech in the extreme, denying that what he is doing is "hate radio."
Finally, we get to vote on the extent to which we agree or disagree with
statements concerning free and hate speech ("I protest whenever I hear
hate speech" is one example). After each question, we see our responses
tallied on the big screen. The narrator reminds us, "Words are tools . . .
they can be used constructively or destructively." The overall issue is one
of taking responsibility for one's words; otherwise, there may be fatal consequences.

Inside the Point of View Diner are placards on the tables that read:
"People often feel their opinions don't matter. This is NOT true. A SINGLE
VOICE can save a life or change the world. You're about to see a dramatic
story. Use the video jukebox in front of you to OFFER OPINIONS and ASK
questions. Think about what you see. Your point of view is very important. Your opinion counts." Clearly, the interactive nature of the Point of
View Diner is its major selling point to museum visitors. But the simplistic manner in which that interactivity is played out and in which the
two programs on offer are presented raises questions as to the real extent
of the display's impact. Indeed, no outlet actually exists for visitors to "offer opinions" or "ask" anything other than canned questions, aside from
turning to the museum docent. I suspect that, as visitors leave the diner
for the "Other America" display and move into the as-yet-unchanged re-
mainder of the Tolerancenter they are more, rather than less, confused
about what they are meant to experience here. More a part of the flow of
media culture around us than distinct from it, the material at the Point of
View Diner runs the risk of washing over museum visitors rather than engaging them in a serious consideration of personal responsibility.

During my visit in 2000, the docent makes it clear that the museum is
divided into two sections. The displays on hidden prejudice and the
"other America" are gone, waiting to be replaced by an updated exhibit

"GLOBALHATE.COM."[59] The Point of View Diner features two new programs, though they are less popular and less frequently screened than the previous two, still the main staples of the café's offerings. Both can be read as returns to more-local, Los Angeles–based issues, and both dispense somewhat with the artifice of a news documentary casually stumbled upon in favor of a more directly programmatic style. One, *Scared to Death*, shows Grandma Castillo being robbed in her home by members of the Eastside Angels, a Los Angeles gang, during a heat wave (recalling the riots perhaps?). This leads into a community debate about gang injunctions, neighborhood watches, job-training programs, and curfews; a city councilwoman worries that civil liberties groups will protest against any severe restrictions meant to curb the violence. The next night, Mrs. Castillo hears shots outside and barricades herself in her apartment. She dies in her sleep. Was it fear that killed her? The city council holds the Angels responsible, and it imposes a gang injunction prohibiting assembly, gang colors, and signs and institutes a curfew. The issue is one of balancing rights, and we are asked a broad range of questions regarding the importance of various factors in curbing gang violence, including injunctions, the presence of father figures, and better education.

The second new interactive video program, *Till Death Do Us Part*, deals with issues of stereotyping. It runs, however, like an advertisement for the Los Angeles Police Department. It opens with an incident in which an officer is shot during a drug bust. After he returns to duty, he responds with his partner to a domestic violence dispute. With the police there, the woman declares she is leaving her husband. Suddenly, the husband pulls a gun and grabs his wife, threatening to kill her. The officer shoots and kills the man. Three months later, the officer and his partner hear that the woman is suing the officer for "murdering" her husband. We then question the officer and the woman. In the officer's responses he denies that he panicked or that he could have waited or only shot to injure, not kill, the man. He says that he wishes people could stand in the shoes of the police. In the woman's responses she denies that she was in any real danger and suggests the officer overreacted. Disturbingly, in a program designed to counteract stereotyping, the woman appears as a stereotypical "abused wife," unable or unwilling to break free of her abuser. Viewers are finally asked questions: Was the officer justified in firing? Is the suit warranted? What has *my* experience of the police been like? Are the police unfairly criticized? At the end, the big screen features a pitch for avoiding stereotyping, arguing that cops *are* us, not different from us. Both programs do not appear to add much to the overall impact of the Point of View Diner.

As we leave the diner, we pass the soon-to-open Millennium Machine, the latest addition to the Tolerancenter's ongoing efforts to engage visitors in issues of personal responsibility, the power of words, and values and morals on a global scale. While the museum was still busy fine-tuning the display during my visit in August 2000, an assistant allowed me to preview it briefly. An impressive high-tech media environment, the Millennium Machine offers video scenarios dealing with the issues of the exploitation of women and children, prisoners and refugees, chemical and nuclear warfare, and terrorism. Each program is followed by a battery of factual multiple-choice questions meant to check the level of our knowledge of issues related to the video program. Then, each unit of six visitors is asked to discuss with one another key related ethical issues and vote on the application of those issues. The experience ends with links to further resources on the issues raised.[60]

One proceeds now past the historical time lines "Intolerance Persists" and "In Pursuit of Tolerance," which frame the video presentation *Ain't You Gotta Right*. The time lines end opposite two interactive TV screens, remnants of the Los Angeles riot displays that once stood as the focal point of the Tolerancenter. In this way, the MOT preserves its own ever changing history. Nearby, a new three-screen theater has been installed, serving as an interlude before the Holocaust section of the museum. *In Our Time* is more up-to-date than *It Is Called Genocide* was, both contextually and stylistically. Opening with the end of World War II, it moves quickly to present words and images of more recent atrocities in the former Yugoslavia, Rwanda, and generally in contemporary society. At its end, the film declares: "We seem to have forgotten what it was we were supposed to remember." Indeed.

SIMULATION (1995–97)

Entrance into the next section of the exhibit is restricted; while in the first section we were free to explore at will, here we must wait for the next guided "tour" to begin. The style of the mediated museum experience is different as well. Instead of the occasional video-host provocateur of the Tolerancenter, our journey through Beit Hashoah is consistently led by the voices of three figures identified as a historian, a researcher, and a museum designer—"cast out of plaster, three-quarter sized (scale as a way of manipulating performance space), and unmoving."[61] These three characters serve to frame and filter the experience for us; they are the computerized guides who move us through the exhibit, processing us and our

museum experience. In this way, the entire character of the visitor's experience shifts radically from interactive participation in multimedia displays to the activities of a passive voyeur. Comparing the museum experience here to that of TV watching, Nicola Lisus argues that, as visitors
move into Beit Hashoah, the "'power of the remote' is displaced from the
viewer's hand to the hand of the Museum." Moreover, she continues, the
museum has effected a shift in this section that at once controls and en-
tertains the visitor: "The aesthetics of emotion becomes the aesthetics of
control."[62] The shift into this second section of the museum is indeed radical. Museum literature sets the stage: "Upon entering the darkened area,
visitors are asked to be witnesses—as if brought back to the scene of the
crime—in a timed tour that moves people from exhibit to exhibit with
synchronized computers."[63] But before we embark on our trip and cross
the threshold (recall the initiatory experience in the USHMM), we are invited to take with us "photo passports," machine-readable cards bearing
likenesses of real children who had been caught up in the maelstrom of
the Holocaust. These passports, necessary talismans for crossing into this
new zone and exploring history (since "the past is a foreign country"),
heighten our museum experience as they encourage our identification
with victims of the Holocaust.[64]

Thus, as we begin our tour through this second and larger section of
the museum's permanent installation, we immediately realize we are
in a different world altogether. Though devoid of artifacts, like the Tolerancenter, Beit Hashoah features no interactive displays, less variation, and no real choice.[65] Instead, we are moved through a series of dioramas that Shandler likens to a "simulation of walking through a
documentary film," first visiting the researcher's and designer's offices
to take a crash course on post–World War I Germany and the rise of
Nazism, "taught" with archival photos and films.[66] We arrive next at a
1932 Berlin street scene, featuring shop window displays and a café in
which we eavesdrop on conversations (see figure 11). In each of the dioramas the stage is set with gray figures (reminiscent of George Segal's
work) that, though almost life-sized, are hardly lifelike. While the window displays are more realistic, it is clear to the visitor to the first part
of Beit Hashoah that this is very much a stage set, not a re-creation.[67]
Lending a somber and colorless tone to the exhibit, these dioramas
present history as staged, reinforcing the developing notion that nothing we are viewing is *real*.[68] We encounter more dioramas in which we
learn about Hitler's rise to the chancellorship and the Nuremberg Laws
before we enter a room in which we are surrounded by large video

Figure 11. Café street scene, Simon Wiesenthal Center Museum of Tolerance, Los Angeles.
Photograph by Jim Mendenhall, © 1992, courtesy of the Simon Wiesenthal Center.

screens, viscerally experiencing a Nuremberg rally as the images and
sounds wash over us.

At this point the visitor experiences a shift in perspective, now being
more part of the display than distinct from it.[69] By 1999 this program was
replaced with another film, *Ordinary People, Ordinary Lives,* which,
while focusing less on the visceral experience of Nazism, nonetheless
still places the viewer in the midst of an intensified media environment.
As if in response to Christopher Browning's excellent book, *Ordinary
Men,* as well as the more well known and problematic *Hitler's Willing Executioners* by Daniel Goldhagen, this segment of the museum focuses
both on the participation of ordinary people in the implementation of the
Final Solution and on the lack of response from the rest of the world. The
film also serves as a link between sections that deal with prewar restrictions on Jewish life and wartime activities, outlining the historical progression between them and framed by images of "ordinary people." If in
the first section of the museum the visitor is brought closer to the "ob-

jects" on display (here, the ideal of tolerance) via interactive media, here he is brought closer still through his physical emplacement in the midst of a (now noninteractive) media set, so that he must assume the mediating role himself (recall the mediating responsibility thrust on the viewer of Holocaust videotestimonies, which this parallels). At this stage in the narrative of Beit Hashoah, "the visitor is inducted as an extra within the production" of the Holocaust "docudrama" unfolding around him.[70]

Now halfway through the Holocaust exhibit, we stop at passport control and are invited to insert our cards into computers and read updates on our alter egos' experiences during the time period we have just "walked through." This break in our experience of witnessing the events of the Shoah brings us back, temporarily, to an interactive environment, where we are reminded of the stories of the children whose photographs we carry on our temporary passports. Meanwhile, on the opposite wall, through a window, we see a table set up for the Wannsee Conference and "eavesdrop on the secret meeting."[71] The pace intensifies, as more exhibits describe the roundups, deportations, attempts at emigration, the St. Louis incident, and the acts of the *Einsatzgruppen* (mobile killing units operating in Eastern Europe). We are soon invited to sit (along with the figure of the historian) in the brick ruins of the Warsaw Ghetto and see a film describing acts of Jewish resistance, including secret Torah study in the ghetto. As the carpeted floor gives way to rough concrete ("like a camp," noted one guide accompanying the Arlington High group), we find ourselves walking through a replica of a death camp gate,[72] past a miniature diorama of the camp, and through one of two brick tunnels labeled "Able-Bodied" and "Children and Others" (see figure 12).

Unlike the doors we first encountered at the start of the Tolerancenter, these are both open; where self-selection was denied earlier because one door was locked, here self-selection does not matter (as it did not for so many of the murdered) because both tunnels lead to the same place. That is, there is the illusion of choice, reinforced by a docent who suggests we keep this ability to choose in mind, even as real choice is once again denied. Putting the final stamp on our Holocaust "experience," we now enter the cold concrete Hall of Testimony, somewhat reminiscent of a gas chamber (see figure 13). But here the air is filled with sounds and images rather than deadly zyklon-B, as photomontages are displayed on the wall, accompanied by accounts of victims, perpetrators, and witnesses (read by professional actors).[73] "That the Museum of Tolerance in Los Angeles re-creates a gas chamber, which functions as a gallery for videos," observes Barbara Kirshenblatt-Gimblett, "reflects its more theatrical (rather than evidentiary)

Figure 12. Death camp gate replica, Simon Wiesenthal Center Museum of Tolerance, Los Angeles. Photograph by Jim Mendenhall, © 1992, courtesy of the Simon Wiesenthal Center.

Figure 13. Hall of Testimony, Simon Wiesenthal Center Museum of Tolerance, Los Angeles. Photograph by Bart Bartholomew, © 2001, courtesy of the Simon Wiesenthal Center.

approach to display."[74] Filing past the words of Simon Wiesenthal, "Hope lives when people remember," we emerge to consider "Who Was Responsible?" and to reflect at the Wall of the Righteous (which lists names of some non-Jews who helped Jews survive). Inserting our passports into machines, we now receive a printout of the complete story of the child who accompanied each of us on this journey, putting to an end the suspense concerning his or her fate (the card reader tells us that "the printer is now printing a fuller account of this young person's life—take it with you and Remember").[75] Passing the "Global Situation Room, where monitors flash up-to-the-minute information on current worldwide incidents of antisemitism and intolerance," we may choose to watch a film, *Echoes that Remain*, about Jewish life before the Holocaust. But it is more likely that we simply end our tour through the permanent exhibit and go upstairs.[76]

DECONTEXTUALIZATION

What kind of museum is this? Critics have suggested that it has the feel of an "indoctrination center," with a narration that "predigests the Holocaust and beams it back out in a way that is supposed to ensure that everyone gets the message." Gary Kornblau states that it "takes its cues from

infotainment, providing a sort of It's a Small World for liberals of all ilk."
He adds: "The format is reminiscent of the old Carousel of Progress attraction at Disneyland, but here one ends up in a recreated gas chamber,
sitting on concrete benches, and watching a television documentary.
Clearly, this museum assumes people can't or won't think for themselves."[77] One reviewer has even suggested that, with the museum's opening, "the emotional manipulation school of Holocaust remembrance has
found its spiritual center."[78] MTV, however, as quoted on the cover of an
old museum brochure (which, incidentally, makes no mention of the
name Beit Hashoah), has called it "very moving." Clearly, everyone has
been strongly affected by the museum's technologically sophisticated,
antiartifactual, multimedia approach to its permanent exhibit. Is there
anything really wrong with this? Surely we cannot fault the Wiesenthal
Center for trying to use the best means available to get its message across
to its target audience of schoolchildren, and an object-driven exhibit certainly has its problems, as we have seen. The past is always mediated,
whether it be through artifacts or not, so what difference could this particular style of mediating tradition and constructing culture make over
other approaches?

One possible answer is, It makes little to no difference at all. In this
view, we must accept the character of contemporary media and work
with them, rather than look back with regret to some imaginary former
era. "Live with the times," the Wiesenthal museum officials might say.
Indeed, it is understood at the MOT that dean of the Simon Wiesenthal
Center Rabbi Marvin Hier's overarching interest has consistently been to
keep changing, to remain up-to-date.[79] Considering that our culture has
already been transformed by video and other new media and realizing that
there is no way "back," it has been suggested that "educators and in-
tellectuals alike get beyond lamentation, beyond the sense of violation,
of being forced into an unwelcome and unwelcoming arena, beyond
the sickening sense of vertigo that the ground has gone from under us,
that we have lost any grip on our children, that we will not recognize
where we are already. In particular, it may be very valuable to get beyond nostalgia for some time when the literary, philosophical, and religious canons were (supposedly) in their place and all was right with the
world."[80] Indeed, all may never have "been right with the world," and perhaps the only route to recognizing where we are now is forward, into the
spectacle, as it were. The traditional recollective strategy of the object-
driven museum may breed the kind of nostalgia of which the Parrs speak,
a process similar to the dis- and misplacement of memorial activity on

which I have already commented. Does the Wiesenthal museum offer a viable alternative?

The answer to this question may be found in the observations of one media theorist, Hans Enzensberger.

The new media are oriented towards action, not contemplation; towards the present, not tradition. Their attitude to time is completely opposed to that of bourgeois culture, which aspires to possession, that is to extension in time, best of all, to eternity. The media produce no objects that can be hoarded and auctioned. They do away completely with "intellectual property" and liquidate the "heritage," that is to say, the class-specific handing-on of nonmaterial capital.

That does not mean to say that they have no history or that they contribute to the loss of historical consciousness. On the contrary, they make it possible for the first time to record historical material so that it can be reproduced at will. By making this material available for present-day purposes, they make it obvious to anyone using it that the writing of history is always manipulation. But the memory they hold in readiness is not the preserve of a scholarly caste. It is social.[81]

Enzensberger's somewhat ideological critique is well-taken, for he articulates the situation in which we find ourselves at the Museum of Tolerance. Here, memory is indeed public and social, not restricted to an intellectual elite, though manipulated nonetheless.[82] Here, claims to propriety over Holocaust symbols are undercut by the liquidation of their "heritage." Here, mediation of the past leads visitors to an awareness of the present, not of tradition, orienting us toward our own contemporary milieu and resisting the museological impulse to freeze time (in this regard, it is fitting that the Museum of Tolerance is evolving faster than this chapter could ever seize it). The museum, in this paradigm, is an enlivening institution, revivifying a stale memory and making it accessible to as wide a public as possible.

But all this leads to a process of displacement distinct from the one described by Young. There, memory-work was distracted and displaced by the material witness of artifacts; in this museum, memory-work is displaced by simulation and spectacle and the liquidation of tradition. It is all well and good if a contemporary museum can offer an alternative to the apparently deadening effects of traditional museum organization, but what actually takes its place? In the Museum of Tolerance, the past and its evidence are all but erased or, at best, relegated to the margins of the museum, sideshows to the main attraction. Representations and reproductions constitute the central narrative here, and as Walter Benjamin has taught us, the technique of reproduction threatens the aura of authenticity surrounding the original object, separating it from tradition; simulation, however "real," is inauthentic.[83]

The ground *has* gone out from under us, and without any artifacts holding us down and helping to maintain a sense of history and coherence (however "fictional" their representational scheme may be), we travel weightless through the spectacle, unsure of what exactly has been represented or seen.[84] What is more, Lisus suggests, the spectacle itself has become the real: "The difference between the signifier and the signified collapses in on itself." Or as Anton Kaes argues, "If distinctions between object and representation are breaking down and the contrast between the imaginary and the real . . . is no longer discernible, then the real itself is absorbed in the simulation: history dissolves into a self-referential sign system cut loose from experience and memory."[85] In this way, the permanent exhibit of the Los Angeles museum becomes something like a grand work of installation art, inasmuch as, without anything on display, it ends up displaying itself, self-referential to the point that the exhibit becomes its own context. Instead of the small risk of not remembering the Holocaust because of the overwhelming claims of material evidence, media that speak for themselves, we run the much greater risk of failing to remember because nothing is *there* to remember—we are mediating our own experience. In this context, as Vivian Patraka observes, "we are asked to become performers in the event of understanding and remembering the Holocaust."[86] But are museum visitors up to the task?

Some of the risk of failing to remember arises, as I have suggested already, from the split personality of the Simon Wiesenthal Center's museum. Beit Hashoah-Museum of Tolerance sends us mixed messages: in the Tolerancenter, we are encouraged and challenged to choose and think for ourselves, eventually coming to the point where we may mistrust the very media with which we have been interacting. But in Beit Hashoah, it seems we are not trusted to make choices for ourselves anymore; rather, we must be led through a preprogrammed experience. Perhaps this is meant to increase our identification, as through the passports we carry, with those who suffered through the Holocaust, who themselves had few choices at the time. Carrying those passports does succeed in "rehumanizing" the victims, as Young would argue. But, as he discusses the virtually identical program planned for the USHMM, he finds a not insignificant act of "deception" here: "For by inviting visitors to remember their museum experience as if it were a victim's Holocaust experience, the personal identity card asks us to confuse one for the other. . . . Imagining oneself as a past victim is not the same as imagining oneself—or another person—as a potential victim, the kind of leap necessary to prevent other 'holocausts.' All of which obscures the contemporary reality of the Holocaust, which is not the event itself, but *memory* of the event, the great distance between then and now, between there and here."[87] Either we travel back in time to identify with the children whose photographs are on our passports and lose the connection to the contemporary relevance of the Holocaust (the ultimate lesson of the Tolerancenter, now too far away in symbolic space and time), or we bring those same children forward to join us in our journey through simulation and lose a sense of the reality of their experiences. In both cases the past is not mediated, and both strategies result in the eliding of memory and the blurring of temporal and spatial distinctions, a process that runs throughout Beit Hashoah.

The issue of spatiality is crucial here, as it is in the USHMM. What is the nature of the museum space created at the Museum of Tolerance? Patraka, in a discussion of the contemporary cultural "performance" of the word "Holocaust" that considers the two museums analyzed here, turns to Michel de Certeau's useful distinction between "space" and "place." As Patraka reads him, the distinction concerns the different narratives of meaning associated with each term. *Place* invokes stability and the "law of the 'proper,'" where two things cannot coexist in the same location, whereas *space* is multiple, so that it "'occurs as the effect produced by the operations that orient it, situate it, temporalize it, and make it function in a polyvalent way.'"[88] In this way, place is determined by the object, while space is determined by the subject.[89] Patraka carries the distinction forward to consider the different strategies of memorialization put into motion in relation to the degree to which Holocaust "place" becomes Holocaust "space" at the two museums and, especially, in their public faces as evidenced in their fund-raising materials. What is revealed is the tension between conflicting needs for, on the one hand, spaces open to visitors' performances of interpretation and, on the other, the stricter imposition of the "monumental meaning of the Holocaust" as expressed in the "logic" of place. There appears to be a need as well to convert the "'place' of the gawking bystander . . . into the 'space' of ethically engaged witnessing" (similar, I would add, to the "space" of engagement created in the viewing environment of videotestimonies).[90]

In the end, a museum such as the Museum of Tolerance seems to move from space to place, so that, "despite its emphasis on the interactive, by ending with the gates of Auschwitz the museum takes the space it tries to open up for a consideration of the interconnections among oppressions and re-contains it into a (computer-synchronized) place. Auschwitz becomes a monumental metonymy for the Holocaust, for all anti-Semitism(s), and for the consequences of intolerance."[91] In spite of great efforts to the contrary, the Los Angeles museum ends up with the same shortcomings of metonymic representation it may have been trying to overcome. Indeed, it would appear that the USHMM moves in the opposite direction (and this may account, in part, for its success), so that the negotiation of place between Washington and Europe in the re-placing of artifacts gives way to the kind of reflective space for individual negotiation of meaning that Patraka advocates (and Freed designed into the building itself).

In addition, although the connection between the Holocaust section and the tolerance section of the museum in Los Angeles is obviously encouraged, the distinction between them is still maintained to such an extent that the Holocaust is never really contextualized—what remains is a hyphenated, double museum. But contextualization is crucial. Critics of current trends in American Judaism argue that our identity depends too much on the Holocaust, leaving out the rest of a collective Jewish history and memory, *de*contextualizing the Shoah, as it were.[92] Young argues that "without the traditional pillars of Torah, faith, and language to unify them, the majority of Jews in America have turned increasingly to the Holocaust as their vicariously shared memory."[93] Indeed, the Simon Wiesenthal Center's museum appears to support this decontextualization, denying Beit Hashoah much of its potential traditional context and historical evidence while effectively encoding its Jewish references, perhaps so as not to offend visitors with perceived claims of propriety.[94]

In fact, the museum seems to want to have things both ways at once. It seeks to place the Holocaust in the context of a vaguely determined "Judeo-Christian" ethic of "tolerance," an indeterminate locus of social responsibility that has little real basis in tradition or culture and whose parental abstraction tends to erase the Jewish side of the marriage at the same time as it tries to maintain its separate, unique status.[95] In other words, the "Judeo-Christian" parallels the naming of the museum itself, so that embedded within the public performance of the name "Beit Hashoah-Museum of Tolerance" is an erasure of the "Judeo" in favor of the "Christian," even as the museum attempts to isolate the specificity of the "Judeo" (i.e., the Holocaust section). This is borne out by the erasure of the name "Beit Hashoah" in all current MOT literature. Omer Bartov goes even further, cynically suggesting that the MOT's strategy is one totally infused with Christian "love":

Just as the medieval Catholic Church had insisted that man's station in society was divinely ordained, and all that was needed was love and acceptance, so too the Simon Wiesenthal Center accepts the conditions that breed prejudice while calling for the replacement of prejudice with love. If the 1960s celebrated love as a transforming social force, the 1990s seem to celebrate love (of oneself, one's group, one's nature) as an antidote to social upheaval in the face of potential explosion. Ironically, this museum, which attempts to find a relationship between present intolerance and past genocide of the Jews, interprets the past through a Christian prism of infusing matter with spirit, allowing things to remain precisely as they are while simultaneously arguing that they have been transformed in their essence through love (and faith). The possibility that love, or at least human dignity and mutual respect, can only be created through a change in the material conditions of humanity, does not seem to occur to the organizers of the Hall of Tolerance.[96]

While Bartov may overstate his case, he nonetheless highlights a spiritual displacement that, curiously, reflects back on the material displacement at the heart of the MOT's representational strategy.

Nevertheless, the idea of making a museum of/to tolerance is no doubt admirable, especially when we recall Ivan Karp's suggestion that museums participate in the framing of the "ever-changing constitution of civil society." Indeed, Patraka credits the museum with making a significant gesture in beginning to put the "mechanisms of oppression (and not simply diversity) into public discourse."[97] But Karp's point is that such a constitution emerges through a process of negotiation and debate over social ideas and identity, not via the articulation of one theme. And when we shift to the presumed theme of "never again" enshrined in the Holocaust section, we have, at best, the continuation of the earlier theme of tolerance (with little variation) and, at worst, the manipulated simulation of history overshadowing its referent and thus obscuring its lessons. An interpreted narrative of the Shoah is necessary, of course, for a museum's message to get across, but a hermeneutics of the Holocaust, as Harold Kaplan suggests, "cannot be a single monothematic interpretation. The questions held before us are, How does this story instruct the future? How does it discover important values? How does it decide what is human?"[98] This museum does not provide sufficient answers to these questions.

In fact, it runs the risk of doing something much worse: encouraging identification rather than understanding, even at the expense of understanding.[99] In his biting critique of the contemporary American impulse to trivialize tragedy, as at the USHMM, in *Schindler's List*, and elsewhere, Jonathan Rosen makes comments I think best apply to the MOT. Critical of museums and historical theme parks that "go so far as to make visitors feel that they are the people whose fate is on display," Rosen argues that the American way is increasingly to make tragic history into "tragic theater, instilling fear, pity, and, ultimately, purgation." The catharsis such exhibits offer provides the "closure that historical tragedy never possesses" (recall the enduring effects of trauma on survivors' lives and life stories).[100] This embodiment of memory ultimately stands in the way of real understanding, and Rosen makes the provocative and important claim that, rather than teach us something positive about the world, "some history" might lead to the opposite conclusion. "What if studying radical evil does not make us better? What if, walking through the haunted halls of the Holocaust Museum, looking at evidence of the destruction of European Jewry, visitors do not emerge with a greater belief that all men are created equal but with a belief that man is by nature evil?"[101] In this context the MOT may not be teaching tolerance at all, but intolerance.

So, without much of a sense of tradition, artifactually based or otherwise, the Simon Wiesenthal Center's Beit Hashoah-Museum of Tolerance strikes me as ultimately forgetful. How different it might have been if the designers had considered incorporating something like Rabbi Hillel's famous ethical lesson: "What is hateful unto you do not do unto your fellow human being. This is the entire Torah; the rest is commentary; go study."[102] An insertion such as this could have given the entire exhibit on tolerance more resonance with "tradition" (framed in one of a variety of ways), while helping to forge a solid connection with the Holocaust section, grounding it, as it were. Such a reference might also have helped mediate between the past being represented and the present perspective and sociohistorical context of the museum visitor, a role not successfully played by any of the "media" at the museum. Instead, what we have is symbolized in the Hall of Testimony at the end of Beit Hashoah where one can hear, if one is listening and if one can recognize it, the Jewish prayer in honor of the martyred dead, El Maleh Rahamim, piped into the background of the audiovisual display on the cold concrete walls. Here, tradition and memory are largely ignored, pushed to the sidelines in favor of a multimedia spectacle that ultimately fails to mediate much of anything.

HOLOCAUST MUSEUMS ultimately serve to tell stories, to find ways of speaking out of the silence that is the abyss of the past and of conveying such speech to visitors. More emplaced and embodied than videotestimonies (indeed, both the United States Holocaust Memorial Museum and the Museum of Tolerance will one day serve as repositories for Spielberg's Survivors of the Shoah Visual History Foundation, so that even structurally the museum will encompass the video), but less so than ritual-commemorative activities (which I will discuss in the next chapter), such museums are situated in places and spaces of mediation. Located between presence and absence, mystery and revelation, these two very different museums communicate, in the end, the precarious and paradoxical role of Holocaust memory as reconstituted in the present, in America. What happens, however, when Americans go abroad in search of heritage and memory at the sites of history themselves?

CHAPTER FIVE

Performing Memory

TOURISM, PILGRIMAGE, AND THE RITUAL
APPROPRIATION OF THE PAST

To understand how collective memory works, we cannot restrict our inquiries to tracing the vicissitudes of historical knowledge or narratives. We must also, and I believe foremost, attend to the construction of our emotional and moral engagement with the past. When looking at public discourse, this translates into questions about how the past is made to matter. Framing events, heroes, places as worthy of remembrance and honor is quite different from defining whole historical chapters as a burden to be mastered.

—IWONA IRWIN-ZARECKA, *Frames of Remembrance:*
The Dynamics of Collective Memory

SEEKING MEMORY

THE COMMITMENT to Holocaust memory has increasingly become a concern to a new generation intent on appropriating that memory. The strategies developed for and by these memory tourists for the memorialization of the Holocaust often go far beyond iconic inscription and technological mediation to (almost) the logical extreme of embodiment. Whereas iconic mediations of the Shoah can offer models for representation that establish the symbolic language for remembrance and whereas museums and videotape archiving projects, to a large degree, also attempt to stabilize memory in order to mediate it for contemporary culture, ritual commemorative activities take mediation (and memory) beyond these techniques geared toward preservation and permanence and accentuate the performative, transitive qualities of memorialization. Though they appropriate the stable logics of place so as to ground memory in the concrete and the "real" and to build lasting structures for Holocaust memory, commemorations bring the practice of memory into the present through the activities of those doing the remembering. Thus Holocaust memory becomes a public, social phenomenon. Following the maps established by historians and geographers, survivors and political leaders, the memory pioneers of the next generation negotiate spaces for the production of Holocaust memory that have their own internal rationales. Building on the structures created by religion and ideology as well as by expectation, today's explorers of the landscape of memory proceed far beyond the constraints established by icons, video frames, and museums to embody the past themselves and find ways *into* the Holocaust. That this may be the same Holocaust those who "were there" may want to find ways *out of* only highlights the difference and importance of the contemporary quest for remembrance.

In this chapter I discuss those ritual strategies and appropriations in the context of one particular case of Holocaust commemorative activity: the March of the Living. Because the march itself has come to dominate the culture of such memory tourism, and because its structure and itinerary are paradigmatic of both the large majority of such tours and the problems and pitfalls of these excursions in their most extreme forms, this analysis well addresses the most essential issues involved in the ritually embodied, commemorative forms of Holocaust memorialization. Indeed, no less an authority than Martin Gilbert, noted British historian, led a tour of Holocaust sites in Europe for his graduate students in 1996, about which he subsequently wrote. Though the book resulting from that experience makes clear that his was an itinerary deeply informed by historical awareness, steeped in archival research into the background of Jewish communities before the war as well as their wartime destruction, it nonetheless reveals the prominence of Holocaust tourism as a way of seeking memory and engaging the past.[1] This mode of memorializing is all the more pronounced in the case of the march, whose underlying religious, ideological, and cultural structures reinforce the construction of memory. In this most highly negotiated and deeply appropriated genre of the contemporary cultural memory of the Shoah we also find more ways in which memory is made meaningful—ways it engenders commitment in the present and to its own future.

I will begin to explore this terrain at the end, as it were—the ruins of Crematorium Chamber II at Auschwitz II-Birkenau, in a place that is framed as original, in starkly religiomythic terms:

We are assembled here again, marching against death, in the march that has no end, on the awful road of death and destruction in Auschwitz. . . . Here, each year anew, the Jewish nation begins its march to freedom, and to its homeland. This is the March of Life, the lives of their children, grandchildren, and great-grandchildren. . . . This is the March of Remembrance, of those who swore to remember and never forget. . . . This is also the March of the Dead, who never stopped marching and still march today with us and accompany us like the pillar of fire that led the Jewish camp in the Bible, today serving as a reminder and as a witness. They march with us today; they will march with us tomorrow and next week; and they will return with us to Eretz Yisrael.[2]

How can we begin to unpack this arresting series of assertions and declarations linking past, present, and future, myth and history? Clearly, as framed by march organizers, the activities of the March of the Living are communally and perhaps cosmically significant. Yet, if we were to follow the late iconoclast Yeshayahu Leibowitz, none of these mythic-memorial constructions would make any difference. According to his clearly singular and idiosyncratic views, the religious significance of historical events depends solely on whether or not such events occurred for religious reasons, under religiously determined circumstances. In this view, "the Holocaust of our generation is religiously meaningless. The Holocaust belonged to the course of the world, it merely exemplified the lot of the helpless who fall prey to the wicked. What was not done for the sake of Heaven, is indifference from a religious point of view. Since the establishment of the state of Israel was not inspired by the Torah nor undertaken for the sake of the Torah, religiously speaking, its existence is a matter of indifference."[3] Thus, not only would the Holocaust fall outside the realm of religiomythic relevance, so too would the foundation of the State of Israel. The ritual-commemorative mode of Holocaust memory, as played out in the March of the Living, stands, as it were, between these two statements. On the one hand, it raises powerful associations with the trappings of tradition and the positive construction of memory. On the other, it demands analysis as to its position in the landscape of religious and cultural responses to the Shoah, questions as to its role in promoting certain ideologies of remembrance. These two quotations will therefore serve as the poles between which I will chart my explorations.

Indeed, ever since the Israeli Knesset enacted the Holocaust and Heroism Memorial Day Law in April 1959 and, two years later, legislated that Yom ha-Shoah veha-Gevurah (literally, "the day of Holocaust and Heroism") be observed in a Jewish ritual manner (for instance, that it begin at sundown the previous day), ritual commemorative activity around the Holocaust, bounded by these two poles, has grown substantially.[4] That is, despite the non-Halachic (and even idolatrous, as Leibowitz might argue) nature of such commemoration, Jews seem increasingly interested in, rather than indifferent to, marking the memory of the Shoah through symbolic activity, much of it colored by tradition. In 1988 a new form of such symbolic activity was inaugurated: the "March of the Living."[5] The "march" itself is an annual silent walk from Auschwitz I to Auschwitz II-Birkenau on Holocaust Memorial Day, undertaken by a group of international Jewish high school students accompanied by adult educators, survivors, medical professionals, and community leaders, culminating in a mass commemoration ceremony at the Birkenau memorial; in 1994 (the year I participated) the march involved over six thousand teens from over forty countries.[6] But the march is also much more: all six thousand students who participated in 1994 crisscrossed the Polish countryside in convoys of tour buses exploring the landscape of Jewish memory and history; for the fifteen hundred American students who went and for all other march groups, the March of the Living was the entire two-week expedition to and tour of Poland and Israel that framed the Holocaust Memorial Day walk. On this trip (April 4 to April 18 in 1994) the students generally visit Warsaw and Kraków, Majdanek and Treblinka, and various important symbolic-political sites in Israel, including the Western Wall, Masada, and Jerusalem's Ammunition Hill, in addition to the Auschwitz camps. Throughout the tour of Poland, students participate in (and even initiate) organized and improvised ceremonies of remembrance for the murdered Jews and their destroyed world, while in Israel more ceremonies occur marking and celebrating the Jews' "return into history" in a sovereign state. What kind of memory is established through this activity, and how can we contextualize it?[7]

One can begin to answer these questions by understanding the march on its own terms, as a pilgrimage of memory. I argue that the symbolic behavior of the teenagers throughout the two-week tour must be understood in a religiohistorical context; the rites of remembrance, in all their variety, are symbolic interactions with sacred sites of memory, what Pierre Nora has called *lieux de mémoire,* augmented by traditional and innovative liturgy and explorations into history and ideology.[8] Indeed, the superstructure of the entire March of the Living and its itinerary is designed to evoke a strong connection between the student participants and their past/heritage through a Zionist ideology of history that follows the contours of collective, popular memory more than it adheres to strict historical realities: Israeli flags, for instance, are seen everywhere on the tour in Poland, (re)claiming symbolic space for a country that did not exist during the time and history the pilgrims are exploring. But beneath this enforced *communitas* lies a realm of competing discourses about history, memory, and the sacred in which the students, from a wide variety of social and religious backgrounds, actively struggle to find their place. Whether they are traveling the Polish countryside in buses while listening to their *madrikhim* (guides) narrate the "sacred" history of the Holocaust through its various texts, exploring on foot the symbolic geography of memory of the camp-memorials, praying on Shabbat in the only remaining Warsaw synagogue, or observing Yom ha-Zikkaron and celebrating Yom ha-Atzma'ut one after the other in Israel, each day of the tour is fraught with significance, as identity and experience blend and the participants construct a viable Holocaust memory (or have it constructed) for themselves. Understanding the strategies of symbolic appropriation and expression invoked throughout the march will lead us to a better understanding of the contours of collective Holocaust memory in its most active and embodied construction in ritual performance.

THE MARCH OF THE LIVING: PREPARATION AND EXPECTATIONS

Preparation for participation in the march is involved; this is no holiday tour, at least it is not presented as such. Prospective participants must apply, and the brochures warn that not all applicants are accepted into the program. The main concern of the organizers seems to be that the students be mature enough to handle the strong emotional and physical burdens of the two-week tour. After acceptance into the program, participants are mailed a packet of preparatory readings presented as a study guide and created by the Central Agency for Jewish Education in Miami, the first U.S. community to be involved in the march and still the trailblazer for its continued expansion and development (though the march is now administered in New York). The study guide offers basic, easily digestible selections organized into units titled "Danger Signals," "The Persecution Years," "Israel," and "Israel Today" and including excerpts from Holocaust literature, histories, songs, memoirs, maps, and traditional Jewish sources, along with thought questions, exercises, and activities. (A final section of the study guide is mailed out separately upon return to the United States following the march.)[9] Participants are then given reading and homework assignments selected from the guide in the weeks or even months prior to departure. Students living in or near major metropolitan areas (such as Los Angeles and San Francisco, cities whose contingents I studied and accompanied, respectively, in 1994) get together for a series of meetings with one or several of their madrikhim to discuss these readings, watch films, hear presentations, and even role-play, while the others prepare correspondence course–style. All this serves to set a tone of seriousness and community, as well as to establish a common background of knowledge.

The students themselves come with a range of educational backgrounds and interests, but most seem to have had some previous interest in the Holocaust, as well as in Israel and in their Jewish communities. Many seem to have heard about the march from friends or in their Jewish youth groups. Responding to a questionnaire item that asked, "How did you decide to go on the March of the Living? Who, if anyone, or what encouraged you to go?" one student wrote: "I knew I had to go after I heard my friend speak about it two years ago. Even though he only spoke about the torture that went on in Poland, he later told me that it was the best time of his life. I also wanted to see for myself what happened, so I could actually believe it—let myself feel it. I have always acknowledged the Holocaust, but made myself put up a shield for my emotional protection. I feel I am ready to surrender my shield."[10] Another participant had this to say: "I have always been told that visiting the concentration camps and visiting Israel is a necessary part of being Jewish. I did not feel that I was mature enough or emotionally ready to visit Poland, until now. [The] March of the Living was the perfect opportunity for me to remember the Holocaust. It did not take long to get me interested in the program. I was encouraged by *everybody* to go on the trip. I am so lucky to be able to go. And I hope that I will bring back memories/stories for those who were not fortunate enough to be able to go." Taken together, these two responses display both long-standing interest in the Holocaust as well as a certain apprehension regarding its brute reality or lessons, expressed nonetheless in the context of positive expectations. One can read a sense of obligation (even religious obligation) in the second of the two, echoed by one student who wrote, "I decided to go because I believe it is my obligation to see the atrocities first hand." This feeling of responsibility is important, as noted by anthropologist Jack Kugelmass: "For Jews, visiting Poland and the death camps has become obligatory: it is ritualistic rather than ludic—a form of religious service rather than leisure."[11] Participants also voiced a certain insistence that the decision to go was theirs alone and that no one talked them into it: "My mother saw the advertisement in the Jewish Bulletin and encouraged me to call, but I knew I wanted to go and it was my choice"; "I have always been interested in the Holocaust and I have read several books and watched movies, but I have always wanted to see for myself, what my relatives and fellow Jews went through. I think it is important that everyone go see the camps, not just the Jews. No one encouraged me at the beginning to go but after people learned more about the trip, they got excited for me."

A look at some of the participants' expectations and preconceptions is also instructive. When asked, "What do you think of when you think of Poland?" and "What do you think of when you think of Israel?" participants responded in sharply dichotomized terms: "When I think of Poland I think of the color grey, cold weather and cold faces. I think of sadness and death and what could have been. When I think of Israel, I think of trees, color, and new life. I can see smiles and hear laughter and can imagine people dancing." "[Poland is] anti-semitism, hatred, darkness; [Israel is] happiness, being free, home, beauty." Almost all the respondents mentioned the notion of Israel as a Jewish homeland, and while images of Poland were more varied, almost all reflected a negative impression: "I think of death, bitter cold, racism, and hatred. To be honest, I am frightened about what I am going to see there and how I am going to react. Israel is happiness. Although there is still and probably always will be war there, I can do nothing but smile and feel warm inside when I am there."

Turning to more general expectations, I found mixtures of apprehensiveness and excitement and, sometimes, a curious denial of expectations at all. Responding to the question, "What expectations and concerns do you have for your trip to Poland and Israel? Specifically, how do you think it might affect (1) your sense of Jewishness and (2) your relationship to the Holocaust?" one student wrote, "I expect nothing, but I know that it will change my outlook on humanity and strengthen my faith in *Hashem* [God]." Another wrote: "I think this trip will help me identify with the Holocaust. Make me actually see the truth. I've read so much, but I want to see for myself. I'm scared to find out the truth at the same time, scared of learning something about my beliefs. Scared of being categorized/generalized by people." Finally, two respondents expressed, among other things, concern over their return and the kind of people they would be after the march:

I have been waiting for this trip for months and I can't believe it is almost here. I'm getting very anxious and excited, but also a little nervous. I don't know how I'm going to react when I walk into the concentration camps. But I know that I will meet so many people that will be there for me. After this trip, I will be a stronger Jew and will be prepared to deal with difficult things when I get back. I will also have a personal reaction to the Holocaust, which will allow me to carry on the memories and stories of the 6 million Jews.

I fear that when I see the camps in Poland that I may lose all faith and hope of a good future and peace of mankind. I don't know where my Jewishness will go, it could to non-believer or super-believer. I hope that I'll have a better understanding of the 6 million killed and that I will understand their pain. My main concern is that I have no idea how I will be able to fit back in with my life once I return.

Overall, there is a sense of expectation that the march will instill knowledge that will lead to understanding and an integration of the "Holocaust" into the lives of these teenagers. This integration, it is clear, is expected to make its bearers inheritors, to a certain extent, of the Holocaust's lasting cultural, social, and religious effects.

THE ITINERARY: "SACRED" SITES IN POLAND AND ISRAEL

The pace of the march-tour is exhausting.[12] After a fun-filled, sleepless night of excitement on the plane, our group landed in Warsaw and hit the ground running, so to speak. The first day in Poland was spent exploring the memory of the Warsaw Ghetto and its uprising, largely via the "memorial route" that stretches between the Umschlagplatz (the main gathering place from which many Jews were deported)[13] and the monument designed by Nathan Rapoport. In between, the route included stops at the Mila 18 memorial (at the site of the headquarters of the Warsaw Ghetto resistance), where we recited Kaddish (the prayer, recited in memory of the dead, which attests to God's greatness), and various markers named for specific ghetto figures.[14] Along the way competition with other march groups was sometimes fierce for access to the memorial spaces, especially at Mila 18. That tour culminated in a memorial ceremony at the Rapoport monument for our entire convoy (five busloads of approximately thirty people each) consisting of readings by student participants, El Male Rahamim (a prayer in honor of Jewish martyrs), and "Ha-Tikvah" (Israel's national anthem), and interrupted by (then) Israeli minister of education Amnon Rubenstein, who laid a wreath at the monument and said a few words to our group.[15] That evening we drove to Kraków in the numbered buses that were not only the source for our temporary group identity ("Bus 544, over here!") but also the places where we unwound, reflected, chatted, wrote in journals, listened to music, and had briefings about upcoming sites.

The next day we toured both the Auschwitz I camp-museum and the vast remnants of Auschwitz II-Birkenau, in advance of our more ritualized and less exploratory visit the next day, the day of the memorial walk itself. The theme of "seeing with our own eyes," first established almost as soon as we landed and began exploring the remnants of the Warsaw Ghetto, reached the first of several peak moments of expression in the reconstructed gas chamber and crematorium of Auschwitz I, where we gathered after hearing one of the survivors accompanying us, Fred Diament, tell of "life" in the camp and after visiting the museum exhibits at the camp-memorial. The leader of the entire five-bus convoy, Chicago's Dr. Gerald Teller, spoke to those of us gathered inside the crematorium, framing the focal point of our group's experience for the day thusly: "the fire . . . burned day and night [here], just like the fire on the altar in the Holy of Holies in the Holy Temple burned day and night. And it was a fire which consumed . . . anything and everything that was in its way."

This powerful, though somewhat misinformed, conflation of the sacred and the profane raises the disturbing connotation of sacrifice to God (recall that the word "holocaust" originates in the Greek translation of the term for the "wholly burnt sacrificial offering" in the Hebrew Bible) and suggests the *Ner Tamid* (eternal light) of the Temple (and the modern synagogue). But it was surely meant to underscore the utter depravity of the Nazi assault on Judaism (and also drew strong associations for the candle lighting to follow). It was, however, heard by only half the group, as the space of the crematorium room could not handle all of us at once. Furthermore, there was also no mention of the *reconstructed* nature of the space in which the participants were being asked to act symbolically.[16] Finally, it was a misinformed statement because there was neither fire nor altar in the Holy of Holies, the innermost sanctuary of the Jewish Temple in ancient Jerusalem, which was empty; in any case, only the high priest would go inside that place, and only on Yom Kippur. The sacrificial altar was well outside the inner chambers of the sanctuary.

We can understand, here, something of how the contours of memory can be shaped with little regard for accurate historical, or even symbolic, details. Rather than harshly criticize, though, we can learn from this example how strongly the force of memorialization pulls us into symbolic associations. As if in response to Teller's words, after the El Male Rahamim and the Kaddish, participants lit memorial candles, placing them in and around the ovens. There was also a student-led ceremony inside one of the barracks at Birkenau, one of many introduced over the course of the trip to ritualize memory. We then went to Kazimierz (the "city of the Jews" just outside Kraków), to its old Jewish square, and visited the Rema Synagogue. At the synagogue one of the rabbis accompanying the group gave a talk in which he reflected on the construction of Jewish community and the transmission of the living Torah through the generations. This talk reflected another interest of the organizers: to balance images of death and life against each other every day, each serving as a reminder of the other. The sense of life, however, was not one of vibrancy but of a fading, barely present reality. The synagogue, for instance, was celebrated as still in use, but when one of its members spoke to us briefly (in Yiddish, through a translator) he was barely comprehensible and obviously very old. The "life" that was presented to us, therefore, in that museum-like, empty (without us) shul in the midst of an ancient cemetery was really just the reflection of the life that we, as march participants, brought there ourselves, and it strikes me that we took it with us when we left Poland. The balance sought by the organizers, then, was really only a turning inward of the commemoration process, and this would recur throughout the first week of the trip.

The following day, April 7, Yom ha-Shoah, the "March of the Living" itself took place. After short visits in the cold snow to the areas of the former Kraków Ghetto and the Plashow labor camp (the site of much of the story recounted in the film *Schindler's List*, today marked by an imposing monument), we arrived at Auschwitz I and parked among many other buses. As the other groups lined up, we once again listened to Auschwitz survivor Fred Diament, who read a prepared piece in front of the notorious "shooting wall" next to Block 11, memorializing some of his comrades who were involved in camp resistance, one of whom was his brother. This emotional moment concluded with a recitation of El Male Rahamim and the Kaddish. After this the "march" began, led by eighteen participants (selected perhaps because it is the numerical equivalent of the Hebrew word *chai*, for "life") bearing the national flag of Israel. They were followed by VIPs and the national contingents in alphabetical order after the Israeli one, with participants instructed to walk silently in rows of six. The "march" proceeded through the Arbeit Macht Frei gate at Auschwitz I,[17] down a road (where police officers kept local Poles from crossing until after we had passed), up and over a bridge crossing several railroad tracks, and down past some residences on the way to the gate at Birkenau.[18]

Marchers broke ranks to photograph themselves at three major sites: the Arbeit Macht Frei gate, the bridge over the railroad tracks (from which, owing to the elevation, there was a good view ahead and behind at the sheer size of the "march" and under which passed several trains, themselves eerie reminders of the mechanics of deportation), and the walkway and railway tracks leading up to the gate at Birkenau. The first and last of these can be understood as mnemonic markers—icons—recognizable sites that, both because of and despite their recognizability, needed to be captured as snapshot mementos to remind the participants that they were indeed there. Additionally, as Marianne Hirsch argues, "the two gates are the thresholds that represent the difficult access to the narratives of dehumanization and extermination," thus reinforcing the need for marchers to "remember" their experience of passing through them via photography.[19] The second of these three sites served as a literal and symbolic vantage point from which participants could view and capture the unfolding commemoration in visual context.

Once inside the Birkenau gate, the "march" continued (now to the accompaniment of lists of victims' names read by representative participants) along the tracks until the memorial at the end. Next to the memorial, on the ruins of Crematorium II, a long ceremony was conducted in front of an array of ten Israeli flag bearers standing on top of the ruins. The ceremony, largely in Hebrew, consisted of a series of speeches, readings, and songs (including "Eli, Eli" and the "Partisans' Song") by the Ashkenazi chief rabbi of Israel, march organizers, dignitaries, and student participants. It ended with the lighting of six memorial torches, El Male Rahamim (as noted, a memorial prayer in honor of the dead modified for a Holocaust context), the Kaddish, "Ani Ma'amin" (a setting of one of Maimonides' thirteen essential principles of Judaism, the belief in the coming of the Messiah), and "Ha-Tikvah." After this, participants were urged to plant memorial plaques (see figure 14), as well as to join those on the "stage" in *davening minha* (reciting the afternoon prayer).

On Friday, April 8, we traveled to Treblinka, at which students conducted a ceremony involving readings, the Kaddish, and a group sing-along of "The Sound of Silence" (with an added verse, written by students, relating to the Holocaust). This was performed around a sculpture made to look like a fire pit in which bodies were burned. Participants were then encouraged to explore the grounds and make rubbings onto paper of some of the thousands of memorial stones.[20] We then drove back to Warsaw for Shabbat, joining many of the other participants; activities included, on Saturday, a walk to and services at Warsaw's only remaining shul, the Nozyck Synagogue, usually almost empty but overflowing with march participants on our visit. This example again shows the organizers' interest in pairing or balancing images of death with the celebration of life; the observance of Shabbat in a former Jewish cultural center now almost completely empty of Jews was surely intended as an oasis of calm in the midst of a veritable memorial sandstorm. But the life we celebrated was once again almost completely the life we brought ourselves: the shul and its few regulars provided only the faint echo of former glory in the desert of Polish-Jewish memory.[21]

The next day, our last in Poland, we drove to Lublin and nearby Majdanek. At the former, we attempted to revive the sleeping ghosts of Jewish memory through Hasidic stories told during our visit to the old Lublin yeshiva building (now a medical college), before moving on to the death camp on the outskirts of town. Our visit there, to perhaps the most emotionally difficult camp-memorial of all, involved a long walk from Wiktor Tolkin's imposing monument at the gate, through the camp's first gas

Figure 14. March of the Living participants planting personally inscribed memorial plaques along the railroad tracks at Auschwitz II-Birkenau, Yom Hashoah, April 7, 1994. Photograph by the author.

chambers, past and through several barracks containing various displays (three of which are filled with shoes that once belonged to camp inmates and transients and were now picked up and touched by the occasional march participant), up to the mausoleum and the adjacent crematorium at the far end of the camp. The former contains several tons of human ash, flecked with bone fragments, held in a huge domed, open, marble bowl.[22]

For our last ceremony in Poland we gathered in the open space between the mausoleum and the crematorium (because another, even larger contingent from Miami was holding theirs at the dome). First forming a circle and then spiraling in toward the center, we listened as Joe Findling, another survivor traveling with our group, provided a moving reflection on memory, family history, and faith, as he recounted his experiences the previous day, when, returning to his boyhood village to say Kaddish for his father, he discovered a plaque placed there by unknown relatives and, hence, a family he never knew he had. That moment is mentioned by many participants in our convoy as one of the most moving and memorable of the entire trip, and we can understand it as a profoundly symbolic passing of the memorial torch, as it were, from one generation to the next.[23] Gathered tightly as a literal and symbolic community, participants found themselves listening to a narrative recounting the surprisingly redemptive power of the memorial quest, made all the more potent by "Uncle Joe's" concomitant provisional reconciliation with God. The tightly packed spiral, with Joe at the center, suggested a radiating outward of memorial responsibility, as well as a palpable sense of hope made stronger by the fact that we would soon be on our way to the land of milk and honey. Following Joe's story, the members of our convoy said the usual prayers, sang "Ha-Tikvah," and returned to the buses. That night we flew to Israel.

In Israel our schedule was both less hectic and less prescribed. We now traveled in individual buses, so that, after a few days, each group had its own program structured around common meeting times (usually meals) or events planned for the convoy or larger groups. The marked change in mood, setting, and structure was symbolized immediately upon arrival, as each participant was handed a snack pack as he or she boarded our newer, more modern buses at the airport. Inside we found refreshing chocolate milk, an apple, and several dates, in sharp contrast to the food served throughout our visit in Poland, where, for example, we never had any fruit.[24] On our first day (April 11), we visited three sites in the north. First, the prestate immigration/refugee camp at Atlit, then the Haifa panorama (at which we sang Shehekhiyanu, a prayer of renewal, used primarily for expressing gratitude for God's sustaining the Jews and bringing them to new experiences in the present), and finally Safed, before an evening barbecue and disco-boat ride on the Kinneret. The stop at Atlit served to remind participants that, even though survivors (and the march) had finally arrived in the land of Israel, their trials were not yet over.[25] The message was that the memory of hardship could not immediately be forgotten, though the activities during the rest of the day did much to overshadow this lesson. The following day brought our bus to the poet Rachel's tomb, Tel Aviv, and, finally, Jerusalem. In the evening, we attended a special erev Yom ha-Zikkaron ceremony for most march participants in Jerusalem. Here we were taught the meaning of Memorial Day for Israelis in speeches by Israel's president and the father of a soldier killed in the Lebanon War. Naomi Shemer also communicated this message by leading the audience in her own "Yerushalaim shel Zahav" ("Jerusalem of Gold"), the song which won the Israel song festival shortly before 1967's Six-Day War and which, with a few lyric changes, came to be associated with Israel's recapture of Jerusalem's Old City in that war. This song is an emotional trigger with strong associations (for Israelis) with that seemingly miraculous victory.[26]

The next day, April 13 and Israel's Memorial Day, we toured the Jewish Quarter of the Old City of Jerusalem, ending at the Western Wall. Arrival at the wall was moving for many of the participants and was heightened when, just then, the second siren of Yom ha-Zikkaron sounded. As most everyone in the Western Wall plaza stopped, we too solemnly observed the moment of silence and stillness for Israel's fallen. Don Handelman and Elihu Katz describe this moment in its general context: "On the appointed minute, and for one minute's duration, siren blasts shriek in every village, town, and city in the land. Human life stands still: people stop in their tracks, vehicles stop in mid-intersection; all is silent, yet all silent space is pervaded by the fullness of the same wail. These sirens also announce crisis and the activation of emergency procedures. The sole difference is not of intensity nor pitch of sound, but of modulation: to announce crisis, the wails rise and fall; to declare bereavement their note is steady and uniform. . . . The sound synthesizes mourning and action, absence and presence."[27] Indeed, our first visit to the Western Wall was structured, I would argue, to serve as a powerful countersymbol to the central commemorative event at Auschwitz: the "March of the Living" walk itself.[28] By participating in the communal national minute of observance at the wall, itself a national shrine and site of remembrance, the participants experienced a more cathartic and constructive ritual of commemoration than the largely self-reflective act of the "march" itself, as students were able to sense more directly their connection to the people of Israel at "home" in their own nation rather than to the more artificial collective, established by imaginal association and not by actual participation in the context of the "march."[29] That evening, like many Israelis, we took to the streets of Jerusalem to mark the end of mourning and the beginning of celebration in the transition from Yom ha-Zikkaron to Yom ha-Atzma'ut in a festival atmosphere of release all the more pronounced by our experiences in Poland just a few days earlier.

On the next day, Israel's Independence Day, we followed a path marking national celebration as well as commemoration and self-sacrifice. We first visited Ammunition Hill, site of fierce conflict in 1967, and then traveled to the memorial and museum at Latrun, site of bloodshed in 1948.[30] After a lunchtime visit to a paratroopers' memorial, we made our way to the Palmachim army base, where we met up with most of the other march groups (except Israel's and Sweden's) for an evening of food, entertainment, singing, and dancing, in direct opposition, I would argue, to our mass gathering at Auschwitz II-Birkenau. It is significant as well that this gathering was at an army base, symbol of Israel's military might and the best insurance for the philosophy of "never again," from the Israeli perspective. Instead of the pattern of balance established in Poland, where representations of death were offset by somewhat hollow simulacra of life, a new pattern arises in the march activities of Yom ha-Zikkaron and Yom ha-Atzma'ut, in which more complete manifestations and commemorations of life in Israel are set up in contrast to (and perhaps with the intention of replacing) the commemorations of death in Poland.

The following day we awoke early and climbed Masada, where we explored the fortress and discussed its importance for Israeli and Jewish memory and history.[31] After lunch, we returned to Jerusalem for Shabbat, which many participants used to visit with friends and family. The following evening we roamed the Ben-Yehuda shopping area of Jerusalem. Sunday, April 17, our last day in Israel, our itinerary was most significant. We first visited Yad Vashem, stopping only at its Valley of Lost Communities, Children's Memorial, Hall of Remembrance, and various outdoor sculptures.[32] We then visited Hanna Senesh's grave on Mount Herzl, where we had a brief ceremony, singing a final "Eli, Eli," one of our "liturgical" staples, in her honor.[33] Following that, we stopped at the Ben-Yehuda pedestrian mall one last time before going to the Old City for a last look at the Western Wall. After that, we drove to Mount Scopus for dinner and a final ceremony with our entire bus convoy, circling and spiraling once more for some last songs, tears, and words about passing on what we had learned over the past two weeks. The essential message was that the student participants had now graduated, as it were, to the status of "the next generation of survivors and witnesses." Indeed, a number of participants used this kind of language to refer to themselves after their return. Following our good-byes, we drove to the airport for the flight home.

THE JEWISH CONTEXT

By embodying Holocaust memory and ideology through their two-week journey in Poland and Israel, participants in the March of the Living also engage in and embody the very sacred symbols drawn from tradition that contribute to such ideology in the first place. Victor Turner offers some instructive and critical comments relevant to participation, memory, and intensity (what I would call commitment and embodiment):

A pilgrim's commitment, in full physicality, to an arduous yet inspiring journey, is, for him, even more impressive, in the symbolic domain, than the visual and auditory symbols which dominate the liturgies and ceremonies of calendrically structured religion. He only looks at these; he participates in the pilgrimage way. The pilgrim becomes himself a total symbol; indeed, a symbol *of* totality; ordinarily he is encouraged to meditate as he peregrinates upon the creative and altruistic acts of the saint or deity whose relic or image forms the object of his quest. This is, perhaps, akin to the Platonic notion of anamnesis, recollection of a previous existence. However, in this context it would be more properly regarded as participation in a sacred existence, with the aim of achieving a step toward holiness and wholeness in oneself, both of body and soul. But since one aspect of oneself consists of the cherished values of one's own specific culture, it is not unnatural that the new "formation" desired by pilgrims should include a more intense realization of the inner meaning of that culture. For many that inner meaning is identical with its religious core values. Thus social and cultural structures are not abolished by communitas and anamnesis, but . . . the sting of their divisiveness is removed so that the fine articulation of their parts in a complex heterogeneous unity can be the better appreciated.[34]

There is certainly some connection effected, during the entire two-week march experience, with the religiocultural core values of Judaism. On the simplest level, this means that virtually all the students who go are Jewishly identified; non-Jews, generally, do not participate (though in the past few years there has been increased interaction with young, mostly non-Jewish, Poles).[35] These teenagers come from a variety of backgrounds in terms of observance and tradition, ranging from the "cultural Jew" who has almost no familiarity with Jewish daily practice to the Orthodox Jew who prays three times daily. Out of respect for the observant participants (but perhaps for other reasons as well), the march conducts all its activities within a fairly observant context: the students (especially the non-observant ones) were told ahead of time that they would be praying *shaharit* (the morning prayer) in groups every morning during the trip and that both Sabbaths would be traditionally observed. Additionally, all meals arranged as part of the trip were strictly kosher; the food was flown in daily from Israel in a significant logistical operation.

Some might see this as curious. Why enforce even a rudimentary sort of religiosity—possibly creating additional concern and tension for some participants—in a setting that already threatens to overwhelm through its symbols, imagery, and historical associations? One possible response to this is commonsensical: "The Holocaust is so laden with religious symbolism and associations that it evokes and strengthens a sensitivity to the religious tradition and the Jewish people. Death naturally evokes religious associations."[36] Though true, this statement does not really speak to the phenomenon of religiosity in extreme situations. "Celebrating the memory of the dead" does seem to involve the use of religious symbols, but we still need to understand more about the connections between the two.

In particular, we must consider the notion that the Holocaust, as an eruption of radical evil in the space of human history, represents an encounter with the "absolute." We can approach this encounter in terms of thinking about sacred space and place (recall chapter 4). According to the late historian of religions Mircea Eliade, "A sacred place is what it is because of the permanent nature of the hierophany that first consecrated it. . . . The hierophany therefore does not merely sanctify a given segment of undifferentiated profane space; it goes so far as to ensure that sacredness will continue there. *There*, in *that* place, the hierophany repeats itself. In this way the place becomes an inexhaustible source of power and sacredness and enables man, simply by entering it, to have a share in the power, to hold communion with the sacredness."[37] Ignoring for the time being the theoretical incompatibility between Eliade's essentialism and my more "constructivist" approach, we may still benefit from an understanding of the symbolic potency of Holocaust territories. If we consider that the events of the Holocaust may have permanently "sanctified" the sites of mass death visited by the marchers during their week in Poland, then we can better understand not only the pull toward commemoration in these places but also the tendency toward the use of religious symbols.

At the same time, one should be careful not to misinterpret this "sanctity" so as to avoid straying into the dangerous and anti-Judaic territory in which the events of the Holocaust are understood as redemptive sacrifices to God. Rather, one must understand the "sanctity" of these places, and the hierophany manifested there, as inverted, radically negative. The "sacred" with which we have communion is a very different kind of sacrality from what we are normally used to dealing with in the history of religions, but it is powerful and inexhaustible nonetheless. And this might help explain why religious practices and symbols seem to find a natural connection to Holocaust commemoration: especially at the sites of the destruction, the invocation of symbols may provide a necessary defense against the almost gravitational pull of nihilism and despair inherent in the black holes of the death camps, offsetting chaos and providing needed structure. Both memory and religion have this in common; each chronotopically condenses time and space into the mythic, setting certain "sacred" areas off from the rest of time and space and making them suitable for commemoration, so that, as Jack Kugelmass argues, "memory culture has typically conflated time into the few short years of the Holocaust, and place into a few of its principal camps of extermination—Auschwitz, Treblinka, and Majdanek."[38] In this way, the territory is made ripe for religious activity.

These religious arrangements may have been necessary for the success of the trip (simply put, it is easier for nonobservant Jews to eat kosher food than it is for observant Jews not to, notwithstanding the possible compromise on the nonobservant Jews' ideals). In addition, Kugelmass has argued, in a more general context, these often unfamiliar, "self-sacrificing . . . practices contribute to [such marches'] 'time out of time' quality. Their very liminality suggests to participants that what they are experiencing is important."[39] I would go even further, arguing that these arrangements also served to reinforce a sense of community in the participants; many came not only from a variety of backgrounds but from a variety of locales, and they knew few of the other participants before the march. Some moderate enforcement of traditional Jewish practice, then, on a generic level, served to integrate everyone into one temporary, functioning Jewish community (a mobile "shtetl," as it were), which subsequently served as a support network for the difficult and emotional stages of the trip. Such communal identification also reinforced a vibrant link between the march participants and the Jewish past(s) they were exploring and helped establish a real sense of Jewish peoplehood.

Furthermore, creating a sense of community may also be understood as a powerful response to the very reality of the Shoah and the necessary qualities of its commemoration: "Holocaust Day . . . commemorates the horrific destruction of European Jewry, a terror that in explicit Nazi intentions towards the whole of European Jewry was utterly indiscriminate and totally final. More abstractly, the Holocaust signifies the disconnection from one another of all vital values, the uncoupling of all essential relationships, the dismemberment of all community and collectivity, of social body and human body, leading inevitably to the denial of humanity and to death. Through its absolute negation of the human, the Holocaust is ramified disorder on the cosmic scale. For Jewry, it is the experience of the extinction of cosmos, of primeval chaos."[40] In this light, each symbolic activity during the march period which helped create a sense of community by reconnecting participants also helped, in no small way, to reestablish the order of the cosmos, to engage in temporal and spatial mythic reconstruction. This is a remembering on a grand scale, especially in the rituals of Yom ha-Shoah, most of all in the "March of the Living" itself. For example, the march participants, congregated at Auschwitz I, began their three-kilometer silent walk to Auschwitz II-Birkenau in 1994 with the playing of Kol Nidrei by Yaacov Strumza, a survivor living in Israel who had been for two years the first violinist of the Auschwitz orchestra. The Kol Nidrei melody is an emotional trigger for many Jews, who recognize it from the Yom Kippur liturgy as a haunting prayer sung by the cantor at the beginning of the services marking the Day of Atonement (though many Jews would be hard-pressed to identify the meaning of the prayer's text). Indeed, several participants commented on how that melody brought them into focusing on the ritual act on which they were about to embark. Thus, Kol Nidrei has significant associations with the "tradition" for many Jews whose own observance may not involve anything more than Yom Kippur.

Following this, a shofar was blown by two different men to signify the beginning of the "march"; this act also has powerful associations, specifically with the High Holidays and the opening of the gates of heaven, and generally and traditionally as the Jewish call to assembly and to action since biblical times. In addition, all the commemorative ceremonies (except, of course, those on Independence Day) during the trip included the lighting of memorial candles, the recitation of the Mourner's Kaddish, as well as various prayers such as the El Male Rahamim and the Ani Ma'amin. These all provided a constant and increasingly familiar liturgy to which the participants could turn again and again throughout the course of their commemorative journey. Here, liturgical language works in a powerful way; it is one of the essential elements of commemoration.

As Paul Connerton argues, such language is a "form of action."[41] The central properties of liturgical language, he continues, are the performativeness and the formalism of ritual, together contributing to the success of commemoration as a ritual activity.

Furthermore, I would suggest that not only do the ritual activities of the march contribute to a viable sense of community during the trip, calling to mind a sense of "tradition," but the collective ritual activities also serve to reinforce that sense of "tradition." Sally Moore and Barbara Myerhoff attribute that reinforcement to the formal properties of ritual. These formal properties, for the authors, include repetition, acting, stylized behavior, order, evocative presentational style and staging, and the collective dimension.[42] Altogether, a certain mutually interactive quality exists in the use of traditional Jewish symbols and forms for the ritual activity during the March of the Living: they both help sustain a connection to the community and tradition, and they in turn contribute to the definition and celebration of such a tradition and community.

Finally, many of the ceremonies (certainly all the major ones) also included (and often ended with) "Ha-Tikvah," the Israeli national anthem. This last point, however, suggests the merging of the "purely religious" with the national and political in the Jewish context of the march, to which I will return below.

THE LITURGICAL-COMMEMORATIVE CYCLE

The March of the Living trip takes place at a specific and significant time of the year, linking itself symbolically to both the traditional Jewish calendar and the modern Israeli one (which are already necessarily linked): "YOM HASHOAH and YOM HA'ATZMAUT are two of the most important days in modern Jewish times. By taking part in these special events, you will share unforgettable moments in Jewish history and bear witness to the undying spirit of the Jewish people."[43] Indeed, reflection on the significance of the timing of the trip and the days of civil and religious commemoration it incorporates (as well as reflection on those days' histories) tells us much about the meaning and message of the March of the Living, which goes far beyond the choice for Yom ha-Shoah veha-Gevurah as the day for the "march" itself.

In discussing the Israeli government's choice of the twenty-seventh of the Hebrew month of Nisan as the day marking the public commemoration of the Holocaust (and thus setting it apart from strictly religious days of public mourning for national catastrophes such as the ninth of Av and the tenth of Tevet), James Young effectively summarizes the day's significance:

Pulled from both the middle of the six-week [Warsaw] Ghetto uprising and the seven-week Sfirah [the counting of the omer, a period of semimourning in Jewish tradition], this day retained links to both heroism and mourning. Coming only five days after the end of Passover, . . . [the day] extended the festival of freedom and then bridged it with the national Day of Independence. Beginning on Passover (also the day of the [start of the] Warsaw Ghetto uprising), continuing through Yom Hashoah, and ending in Yom Hatzma'ut, this period could be seen as commencing with God's deliverance of the Jews and concluding with the Jews' deliverance of themselves in Israel. In this sequence, biblical and modern returns to the land of Israel are recalled; God's deliverance of the Jews from the desert of exile is doubled by the Jews' attempted deliverance of themselves in Warsaw; the heroes and martyrs of the Shoah are remembered side by side (and implicitly equated) with the fighters who fell in Israel's modern war of liberation; and all lead inexorably to the birth of the state.[44]

In this context, recall Avraham Hirchson's words from the "stage" of the crematorium ruins naming this site as the origin of the Jewish nation's "march to freedom, and to its homeland." The resonance with the exodus paradigm is pronounced.

These important symbolic links are expressed differently by Handelman and Katz, who note that the week between "Holocaust Day" and "Remembrance Day" corresponds to the traditional Jewish period of mourning immediately following death, *shiva* (literally, "seven"). The authors add that, "following the exemplar of biblical creation, the arithmetic unit of seven is thought to sign completion, closure, and unity. Implicitly, in this instance, the seven days between Holocaust Day and Remembrance Day, and the implication of this number for the completion of a basic duration of mourning, may point to the closure of the diaspora chapter of Jewish history, in accordance with Zionist visions of the period."[45] This astute observation shows how the spacing of these key commemorative dates recapitulates a traditional sense of the rhythm of time, reproduced in the Jewish week, culminating in the peak day of the Sabbath. This, the authors suggest, constitutes a pulsation that goes beyond merely structuring the week, "for this rhythm of temporal pulsation is deeply embedded in numerous units of time in Jewish culture. The pulsation may be described as a beat or impulsion from lower to higher, from ordinary to extraordinary."[46] One could go further: if there are seven days separating Yom ha-Shoah veha-Gevurah from Yom ha-Zikkaron, there are eight marking it off from Yom ha-Atzma'ut; if seven is a number representing completion and culmination, eight (as in the marking of time for a boy's *brit milah*, or circumcision ceremony) traditionally represents a higher, more spiritual level. Here, the rhythm of eight days marks the attainment of a new level of being, a new order of awareness (parallel, it might be said, to the beginning of a higher octave in Western musical notation).

Understanding these rhythms, then, allows us to understand more fully the dual quality of both sacred and secular time on which this particular commemorative sequence feeds. Handelman and Katz argue that this temporal progression is "accepted as natural and appropriate by Israeli Jews. . . . It is a statist version of modern Jewish history, but one of cosmological, temporal harmonics that are embedded in Zionist ideology."[47] Moreover, this version of history and ideology also recapitulates a familiar paradigm in a secular but "no less mythic" framework, as Saul Friedländer contends, for selecting the twenty-seventh of Nisan works "to reinsert the Holocaust into an historical series of Jewish catastrophes and to suggest a mythic link between the destruction of European Jewry and the birth of Israel—i.e., catastrophe and redemption—which, in turn, give a new dignity to the Jews of the Diaspora, as victims or survivors."[48] In other words, the mythic link of catastrophe and redemption works in a classically cosmogonic fashion, offering a narrative explanation for how the world (in this case, the State of Israel) came to be, fully in line with Zionist mythology.

Though some religious patterns and paradigms may be maintained here, the choice for the date of Yom ha-Shoah itself was far from traditional. For example, Tisha B'Av (the ninth day of the Hebrew month of Av) had long served as the great commemorative sponge for all Jewish tragedy: the idea of creating a new day of mourning in the calendar was considered "presumptuous" in the traditional attitude, as Irving Greenberg notes, so that commemoration of all tragedy was subsumed under the commemoration of the destruction of the Temple. "Perhaps it was just as well that this conclusion was reached, for otherwise the Jewish calendar might have become one mass of never-healing wounds, each day sporting the stigmata of yet another community massacred, another collective martyrdom. Still, the net result was that the rabbinic tradition that had so powerfully articulated a partnership model for covenantal living had now turned into an ethic of theological as well as historical powerlessness."[49] This important point suggests that what contemporary rabbis did not realize as they were looking for a way to commemorate the Holocaust was that, beyond the possibility that it was too great to be assimilated into

Tisha B'Av, such assimilation would continue the ethos of powerlessness so many in the emerging state were trying to surmount.

Similarly, Greenberg comments on the tenth of Tevet, the date traditionally associated with the beginning of the siege of Jerusalem which led to the destruction of the Temple and which has been adopted as the official religious day of mourning for those Jews whose death dates are not known. Selecting it as the possible date for Holocaust commemoration "reflects the idea of incorporating the newest tragedy into the chain of tradition without introducing any halachic innovation. This decision affirmed that the destruction of the Temple remains the paradigm and acme of Jewish tragedy." But Greenberg notes as well that, among other problems, this decision was also clouded by an ulterior motive of strengthening what was a weak and marginal fast day.[50]

Such traditional alternatives and challenges to what became Yom ha-Shoah continue to crop up. Greenberg cites Rabbi Pinchas Teitz's suggestion in 1984 to set the date for commemoration according to the anniversary of Hitler's death, itself seemingly preset to fit into the Jewish calendar. Hitler's suicide was on the seventeenth of Iyar, the eve of the Lag B'Omer holiday, "which is already a day of semirejoicing, breaking the gloom of the Omer period."[51] Another alternative date is suggested by Michael Strassfeld, author of the popular *Jewish Catalogues* and an opponent of the twenty-seventh of Nisan as the date for Yom ha-Shoah because of its close proximity to Yom ha-Atzma'ut. Strassfeld would prefer to see no connection between the Holocaust and the founding of the State of Israel (against prevailing Zionist readings of history and memory), and he also rejects the assimilationist theology of the fast days because those are observed traditionally as atonement for sins. He would set the date of Holocaust commemoration on the sixteenth of the Hebrew month of Heshvan, corresponding to the tenth of November 1938, or Kristallnacht. "Heshvan also seems appropriate," Strassfeld argues, "for it is the only month of the year without any commemorative days. The rabbis called it *marheshvan*—'bitter Heshvan.' Heshvan-the-bitter is also, according to tradition, the time of the biblical flood when all humans and animals were destroyed except for those in Noah's ark. After the flood, God promised that He would never again destroy the world and placed a rainbow in the sky as a sign of that promise. Yet it is still within the power of human hands to destroy the world. . . . Heshvan is the darkest period of the year, the moment before any sign of life appears, a time of death and decay."[52] Such alternatives indicate that many people are uncomfortable with the twenty-seventh of Nisan as the date for the commemoration of the Holocaust. That discomfort is not surprising, for the date is really a compromise that both accepts and rejects others' interpretive paradigms for commemoration (such as the heroic or the theological); it is a negotiated date by committee that accords some respect to a variety of models of interpretation. Yom ha-Shoah is fixed here on a "'broken' date (drawn from a broken paradigm)," as Greenberg puts it, affirming the "broken" (but nevertheless still applicable) character of Jewish theological (and commemorative) thinking after the Holocaust and as such reinforcing the human role in maintaining the covenant.[53]

That human role involves the active commemoration of history via religious forms and symbols in the context of a carefully planned progression of dates, which resonate successfully with mythic paradigms of catastrophe and redemption and effectively contextualize the commemoration of the Holocaust. Greenberg would have us keep the tension between catastrophe and redemption in mind, arguing that the "State of Israel is not a reward or a product or an exchange for the Holocaust; it is a response. . . . Yom Ha'Atzmaut is neither recompense for nor resolution of the Holocaust. The two orienting events confront each other in unrelieved dialectical tension. As long as memory and faith exist, they will continue to cast their shadow and duel for dominant effect in the mind and heart of Jewry and of the world. The two days are forever twinned, without softening the tension between destruction and redemption and without betraying the character of either event."[54] Though Greenberg's point is an admirable ideal, it is more likely that the Zionist narrative is too strong *not* to overcome that crucial tension. Therefore, it is not difficult to see the wisdom of the timing of the March of the Living: more than a mere Holocaust commemoration, the entire two-week journey is structured and organized calendrically to coincide with and encourage active participation in a symbolic-mythic journey from darkness to light, from slavery to freedom, and from exile to redemption in Jewish national sovereignty in the State of Israel.[55]

MEMORIAL PILGRIMAGE

It is the way the teens are encouraged to *participate* in this symbolic journey that encourages me to think of it as a pilgrimage, albeit a contemporary one. Consider the language used by Rabbi Peretz Wolf-Prusan, one of the leaders of the San Francisco Bay Area bus on the 1994 March, as he spoke to participants on the way to the area of the former Warsaw Ghetto from the airport on our first day in Poland: "There are three great pilgrimages the Jews would take in biblical times: Pesach, Shavu'ot, and Sukkot. And we would pack in from all the parts of Judea, Samaria, the south, and head off towards Jerusalem. And that ceased, of course, after the destruction of the Temple. We still remember why we made those pilgrimages. That's what you're doing right now; you're making a pilgrimage. There are only two new holidays in the Jewish calendar since Talmudic time: Yom ha-Shoah, this Thursday, and Yom ha-Atzma'ut, the week after. We are actually taking part in a pilgrimage, to recover memory and to find out who we are and where we're going." But his view is also supported by the march literature itself, as in the introductory message by president and founder Hirchson to the informational pamphlet *To Know and to Remember*, published by the march organization in Israel: "We are going on a pilgrimage to the 'Valley of Death,' to stand there and remember the dead in the very same places they were murdered, to cherish their life, to mourn their death, and to say 'Kaddish' over them, because their death turned our people into orphans."[56] These two descriptions are instructive: the latter emphasizes the importance of place in the pilgrimage quest and focuses on the aspect of mourning and loss central to at least the first half of the march experience. The former places emphasis on sacred time and, in light of the previous discussion, resonates well with the historical, theological, and mythic paradigms of catastrophe and redemption, even as it expresses the contemporary commemorative need to emerge from the shadow of the destruction of the Temple. I find Rabbi Wolf-Prusan's notion of the collective need to recover memory (implying that it was once lost) through ritual to be both powerful and thought-provoking.

The most common context for Jewish pilgrimage is that of the visit to a saint's—or some revered person's—tomb, understood as a meeting point of the divine and earthly realms wherein symbolic and sacred power lies.[57] Here worshipers will also invoke the merit and sanctity of the dead, just as Jews often invoke that sanctity verbally in speaking about the dead, saying *zikhrono livrakha*, "his memory shall be a blessing." I would maintain that the March of the Living invokes the same kind of sentiment and symbolic dynamic in visiting the landscape of murder in Poland. But much more is involved. First, there is a structural similarity between the march and pilgrimage as it has been classically defined. Victor Turner has described pilgrimage as a liminal or liminoid phenomenon, comparing it with the liminal phase in rites of passage as described and analyzed by Arnold van Gennep, a phase in which one is separated in space and time from normal social structures and their constraints: "The

peripherality of pilgrimage shrines and the temporal structure of the pilgrimage process, beginning in a Familiar Place, going to a Far Place, and
returning, ideally 'changed,' to a Familiar Place, can be interestingly related to van Gennep's concept of the rite of passage, with its stages of separation, margin or limen, and reaggregation. The liminal stage, when the
subject is in spatial separation from the familiar and habitual, constitutes
a cultural domain that is extremely rich in cosmological meaning, conveyed largely by nonverbal symbols. Liminality represents a negation of
many of the features of preliminal social structures, and an affirmation
of another order of things, stressing generic rather than particularistic
relationships."[58] For Turner, this liminal sense of being "betwixt and between" established modes of existence and behavior leaves pilgrims with
a sense of freedom and creativity and allows for a sense of "communitas,"
a "spontaneously generated relationship between leveled and equal total
and individuated human beings."[59] I have already pointed out how the
Jewish context of the trip helps the participants establish a sense of community; here I would add that the pilgrimage aspect reinforces this sense.
As in the classically described pilgrimage, the participants undertake an
arduous journey to a "faraway place" invested with symbolic (and perhaps sacred) significance and return to their normal lives and structures
changed. Perhaps this is something inherent in the journey—a quality the
march organizers have capitalized on. Young writes, "We must . . . recognize that this awful place [Auschwitz] remains sacred only in the great
distance between it and ourselves, between its past and our present. The
site retains its symbolic power over us partly because we don't live here,
because we must make this pilgrimage to memory."[60] In going there
(rather than bringing its objects over "here," as at the USHMM), we engage the past on its own terms.

Some would downplay the potential for change in the interaction with
sacred power that I would argue is built into this "pilgrimage." Kugelmass, for example, contends that those who go on such trips largely express through such "secular ritual" their identities as American Jews.[61]
For Kugelmass, this self-confirmation of (American) Jewish identity is
"secular" rather than "religious" because it does not conform to more traditional patterns of Jewish religiosity. But we have already seen how powerfully the march activities invoke religious symbols and forms and how
religious the basic structure of Holocaust commemoration is, and therefore downgrading march activities to the level of secular ritual is missing
the point. Kugelmass may merely be trying to maintain an artificial distinction between national (read "secular") and religious elements within

Jewish culture, which are not so easily separable, especially when considering the complexities of Jewish identity. Rather, as we well know, religious and national elements are constantly intermingling and feeding off notions of peoplehood, the land, and the Torah. As such, the notion that Jewish secularity can be split off from Jewish religiosity is suspect.[62]

The marchers, then, are not simply confirming (or reconfirming) their (American) Jewish identity but are involved in a process of creating and defining that identity, returning, postliminally, to their social structures with a new status in their "community." For the likeness between pilgrimage and rites of passage is also evident here: the student participants on the March of the Living are, I would argue, actually being trained and prepared for their entrance, upon return to the United States, into adult American Jewish society, with all its responsibilities. The march, as I understand it, effects a transformation in its participants as it seeks to change them from schoolchildren with no profound investment in the Jewish community and its future to adults who are active participants in that future. Indeed, one of the Miami-based founders of the march, Gene Greenzweig, makes the startling suggestion that in twenty years, "ninety percent of Jewish leaders from all over the world will have been on the March of the Living," so that the vast majority of these future leaders "will have a common memory."[63] The participants are encouraged to return to the States and report on what they have seen and experienced,[64] to represent Israel positively to others, and to become full members in what has been described as an American Jewish civil religious community.[65] Of course, there is a significant amount of tension and contradiction in this view, but it parallels the contradictions inherent in American Jewish identity. It is the qualities of civil religion that, I suggest, are the driving forces behind much of the meaning of the march/pilgrimage.

Charles Liebman and Eliezer Don-Yehiya have argued that the "objective of civil religion is the sanctification of the society in which it functions" through three main expressions: integration, legitimation, and mobilization.[66] Jonathan Woocher expands on these modes of sanctification: "Civil religion integrates, legitimates, and mobilizes by producing in its adherents the sentiment that the society or group is tied to a sacred order, that its history and activity point beyond themselves to a higher realm of purpose and significance. Thus, the members of the society are induced to support its endeavors, to protect its unity, and to find meaning for their own lives through identification with the collective's ventures." Civil religion seems uninterested in the transcendent (though divinity is often invoked in its rhetoric), since its "focus and locus" are in political and civic institutions that provide a "'meta-ideology' for the political community in a sacred key."[67] But it nonetheless remains reliant on the articulation of myths and rituals for the success of its processes of integration, legitimation, and mobilization. Thus it taps into the traditional memorial patterns described above by Friedländer and also links contemporary Jews to Judaism's traditional religious paradigms. Civil Judaism's first central myth, for instance, "is the story of 'Holocaust to Rebirth,' the retelling by American Jews of the two most significant Jewish events of the twentieth century . . . so as to make them a paradigm for Jewish history and a continuous inspiration for Jewish action."[68]

This story is nothing more than the "catastrophe and redemption" paradigm invoked throughout the march (indeed, inherent in its very structure and timing, as I have discussed); as a central myth of the American Jewish civil religious worldview, it effectively allows American Jews to insert themselves into a "sacred" narrative to which they remain largely marginal. The insertion is somewhat problematic, and Woocher recounts Jacob Neusner's criticism of this essential myth as "respond[ing] to the ambiguous and ambivalent character of American Jewish existence by projecting a process of death and redemption in which the American Jew can vicariously participate. . . . For Neusner, the myth of 'Holocaust to rebirth' is a veil which American Jews place between themselves and the daily reality of their lives, at once profoundly functional in sustaining Jewish group commitment and activism (primarily in defense of Jewish survival), and deeply dysfunctional in deflecting American Jews from the task of creating a mode and myth of Jewish religious existence faithful to their own chosen condition."[69] The point is well-taken, for it is the dysfunctionality of the participants' American Jewish identities which the march ultimately reinforces. Nonetheless, such a myth is very effective not only in integrating American Jews (like the marchers) into one community (supporting the discussion above) but also in helping them legitimate their worldview (as expressed in the ideology of the march) and mobilize their activities (as in the march participants' new sense of responsibility and purpose upon their return to the United States).

Indeed, the key findings of an unpublished sociological study (funded by the March of the Living) of past participants indicate that the March of the Living has had profound long-term, positive effects on marchers' Jewish identification, attitudes toward Israel, and social responsibility, reflecting several of the central tenets of the American Jewish civil religion as described by Woocher.[70] Such activities as the March of the Living are not new in the realm of American Jewish civil religious undertakings.

The march owes some of its success to the precedent of "missions" such
as the United Jewish Appeal's Young Leadership Programs, which, like
the march, take American Jews through Eastern Europe and then to Israel,
though they are not structured to coincide with the commemorative calendar in the same powerfully symbolic manner. Woocher provides an excellent summary of the ideology and success of such "missions," which
is equally applicable to my discussion:

Missions work. They transform mildly supportive individuals into dedicated contrib-
utors and activists, and committed workers into driven leaders. Like all good rituals
they are artfully manipulative, playing with the emotions, overwhelming mind and
body with a flow of sensations. But they work primarily because they are enormously effective *mediators* of the fundamental religious myth and experience of
civil Judaism. Critics contend that missions present a distorted picture of Israel, and
in one sense that is probably correct. Yet, they are brilliantly successful in presenting the Israel of civil Jewish mythology, in all its confused profusion of meanings:
the Israel of strength, and Israel threatened; the bold, new, technologically sophisticated Israel, and the Israel of ancient Jewish tradition; the Israel which is exotic,
and the Israel which is "home."

The American Jews who go on a mission are experiencing a ritual of anti-
structure and communitas. Removed from their familiar surroundings, they are
thrown together on a bus in enforced solidarity. They are enveloped in the story of
a nation built on the ashes of six million dead, rising like a phoenix, struggling at once
just to stay alive and to be a beacon of hope for the world. And they are told what
they must do once they return to their "real world" to maintain the unity they have
come to feel and to continue to share in the destiny they have glimpsed unfolding.
It is a ritual of unique power, a rite of passage which leaves few untransformed.[71]

As rituals, these commemorative pilgrimages are therefore *mediative* in
providing the structure for the personal experience of contemporary
mythology and ideology. Applying a typology developed by Don Handelman, the march experience can be characterized not only as an event-that-
presents or re-presents the lived-in world (an event that acts as a mirror of
social realities) but also as an event-that-models that world (what I would
call an embodiment). This teleological event, in working through its own
built-in contradictions, effects transformations in its participants, who in
turn seek to have an impact on society at large.[72] I wonder if this is also another version of the iconic mode of memorialization, in that it provides a
distilled, symbolic model for effective engagement with the past. In this
view, the construction of memory (and identity) in the March of the Living not only reinforces (and is reinforced by) a particular Zionist worldview
but also contributes to the ongoing reconstruction of that worldview.

PLANTING: ISRAEL AS THE CENTER AND GOAL

But before accepting this characterization, we may want to get a better sense of the true center and goal of the march these "pilgrims" undertake. First, consider one genre of symbolic activity undertaken in various forms by the participants: planting. As I have already mentioned, Israeli flags are very prominent, especially during what appears to be the central event of the trip, the "March of the Living" walk itself. Israeli flags, large and small, crop up everywhere, most notably in a tableau that establishes the backdrop for the long commemoration ceremony at Birkenau at the end of the "march." The stage here is the ruins of one of the gas chamber–crematorium complexes, on which ten flag bearers plant themselves for the duration of the ceremony, behind the speakers' area. This symbolic planting and (re)claiming of territory is reflected and magnified in perhaps the most striking ritual, ceremonial, and symbolic act of the march, wherein the participants, who have been given small wooden plaques and told to write on them the names of family or loved ones who perished in the Holocaust (or, if there are none or the names are not known, then something suitably commemorative), are told at the end of the Birkenau ceremony to go around the camp and plant these plaques anywhere they like and make of the camp a symbolic graveyard, a field marked with specific individual names and messages of commemoration to replace the vast unmarked landscape of generalized mass horror and indeterminate memories (see figures 14 and 15).[73]

The planting of plaques, in turn, has been reflected in Israel on all past marches in the planting of new trees in a specially marked March of the Living forest, further reinforcing the motif of passage from darkness to light established by the march itinerary. Tree planting is a common act of commemoration in Israel, as Amos Elon observes: "In vast afforestation areas many thousands of trees are annually planted and marked in the memory of lost communities and of individual victims. . . . In previous ages, religious ceremony and prayer would have served as mourning, but in Israel, tree planting and building have always been acts of faith."[74] Dara Horn, a student participant in the 1992 march, whose journal excerpts have been published in book form by the American march organizers as a handy promotional and informational guide to the experience, also reflects on this theme: "Today, on Yom HaZikaron, we are planting trees. Almost every tourist who comes to Israel ends up planting a tree, since it's a national project to build up the land, so I've planted trees here several times before. But this time, it meant so much more to me. . . . This was

Figure 15. March of the Living participant walking with an Israeli flag in a field marked
with memorial plaques, Auschwitz II-Birkenau, Yom Hashoah, April 7, 1994.
In the background is one of the camp's intact barbed-wire fences and, beyond it,
the ruins of Crematorium III. Photograph by the author.

my way of remembering, of giving back something living."[75] (In 1994,
trees were not planted because it was a year of *shemitta*, a biblically man-
dated year in which fields must lie fallow. Not planting does, however, reinforce the trip's strong identification with Jewish practice, and in any
case, participants were to receive certificates saying that trees eventually
would be planted in their honor.) Of course, such symbolic activity helps
reinforce a certain sense of symbolic Jewish (and Israeli) sovereignty over
the terrain covered by the march: students "march with unfurled flags, as
if we've come to conquer Poland," former Israeli education minister
Shulamit Aloni said in the fall of 1992.[76] Also, only in Israel is anything "planted" that will live on and grow in the landscape. The flags
and plaques "planted" in Poland are not alive and do not live on past the
march. This practice reflects the wish of march organizers, in my opinion,
to downplay any suggestion that Jewish life is truly viable in Poland, even
today in the face of such life's tentative resurgence.

An interesting series of discourses is being produced here. The territory that the marchers "cover" over the course of their two-week journey (a discovery of the landscape of memory and suffering in Poland, con-
trasted with a discovery of the landscape of joy and redemption in Israel)

is "covered" by flags, trees, and plaques in the process. But this (re)covering of the landscape is ironically meant to effect a recovery of memory (that marchers never had to begin with) and a *dis*covery of the land with which the marchers are truly meant to affiliate, the place where what has been planted can really grow (and thus cover over the ground): Israel. This *dis*covery and discovering can also be construed as ambivalence resulting from the disjunction of (in this case) American students playing out a Zionist ideology of history.

All this supports the argument that Poland—especially Auschwitz— is not the real center of the march experience. Surely, the broadly defined March of the Living itself is significant, especially as an exploration of the physical and symbolic landscape of suffering of the Holocaust (although I am skeptical as to how much of the terrain is truly explored on the trip). But together they define an anticenter, a place of radical negativity whose association with Jewish life exists only in history and memory,[77] stopping here would leave the pilgrimage unfinished and the Holocaust "unresolved." Rather, it is in the progression through what is now configured as a peripheral (but still relevant) place to the "center out there" which is Israel that the full context of the pilgrimage is established.[78] Indeed, Miami organizer Miles Bunder asserts that the March of the Living is really a two-week Israel experience, with Poland as the preparation. This discovery of the "true" center of the march occurs complete with various kinds of rewards (the food is better, for instance, and there is—or at least was—a greater sense of freedom for the participants)[79] and even cathartic, carnival-type celebrations: first, a disco frenzy on a boat on the Sea of Galilee on our first night in Israel and, then, the wild and crowded real carnival of the streets of Jerusalem on the eve of Independence Day. These activities conclude the tour (in terms of its mythic temporal itinerary) and allow participants to perform and inhabit memory in a manageable (rather than an unmanageable) way.[80]

MEMORY TOURISM

How can the March of the Living be characterized and contextualized? Sociologist Erik Cohen has analytically distinguished five main modes of tourist experiences and compared them with pilgrimage as it is traditionally conceived. While modern mass tourism generally seems to be the exact opposite of pilgrimage, a closer analysis of a broad spectrum of its modes reveals some striking similarities, most notably in the fifth and most serious of the modes he identifies: the existential, in which the tourist's visit is "phenomenologically analogous to a pilgrimage." Moreover, as for Zionist Jews, that center may not be merely an elective spiritual one (the main defining characteristic of the existential tourist) but can be a traditional one. Such traditionality is defined by historical and spiritual roots and attachments, so that the visit has the sense of a homecoming, albeit often only a temporary one.[81] This is certainly the attitude of many of the March of the Living tour participants, who, as they make their pilgrimage across time and space, ritually commemorate history and its transformation through memorial activities. At the journey's end they find at least a temporary authenticity in Israel and in their perhaps paradoxical identification with it, even as their identities as American Jews are also reinforced.

But, as cited above, Jack Kugelmass would call the March of the Living a secular ritual, one of many "rites of the tribe" that are clearly distinguished from the traditional ritual of pilgrimage by their "relative cosmological shallowness," "their largely ethnic rather than religious basis," their "sociopolitical" as opposed to cosmological framework, and their tendency toward the spectacle, which relegates the transcendent to secondary importance. These characterizations do not fully apply to the March of the Living. Though Kugelmass's observations concerning these "rites of the tribe" are cogent, useful, and often insightful, I maintain that the March of the Living, though it is certainly a spectacle, is a unique phenomenon with a serious and far-reaching religious and cosmological basis. Furthermore, I am wary of a view that separates the sociopolitical from the cosmological so cleanly, for even traditional rituals surely have sociopolitical characteristics. Certainly, these "secular rituals do not comply with traditional forms but rather appropriate them and in part invent whole new meanings," but it is the *way* these forms are appropriated that is especially interesting and deserving of study. Many of those forms of appropriation have already been discussed; Kugelmass provides one possible summary: "By evoking the Holocaust dramaturgically, that is, by going to the site of the event and reconstituting the reality of the time and place, American Jews are not only invoking the spirits of the tribe, that is, laying claim to their martyrdom, but also making past time present. And in doing so they are symbolically reversing reality: they are transposing themselves from what they are currently perceived as—in the American case highly privileged, and in the Israeli case oppressive—and presenting themselves as the diametric opposite of privilege, as what they in fact were. And it is this image of the self that remains central to the American Jewish worldview."[82] In this view, the March of the Living would be understood as a commemorative act that generates and supports a self-identity that feeds on the historical image of Jews as powerless, thus reversing time and space.

But continued attention to the modes and manner of symbolic appropriation in the March of the Living suggests, following John Eade and Michael Sallnow, that this pilgrimage features a "realm of competing discourses"—both positive and negative. We can perceive these competing discourses on several levels. One is the frame of the experience itself. Thus, as Erik Cohen argues, the existential tourist mode (and, by analogy, pilgrimage) "is particularly amenable to falsification. The tourist, expecting the ideal life at the centre, is easily taken in; he is helped, as it were, to become a 'starry-eyed idealist.' Like traditional pilgrimage centres, centres of 'existential' tourism are advertised and embellished; tours through 'existential tourist space', like traditional pilgrimages, are staged." This may, however, simply be a result of the unmediated nature of "unprocessed experience"; the March of the Living, like any pilgrimage, may simply demand an interpretive frame. Kugelmass observes: "Of course there is in such travel to re-created places and moments in history something that seeks a reality more real than the real. Events witnessed on television, for example, are much easier to accept than those we witness firsthand: unprocessed experience generally lacks a dramatic structure to make it meaningful. Without the authoritative voice of the narrator, experience seems to lack legitimacy."[83]

The March of the Living is certainly staged and placed firmly within a Zionist interpretive framework. But the Zionist narrative of history is only the most overt of its symbolic appropriations; beneath that, I would contend, are a variety of discourses and strategies of appropriation brought to the march by the participants themselves and, at times, at odds with the official discourse. For example, the Mourner's Kaddish, repeated at almost every ceremony on the trip, may have meanings for the nonpracticing Jews on the march which are very different from those it has for the more religious participants. The former may develop here a profound connection between the Holocaust and a largely unfamiliar prayer, whereas the latter may connect the repeated performance of a familiar prayer immediately to their everyday practice. Or, in another example, we might ask what the significance is of the widespread "early planting" (before they were instructed to do so) of plaques at Birkenau by students uninterested in (or perhaps unable to understand) the long recitation in Hebrew of the official discourse of the event from the "stage."[84]

The competition for access to memorial spaces found at Mila 18 and at Majdanek can extend even to the individual participants of one commemorative ceremony, who may be engaged in a variety of activities and discourses at the same time. As Eade and Sallnow argue, "a pilgrimage shrine, while apparently emanating an intrinsic religious significance of its own, at the same time provides a ritual space for the expression of a diversity of perceptions and meanings which the pilgrims themselves bring to the shrine and impose upon it. As such, the cult can contain within itself a plethora of religious discourses."[85] But this kind of internal dissonance may reflect nothing more than the nature of ritual in general. Barbara Myerhoff suggests that "ritual is full of contradictions and paradox. Most paradoxical of all, by selecting and shaping a fragment of social life, it defines a portion of reality. The very act of consciously defining reality calls to our attention that, indeed, reality is merely a social construct, a collusive drama, intrinsically conventional, an act of collective imagination. Rituals are not only paradoxical intrinsically, they are built out of the paradoxes suggested by their symbols. They cope with paradox by mounting the mood of conviction and persuasion which fuses opposing elements referred to by their symbols, creating the belief that things are as they have been portrayed—proper, true, inevitable, natural."[86] Thus, the march seeks to make it seem perfectly natural that Jews should gather on Yom ha-Shoah, walk silently in solidarity from Auschwitz to Birkenau, and participate in a long ceremony of remembrance on top of the ruins of a crematorium complex, all the while downplaying the inherent paradoxes of such commemorative acts: the ahistorical (re)claiming of "sacred" space with Israeli flags, the celebration of largely Israeli identity and an Israel-centered worldview (a central paradox of the American Jewish civil religion) by a majority of non-Israelis, even the explanation for the "march" route itself—organizers claim that the "march" follows the same route taken by "so many of our brethren" to their deaths, and many participants find a strong connection to this, even though it is highly unlikely that more than a small number of Jews (relative to the number of Jewish Auschwitz victims) were actually marched to their deaths from Auschwitz I to Auschwitz II-Birkenau.[87] The March of the Living, as an ideological and religious experience, is an excellent example of commemorative performance in which the desire for memory has outrun the need for history.

Attention to these issues, then, highlights rituals as "dramas of persuasion," as Myerhoff states. In this sense, rituals "must be convincing. Not all the parties involved need to be equally convinced or equally moved. But the whole of it must be good enough to play. No one can stand up and boo. Not too many people can shift about in embarrassment, sigh or grimace. . . . [A]ll must collude so as not to spoil the show, or damage the illusion that the dramatic reality coincides with the 'other, out-there reality.'"[88] As drama, the "March of the Living" walk, as well as many of the commemorative acts throughout the two-week tour, is certainly persuasive, especially as it assists in the integrative, legitimating, and mobilizing processes discussed above. But looking more carefully at the competing discourses beneath the ideology of the organizers, we begin to see gaps and ruptures in the persuasive process, subtle (and not-so-subtle) challenges to the hegemonic discourse of the march. These range from personalizing plaques at Birkenau to bringing home earth from Poland as a souvenir, to devising one's own method of commemoration, and even to wandering off during the long and largely unintelligible ceremony at the end of the "march." Though the ritual commemorative activities of the March of the Living surely invoke Jewish traditional symbols and forms, they simultaneously challenge those structures in a variety of ways in a process of ritual commemorative construction that, as Catherine Bell argues, "can . . . renegotiate the very basis of tradition to the point of upending much of what had been seen as fixed previously or by other groups."[89]

What does this say about memory? Attention to the multiple and even conflicting discourses and strategies of commemoration invoked during the March of the Living brings us back to James Young's interest in exposing the "fundamentally interactive, dialogical quality of every memorial space." Here, as I suggested in the first chapter of this book, it becomes necessary to speak not of a memorial's "collective memory" but of its "collected memory." Young adds: "By maintaining a sense of collected memories, we remain aware of their disparate sources, of every individual's unique relation to a lived life, and of the ways our traditions and cultural forms continuously assign common meaning to disparate memories." Interestingly, Young observes that such ritual construction of memory may be self-perpetuating and self-reinforcing: "At some point, it may even be the activity of remembering together that becomes the shared memory; once ritualized, remembering together becomes an event in itself that is to be shared and remembered."[90] The shared aspect of ritual may help explain the success of the March of the Living in fostering a greater sense of Jewish identity in its participants. Here, memory is ultimately self-reflexive, creating a new discourse for memorialization dependent on ritualized engagement and embodiment.

HOLOCAUST COMMEMORATION: TIME, SPACE, AND MEMORY

The historian of religions Jonathan Z. Smith asserts that "ritual is, first and foremost, a mode of paying attention" and that "place directs attention," so that sacrality is perceived as "a category of emplacement."[91] For Smith, it is the attention to place that generates the sacred, and commemoration would be seen as another form of ritual emplacement. Eliade, on the other hand, focuses more on the temporal realm: "In religion as in magic, the periodic recurrence of anything signifies primarily that a mythical time is *made present* and then used indefinitely. Every ritual has the character of happening *now*, at this very moment. The time of the event that the ritual commemorates or re-enacts is made *present*, 're-presented' so to speak, however far back it may have been in ordinary reckoning."[92] Following this view, commemorative remembering would be understood as ritual re-presentation. Both views are valid and theoretically useful, especially in combination with each other. But, curiously, while both approaches seem overly concerned with ritual *presence* ("emplacement" in the former, "re-presentation" in the latter), they seem to overlook the presence of the very ritual actors who, in no small measure, make the sacred happen.

For it is the ritual *interaction* with space and time, made sacred by that interaction, that defines the March of the Living as a powerful Holocaust commemoration, specifically, as a memorial pilgrimage. And it is in the ritual engagement with sites of memory, with mythic time, and with other actors creating the commemoration that Holocaust memory is constructed and a community of memory is established. Maurice Halbwachs, as I discussed in chapter 1, had already noted that any kind of memory is irreducibly social and, moreover, that collective memory reconstructs the past in light of the constraints of the present.[93] In this light, the March of the Living is simply an extreme example, helpful in calling attention to the nature of Holocaust commemoration activities and, thus, the ritual inscriptions of memory. There are, of course, many different kinds of Holocaust commemorations (whose full analysis falls outside the scope of my book): synagogue services, film presentations and discussions, mass ceremonial gatherings, even cultural performances and individual observances. All these, even private commemorations, serve to connect actors to the community, the past, and the tradition, in the context of present-day concerns.

In chapter 1 I also observed that some critics believe Halbwachs did not go far enough in considering how commemoration works. Paul Connerton, for instance, finds Halbwachs's work lacking in specific attention to the ritual actors and their performances.[94] Connerton's project is to understand "how societies remember" (the title of his book); he argues that commemoration can be achieved only if we bring recollection and bodies together: "One might not have thought of doing that because, when recollection has been treated as a cultural rather than as an individual activity, it has tended to be seen as the recollection of a cultural tradition; and such a tradition, in turn, has tended to be thought of as something that is inscribed. . . . [A]lthough bodily practices are in principle included as possible objects of hermeneutic activity, in practice hermeneutics has taken inscription as its privileged object."[95] In other words, we must pay attention to the active components of memory construction carried out by real people, in real places and at real times.

For Connerton, therefore, social memory depends on commemorative ceremonies, which in turn depend on ritual, bodily performances, as well as the simple "facts of communication between individuals." But these facts are more than telling stories; the "master narrative" of a ritual is "a cult enacted" so that the "image of the past . . . is conveyed and sustained by ritual performances." Thus, Connerton distinguishes ritual activity from mere narrative; commemorations are especially interesting for him because their reenactments (or enactments) of the narratives of past events "do not simply imply continuity with the past but explicitly claim such continuity" (we might think here of the organizing narrative of Auschwitz inmates being marched to their deaths from Auschwitz I to Auschwitz II-Birkenau at the heart of the "March of the Living").[96] They can lay such claims to continuity because the bodily strategies of commemoration of which they consist (Connerton calls them "incorporating practices") are an effective system of mnemonics. These mnemonics depend on their existence through their performance and their acquisition in a manner often unconscious of that performance.[97] In this view, commemorative ceremonies are self-perpetuating and nonreflective, insuring their own continuation, constructing and maintaining memory, and resisting debilitating criticism. Thus, commemoration helps create, revise, and sustain tradition through the bodily, ritual activities of its actors; Holocaust commemoration, in this view, brings the past to the present through the incorporating practices of the people doing the commemorating, producing ritually enacted narratives and thereby creating culturally viable memories for all the participants.

As I discussed in chapter 1, James Fentress and Chris Wickham have also responded to Halbwachs's work critically. Much of what they have to say is compatible with Connerton's conclusions: they too are concerned with the individual actor left out of, or rendered passive in, Halbwachs's observations.[98] They define commemoration as both "the *action* of speaking or writing about memories, as well as the formal re-enaction of the past that we usually mean when we use the word. Within this social perspective, there is an important distinction between memory as action and memory as representation; remembering/commemorating considered as a type of behaviour, and memory, considered cognitively, as a network of ideas." Again, the emphasis on memory as activity here is instructive, setting commemoration apart from cognitive representation. For Fentress and Wickham, social memory is memory articulated (not necessarily in speech), conceptualized, and transmitted, not only through narratives but also as guides to social identity. Most important, the authors remind us of our own often forgotten presence in the commemoration process: "It is we who are remembering, and it is to us that the knowledge, emotions, and images ultimately refer. What is concealed in models of memory as a surface whereupon knowledge of experience is transcribed is our own presence in the background. Whatever memory may be as a purely neurological or purely epistemological object in itself, we can neither know nor experience our memories unless we can first 'think' them; and the moment we 'think' our memories, recalling and articulating them, they are no longer objects; they become part of us. At that moment, we find ourselves indissolubly in their centre."[99] This supports a view that bears repeating, expressed by Yosef Yerushalmi and already cited in chapter 1, which I find most applicable to Holocaust commemorations: "whatever memories [are] unleashed by . . . commemorative rituals and liturgies [are] surely not a matter of intellection, but of evocation and identification. . . . [W]hat was . . . drawn up from the past was not a series of facts to be contemplated at a distance, but a series of situations into which one could somehow be existentially drawn."[100]

Commemoration is highly mediated; there can be no "pure" ritual experience here, certainly not in a carefully orchestrated six-thousand-person pilgrimage through Poland and Israel, but not in any other kind of Holocaust commemoration either. Commemorative activity depends on various narrative (religious/ideological) frames, on symbols, on ritual forms. Therefore, Edward Casey refers to commemoration as "remembering-through": "through this very vehicle, within its dimensions, across its surface. For the past is made accessible to me by its sheer ingrediency in the *commemorabilium* itself. It is commemorated therein and not somewhere else, however distant in time or space the com-

memorated event or person may be from the present occasion of commemorating. . . . *Through* the appropriate *commemorabilia* I overcome
the effects of anonymity and spatio-temporal distance and pay homage
to people and events I have never known and will never know face-to-
face." Thus, "remembering-through" creates connections to the past,
overcoming ruptures in space and time, even mixing and re-creating
space and time, in a process that we recognize, in the context of Holocaust commemoration, as reinforcing a sense of Jewish peoplehood. Here
we arrive at a deeper understanding of the communitas effected by
commemorative ritual activity, which overcomes "the separation from
which otherwise unaffiliated individuals suffer. Still more radically,
commemoration suggests that such separation is a sham."[101] It is exactly
that kind of powerful sense of affiliation, I would argue, that is at the
heart not only of the march agenda but of all other forms of Holocaust
commemoration as well.

For Casey, the memorialization achieved by commemorative ritual
effects "lastingness," the peculiar temporality of memorialization he
prefers to call "perdurance." This is the "enduring-through" of the interpretive encounter that is tradition, what Casey calls a *"via media* between eternity and time."[102] In other words, such rituals as Holocaust
commemoration ceremonies help establish a special kind of temporality
through which memory is articulated (mediated); it is through this form
that memory overcomes the obstacles of human time and space, effectively establishing viable symbolic connections and reconciling past,
present, and future. Thus, commemoration allows the past to perdure not
only into the present but through the present on into the future as well,
the result being that the past never really ends:

Freud would have described such a situation as one of "deferred action" (Nach-
träglichkeit): by being commemorated, what might otherwise end altogether, come
to a definite close, is granted a delayed efficacy. In this respect commemorating enables the past not just to evanesce in the present but, more crucially, to traverse the
present on its way to becoming future. It is as if the very delay in discovery or recognition—or in simple appreciation—empowers the past to gain an increased futurity.
As Freud remarks of deferred happenings generally, the effect seems to exceed the
cause, contravening the Aristotelian-Cartesian assumption that there must be at
least as much reality in a cause as in its effect. Such is the force of commemoration
when it is fully and freely enacted.[103]

Holocaust commemoration here, as a particular way of constructing Jewish
memory, is powerful indeed, sustaining itself through the incorporating

practices of its actors, who (re)connect themselves to Jewish history and tradition (and to each other) and, through their participation in a memorial process of cultural inscription that effects perdurance across time and space, not only make the past present but also make it last into the future. Kugelmass finds that these rites, in this way, create a certain kind of meaning: "In part a meditation on the past, and in part a scripted play about the present, the rites I have described are also rehearsals of what American Jews are intent on becoming or, perhaps more accurately stated, intent on not becoming. How ironic. Poland, relegated to the past by American Jews, has suddenly emerged as a stage upon which to act out their future."[104] In the end, the memory constructed through the March of the Living, which, I have argued, tells us more about the present than about the past, ends up virtually exceeding the constraints of re-presentation in the present and propels its participants, and us, into the future. What is left behind, what is forgotten, as well as the value of such forgetting are the subjects of my concluding chapter.

Conclusion

REMEMBER FORGETTING / FORGET REMEMBERING

The universe is silent in the hand and reborn from this silence through the word. Hence the beginning is absence, appropriate wound of a premature loss of memory.

A new beginning can only mean that we have, in all innocence, forgotten the beginning.

In any case, beginning means forgetting.

—EDMOND JABÈS, *The Book of Questions,* vol. 2

Ordinary facts are arranged within time, strung along its length, as on a thread. There they have their antecedents and their consequences, which crowd tightly together and press hard one upon the other without any pause. This has its importance for any narrative, of which continuity and successiveness are the soul.

Yet what is to be done with events that have no place of their own in time; events that have occurred too late, after the whole of time has been distributed, divided, and allotted; events that have been left in the cold, unregistered, hanging in the air, homeless, and errant?

Could it be that time is too narrow for all events?

—BRUNO SCHULZ, *Sanatorium under the Sign of the Hourglass*

THE FORGOTTEN

HOW, IN THE END, will memory encompass and contain the representation of the Holocaust? Dealing with the Holocaust leaves a sense that we must always begin again. This is not to say that we continually and incessantly return to the origins of memory in order to capture the events themselves as they determine the starting point of experience (though for survivors this is indeed the case, in endless returns to the traumas which allow virtually no escape and no forgetting). Rather, in constructing memorial representations of the past, we always return to the origin because we *cannot* capture beginning in memory. Every attempted representation comes back to this point, if for no other reason than every attempt is inadequate, each one falls short of the monumental task at hand. We nonetheless keep trying. Perhaps we can do this because of our infinite capacity for forgetting.

For memory to matter, it must ultimately deal with forgetting. Forgetting raises its ugly head in every memorial situation, as its double, its ghost brother. The issue of forgetfulness is especially important in the contemporary, technological age, in which historical knowledge appears to be slipping away and everything seems to be focused on the present moment. In addition, the very attempt to totalize and contain knowledge is itself subject to great suspicion. How, ultimately, does Holocaust memory survive the postmodern condition?

In this concluding chapter I consider the "other side" of memory—that is, what is forgotten in the course of engaging and appropriating the past in the desire for remembrance. Forgetting can be characterized in a number of ways, as excess, remnant, absence, margin, limit, trauma, the "real," the "other," the impossible, the supplement. For each of these, we can say that the body itself becomes the site of the "forgotten" or, better yet, the space where what is to be forgotten is negotiated. This negotiation reminds us that memory and forgetting, forever linked to each other, are both distinct from the experiences of the events that have come to be known as the Holocaust. Memory, here and in every case, is always "of" the Holocaust, not the Holocaust "itself." However we define the margin of the "forgotten," it is not the forgetting of the referent that is the Shoah but rather the forgetting of an aspect of its representation. Forgetting, like remembering, remains an index of the trauma. Recognizing this difference is crucial for an appreciation of the efforts and outcomes of remembering *and* forgetting as techniques of engagement with and embodiment of the past.

To approach this complex and multifaceted issue, I would first like to consider four contemporary novels in which the authors engage the idea of forgetting as productive of both knowledge and narrative of the Holocaust. Against this backdrop I can discuss the appearances of forgetting in its varieties in the contemporary critical literature, which will set the stage for a reengagement with and a revisioning of the primary subjects of the book.

Many of the newer popular narratives of the Holocaust in literature confront the very issue of Holocaust remembrance. That they do so is not surprising, for popular fiction often responds to the contemporary culture in which it is situated. This confrontation is all part of a more generalized cultural effort to come to terms with the past and articulate relationships to that past in the present. Such an effort shifts the agenda in the process of literary memorialization from the concerns for the preservation of the past, largely borne by a privileged elite, to the needs of the present, often executed by a variety of actors and authors with varying levels of engagement in determining cultural heritage. Reading popular fiction can therefore tell us much about the age in which we live.

Contemporary Holocaust writing thus establishes "new paradigms" for representation. These often involve the provocative manipulation of symbols and themes of the Holocaust freed from the restrictions of previous conventions of representation, such as the "lamentational" or "covenantal" models (though, of course, seeds for this new freedom were sown throughout the history of Holocaust literature).[1] I discussed two examples of this symbolic manipulation in chapter 2 in the analysis of Art Spiegelman's *Maus* and Emily Prager's *Eve's Tattoo*. These challenges to the presumed propriety of representation go hand in hand with the breakdown of the familial, generational models for representation, as the Shoah becomes part of a more generalized, common cultural heritage subject to the creative scrutiny of writers at various levels removed from the events of World War II. Even for writers whose connections to the Holocaust are direct or "legitimately" inherited, the challenges posed by critical thinking about memory and representation resonate within their fiction. Sometimes these literary treatments of Holocaust memory and the memorializing process self-critically and -reflexively engage the issue of the production and reproduction of memory, as in the works by Spiegelman and Prager that I associate with the iconic mode. But sometimes such fictional responses miss the boat of critical reflexivity and enter the realm of kitsch representation.

THE KITSCH OF FORGETTING

I do not intend this to be a discussion of the nature of kitsch art or Nazi kitsch. Rather, my aim in this section is to highlight some of the more striking and disturbing aspects of one work of Holocaust fiction, in the context of the manipulation of Holocaust imagery and the memorial process, in order to consider the issue of forgetting. The idea of kitsch is merely a loose organizing principle and not a precise fulcrum point for my analysis. To think about kitsch here is only to focus the discussion on some provocative issues and images.

What do I mean by "kitsch"? It is a difficult term to nail down, to be sure, and it can be identified in a number of ways. Once defined as "the principle of evil in the value system of art," kitsch can be generally understood as "an aesthetically inadequate mode of expression, an imitation of art, which aims at getting an unreflective, immediate, emotional response," with a function of either promoting something in commercial terms or reinforcing an identification on ideological terms.[2] Kitsch as imitation is so close to the "real thing" that it is often difficult to distinguish one from the other, making the task of identifying something as kitsch more of a challenge, because the task is often reduced to the judgment of an individual reader or viewer. What concerns me here is not kitsch in general but a particular genre of kitsch, one that Saul Friedländer has identified as part of the "new discourse on Nazism" that first emerged in the late 1960s. This discourse involves the breaking down of protective barriers erected around the symbols of the Holocaust and a return to those symbols and the past they represent, in order to transform, reelaborate, or otherwise attempt to understand that past—processes which reveal an obsession with the Nazi era that can, at times, slip into a profound fascination with and even implication in the internal logic of the Nazi worldview.[3] This obsession, for Friedländer, engenders a connection between kitsch and death that marks this discourse as unique, and it is that connection which informs my explorations here.

For Friedländer, "kitsch emotion represents a certain kind of simplified, degraded, insipid, but all the more insinuating romanticism. All of us live among kitsch; we are plunged into it up to our necks. Hence the importance and the hold this type of imagery and sentiment has on us, a hold that is formed into frisson thanks to the counterpoint of death and destruction." The new discourse on Nazism returns to the potent combination of death and kitsch inherent in the Nazi worldview itself, which creates another level of complexity in analysis, for the kitsch qualities we may perceive in contemporary fiction are such because they represent or imitate Nazi kitsch. This return to the past is a version of obsessive memorialization, a way of making the past present, and it also makes use of the power of myth in a manner much like classic collective memory. For example, Friedländer argues, "Myth, in its function as a revealer of truths and basic and hidden values, is the source of power and inspiration, the vehicle of coherence, the harbinger of an enduring present. . . . Kitsch is a debased form of myth, but nevertheless draws from the mythic substance—a part of its emotional impact—the death of the hero; the eternal march, the twilight of the gods; myth is a footprint, an echo of lost worlds, haunting an imagination invaded by excessive rationality and thus becoming the crystallization point for thrusts of the archaic and the irrational."[4]

This raises a crucial point: a similarity can be perceived between the distillation of history into memory and the distillation of art or ideology into kitsch symbols. Both appear to organize complex structures into discrete packets of easily digestible images and types. Does that mean that collective memory is kitschy? I am not willing to go so far, but I do think the structural parallels between the two can fuel our analyses. Consider, for example, Friedländer's comments on the reconstruction of religious symbols in modern political contexts, where "kitsch is the basis of the act of reconstruction. You light the torches, set the flags waving in the breeze, set the altar, and appropriate the idea of sacrifice, and of the hero dead and resurrected. You simply imitate what was authentic in its religious context and you enter the realm of political kitsch, with its immediate emotional impact. It brings the viewer back to what he senses has been a deep-rooted tradition, to the world of myth—which was natural, which is not anymore, which is now the kitsch representation. It has this direct effect of taking you back." Such a visceral "return" to the past through the construction of tradition has clear parallels with the commemorative process (as I discussed in the previous chapter), especially in the independent life such images have, setting off emotions and tapping into associations. "Once they are set in motion, they operate powerfully on the free-floating imagination."[5] In many ways, this discussion echoes that in chapter 2— one may say that kitsch is another name for the representational processes I called idolatrous (as opposed to iconic). Kitsch memories, like idolatrous ones, do not allow remembering-through but are more opaque. As such, they are also ultimately forgetful.

Throughout this brief analysis, it may be useful to recall a constellation of descriptive terms we might associate with the word "kitsch." Such potentially helpful terms are *false, inauthentic, appropriative, cheap, banal, nostalgic, seductive, sentimental, anti-ironic, uncritical, popular, unreflective.* Kitsch can at times mobilize; it encourages quick, uncritical responses; it operates in a closed system; and it imitates real experiences. The more political expressions of kitsch, such as *fascist kitsch,* operate within a cult of death and vague eroticism. Within the new discourse on Nazism, then, the combination of kitsch and death evokes a distinct uneasiness which "stems, most of the time, from a dissonance between the declared moral and ideological position of the author or the filmmaker, the condemnation of Nazism and the will to understand and the aesthetic effect, be it literary or cinematographic."[6]

I now want to consider Elie Wiesel's novel, *The Forgotten,* in the context of contemporary, popular Holocaust writing and the question of kitsch and forgetting, in the broad terms I have sketched above.[7] The novel directly confronts the issues of a receding past, the survivor's advancing age, and the concomitant contemporary crisis of memory, all in a popular context. Wiesel, the premier Holocaust survivor-spokesperson, can be credited with almost single-handedly putting the Holocaust on the cultural agenda, and in examining *The Forgotten* I wish to take nothing away from Wiesel's stature and accomplishments. As a living embodiment of

Holocaust memory in what can arguably be described as its more mystical mode, Wiesel has long laid rightful claim to the role of the witness-narrator in sharing some part of the sacred mystery of the Holocaust experience. But in this novel Wiesel has moved into interesting new fictional territory, presenting narrative from the World War II period in the form of the fading memories of Elhanan Rosenbaum. As Elhanan's grasp of his own past gradually deteriorates, he asks his son Malkiel to begin remembering *for* him, passing on the stories of his past in a valiant attempt to preserve in the consciousness of his son the memories stored in the now cracking vessel of his own mind. This device means that those memories, as we read them, are presented in the context of Malkiel's own life and his own ongoing attempt to "create a past for himself." In this way, the Holocaust narratives are interspersed with Malkiel's thoughts and reminiscences, all of which might suggest a rich, deep, multilayered narrative with powerful implications as a model for memorial responses to the Holocaust.

But that is not what we find. True, some interesting passages do skillfully blend images of the "past" and "present," often accentuated by the narrative doubling caused by the repetition of characters' names—Malkiel, son of Elhanan, son of Malkiel, son of Elhanan—especially in the sections woven around Malkiel's visit to his grandfather's grave in the old country. But most of the novel is a melancholic and melodramatic blend of cheap sexual intrigue and sentimentality for a receding past, interspersed with pseudoreligious musings on fate and faith and, of course, memory. Listen to this passage, in which Malkiel recounts his first sexual experience with his cousin Rita: "And Malkiel soared to seventh heaven before plunging to seventh hell. In torture, in ecstasy, he wanted to sing and to weep; he had never felt so torn or so whole. 'Was that the first time?' Rita asked. He was ashamed to admit the truth but admitted it anyway, not going so far as to tell her what he felt now: a mixture of guilt and remorse, a sense of defeat. His whole religious memory was suddenly judging him. Had he not violated one of the Ten Commandments? How would he answer at the Last Judgment? What would his uncle think?" (107). Or consider the point at which we are first introduced to Malkiel as he explores the cemeteries of his ancestral village and muses on the local official's wish that he stay a while: "And indeed he might linger. For how long? How could he know? Only God knew all, always. Only God pierced the mystery of the future. Yesterday, tomorrow, never. These words don't have the same meaning in New York and Bombay. The beggar and the prince move toward death at different paces. What separates an individual from his fellowman? What keeps the past from biting into the future? All men need rain, prayer and silence; all forget, all will be forgotten. Me too? Me too. And my father, too? And God? He, too?" (25).

Wiesel's novel presents a kitsch version of memory's complexity, but it is difficult at times to tease out passages that clearly identify it as such. And that is exactly the point: kitsch and death, the popularization and propriety of Holocaust imagery, and even the interplay between memory and forgetting are all concerned with border crossing, with violating boundaries. When certain works hover at the borderlines, they are challenging and provocative, and they can serve as models for other cultural grapplings with Holocaust remembrance. But when a work crosses the line, so that it uncritically manipulates emotions and symbols and serves more as a model of inauthenticity, then the sense of uneasiness of which Friedländer speaks is magnified. This becomes clear in the central event of Wiesel's novel, where the author retells the awful story of the partisans' reconquest of Feherfalu, Elhanan's hometown. Having joined the partisans during the war, Elhanan returns with them in advance of the Red Army to a ghost town to find that all the Jews have been taken away and to hear about the atrocities committed by the local Nazi sympathizers, one Zoltan in particular. His comrade Itzik vows revenge and disappears. Later, as Elhanan is wandering the streets dumbly, he hears a woman's cry for help. Investigating, he finds to his horror that Itzik is raping a young woman. Unable to act to stop Itzik and save her, Elhanan leaves the house and vomits in the street. He returns later on to try to comfort and apologize to the woman for what his friend did. He finally confronts Itzik and tells him he was wrong, but he remains uneasy: "Perhaps he felt guilty for not acting quicker to keep his friend from going too far, not fighting for the raped young widow, a victim of uncontrollable Jewish rage and suffering" (141–47; quotation on 147).[8]

The events described in these few pages are clearly integral to Wiesel's   .
narrative, and making the reader a voyeur to this violence may be necessary for the author's desired effect, but it remains a manipulative episode. What is more disturbing is the way the event is transmitted within the bounds of the novel itself. It is central to the narrative because Elhanan has never forgiven himself for not acting on the woman's behalf, and as a result, he passes this feeling of guilt on to his son. It is a defining trauma for the father, and it is central to his memory. It can never be forgotten as long as Elhanan has a memory. Elhanan wishes to find some vicarious resolution to his guilt, before his memory fades completely and he can no longer remember to forgive himself, so he asks his son to return to Feherfalu to find the woman. At the climax of the novel, Malkiel finally

locates her and, through his translator, Lidia, gradually circles in on her traumatic experience. Resisting, the old woman insists she does not remember, and to interrogate her further, Malkiel repeatedly fights off the feeling that she has suffered enough. He zeroes in on the events leading up to her rape:

> "Stop it," Lidia said. "Can't you see she's suffering? Why do you make her suffer?"
>
> "I did nothing to her," Malkiel said stubbornly. "Someone else made her suffer, not me. I'm part of her present, not her past."
>
> "But you're making her suffer in the present," Lidia said.
>
> "No. She's remembering pain from long ago. It's not the same."
>
> "I don't remember," the old woman said tonelessly. (221)

Malkiel nonetheless relentlessly forces the old woman to reexperience (through recollection) her own traumatic rape, including the scene in which his father attempted to rescue her. Elhanan has become, in this version, an "unexpected knight," much more insistent on stopping the crime than in the original version, at least as we have it (221–22). Nonetheless, in this revisited scene of violence, the sense of uneasiness and the bounds of good taste are exceeded. As a reader I feel angry and ashamed at this kind of manipulation, despite the fact that I recognize this may be the author's intent. This final act of Malkiel's vicarious revenge followed by a curious atonement is self-serving and offensive: though the old woman expresses anger at Malkiel for "rifl[ing] through my memory" (222) and transforming God's compassionate granting of forgetfulness of the rape "into human malediction" (223), she goes on to forgive Malkiel. At the end of their encounter, "Malkiel held her hand in his own. 'I hope you won't be too angry with me, Madame Calinescu. Thanks to you I've learned something useful and perhaps essential: forgetting is also part of the mystery. You need to forget, and I understand. I must resist forgetting, so try to understand me, too'" (223). Madame Calinescu kisses Malkiel's forehead and thanks him, and his father. This uncritical, oversimplification of the "mystery" of memory is certainly not worth the discomfort of Wiesel's creation of a twice-represented, twice-remembered horror. Here, remembrance is a weapon to be wielded at those who would wish to forget. The memory of suffering for Elhanan/Malkiel still wounds, but the claim that Madame Calinescu's memory of suffering also endures in the present is rejected.

Of course, it is possible that *The Forgotten* is a far more subtle and sophisticated novel than I am suggesting, a supercritical representation of kitsch manipulation so complete that it masquerades as its opposite. If so, the reader would be exposed to a kind of memorial violence in order to interrogate such aggressive memory, wherever it may occur. But if that were the case, then it would, somewhere, take occasion to reflect on the complexities it so quickly glosses over. Instead, Wiesel leaves us only with inauthentic reflections on tradition; graphic, voyeuristic images; and a profound uneasiness. Or this could simply be a bad book, in which case I could not fault the author for one black mark on an otherwise impressive résumé. But, even if true, I do not think one can so easily dismiss the novel, if for no reason other than that it exemplifies some of the dangers of memory obsession. Madame Calinescu must relive her suffering for Malkiel to redeem his father's; the old woman's need for forgetting is outweighed by Elhanan's desire to remember before (or, perhaps, beyond the point at which) he forgets entirely (represented by proxy in Malkiel). The memory and experience of trauma is exchangeable here, not only from father to son but between the father (through his son) and the "other," the woman, the victim of her own private suffering at the hands of Jewish revenge. But against what Wiesel would have us think from reading *The Forgotten,* memory, especially the memory of trauma, cannot be exchanged, and it cannot be so easily transmitted from one generation to the next in an ever repeating cycle of inheritance (as marked, for example, in the recurring names Elhanan and Malkiel). If it were so (and, sadly, sometimes this is the case), the world would be filled with Malkiels visiting their parents' rage and failing memories on the nonremembering (or, at least, nonremembering of Jewish experience) population. Perhaps it would be better to recall Madame Calinescu's words to Malkiel: "The truth is that I don't understand you. Aren't you too young to learn someone else's past in addition to your own?" (223).

"It seems to me," Larry Nachman suggests in a symposium published by *Salmagundi,* "that kitsch emerges when tradition is destroyed. . . . The artifice of kitsch is closely related to the artifice of modern society as something constructed and decided upon, as opposed to what societies have always been, that is, societies based on tradition."[9] Elie Wiesel represents the tradition of an almost forgotten mysticism, a nostalgia for an almost forgotten world which he embodies and to which he continually alludes in his writings. He also stands in for the survivor generation as a whole, now "passing into history."[10] In *The Forgotten* the character of Elhanan represents that generation while embodying the "disease" of forgetting that many embody simply in their deaths. That generation's legacy has been and continues to be appropriated in a variety of ways, as I have discussed in this book. But the impending death of the survivor generation is not a forgetting but simply a death, a passing on. Are we to fault them for dying? Additionally, their forgetting is not in any way a death of their memory, though survivors have a right to take their traumas to the grave. But in *The Forgotten*, Wiesel offers a troubling counterweight to those efforts at remembrance. In this novel, memory is not a negotiated outcome of a genuine engagement with the representations of the past or even a naïve encounter with an image of the past taken to be the past itself. No, memory here is a cheap imitation, an impostor. More than naïve, it is insensitive, even cruel. Wiesel's father and son characters embody this inauthentic memory, forgetting the intransitive qualities of memory in the desire for its transfusion, the need to remember everything even as it is slipping away. What is forgotten here is compassion; what is forgotten are the merits of forgetting itself.

FORGETTING AND REDEMPTION

One way the more constructive aspects of memory and forgetting can be explored is through the grounding of memory in imaginative Holocaust writing via a stable reference point. In some cases, such grounding of memory, especially in the case of Holocaust remembrance, involves the memorialization of a specific figure. The creative literary representation of such a process mimics the construction of a monument to the past, where myth and history are bound and transformed into memorial icons. Such a process also reflects back on classical religiomythic strategies of memorialization. As models for such concrete literary memorialization, David Grossman's *See Under: Love* and Cynthia Ozick's *The Messiah of Stockholm* are excellent examples of Holocaust memory oriented toward a common reference point.[11] The novels share an obsession with Bruno Schulz and his lost manuscript *The Messiah*, offering fascinating observations concerning the nature and appropriation of Holocaust memory and mythology, as well as the recovery, redemption, and re-creation of lost texts, hopes, and lives. A comparison of these two novels will illuminate different strategies not only for memorializing the past but also for grappling with the problem of its lasting meanings, in light of the ever looming specter of forgetting.

Ozick's *Messiah of Stockholm* is primarily concerned with recovering a direct Holocaust legacy in the form of patrimony: the protagonist, Lars Andemening, claims he is the long lost, unknown son of none other than Bruno Schulz, the Polish-Jewish writer and artist murdered in the

Holocaust. Moreover, Lars, himself a two-bit book reviewer for a local paper, imagines he has inherited his "father's" words, his language. Lars's only friend, Heidi, accepts this fantasy but scolds him for his cultish attachment to it (33). Heidi is more interested in Schulz's death than in his tales (and this is not fiction): on November 19, 1942—"Black Thursday," as it was called by the Jews of the Drohobycz Ghetto, or "the Wild Action"—Bruno, who had been given a pass to the Aryan side of town by his Gestapo "protector," was shot dead by that Nazi's rival as he was looking for bread outside the ghetto. But for Lars, this is off the track (39): what is important to him is his linguistic and literary patrimony; the disruptions of history get in the way of the continuity of inheritance. Naomi Sokoloff, in her essay comparing these two novels, has observed that Lars's identification with his Jewish past through Schulz's art represents false salvation, and his disinterest in Schulz's murder shows an inability to keep priorities straight and "acknowledg[e] the importance of the collective history of destruction the Jewish people has suffered."[12] For Sokoloff, there is something inauthentic about Lars's project of appropriation. Her observations are valid, but what is more important to me is whether Lars, in his single-minded attention to his so-called "inheritance," will succeed or fail in recuperating his "father's" memory.

Lars is given his chance when a character named Adela (who shares a name with the maid from Schulz's stories and claims to be his daughter) arrives bearing the long-lost manuscript of Schulz's masterpiece-in-progress, *The Messiah.* Lars had already been shown "mooning . . . over the missing *Messiah* . . . and its keeper. . . . If its keeper was shot in the street, was *The Messiah* scattered loose in the gutter, to be chewed over by dogs, to rot in the urine of cats? Or was *The Messiah* shut up in an old dresser in a house in Drohobycz until this day? Or put out with the trash thirty-five years ago? Or left tangled between its keeper's coat and shoes in the mountain of coats and shoes behind a fence in the place of death?" (38–39). That is, could *The Messiah*—and this must be taken in all its multiple meanings: the manuscript, the redemptive personality, the very idea of redemption—have survived the Holocaust? Or was *The Messiah* and the possibility of the Messiah destroyed at Auschwitz?

The *Messiah* text, then, serves as a potential bridge over the abyss of the Holocaust back to the lost memory of Bruno Schulz. The resurrected *Messiah* lying on Lars's "bed of rebirth" (as he calls it, 73) offers a potential victory for the legacy of memory and language over the legacy of history and death. Lars may soon be able to make sense of his "past" and rescue his "father's" (absent) memory from literary obscurity. Thus, he sees the possibility for redemption of and by *The Messiah.*[13]

But what kind of text is this? "These poor battered sheets were erratically paginated, some not numbered at all, and one eddying flowed into another; there were sequences and consequences, parallels and paradoxes, however you shuffled them. . . . So it was with the intelligence of *The Messiah*'s order and number and scheme of succession: everything voluminously overlapping, everything simultaneous and multiform" (106). Is this what Bruno Schulz's lost masterpiece was like—his book of books? Is it simply a jumble of texts, or is it an imitation, a vision, of the intertextuality of Torah? Or perhaps it is some poststructuralist's dream: the thoroughly deconstructed text? It is striking that it is initially described as being nonnarrative and nonlinear—out of time as it were, which is perhaps just what a messianic text would have to be.

But the text *is* somewhat legible: "*The Messiah*, insofar as it could be determined to be 'about' anything (and Lars, amnesiac, forgot almost all of it), was about creation and redemption. It was a work of cosmogony and entelechy" (106–7). Yet, as we read Ozick's imagined version of Schulz's *Messiah*, we are disturbed: it presents a vision of a Drohobycz wholly devoid of humans and "inhabited" by idols, reading more like a World War II nightmare of absolute Nazi victory than a glimpse of the messianic age. The inhabitants have converted to atheism and fled, religion has all but dried up, and the beautifully polished idols bow to one another and eventually sacrifice one another (108–9). The Eastern European ghetto has reverted to a nightmarish, precovenantal, sacrificial age. "The town was on fire, idols burning up idols in a frenzy of mutual adoration. Then—matter-of-factly, with no fanfare—the Messiah arrived. (And almost immediately fell to pieces)" (109). It is a challenging image. On the one hand, this catastrophic vision can be read as an ominous prefiguration of the Holocaust because of the fictional genesis of *The Messiah*; on the other, it reads as a postfiguration because this is, after all, Ozick's post-Holocaust creation.[14]

This messiah's origin turns out to be the cellar of the Drohobycz synagogue, and more than anything else, this messiah resembles a *book* whose pages are covered with illegible, cryptic characters that turn out to be tiny drawings of those same idols which have taken over the town (110). Is Ozick trying to resurrect Schulz's notion of an original text as redeemer—a metaphor for the primordial Torah, perhaps? But this strange book is illegible, and in any case, no one is there to read it. Moreover, this messianic text (within a messianic text) finally collapses—destroyed—as it gives birth to a bird that flies among the idols, touching them with a wand of hay.[15] "And then there rose up out of Drohobycz the sound of lamentation and elegy, as the bonfires were extinguished, and the idols were dissolved into sparks . . . until the town was desolate, empty streets and empty shops and empty houses, and the flecks of sparks fading to ash" (111). So much for idolatry—but so much as well for the messiah.[16]

Perhaps some sense exists in all this: Gershom Scholem, whose scholarship informs our very notion of Jewish messianism, tells us of the doubling of the figure of the Messiah within the tradition. "The Messiah ben Joseph is the dying Messiah who perishes in the Messianic catastrophe. . . . He is a redeemer who redeems nothing, in whom only the final battle with the powers of the world is crystallized. His destruction coincides with the destruction of history."[17] Does this tale, then, represent history devouring itself at the end of time—the messianic catastrophe prior to the true age of redemption? Perhaps Ozick's imagined Schulzian text should be read as a metaphor for the Nazi era of destruction, prior to the age of redemption (which has not yet arrived)? Has anything been redeemed in and by this tale?

Lars, unfortunately, cannot answer these questions, because, upon emerging from his "sacred engagement" with The Messiah, he cannot remember what he has read.[18] It is only the trace of the catastrophe that Lars can recall; beyond that, he is left with the abyss. Perhaps the only legacies here are the all too real traces of pain, lamentation, and elegy. Is it impossible for Lars to remember because one cannot (re)create the memory of an experience not undergone, especially without some kind of traditional/cultural netting as a support network to fall back on and provide the necessary context for such creation?[19] Does Lars, in scrabbling after his artificial patrimony and ignoring everything else, necessarily deny any redemptive power to collective Jewish memory, making it, at best, a parody of "true" inheritance? Finally, is his experience a metaphor for the ultimate failure of literature to redeem?

I think Ozick would answer "yes" to all this and more, for this is the point of her novel. And the final blow comes when Lars "realizes" that the text is a fake—a false Messiah. He has no choice but to reject it. In so doing he resigns himself to another, all too familiar story with its own legacy: "The Messiah went into the camps with its keeper. . . . That's all that could have happened, nothing else. The Messiah was burned up in those places. Behind those fences, in those ovens" (121). As if to drive the point home, Lars offers a final solution to the problem of cultural patrimony, redemptive memory, and messianism: he incinerates the manuscript. Ozick here posits the failure of Jewish memory to reclaim the legacy of the past and redeem a sense of cultural connection from the ashes of the Holocaust. This legacy is one of forgetting, articulated through a narrative depicting forgetfulness.

David Grossman, in *See Under: Love*, offers a different story that we can read as an alternative to Ozick's altogether bleak inheritance. In the second part of the novel (the most cerebral and thus least "popular" of the four I discuss here), Grossman writes a new coda to the biography of Bruno Schulz and, in so doing, creates something approximating a new foundational myth for Holocaust memory and its inscription with provocative implications. While Grossman through his Bruno character admits to knowing the "real" story of Schulz's demise, both choose to ignore it. Instead, Bruno is shown in Danzig, jumping off the town pier into the sea and becoming a fish.[20] This is no mere fantasy; rather, it articulates the beginnings of a program of literary redemption. In this act Grossman not only redeems Bruno from his unheroic death but he also redeems his individuality and his identity from the abyss of mass obliteration and dehumanization. Adopting a decidedly postmodernist style, Grossman presents his Bruno in soteriological terms, in a deliberately confusing and eerily mythological narrative in which the character's thoughts are interspersed with quotations from Schulz's own published words: "Four years of thinking and writing. It was a mistake that spread malignantly before he realized the Messiah would never come in writing, would never be invoked in a language suffering from elephantiasis. A new grammar and a new calligraphy had first to be invented" (89).[21]

This redemption of Bruno's identity is part of a broader struggle for authentic identity embodied by Grossman's protagonist Shlomo (Momik) Neuman. Like Ozick's Lars, Momik is a writer obsessed with Bruno Schulz and *The Messiah*. Unlike Lars, who has "the orphan's terrifying freedom to choose" (Ozick, *Messiah of Stockholm*, 102), Momik is an Israeli child of survivors who grew up in the shadow of a horror about which no one will speak. Thus, Momik must create for himself a link to a past that really *is* his birthright, a link he continues to forge as an adult fiction writer grappling with the Nazi era and the second generation's paradoxical response to it: Grossman constantly reminds us of the difficulties involved in (re)telling the tale that cannot be remembered.

Momik's early struggle with Holocaust memory is marked by one key event. While he is listening to his "grandfather" hum the usually incomprehensible story that Momik believes could connect him to the mystery of life "over there" in the Holocaust world, if only he could make sense of it, suddenly "this time the story sounded clear and he told it nicely with biblical expression, and Momik held his breath and listened to the story from start to finish, and swore he would never-ever-black-and-blue forget a single word of the story, but he instantly forgot because it was the kind of story you always forget and have to keep going back to the beginning to remember, it was that kind of story, and when Grandfather finished telling it, the others started telling their stories, and they were all talking at once and they said things no one would ever believe, and Momik remembered them forever and ever and instantly forgot them" (Grossman, *See Under,* 84). Momik will spend the rest of the novel trying to overcome this amnesia and reconnect to those stories through his own imaginative narrative constructions.

His search for lost time takes him to the seashore, where he prods the queen of the deep for facts about Bruno and *The Messiah* until she coughs up the text. Grossman, like Ozick, gives us the story of *The Messiah,* but Grossman's version is, like a modern-day midrash, written into the space of Schulz's own published work: *Sanatorium under the Sign of the Hourglass.* Moreover, Momik approaches the text not, like Lars, as a priest in search of patrimony but in the very "body" of a character from the extant story by Schulz, "The Age of Genius." Thus Grossman grounds the search for a literary legacy and the redemption of memory and identity in his own finely woven intertextual cloth.

In Grossman's subversive version of messianic mythology, the townspeople of Drohobycz are gathering in the square to celebrate the coming of the Messiah when a man enters on a gray donkey, dismounts, and promptly disappears. The donkey circulates among the people, wagging his tail at everyone and causing them to forget everything, even language, and in their mute interactions their faces register terror and loss (171–73). But it is this disturbing event that allows the people to become "artists" (174), this Messianic Age "'is the Age of Genius we've always dreamed of'" (175). Suddenly, the townspeople have no tradition, no longing for the past; "'these are people without memory, firsthand souls, who in order to continue to exist must re-create language and love and each coming moment anew'" (175).[22] Strangely enough, amnesia is the road toward redemption in this *Messiah* text (177).

But Momik protests. Tradition, he argues, is essential for cultural survival; this messianic age is cruel and too idealistic, and it offers nothing of the order people need to make sense of their lives (175). Bruno counters with what he sees as the supreme value of an age in which the very traces of "'decay and putrefaction, destruction and fear'" in thought would be incomprehensible, likened to our inability to comprehend the "'backward flow of time'" (179). This is the end of history—time out of time (recall the epigraph above from Schulz's own writings). But Momik presses on, bringing up the disturbing story of a certain Nazi "who shot a Jew to challenge his rival," only to be cut off by Bruno, who argues that "'now everyone will understand . . . that whoever kills another human being destroys a uniquely idiosyncratic work of art which can never be reconstructed . . . a whole mythology, an infinite Age of Genius'" (180). In this way, *The Messiah*, along with the novel in which it is embedded, posits the redemption of individuality and identity that were destroyed in the Holocaust. They also redeem Bruno Schulz's identity from its fate at the hands of a fallen world and a swollen language.

But to follow Bruno, to be completely swallowed up by *The Messiah*, would be too much for Momik. He, like the rest of us on this side of the messianic age, cannot discard all history, all memory, all narrative.[23] His encounter with Bruno does, however, offer a model for compromise based on the redemptive value in each person's individuality, the cultivation of personal and cultural identity, and the tireless search for lost stories and memories as challenges to the mass destruction of the Holocaust.[24] And, while Grossman's novel continues, following Momik's ongoing struggle with the redemption of Holocaust memory, the story of *The Messiah* ends here.

But in one last interchange, Momik asks Bruno if he happens to know the incomprehensible story his "grandfather" would always hum. Bruno responds:

"It's a fabulous story, oh yes. . . . Only there's . . . ha! The devil take it! I've forgotten!" And with a smile, as though remembering suddenly, he added, "But of course! That was the essence of his story . . . you forget it and you have to recall it afresh every time!"

"And could someone who never knew it, had never heard it in his life, remember it?"

"Just as a person remembers his name. His destiny. His heart. No . . . there is no one who does not know that story." (181)

This, finally, is the nature of Grossman's imagined messianism, the only redemption available outside the inaccessible world of Bruno's lost *Messiah*: that out of the constant interplay of memory and forgetting that accompanies the representation of the Nazi genocide there emerges a story that, in its eternal retelling, may somehow redeem. The telling of such stories becomes the only literary legacy to which we all can have access.[25]

Geoffrey Hartman has argued that the Holocaust "challenges the cred-
ibility of redemptive thinking." Certainly, as we have seen, the horrors of
the Nazi era threaten a variety of attempts to find meaning in history. But
what about the notion of *literary* redemption? Sidra Ezrahi, in the conclusion to her landmark book *By Words Alone*, asks: "Are we still searching for redemption in literature? Or do we rather condemn the writer who
finds it in the darkest regions?"[26] Literary redemption—the redemption
of, by, and in literature—arises in the engagement engendered in the act
of writing or reading the Holocaust. This may be a pale and paltry form of
memorial embodiment, but in its imagined narrative space of engagement, it nonetheless stitches together a missing swatch of the ruptured
fabric of history.

Moreover, as each author creatively fills in the gap left by Schulz's
death and the lost *Messiah*, each points to the larger gap in memory left
by the Nazi genocide and attempts, in some way, to fill that in. Yosef
Yerushalmi tells us, in a quotation that bears repeating, that "hardly any
Jew today is without some Jewish past. Total amnesia is still relatively
rare. The choice for Jews as for non-Jews is not whether or not to have
a past, but rather—what kind of past shall one have?"[27] In Ozick's and
Grossman's visions of the redemption of Bruno Schulz and his lost *Messiah*, we can read two metaphors for the challenge of remembering the
Holocaust and articulating a Jewish past in the context of forgetfulness.
Ozick, through Lars, a rootless writer with no tradition, describes a failed
appropriation of Schulz and of Holocaust memory. She is thus critical of
the notion of literary redemption and pessimistic about the redemptive
value of Jewish memory in overcoming historical rupture. In Ozick's
novel, forgetting is linked to inauthenticity and is a symbol of skepti-
cism regarding our abilities to connect with the past. Grossman, through
Momik and his engagement with Bruno, describes a more successful
program of literary appropriation and redemption despite its subversive nature,[28] and suggests, ultimately, the possibility for a new literary
commemoration of the Holocaust (indeed, the entire novel is about such
possibility). For Grossman, forgetting itself is redemptive, because it can
lead to the reclamation of authentic identity and human individuality.

So perhaps Bruno Schulz's *Messiah* was never completely lost, only, by
its very nature, forgotten. In the "Age of Genius," Schulz suggested the
possibility that, one day, "the Messiah advances to the edge of the horizon and looks down on the earth. And when He sees it, white, silent, surrounded by azure and contemplation, He may lose sight of the boundary
of clouds that arrange themselves into a passage, and, not knowing what

He is doing, He may descend upon earth. And in its reverie the earth won't even notice Him, who has descended upon its roads, and people will wake up from their afternoon nap remembering nothing. The whole event will be rubbed out, and everything will be as it has been for centuries, as it was before history began."[29] For both Ozick and Grossman, the possibility of redemption risks erasing history, tradition, and any engaged sense of the past. Both deal with a similar kind of imaginative accessibility with re-spect to the Shoah, essentially casting creative lines into the yawning abyss so as to hook onto the image of Bruno Schulz and make it trans-missible and representative. But in the end the nature of messianic am-nesia that results from their quests differs in each author's novel. Never-theless, joined by their attention to and fascination with Bruno, these two versions of forgetting balance each other: we would like to follow Gross-man in the redemptive power of forgetting, but we are restrained by Oz-ick, who reminds us that imagined pasts are also a form of forgetting, and a negative one at that.

THE ARROW OF MEMORY

The last novel I will consider in this short survey of literary models of for-getfulness is neither mystical nor mythical, neither totalizing nor decon-structive. I include Martin Amis's *Time's Arrow* because it fascinates me and because it represents perhaps the furthest shore of memory's narra-tion. Amis tells his remarkable story from the perspective of a doppel-gänger inside protagonist Tod Friendly's head: the narrator experiences everything Friendly does, only *backward*, innocently and understandably perplexed by the most basic of human activities. But once it becomes clear that Friendly is harboring a secret past as a Nazi doctor (a *future*, from the perspective of the narrator, to which he is heading inexorably), Amis's strange narrative style starts making some twisted, perverse sense, even as the reel of this film, so to speak, is playing in reverse.

The narrator's often graphic perspective is, after all, a metaphor not only for the upside-down world of Nazism but also for all human society after the Second World War. Repulsive though the descriptions may be, the gross image is powerful: all life, all meaning, everything, emanates from trash can and toilet bowl. In this world, doctors invariably hurt their patients, always making them look worse when they leave than when they came in. Babies are deftly returned to the womb, dressings and band-ages are consistently removed to expose ever worsening wounds; and speech is generally a string of lies or, worse, incomprehensible. And what

happens to memory in this world? Put in reverse, it is rendered as "the human talent for forgetting: forgetting, not as a process of erosion and waste,
but as an activity."[30] This image is suggestive: though the narrator is confused, we can clearly see that if the past suddenly becomes the future,
memory is literally impossible.

When the narrative finally makes its way to Auschwitz, even though
we have become quite used to its inverted perversity, we are nevertheless
startled by the "sense" it makes: "Not for its elegance did I come to love
the evening sky above the Vistula, hellish red with the gathering souls.
Creation is easy. Also ugly. *Hier ist kein warum.* Here there is no why.
Here there is no when, no how, no where. Our preternatural purpose? To
dream a race. To make a people from the weather. From thunder and from
lightning. With gas, with electricity, with shit, with fire."[31] Rendering the
Nazi hubris at playing God like nothing else I know of in fiction, the devastating image of this backward world nearly overwhelms the reader,
sucking us into the cult of death unbelievably transformed into a cult of
life, just as Nazis would see their own system. And when we approach the
central slogan and marker of Nazi ideology (and Auschwitz iconography),
perverse sense screams out once more: "The overwhelming majority of
the women, the children, and the elderly we process with gas and fire. The
men, of course, as is right, walk a different path to recovery. *Arbeit Macht
Frei* says the sign on the gate, with typically gruff and undesigning eloquence. The men work for their freedom."[32] The aesthetic effect here co-
opts the reader into the inverted and perverted logic of the Nazi worldview. We cannot understand. We understand.

Amis's reversal of time and memory not only inverts the presumed
hierarchy of remembering and forgetting; it renders that hierarchy meaningless. As a narrative construction telling the antithesis of Holocaust
memorialization (because it runs backward and because it is embodied
in a Nazi doctor), it posits forgetting as an activity running alongside remembrance. Not a model for engagement, to be sure, but a suggestion that
complicates such engagement by undercutting the teleology of narrative.
Indeed, all four of my literary examples subvert Holocaust memory's teleological narratives. All four question where memory may lead us. In taking up the theme of forgetting, even in its redemptive qualities, all prob-
lematize the memorial act. This attention to the arrow of memory
highlights an important point: it is not just what memory is *of* but also
what memory is *for* that is of concern here.

Considering memory's teleology is necessary in this age of memorial
obsession with the past, an age marked paradoxically with rampant

amnesia. Since we cannot remember everything (despite our techno-logical marvels), we must necessarily forget. Thus we must gain a clearer sense of where memory and forgetting are going. The most care-ful attention given yet to the teleology of memory and forgetting comes in Barbie Zelizer's thought-provoking book, *Remembering to Forget: Holocaust Memory through the Camera's Eye.* Most crucial to me are Zelizer's observations regarding "forgetting to remember" and "remem-bering to forget."

"Forgetting to remember," according to Zelizer, is a process that emerges when photographic images, stripped of many identifying de-tails, come to take on "a universal, symbolic quality with captions that [tell] of generalized phenomena rather than of specific events—*a* mass burial, *a* shower, *a* survivor." Though Zelizer acknowledges the power and success of such images, often substituting for words, she recognizes as well the forgetting that occurs when atrocities are so generalized. Es-pecially as these images were transposed into other media and made symbolic, memorialization "facilitated a partial undoing of memory, where bearing witness produced a failure to remember salient points about Nazi atrocity." As the culture of memory evolved, then, memory itself (and its embodiments in photography and other media) became the ground of remembrance activities, with forgetting of the original referent bound up in the very memorialization process. For Zelizer, the "period of amnesia" lasted from the end of the 1940s until the end of the 1970s, when "stories and pictures of the atrocities moved into the background of memory."[33]

Change occurred in the late seventies, as public attention was once more drawn to the practices of memory, including its content, in a cul-tural turn that is continuing. Photography here, as Zelizer argues, became the "figure rather than the ground of Holocaust representation. . . . Bear-ing witness [became] a case of remembering to remember." But even in the context of a renewed interest in the past, forgetting remained part of the picture. For example, Zelizer mentions the screening of Claude Lanz-mann's monumental *Shoah* in 1985 as a central event in bringing to pub-lic consciousness the issues surrounding memorialization of the Holo-caust. It "lent renewed cogency to the centrality of memory and to the role of survivors in shaping that memory, though the camps were featured through their absence rather than their presence: *Shoah* was acclaimed precisely because it did *not* feature visual depictions of the atrocities."[34] Thus, in this and other cases, remembering *in order to* remember already contained the seeds for remembering *in order to* forget.

"Remembering to forget" emerges, as Zelizer contends, because, despite our memory-obsessed culture, the desire to remember is also marked by a forgetting through the various media in which we attempt to frame and place our memories. "As memory proliferates in the public imagination, the act of bearing witness is growing thin, and our often empty claims to memory work render us capable of little more than remembering so that we may forget in its shadow."[35] The forgetting Zelizer ultimately focuses on is that of other atrocities: the forgetting of others' suffering owing to a too strong emphasis on remembering our own. This type of forgetting is exacerbated by our having become accustomed to atrocity images—the more we see, the less we understand in our era of technological, political, and moral "habituation."[36] And so, memory is increasingly dependent on the forgetting which comes with the conflation and erasure of the temporal and spatial reference points and distinctions that are both necessary for memory's construction and (potentially) damaging for its continued relevance. According to Zelizer, the "collapse of distance between then and now is precarious, overused, and paradoxical. It is precarious because Holocaust memory lingers like the ground floor of a partially demolished building. The past cannot be cleared away, but neither can it be salvaged. It is overused because it reconfigures not only what we see versus what we remember but also what we remember of the events of yore versus what we need to see of the events of now. And it is paradoxical because our capacity for action may lie in an altered linkage with the Holocaust: we may need to remember it less so as to remember contemporary atrocities more."[37] The arrow of memory, then, points not only to the past, present, and future of Jewish memory but also to the events and memories of an entire age of genocide which cannot be forgotten. If Holocaust memory is to continue to engender commitment in the twenty-first century, it must encourage commitment to other memories as well.

ABSENT MEMORIES

In fact, there is a kind of memory-work which embodies the "other" structure of forgetting and the forgotten through a total renegotiation of the memorial process. Significantly, the bulk of this activity has taken place in Germany. Although Germany and its Holocaust monuments have hardly figured in this study, the critical reflections on the varieties of German critiques of the monument/memorial to the Holocaust raise important issues relevant to these conclusions and the issue of forgetting.

This engagement here is also a personal one: in mining James Young's contributions to this discussion for material related to memory and forgetting, I return to the work that originally inspired me to embark on this project. I remember reading Young's *Critical Inquiry* article "The Counter-Monument: Memory against Itself in Germany Today" when it first appeared and having that rare moment of scholarly epiphany regarding his methodology and observations. It is perhaps ironic that I return to this seminal text in the context of my conclusions relating to forgetfulness.

Over the years, an important portion of Young's research has dealt with what he has variously described as the "counter-monument," the "negative-form monument," the "vanishing monument," or simply the "end of the monument."[38] In each case of creativity Young has considered, forgetting has figured powerfully and centrally as an integral component of the memorial process. The most salient example to me is Jochen Gerz and Esther Shalev-Gerz's "disappearing" *Harburg Monument against War and Fascism and for Peace* (1986–93). This forty-foot-high hollow aluminum, lead-plated pillar offered, since its unveiling, a surface on which visitors could inscribe their own record of engagement with the monument. As each five-foot section of the pillar was covered with graffiti, the "disappearing" monument was lowered into the ground. After the last lowering on November 10, 1993, nothing above ground was left of the memorial save for the memories (and recorded images) of those who visited it. "By inviting viewers to commemorate themselves, the countermonument reminds them that to some extent all any monument can do is provide a trace of its makers, not of memory itself."[39] Inverting the monument in this way, the Gerzes also play with the structure of memory as gradually receding, reminding us, as it were, that forgetting is part of that structure and incorporating that aspect of memory into their creation.

In general, the strategies of which the Harburg countermonument is but one example reflect back on the social aspects of memory. Reading into his analyses the ongoing German debates about memory and Germany's relationship to its Nazi past, Young has supplemented the consideration of artistic attempts to make memory matter (literally and figuratively) with an assessment of the public self-consciousness about the matter of memory. The artists he considers consistently work against the forgetting that accompanies traditional monuments: "They contemptuously reject the traditional forms and reasons for public memorial art, those spaces that either console viewers or redeem such tragic events, or indulge in a facile kind of *Wiedergutmachung* or purport to mend the memory of a murdered people. Instead of searing memory into public consciousness, they fear, conventional memorials seal memory off from awareness altogether. For these artists such an evasion would be the ultimate abuse of art, whose primary function, to their mind, is to jar viewers from complacency and to challenge and denaturalize the viewers' assumptions."[40] Thus, they substitute one kind of forgetting—the countermonument—for another—the monument as an amnesiac construction—to remind visitors of the problematics of memorials as much as their less self-consciously configured aims. In this way countermonuments also highlight the contingency and changeability of memory.[41] Germany's countermonuments present, therefore, a model of forgetting integrated into the very fabric of memorialization. The negative spaces of the German countermonuments remind us, most of all, of the negative spaces in memory itself: the murdered, the traumatized, the lost, the absent victims (the "true witnesses," as Primo Levi called them) in whose name memory is often constructed but of whom it is rarely truly cognizant in the flurry of remembrance activities. Forgetfulness, as a natural and inevitable part of life and memory, is thus incorporated into the memory-work of several contemporary artists in Germany, bringing into the light the ongoing struggle to respect both memory and forgetting in the present-day memorial landscape.

REMEMBER FORGETTING

Young's work highlights the extent to which forgetting must be integrated into the work of memory, especially memory as it is configured teleologically. This remembering of forgetting occurs as soon as we realize how much memory is not actually opposed to forgetting but constituted by it. Indeed, Andreas Huyssen asks rhetorically, "Does it even make sense to oppose memory with forgetting, as we so often do, with forgetting at best being acknowledged as the inevitable flaw and deficiency of memory itself? Paradoxically, is it not the case that each and every memory inevitably depends both on distance and forgetting, the very things that undermine its desired stability and reliability and are at the same time essential to the vitality of memory itself?"[42] Memory and forgetting are forever joined in a dialectical duet that is itself productive of the synthesized meaning of remembrance. This process is one of dual recovery and relinquishing, as suggested by Yael Zerubavel's studies: "While some aspects of the past are uncovered or shift from the margins to the center of our historical consciousness, other aspects of the past are marginalized or fade into oblivion. Any remembrance thus entails its own forgetfulness, as the two are interwoven in the process of producing . . . commemorative narratives. This interplay and constant tension between these two forces contribute to their dynamic character and explain why memory has not vanished in the modern era despite the rise of history."[43]

In the analyses of memory's construction in this book, I have not yet directly discussed this kind of dialectical memorialization. It is there nonetheless in every medium of memory I have considered. For what are Holocaust icons, after all, if not symbols embodied and infused with both the memory and the forgetfulness to which they point? For a Holocaust-era boxcar to function effectively in a memorial context, it must both encompass and resist identification with the victims who once (may have) occupied its inner space. As much as we visitors to this memory must make the connections between the victims' fates and the evidence before us in the railway car (thus remembering those who suffered), we must also recognize the difference between their stories and ours—there and here (or wherever we come to find the icon in its new home), then and now, history and memory—thus "forgetting" momentarily the experiences of the victims. So too is forgetting integral to Spiegelman's and Prager's imaginative remembering of Holocaust narratives through the very revision of the symbolic language of Nazism: some of what they memorialize must necessarily be suspended so that readers may pay attention to the needs of the present and the memorial processes in which they and their protagonists are engaged.

In Holocaust videotestimonies, forgetting is, in many ways, part of the structure of the recollection and narration of trauma. For it is only in finding some distance from the events of World War II that those who give testimony may find the ability to tell those events in memory. In that telling, they of course point to those not there, those who did not survive, those who are both remembered *and* forgotten by the survivors who necessarily tell their own tales, not theirs. Within the frame of testimony there is always a forgetting: forgetting what was then in favor of what is now, or forgetting the present in favor of the past. Within the listener-voyeur's frame of reference, in order to be engaged, there is a forgetting of self in favor of the remembrance of the "other" on the opposite side of the television screen. And for the institutions devoted to videotestimonies, there can often be the forgetting of the individual story in favor of that of the collective.

More complex forms of forgetting accompany increased embodiment. Museums of Holocaust memory continually struggle against forgetfulness simply by their existence, and yet within their walls is housed the forgetfulness that comes with the displacement and replacement of artifacts. What is more, when those artifacts are themselves displaced (as at the MOT), forgetting runs the risk of spinning away from its dialectical other in remembrance in the media play of spectacle and simulation. Finally, when memory tours of the landscape of death in Poland negotiate their participants' relationship to the past, they negotiate as well the forgetting of the ground of memory, both then and now, in favor of a remembrance in and of the future. Forget Holocaust, remember redemption; forget Poland, remember Israel. These could be the slogans for the March of the Living.

MEMORY'S PROPRIETY

This interplay, finally, brings me to the dangers of forgetting and remembering. It bears little repeating or analysis that wholesale forgetting of the Holocaust is dangerous and destructive. We all know George Santayana's famous "Those who forget the past are doomed to repeat it." But what of those who remember too well? What damage can they cause? Are there dangers that accompany a surplus of memory? We can well imagine the survivor forever traumatized by memories that will not go away, the atrocity album whose photographs disturb too fiercely, the museum of intolerance. But what of the impact on the inheritors of memory or on those pilgrims to the past? What of those who adopt and appropriate memory, vicarious rememberers in their imagined communities of suffering? Alain Finkielkraut has dissected these living embodiments of unlived lives:

They are not religious, at least most of them; in vain they cherish Jewish culture, possessing only its sorry relics. They have not performed their apprenticeship to Judaism under the gaze of the Other. Neither ethnic nor denominational definition nor the Sartrian scheme could suit them. They are unwavering Jews, but armchair Jews, since, after the Catastrophe, Judaism cannot offer them any content but suffering, and they themselves do not suffer. In order to deny this contradiction, they have chosen to pass their time in a novelistic space full of sound and fury that offers them the best role. Like fanatics of the printed word who flee, by reading, the provincial boredom in which they languish, like spectators who project their desires, their frustrations into a panting plot they will never live—spellbound, these young people live in borrowed identities. They have taken up residence in fiction. The Judaism they invoke enraptures and transports them magically to a setting in which they are exalted and sanctified. For these habitués of unreality, more numerous than one might suppose, I propose the name "imaginary Jews."[44]

Could it be that Holocaust memory culture too easily encourages this kind of forgetfulness? How is that culture implicated in the fabrication of imaginary Jews? Can Holocaust memory be a pollutant, a poison? Zygmunt Bauman thinks so:

> We often say that violence breeds more violence; we remind ourselves much too rarely, though, that victimization breeds more victimization. Victims are not guaranteed to be morally superior to their victimizers, and seldom emerge from the victimization morally ennobled. Martyrdom—whether lived in a real or a virtual reality—is not a warrant for saintliness.
>
> Memory of suffering does not assure life-long dedication to the fight against inhumanity, cruelty, and the infliction of pain as such, wherever they happen and whoever are the sufferers. At least an equally probable outcome of martyrdom is the tendency to draw an opposite lesson: that humankind is divided into the victims and the victimizers, and so if you are (or expect to be) a victim, your task is to reverse the tables ("the stronger lives"). It is this lesson that the specter of the Holocaust whispers into many ears. And for this reason we cannot be sure whether the lasting legacy of the Holocaust was not the very opposite of what many had hoped and some anticipated: the moral reawakening or ethical purification of the world as a whole or any of its sections.[45]

I cannot now conclude the discussion of the legacy of victimization, especially as it still has not played itself out. But I can point out that the adoption of the memory of the offense by those who follow in its wake and are obsessed with its continuation does not attend to the forgetting of the differences between then and now, there and here (or anywhere), that is itself part and parcel of these vicarious memorialists' quest.

Perhaps what is needed is, finally, a provisional letting go of remembrance. Not to forget entirely, or even partially, what happened. But to forget, now, that attachment to what many feel is still happening. As Peter Novick has argued, the Holocaust, "like many other national myths" in American Jewish consciousness, has come "to define an enduring, perhaps permanent, Jewish condition." Is this what we wish the legacy of Holocaust memory to be? Novick cites Yehuda Elkana as providing something of a response: "For our part, we must *forget!* Today I see no more important political and educational task for the leaders of this nation [Israel] than to take their stand on the side of life, to dedicate themselves to creating our future, and not to be preoccupied from morning to night, with symbols, ceremonies, and lessons of the Holocaust. They must uproot the domination of that historical 'remember!' over our lives."[46] But truly to uproot this deep-seated construction, we must let go of one of the most central "memories" established in Holocaust memorial culture and one of the most difficult to relinquish: the desire for lessons. The Holocaust, especially as Novick has argued, does not by itself teach anything, does not, at the extreme, *mean* anything. Once we let go of this desire for lessons, we can remember simply that it happened. Perhaps this is the only, and most significant, lesson to be learned and meaning to be gleaned. Novick argues, "If there are lessons to be extracted from encountering the past, that encounter has to be with the past in all its messiness; they're not likely to come from an encounter with a past that's been shaped and shaded so that inspiring lessons will emerge."[47]

Does this mean the Holocaust is ultimately meaningless? No. But it does mean we may wish to let go of our desire for meaning, to let go of our desire for memory unconnected with forgetting. I have always wondered what the following biblical text means: "Remember what Amalek did to you. . . . Do not forget."[48] Why the rewording, the extra reminder? Perhaps it is this: "remember without forgetting," rather than "remember with forgetting." This commandment is difficult to keep. Might we endorse paradox instead? We cannot ask survivors to forget, but we can remember forgetting. We cannot ourselves remember, so we must forget remembering. The result sustains our continued engagement with the mediations and embodiments of the Holocaust and its memory in the present and into the future. We cannot remember. We remember. We cannot forget. We forget.

Notes

ONE. REMEMBERING MEMORY

1. See, in this regard, Boym's monumental *Future of Nostalgia*, and Spitzer, "Back through the Future."

2. Kugelmass, "Jewish Icons," 49.

3. Funkenstein, "Collective Memory and Historical Consciousness," 6.

4. See Casey, *Remembering*, 273.

5. Peter Novick notes a "grim appropriateness in adopting Halbwachs's approach to the study of Holocaust memory. When, in occupied France, he protested the arrest of his Jewish father-in-law, Halbwachs was sent to Buchenwald, where he died." *The Holocaust in American Life*, 3.

6. Halbwachs, *Les cadres sociaux de la mémoire*. See also *La topographie légendaire des évangiles en terre sainte*. Excepts from both texts are available in English translation as Halbwachs, *On Collective Memory*. See also Halbwachs, *Collective Memory*, originally published as *La mémoire collective*.

7. Halbwachs, *On Collective Memory*, 38, 40, 45.

8. Ibid., 52–53. This view suggests that discourse is mediative, which is also the view of Hayden White. See "Introduction: Tropology, Discourse, and the Modes of Human Consciousness," in *Tropics of Discourse*, 1–25.

9. Halbwachs, *On Collective Memory*, 50.

10. Ibid., 88.

11. Ibid., 98, 119.

12. Ibid., 167–89. See also Halbwachs, *Collective Memory*.

13. Halbwachs, *On Collective Memory*, 183, 188–89.

14. Halbwachs, *La topographie légendaire des évangiles en terre sainte*. The conclusion to his work is available in translation as the second part of *On Collective Memory*, 193–235.

15. Halbwachs, *On Collective Memory*, 215, 219.

16. Ibid., 229, 234–35.

17. Fentress and Wickham, *Social Memory*, ix.

18. Funkenstein, "Collective Memory and Historical Consciousness," 7.

19. Ibid., 11, 12, 18, 19.

20. Another important author concerned with the relationship between memory and history is Yael Zerubavel, who in some sense turns Funkenstein around and analyzes how memory-work relies at least in part on historical constructions of the past. Zerubavel brings particular attention to the dynamics of collective memory in discussing commemorations and their evolution in the Israeli national case. In each example she focuses on the formation of what she calls the "master commemorative narrative," the "basic 'story line' that is culturally constructed and provides the group members with a general notion of their shared past" (6), while recognizing its interaction with counternarratives of nationhood and thus

the interplay between memory and forgetting. See Zerubavel, *Recovered Roots*. See also my review essay dealing with Zerubavel's book, "Memory Matters." For an argument against the very concept of collective memory, see Gedi and Elam, "Collective Memory—What Is It?"

21. Novick, *Holocaust in American Life*, 4; Novick's emphasis.

22. Ibid., 267–68.

23. Nora, "Between Memory and History," 7.

24. I borrow the notion of entanglement from Marita Sturken: "I would posit cultural memory and history as *entangled* rather than oppositional. Indeed, there is so much traffic across the borders of cultural memory and history that in many cases it may be futile to maintain a distinction between them. Yet there are times when those distinctions are important in understanding political intent, when memories are asserted specifically outside of or in response to historical narratives." See *Tangled Memories*, 5.

25. Irwin-Zarecka, *Frames of Remembrance*, 4, 13.

26. Sturken, *Tangled Memories*, 2–3.

27. Gillis, "Memory and Identity," 3.

28. Zerubavel, *Recovered Roots*, 5.

29. Irwin-Zarecka, *Frames of Remembrance*, 18.

30. Sturken, *Tangled Memories*, 7.

31. Lipsitz, *Time Passages*, 5.

32. Halbwachs's legacy extends far beyond the works cited above. A sampling of other important explicit or implicit reactions to his work could include Linenthal, *Sacred Ground*; Boyarin, *Polish Jews in Paris*; Glassie, *Passing the Time in Ballymenone*; Bal, Crewe, and Spitzer, *Acts of Memory*; and Kammen, *Mystic Chords of Memory*.

33. Young, *Texture of Memory*, xi.

34. Young, *At Memory's Edge*, 3–4.

35. Hirsch, *Family Frames*, 22.

36. Michelle Friedman has developed a notion of "rememory" drawn from Toni Morrison's introduction of the neologism in *Beloved*. Friedman argues that "rememory" bears within it the ghostly presence of past events continuing in the present, the presence of a repetition that, like "postmemory" and "vicarious memory," highlights the simultaneous joining of past and present in the memory construct and, thus, the importance of mediation. See Friedman, "Reckoning with Ghosts," especially the chapter titled "Reckoning with Ghosts: Remembering the Holocaust in America."

37. Yerushalmi, *Zakhor*, 9.

38. Deut. 25:17–19, from *JPS Hebrew-English Tanakh*, 2d ed. (Philadelphia: Jewish Publication Society, 1999). David Roskies recounts how, when visiting a friend in Israel, he brought her a fountain pen as a gift; she tested it (as she remembered her father doing) by writing "Amalek" and crossing it out. Here, memory "is an aggressive act." See Roskies, *Against the Apocalypse*, 10.

39. See Yerushalmi, *Zakhor*, 14–15.

40. Ibid., 110. Yabneh was also, interestingly enough, a fortress of symbolic death, as Bernard Lewis reminds us; legend holds that Rabbi Yohanan ben Zakkai managed to escape the besieged city disguised as a corpse, carried out in a coffin.

"Some modern critics," he writes, "have found a bitter appropriateness in Rabbi Yohanan's survival disguised as a corpse. Others have reminded the Jews that it is from that corpse and his bearers that, figuratively speaking, they are all descended." See Lewis, *History*, 21.

41. Yerushalmi, *Zakhor*, 18.

42. Roskies, *Against the Apocalypse*, 25. The critic George Steiner understands this transformation of the textual experience of memorialization as a literal calling: "To experience the Torah and Talmud as *mikra* [convocation], to apprehend these texts in cognitive and emotional plentitude, is to hear and accept a summons. It is to gather oneself and the (inseparable) community in a place of calling. This summons to responsible response, to answerability in the most rigorous and intellectual and ethical sense, is simultaneously private and public, individual and collective. The concepts and association that attach to *mikra* make of the reading of the canon and its commentaries the literal-spiritual locus of self-recognition and of communal identification for the Jew." See Steiner, "Our Homeland, the Text," 4. Steiner's argument in this article is highly controversial, as he opposes Jewish rootedness in the text to the Jewish spatial homeland so completely that, by the end of his essay, he criticizes the substitution of the Zionist State of Israel for that age-old textual home. Needless to say, though I find Steiner's musings useful and provocative, such a total resistance to the spatial component of Judaism makes it difficult to posit the existence of a collective memory that depends on both time and space. For responses to Steiner's essay, see Marmur, "Struggle between Text and Land in Contemporary Jewry," and Wyschogrod, "The Mind of a Critical Moralist—Steiner as a Jew."

43. Neusner, "Map without Territory," 150, 152.

44. See Roskies, *Against the Apocalypse*, 35–36.

45. Roskies writes: "After the exile, the book that had been regarded as the inviolable source of the law and as the chronicle of the people's beginnings took on a radically new dimension, becoming the blueprint for its future as well. This placed the burden of historical recapitulation and interpretation squarely on the shoulders of man. Of course, only God could ever be expected to know and remember everything in its finest detail, but since the God of History was not imprisoned in history, it was sometimes left to man to remind Him, as it were, of His promise that each exile would be followed by a new exodus to freedom. The resort to history had to be the resort to human parallel. The 'reminding of God' was the reassertion of human continuity: *we* remember; we've stored away the promises all the way back to Abraham and Adam." See ibid., 23.

46. Yerushalmi, *Zakhor*, 40.

47. Ibid., 44. See also, on the issue of actualization and reactualization, Childs, *Memory and Tradition in Israel*.

48. Yerushalmi, *Zakhor*, 86, 94.

49. Ibid., 99.

50. Roskies, *Jewish Search*, 3, 9. Other important responses to Yerushalmi's study include Shavit, "Review of *Zakhor*"; Morgan, "Overcoming the Remoteness of the Past"; Myers, "Remembering *Zakhor*"; and Funkenstein, "Response from Amos Funkenstein."

51. Roskies, *Against the Apocalypse*, 305.

52. Roskies, *Jewish Search*, 14.

53. Ibid., 15.

54. Webber, *Future of Auschwitz*, 20.

55. Novick, *Holocaust in American Life*, 226.

56. See, for example, Ezrahi, *By Words Alone;* Amishai-Maisels, *Depiction and Interpretation;* Young, *At Memory's Edge;* Zelizer, *Remembering to Forget;* Doneson, *Holocaust in American Film;* and Shandler, *While America Watches*, to name but a few studies.

57. Sturken, *Tangled Memories*, 9.

58. Ibid., 10. Sturken cites Michel Foucault's important "Technologies of the Self," in *Technologies of the Self*, ed. Luther Martin, Huck Gutman, and Patrick Hutton (Amherst: University of Massachusetts Press, 1988), as a source for her discussion.

59. Huyssen, *Twilight Memories*, 259. See also Friedman, "Labor of Remembrance," which is a riff on Huyssen's suggestion.

60. Huyssen writes, "Such mimetic approximation can only be achieved if we sustain the tension between the numbing totality of the Holocaust and the stories of the individual victims, families, and communities. Exclusive focus on the first may lead to the numbing abstraction of statistics and the repression of what these statistics mean; exclusive focus on the second may provide facile cathartic empathy and forget the frightening conclusion that the Holocaust as a historical event resulted, as Adi Ophir put it, from an exceptional combination of normal processes" (*Twilight Memories*, 259).

TWO. INSCRIBING MEMORY

1. Shandler, *While America Watches*, xii.

2. Ibid., 212.

3. Cole, *Selling the Holocaust*, 18.

4. Yehuda Bauer, "The Significance of the Final Solution," in *The Final Solution: Origins and Implementation*, ed. David Cesarani (London: Routledge, 1994), 306, cited in ibid., 18.

5. Alvin Rosenfeld, "Popularization and Memory: The Case of Anne Frank," in *Lessons and Legacies: The Meaning of the Holocaust in a Changing World*, ed. Peter Hayes (Evanston: Northwestern University Press, 1991), 245, cited in Cole, *Selling the Holocaust*, 25.

6. Cole, *Selling the Holocaust*, 46.

7. Cole, 80, 177.

8. Zelizer, *Remembering to Forget*, 1, 8.

9. Zelizer, 147, 160, 204, 225. It is possible, however, to see such photos from the Holocaust not as "crowding out" our concern for contemporary atrocities but rather enhancing that concern and mobilizing memory. See, in this regard, Linenthal, *Preserving Memory*, 260–72.

10. Shandler, *While America Watches*, 5, 17, 145, 190.

11. Ibid., 203. Novick observes: "Elie Wiesel, of course, became the emblematic survivor. His gaunt face, with its anguished expressions, seemed to freeze time—to be staring out from a 1945 photograph of the liberation of the camps. Nu-

merous Jewish critics—occasionally in print, more often in private—have been acerbic about what they see as Wiesel's carefully cultivated persona as symbol of suffering, as Christ figure. Such criticism ignores the extent to which this stance is thoroughly authentic, reflects Wiesel's immersion, even before his Holocaust experiences, in the depths of Jewish mysticism and asceticism" (*Holocaust in American Life*, 273–74). Indeed, Wiesel is known to some for "staring out" from just such a photograph; he identified himself as one of the prisoners in the famous shot of survivors in the Buchenwald barracks, a photo that has had an interesting afterlife (see Zelizer, *Remembering to Forget*, 103, 183–88, esp. 186).

12. Shandler, *While America Watches*, 253.

13. Ibid., 197.

14. Zelizer, *Remembering to Forget*, 220. For a further discussion and contextualization of Moreira's cartoon, see Amishai-Maisels's monumental overview *Depiction and Interpretation*: the boy, "along with women wearing similar headgear, is being deported by a monstrous Jewish soldier whose helmet now sports a Jewish star. Moreira not only turns the Israelis into Nazis, but adopts the Holocaust itself as a symbol of the plight of the Palestinians, suggesting that they are being shipped to an Israeli version of Auschwitz" (349).

15. Hirsch, "Projected Memory," 10.

16. Shandler, *While America Watches*, 198, 199.

17. For the seminal discussion of this issue, see Friedländer, *Reflections of Nazism*.

18. Richard Lauterbach, "Murder, Inc." *Time*, September 11, 1944, 36, cited in Zelizer, *Remembering to Forget*, 55.

19. Cole, *Selling the Holocaust*, 61–62. Cole cites M. Pearlman, *The Capture and Trial of Adolf Eichmann* (London: Weidenfeld and Nicolson, 1963), 304, as evidence for the Eichmann trial testimony.

20. Marita Sturken notes how the icon of the shoe has been transferred into another context: "In September 1994, gun-control advocates brought 40,000 shoes to symbolize those who had been killed by guns to line the reflecting pool on the mall in a 'Silent March.' The shoes, many of which were accompanied by photos and notes, were there to provide physical evidence of the immense toll of gun-related violence. . . . The shoes included both those of people who had been killed by guns and those who wanted to offer support. After the display, the shoes were donated to charity. According to [J. Michael] Kennedy [in his *L. A. Times* article], the idea of the shoes was borrowed from the Holocaust Museum, with its display of shoes from the Maidanek concentration camp" (*Tangled Memories*, 263 n. 19).

21. Halbertal and Margalit, *Idolatry*, 3.

22. See Young, *At Memory's Edge*, 2.

23. For more information on the USHMM's railway car, see Linenthal, *Preserving Memory*, 158–59.

24. See Walter Loebenberg's comments in the videotape, *The Story of the Boxcar*.

25. See <http://www.flholocaustmuseum.org/fhmcontent.cfm?page_name= store>.

26. For another discussion of these uses of Holocaust-era boxcars, see Cole, *Selling the Holocaust*, 160–61, 164–65.

27. See <http://www.yad-vashem.org.il/visiting/sites/deportees.html>.

28. See <http://cac.mcgill.ca/safdie/Biography/biopage.asp>.

29. Yad Vashem, on Jerusalem's *Har ha-Zikkaron* (literally the Mountain of Memory), sits on the backside of *Har Herzl* (Mount Herzl), named for the founder of the modern Zionist movement and known as the burial site for Zionism's and Israel's most notable dead, including Hannah Senesh and Yitzhak Rabin.

30. <http://cac.mcgill.ca/safdie/SearchEngines/showrecord.asp?GuideNo=110>.

31. Pagis, "Written in Pencil in the Sealed Railway Car," in *Selected Poetry,* 29, reprinted by permission of the publisher. For the Hebrew see "Katuv be-'iparon ba-karon he-hatum," from *Gilgul,* in *Kol Hashirim,* 135. I have substituted the more literal "elder son" for Stephen Mitchell's "other son" in the translation.

32. Ezrahi, "Dan Pagis—Out of Line, 343–45; Ezrahi, *Booking Passage,* 161.

33. Ezrahi, *Booking Passage,* 161; Ezrahi's emphasis.

34. It is also possible to read the poem in a circular, cyclical fashion: "tell him that i / [am] here in this carload." This circular reading works a bit better in the original Hebrew: "tagidu lo she-ani / caan bamishloach ha-zeh." This circular reading is one encouraged by educators (see ibid., 162 n. 12).

35. The railway car was not always symbolic of Jewish suffering. Ezrahi writes, in a consideration of Sholem Aleichem's "Railroad Stories," "Trains shuttled Jews back and forth in the Pale of Settlement and provided the locus for their stories and jokes for several decades before becoming the metonymy of their collective doom." See *Booking Passage,* 109.

36. Young, *Texture of Memory,* 14.

37. Mitchell, *Iconology,* 10–11.

38. See Young, *Texture of Memory,* 127–28.

39. Young, *Texture of Memory,* 132.

40. Ryback, "Evidence of Evil," 68.

41. For an extended discussion of the USHMM's debates concerning the display of hair, see Linenthal, *Preserving Memory,* 210–16. Responding to a draft of this chapter, Michael Berenbaum suggested that the issue of the display of women's hair is not ethically complex but "museologically complex—a powerful artifact, which some feared would be so overpowering that it would transform the Museum into a chamber of horrors. But the museological question was whether we could use its power effectively or [whether] it would be so overpowering that it would obscure the issue. The entire issue masked the question of whether vulnerability should be confronted directly in the Museum or elliptically" (personal email communication, April 11, 2002).

42. Van Alphen, *Caught by History,* 10.

43. Ibid., 11.

44. The original experience of the Holocaust is left only to those who were there. And for them, curiously, the experience can be original more than once: because of the structure of traumatic memory, survivors who give testimony of their experiences, for example, are often creating knowledge that they do not yet possess. This knowledge emerges only in the telling of their story to the one listening to it, who authorizes it and mediates its birth. See Dori Laub, "Bearing Witness, or the Vicissitudes of Listening."

45. On the issue of discursive frameworks and religiosity in the post-Holocaust environment, see also Braiterman, *(God) after Auschwitz*, esp. his conclusion, "Discourse, Sign, Diptych: Remarks on Jewish Thought after Auschwitz," 161–78.

46. Halbertal and Margalit, *Idolatry*, 2. See also Kochan, *Beyond the Graven Image*.

47. Bland, *Artless Jew*, 8.

48. Spiegelman, *Maus: A Survivor's Tale*, and *Maus II: A Survivor's Tale*. Hereafter cited as *Maus* and *Maus II*, respectively.

49. On the issue of recycled images from Holocaust photographs, Hirsch writes, "Spiegelman's use of these repeated images reminds us how much we may need and rely on canonization and repetition in our postmemorial discourse. In his text they have the function of memory itself. His graphic versions recall the photographs we have all seen, reinforcing a common canon of shared images that will extend into the next generations. In participating in the repetition, Spiegelman reminds us that memory also depends on forgetting, that reduction and canonization, and also figuration, are indeed crucial to the work of postmemory. And in translating the photographs into a new graphic idiom he unhinges them from the effects of traumatic repetition, without entirely disabling the functions of sense memory they contain." See Hirsch, "Surviving Images," 238. Some of the material in the following discussion of *Maus* originated in a paper I wrote with Gary Laderman and Richard D. Hecht, "Art Spiegelman's *Maus* and the Crisis of Representing the Holocaust." The paper was first presented at the University of California, Santa Barbara Religious Studies Departmental Colloquium Series "On the Frontiers," November 10, 1993, and subsequently delivered at the American Academy of Religion meeting that same year. I thank Professors Laderman and Hecht for allowing me to build on our initial collective discussions here.

50. Graham-Dixon, "Deliverance for Art's Sake"; Rothberg, *Traumatic Realism*, 203.

51. The inescapability of destruction is echoed in the manner in which Spiegelman depicts Vladek and Anja walking the path of the swastika, meant to symbolize visually their inevitable fate. See *Maus*, 125.

52. See Young, *At Memory's Edge*, 33.

53. See ibid., 32, and Gopnik, "Comics and Catastrophe," 33. For Young, this technique serves "not to show humans and to show them at the same time," while for Gopnik it highlights the difference between classically sacred imagery and the contemporary representation of its opposite.

54. See also Kochan, *Beyond the Graven Image*, 126–27.

55. Gopnik, "Comics and Catastrophe," 31.

56. Young, *At Memory's Edge*, 33. See also Andreas Huyssen, "Of Mice and Mimesis: Reading Spiegelman with Adorno," in Zelizer, *Visual Culture and the Holocaust*, where Huyssen compares *Maus* with the Nazi propaganda film *The Eternal Jew*, and its recurring images of vermin, to show how it "revers[es] its implications while simultaneously keep[ing] us aware of the humiliation and degradation of that imagery's original intention" (34).

57. Quoted in Cantor, "Kat and Maus," 39; *Maus*, 147, 136.

58. *Maus*, 136; Rothberg, *Traumatic Realism*, 210.

59. *Maus II*, 41. Rothberg notes that this one frame "has attracted the attention of nearly all commentators" (*Traumatic Realism*, 216).

60. *Maus II*, 79.

61. I borrow the phrase "distanced realism" from Saul Friedländer, who writes, "Reality is there, in its starkness, but perceived through a filter: that of memory (distance in time), that of spatial displacement, that of some sort of narrative margin which leaves the unsayable unsaid." See his introduction to *Probing the Limits of Representation*, 17.

62. Art Spiegelman, "Maus and Man," *Village Voice*, June 6, 1989, 22.

63. David Firestone, "A 'Maus' Tour in Queens," *New York Newsday*, pt. 2, November 11, 1987, 13.

64. Gopnik, "Comics and Catastrophe," 32–33.

65. Weinberg and Elieli, *The Holocaust Museum in Washington*, 122.

66. Levi, *Survival in Auschwitz*, 23.

67. Prager, *Eve's Tattoo*, 24. All further page references will be given parenthetically in the text.

68. This act reminds me of the climax of David Roskies's Holocaust midrash *Nightwords*, which is read, incidentally, in public performance annually as part of the University of California, Santa Barbara, Yom ha-Shoah veha-Gevurah (literally, the Day of Holocaust and Heroism) commemorations. In Roskies's text the participants pass a ballpoint pen around the reading circle, writing consecutive numbers on neighbors' forearms while simultaneously intoning the digits solemnly. Of course, those tattoos wash off.

69. In a fascinating and revealing essay, "The Tattooed Jew," art historian Dora Apel examines the contemporary practice of tattooing among Jews, despite its anti-Halachic status. She also points out other cases similar to the one fictionalized in Prager's novel. For example, she cites the decision by the artist "Chinchilla" to adopt the number of an infant girl born and killed at Birkenau: "In an act of personal commemoration for an unknown child, Chinchilla had the same number tattooed on her own arm on what would have been the baby's fifty-first birthday" (303). She focuses mostly on photographer Marina Vainshtein's own efforts to express Jewish identity through her "permanent bodyart. By the age of 23 Vainshtein had tattoos of graphic Holocaust imagery over most of her body" (306). For Apel, these tattoos are the "'internal scars' of a people made visible on the body of one of its young. To demonstrate her belief that the postwar generations must carry on the memory of the Holocaust, she places her own body between the past and future as a barrier to forgetting" (308).

70. Think, for example, of our paradigm for the woman's experience of the Holocaust, our only female icon: Anne Frank. Yet we do not think of Frank as a woman, with women's concerns and thoughts, but rather as a young girl, as the title of the popular version of her "diary" suggests. Indeed, the popular rendition of her journal had most of the parts referring to her sexual awareness and womanhood excised, and it is only in the critical edition of the diary that the entire text is restored. Compare *Anne Frank: The Diary of a Young Girl* with *The Diary of Anne Frank: The Critical Edition*. For a discussion of Anne Frank as cultural icon, see Cole, *Selling the Holocaust*.

71. The second tale, about "Eva Hoffler," a loyal Protestant supporter of

Hitler's policies, is interesting in terms of the question of racial identity. This Eva's fate turns when it is discovered she is of "Jewish ancestry"—orphaned of Jewish parents but raised all her life as a Lutheran—but up to her death at Auschwitz she could not comprehend her own "Jewish blood" (43–47).

72. See, in this regard, Koonz, *Mothers in the Fatherland*, 4. Note that such symbolic appropriation is also part of the tattoo culture, well represented in Prager's novel by this description of one of Big Dan's arms, which "featured Nazi Germany. On his bicep, the full insignia of the elite Totenkopf, or Death's-Head squadron of the SS, was perfectly inked with its lightning bolts and skull, and then along the forearm, swastikas and iron crosses, ending on top of his hand with ACHTUNG around which coiled a naked blond with red lips and a rolled hairdo from the 1940s" (6–7). On the eroticization of the Jewish woman victim, see also Horowitz, "Mengele, the Gynecologist."

73. According to Jane Flax, this latter view argues that "if [the woman] thinks she enjoys genital heterosexuality, she is only motivated by and is displaying a profoundly disturbed false consciousness." Though Eve may indeed display such a disturbed false consciousness on a different level, in her sexuality she is giving expression to the "autonomous female, internally motivated sexuality" repressed in the radical feminist discourses about which Flax writes. See Flax, "Re-Membering the Selves," 101.

74. See Levi, "The Memory of Offense."

75. Koonz argues: "Memoirs of male survivors suggest that they underwent a certain 'feminization' similar to soldiers' experiences on the front in wartime. They learned to share, trust, and comfort one another, admit their fears, and to hope together. But most men had to learn behaviors women already knew." See *Mothers in the Fatherland*, 380–81.

76. Horowitz, "Mengele, the Gynecologist," 210.

77. The scar is "like a thick stroke of White-Out where the tattoo has been" (179).

78. The context here is actually the Nazi euthanasia program; the entire citation reads: "No matter what the Nazis claimed, Eve thought . . . the killing of 'worthless Aryan life' was not about killing another race. It was a self-disembowelment. . . . The killing of 'other' was a tradition in human history. The killing of 'self' was new. Surely this first killing of 'worthless self' was intricately connected to the mass killing of 'other' in Nazi Germany. Surely in understanding why mass murder of other, one had to understand this self-murder first" (126).

79. Kaveny, "Suffering in Style," 21. My thanks to Rachel Bargiel for providing me with this reference.

80. I am thinking of Carol Rittner and John K. Roth here, who ask: "How does one confront the past? How should one remember and memorialize, recognizing that our identities and needs are both those of a shared humanity and of a varied particularity—cultural, ethnic, national, religious—without which humanity is lost? As each generation grows further and further from Auschwitz and what led to it, people find it more and more difficult to remember together, particularly when they already remember differently." See Rittner and Roth's introduction to *Memory Offended*, 7.

81. Young, *Writing and Rewriting the Holocaust*, 133. This is the conclusion to Young's discussion of Sylvia Plath's poetry, but it is surely applicable here. Earlier in the same chapter Young writes: "For the most part, the critics of Plath's Holocaust figures object primarily to the want of apparent empirical connections between Plath's life and the death camps, as well as to the 'impropriety' of her borrowing from what they consider the emotional 'reserves' of the Holocaust" (129).

82. Novick, *The Holocaust in American Life*, 11. For a fascinating discussion of Holocaust survivor-icon Elie Wiesel's own self-translation into and for a Christian milieu, see Seidman, "Elie Wiesel and the Scandal of Jewish Rage."

83. See <http://www.yad-vashem.org.il/visiting/sites/deportees.html>.

84. See Friedländer, in collaboration with Seligman, "Memory of the *Shoah* in Israel."

85. This blending of past and present can have some interesting consequences. Vivian Patraka, in discussing her own experience of the railway car, notes how she was approached in the museum by an elderly couple (the Zissmans) who had been involved in resistance activities in Poland. Speaking to the couple about their experiences during the war in the shadow of the railcar forced Patraka to "negotiate their 'unofficial' story with the 'official' one surrounding it" and also to consider the tension between the museum's images of suffering and liberation and the Zissmans' narratives of resistance. See Patraka, *Spectacular Suffering*, 116–17.

86. Ezrahi, *Booking Passage*, 23; Ezrahi's emphasis.

THREE. FRAMING MEMORY

1. Survivors of the Shoah Visual History Foundation, promotional video.

2. Friedman, "Steven Spielberg," 22.

3. Kim Feinberg, interview by author, June 1997, Johannesburg, South Africa.

4. From a full-page advertisement for the foundation seeking donors that appeared in the November 13, 1997, issue of the *Jerusalem Report*. The goal of fifty thousand recorded testimonies was reached in January 1999, marked by a ceremony on January 31. Following this milestone, the VHF shifted its focus from collecting testimonies to indexing and cataloguing them, resulting in a marked decrease in recordings. VHF statistics as of May 2001 cite 51,533 testimonies in 57 countries and 32 languages totaling 116,277 hours of testimony (email communication from Janet Keller, media relations manager at the VHF, June 8, 2001); shortly thereafter the foundation ceased recording testimonies.

5. See Shandler, *While America Watches*, 27.

6. For a discussion of this demand for documentation, see Rothberg, *Traumatic Realism*, esp. his introduction.

7. Huyssen, "Monument and Memory in a Postmodern Age," 11.

8. Rothberg, *Traumatic Realism*, 118.

9. Langer, *Holocaust Testimonies*, xiii. See also Rothberg's excellent reading of Langer's interpretive perspective, in *Traumatic Realism*, 118–29.

10. Hartman, "Learning from Survivors: The Yale Testimony Project," in *Longest Shadow*, 140.

11. I owe a great deal to Iwona Irwin-Zarecka's *Frames of Remembrance*, for inspiring me to think critically about the processes of "framing."

12. T-216, Father John S., Fortunoff Video Archive for Holocaust Testimonies, Yale University Library. All transcriptions from the Yale videotestimonies are my own unless otherwise noted. It is worthwhile to set this excerpt against another, with a parallel though entirely opposite image: "There was a little hole in the cattle train where I looked out and I seen scenery that in my life I never saw such a beautiful area, but our heart was crying for pain." T-584, Eva W., Fortunoff Video Archive for Holocaust Testimonies, Yale University Library. I note as well that the sounds of passing local trains are audible throughout Ms. W.'s testimony, creating an eerie audial backdrop to her testimony. In another parallel, Andrea Liss discusses an art installation by Suzanne Hellmuth and Jock Reynolds, *In Memory: A Bird in the Hand* (1987), in which visitors encounter a peephole at the end of the exhibit wall. Through this peephole, stooping, one views "a reproduction of an archival photograph depicting four male inmates facing the wall of a Gestapo prison yard as they await the next horrific stage in their transport." Liss notes how the exhibit forces visitors to confront the issue of voyeurism. See Liss, *Trespassing through Shadows*, 87–88.

13. See <http://www.library.yale.edu/testimonies/about/index.htm>. Hartman adds: "The interviewer . . . is a listener and companion; he or she asks a minimum of questions in the hope that memories will emerge from a deeper, more spontaneous level" ("The Longest Shadow," in *Longest Shadow*, 22).

14. Hartman speaks to the fortuitousness of what was initially a forced choice in the setting: "There was so little funding that space provided free on the unoccupied floor of a building became a makeshift studio and more feasible than transporting equipment and interviewers from one home to the other. The makeshift studio was sparsely furnished; chairs as necessary, a backdrop curtain, and sometimes a plant. What we sacrificed was the kind of colorful, personal setting we would have found in the survivors' homes, and which helps when videography has a film in mind; what we gained (this realization came later, and we stuck with our ascetic decision) was not only simplicity or starkness but a psychological advantage. The interviewees, in a sparse setting, entered their memories with less distraction, or, to put it differently, they could not divert their attention to this or that familiar object. There were also fewer disruptions—such as a child crying, a dog barking, a telephone ringing—to disconnect the flow of thought." See Hartman, "Tele-Suffering," 116–17. I surmise that Hartman is referring to projects such as the VHF's in his comments about having a "film in mind."

15. Young, *Writing and Rewriting the Holocaust*, 159.

16. Much of the background for this discussion comes from a month-long visit to the FVAHT in August 1993, during which I viewed tapes at the archive every weekday. Thanks to Joanne Rudof and her staff for their support and advice.

17. For another view on the videotestimony interviewing project, see Blum-Dobkin, "Videotaping Holocaust Interviews." Blum-Dobkin, the chief interviewer for the Museum of Jewish Heritage: A Living Memorial to the Holocaust (whose collection is affiliated with Yale's and will be a repository for the VHF), notes, for example, that the tapes her institution records "are more life histories than conventional Holocaust interviews" (46).

18. See Bloch, "Redeeming the Holocaust."

19. Van Alphen, *Caught by History*, 45, 53–54.

20. It could be suggested that this itself represents a not-too-subtle appropriation, or even colonization, of Holocaust memory by the English-, particularly American English-, speaking world: the bulk of the money for such projects comes from the United States, hence American English is increasingly becoming the dominant language of memory's narration for videotestimonies. Statistics from the VHF show, for example, that, as of February 5, 2000, 24,608 testimonies were recorded in English, making up 48.64 percent of the archive (Russian at 13.78 percent and Hebrew at 11.81 percent run a distant second and third), while 19,521 testimonies (38.59 percent) were recorded in the United States.

21. T-3, Sally H., Fortunoff Video Archive for Holocaust Testimonies, Yale University Library.

22. Van Alphen, *Caught by History*, 59.

23. T-107, Edith P., Fortunoff Video Archive for Holocaust Testimonies, Yale University Library. The excerpt is also available online at <http://www.library.yale.edu/testimonies/excerpts/edithp.html>. This tape displays some of the "excessive camera work" that marks the early Yale archive tapes, "zooming in and out, creating Bergmanesque close-ups," as Hartman notes. "Eventually we advised that the camera should give up this expressive potential and remain fixed, except for enough motion to satisfy more naturally the viewer's eye." See Hartman, "Tele-Suffering," 116.

24. Young, *Writing and Rewriting the Holocaust*, 160; for the poem see Celan, "Death Fugue."

25. T-107, Edith P., Fortunoff Video Archive for Holocaust Testimonies, Yale University Library; emphasis added to reflect that of speaker in the original.

26. T-641, Martin S., Fortunoff Video Archive for Holocaust Testimonies, Yale University Library.

27. Jeffrey Shandler writes, regarding a mass demonstration on the Washington Mall held the same week as the opening of the USHMM: "Many . . . displayed examples of the gay rights movement's ongoing use of Holocaust imagery. Chief among these is the adoption of the pink triangle badge, with which Nazis stigmatized homosexual men incarcerated in concentration camps, as an emblem of gay identity that is displayed on signs, buttons, flags, articles of clothing, and the like" (Shandler, *While America Watches*, 248). See also Shandler's comments in "'City of Jews, City of Gays.'"

28. Young, *Writing and Rewriting the Holocaust*, 161.

29. Agamben, *Remnants of Auschwitz*, 17.

30. Ibid., 19.

31. Ibid., 149–50.

32. T-1317, Sigi Z., Fortunoff Video Archive for Holocaust Testimonies, Yale University Library.

33. Langer, "Memory's Time," 268–69.

34. Hartman, "Learning from Survivors," 133.

35. Laub, "Bearing Witness," 65.

36. T-943, Dr. Fred O., Fortunoff Video Archive for Holocaust Testimonies, Yale University Library.

37. Rothberg, *Traumatic Realism*, 3–4, 9, 100.

38. Felman, "Education and Crisis," 24; Felman's emphasis.

39. Felman, "Education and Crisis," 5. For van Alphen, few escape owing to the ambiguous or even negated nature of the witnesses' subject positions, so that the possibility for discourse itself is disrupted at its source. See van Alphen, *Caught by History*, 45–50.

40. Laub, "Bearing Witness," 58.

41. Langer, *Holocaust Testimonies*, 174; Rothberg, *Traumatic Realism*, 21; Mikhail Bhaktin, *The Dialogic Imagination*, trans. C. Emerson and M. Holquist (Austin: University of Texas Press, 1981), 84, cited in Rothberg, *Traumatic Realism*, 27.

42. Langer mistakenly describes the cattle car as a "crowded room" in *Holocaust Testimonies*, 101.

43. T-107, Edith P., Fortunoff Video Archive for Holocaust Testimonies, Yale University Library.

44. Langer, *Holocaust Testimonies*, 174–75.

45. T-3, Sally H., Fortunoff Video Archive for Holocaust Testimonies, Yale University Library.

46. See Langer, "Memory's Time."

47. Hartman, "Holocaust Testimony, Art, and Trauma," in *Longest Shadow*, 153.

48. T-972, Jolly Z., Fortunoff Video Archive for Holocaust Testimonies, Yale University Library; emphasis added to reflect that of speaker.

49. Laub, "Event without a Witness," 75.

50. Hartman, "Holocaust Testimony, Art, and Trauma," 156.

51. Laub, "Event without a Witness," 85.

52. This is echoed in Felman and Laub's introduction to *Testimony*, where they seek to articulate a relationship between testimony and "culture," thereby identifying a sense of the past in the present (another chronotope): "The present volume will endeavor to suggest, therefore, the first stage of a yet uncharted, nonrepresentational but performative, relationship between art and culture, on the one hand, and the conscious or unconscious witnessing of historical events on the other. This is then a book about how art inscribes (artistically bears witness to) *what we do not yet know of our lived historical relation to the events of our times.*" See Felman and Laub, "Introduction," xx; Felman and Laub's emphasis.

53. Van Alphen, *Caught by History*, 36.

54. Laub, "Event without a Witness," 85.

55. Laub, "Bearing Witness," 62.

56. Hartman, "Learning from Survivors," 139.

57. Patraka, *Spectacular Suffering*, 4.

58. Primo Levi, *The Drowned and the Saved*, trans. Raymond Rosenthal (New York: Random House, 1989), 83–84, cited in Agamben, *Remnants of Auschwitz*, 33.

59. Agamben, *Remnants of Auschwitz*, 34, 82.

60. Rothberg, *Traumatic Realism*, 150–51, 159.

61. Agamben, *Remnants of Auschwitz*, 120.

62. Rosenfeld, "Americanization of the Holocaust," 136–37. Peter Novick observes, "American Jews . . . would have been incredulous at the idea, later a commonplace, that survivors' memories were a 'precious legacy' to be preserved. There is, in fact, an eerie symmetry between the messages survivors received in the forties and fifties and those of the eighties and nineties. Earlier, they were told

that even if they wanted to speak of the Holocaust, they shouldn't—it was bad for them. Later they were told that even if they didn't want to speak of it they must—it was good for them. In both cases, others knew what was best." See Novick, *Holocaust in American Life,* 83–84.

63. Novick, *Holocaust in American Life,* 67. Novick cites Werner Weinberg as objecting to this description and describing survivorship as "terminal. . . . To be categorized for having survived adds to the damage I have suffered; it is like wearing a tiny new Yellow Star. . . . It is a constricting designation that can easily make its bearer appear—to others and to himself—as a museum piece, a fossil, a freak, a ghost." See Werner Weinberg, *Self-Portrait of a Holocaust Survivor* (Jefferson, N. C., 1985), 150–52, quoted in ibid., 67.

64. Rothberg, following Charles Sanders Peirce, calls this the "traumatic index": "An index is a sign that relates to a referent as an effect relates to a cause—the classic example is the weathervane that points in the direction that the wind is blowing. However, the index in traumatic circumstances functions differently than in the traditional version. Instead of indicating an object or phenomenon that caused it, and in that sense making the referent present, the traumatic index points to a necessary absence" (*Traumatic Realism,* 104). For a thoughtful treatment of the themes of silence and absence, see Horowitz, *Voicing the Void.*

65. Laub, "Bearing Witness," 57. Laub says, "Testimonies are not monologues; they cannot take place in solitude. The witnesses are talking *to somebody:* to somebody they have been waiting for for a long time" (ibid., 70–71).

66. This idea is embedded in language: we speak of someone "*giving* testimony"; we therefore must consider to whom such testimony is being given. What is the nature of this legacy, this inheritance?

67. T-641, Martin S., Fortunoff Video Archive for Holocaust Testimonies, Yale University Library.

68. LaCapra, *Representing the Holocaust,* 198.

69. Hartman, "Holocaust Testimony, Art, and Trauma," 152. The greatest risk here, for Hartman, is that "routine exposure" to such secondary trauma would "habituat[e] and fascinat[e] and ten[d] to produce feelings of indifference."

70. Felman describes it as a "story of how I became, in fact, myself a witness to the shock communicated by the subject-matter; the narrative of how the subject-matter was unwittingly *enacted,* set in motion by the class, and how testimony turned out to be at once more critically surprising and more critically important than anyone could have foreseen" ("Education and Crisis," 7).

71. Ibid., 47; Felman's emphasis. Note the redemptive desire here. See also the article by Brenner, "Teaching the Holocaust in Academia."

72. Felman, "Education and Crisis," 48.

73. Novick says, "Early indications suggest that the way in which the testimonies have been collected and presented by Spielberg's Survivors of the Shoah Foundation will result in a meretricious, Hollywood-to-the-max sort of evocation. Most interviewers have only the sketchiest knowledge of the Holocaust. The format of the interviews (at Spielberg's insistence) manipulates them in a 'redemptive' direction, with all narratives ending with the survivor surrounded by his or her family. The way in which the material is presented to the public also bodes ill. The foundation's first educational CD-ROM is narrated by teenage sex idol

Leonardo DiCaprio" (*Holocaust in American Life*, 351 n. 24). More accurately, the CD-ROM features commentary by DiCaprio and Winona Ryder.

74. Janet Keller, media relations manager at the VHF, email communication, June 8, 2001; "Meet Our Robot," *Past Forward: The Newsletter of the Shoah Foundation*, fall 2000, 7. The same article announces a recent upgrade of the robot to accommodate 408 terabytes.

75. "Questions and Answers 2001," available for download ("Frequently asked Questions") at the foundation's Web site, <http://www.vhf.org/ato/07_03_01_FAQ.pdf>, response to question 5, "Is the Shoah Foundation still interviewing Holocaust survivors and other witnesses?" p. 3 (dated 7/30/01); "Shoah Foundation Embarks on New Mission," 2.

76. Matthew Chuck, interview by author, VHF, December 11, 1997. All quotations attributed to Chuck are taken from this interview.

77. To date, only a cache of about 150 testimonies had been established at the Simon Wiesenthal Center (SWC), along with a dedicated fiber-optic link to the VHF donated by GTE. The link was active from mid-1999 through early 2001 and was tested successfully for data transfer, both from the cache and from the robot at the VHF. Visitors to the Wiesenthal Center's Museum of Tolerance were able to experiment with searching the database with an SWC staff member on request. Michael Berenbaum asserted in 1999 that the technological hurdle to making the repositories active had been overcome but that a proper interface for use of the repositories was missing. He also speculated that the significance of the repositories would come only with the passing of the survivors (Berenbaum, interview by author, VHF, June 25, 1999). In 2000, VHF executive director Ari Zev informed me of the "smart card" integration of thirty videotestimonies available on the SWC cache. Visitors whose "passports" (see chapter 4) belong to one of the thirty can now proceed upstairs at the end of their tour of the Museum of Tolerance and view the entire testimony of the survivor whose "passport" they hold (Zev, interview by author, VHF, August 21, 2000). Owing to financial constraints, however, the fiber-optic link between the SWC and the VHF was terminated in 2001 (Ari Zev, phone conversation with the author, September 17, 2002).

78. Michael Berenbaum, interview by author, VHF, December 11, 1997. All quotations attributed to Berenbaum are taken from this interview unless otherwise noted.

79. "Shoah Foundation Embarks on New Mission," 2.

80. Mintz, *Popular Culture and the Shaping of Holocaust Memory in America*, 180. Interviewers and interviewees work together prior to the recording of testimony filling out a preinterview questionnaire (PIQ), which determines the basic outline of the witness's story and is used subsequently to provide crucial biographical information essential to the cataloguing and indexing process. A short version of the PIQ has now been established and is being used to enter all fifty thousand testimonies into a database to pave the way for future cataloguing of complete videotestimonies (Ari Zev, interview by author, VHF, August 21, 2000).

81. This is reminiscent of an episode of the famous television program *This Is Your Life* broadcast on May 27, 1953, and analyzed in *While America Watches* by Jeffrey Shandler, in which Holocaust survivor Hanna Bloch Kohner was the "guest

of honor." The set evoked a "posh living room" (30) in which Kohner was subject to the usual parade of surprise visitors from her past. Its broadcast "reveals how . . . television could shape the telling of a Holocaust survivor's life story" (34) by staging a "series of dramatic climaxes" that "transform[ed] Hanna's experiences of rupture, loss, and displacement into a cohesive narrative of triumph over adversity" (36). In this way, Shandler asserts that "although the program was presented as a tribute to her, Hanna often appeared to be more its victim, the camera fixing on her face in extended close-ups throughout the broadcast. [Host Ralph] Edwards only nominally involved Hanna as an active participant in the proceedings, asking her occasional rhetorical questions to which she could give only the briefest of answers" (38). While I am by no means suggesting that the VHF is duplicating this "victimizing" structure of staging and framing, the case of Kohner's television appearance serves as a warning about the dangers of framing the witness in the service of a broader representational agenda.

82. Some indication of the evolving agenda of the VHF is visible in "A letter from Ari C. Zev," executive director and chief operating officer, published in *Past Forward*, fall 2000: "As the Foundation shifts its focus from collecting survivor and witness testimonies to disseminating them, we continue to explore the best methods of sharing the vast Archive with the world. Although we are still in the early stages of this process, our goal is clear: That the survivors and witnesses who have so generously given testimony will now become teachers, providing moving personal lessons in cultural, religious, and racial harmony today and for generations to come" (5).

83. Michael Nutkiewicz, interview by author, VHF, August 21, 2000.

84. Lisa Goodgame, phone conversation with the author, August 30, 2002.

85. Shandler, *While America Watches*, 177. See also Miller, *One, by One, by One*, 266–75.

86. Hartman speaks to this issue: "As distance learning becomes standard, and machine-readable cataloguing takes over, archives of conscience like ours may not be able to resist being turned into gigabytes of information, electronic warehouses of knowledge that marginalize the other values I have mentioned. This greed for more and more information, for positivities, which has already accumulated an extraordinary and melancholy record on the Holocaust, has not yielded appreciable ethical lessons. The heaping up of factual detail may even be an excuse to evade the issue of what can be learned" ("Tele-Suffering," 119).

87. Derrida, *Archive Fever*, 7. For a critical overview of the Holocaust's "new archive" of videotestimonies, see Mintz, *Popular Culture and the Shaping of Holocaust Memory in America*, 178–86.

88. Derrida, *Archive Fever*, 91.

89. Ibid., 36.

90. Agamben, *Remnants of Auschwitz*, 143, 144.

91. Berenbaum suggested to me after he was no longer working at the VHF that the only other archive of comparable size is that of the Cable News Network (CNN) (Berenbaum, interview by author, Los Angeles, August 22, 2000). This raises the issue of size once more. Elsewhere, Berenbaum also provided a rationale for why, though Spielberg "could easily write one check to cover this entire proj-

ect," he had not. Not only would the foundation become the filmmaker's (though in the public mind perhaps it is), but it would also become associated with his filmmaker's many "fantasies," Berenbaum argues. Berenbaum quoted in Dubner, "Steven the Good," 235.

92. The editors of the companion volume to the video documentary, introducing the book but no doubt referring to the video as well, suggest: "*Witness* weaves together testimony from differing and often contradictory angles of vision. The result is a complicating of our thinking about the events being described. A memoir provides us with the continuity of one individual's personal odyssey. In a multivoice narrative such as *Witness*, we discover that such continuity can be misleading. Complexity and contradiction can often be greater tools for approaching an understanding of what happened." See Greene and Kumar, *Witness*, xxiv. Quotation in text from ibid., xxv.

93. Dubner, "Steven the Good," 234. (Strictly speaking, the VHF is not a Holocaust-studies center.) A cursory study of the mastheads of the foundation over the years shows an evolution from a Hollywood movie model (with executive producers and producers) to a corporate model (with president/chief executive officer, several vice presidents, and a board of directors).

94. *Survivors: Testimonies of the Holocaust*, prod. and dir. Barish. Other VHF products include eight documentaries: *The Last Days* (discussed below), *The Lost Children of Berlin*, *Survivors of the Holocaust*, and *Broken Silence*, a series of five foreign-language documentaries for television broadcast in Hungary, Russia, Argentina, Poland, and the Czech Republic. The Shoah Foundation has also produced a German-language CD-ROM, *Erinnern für Gegenwart und Zukunft* (*Remembering for the present and future*).

95. Rothberg, *Traumatic Realism*, 209.

96. One the issue of "playing" with the Holocaust, see James E. Young, "David Levinthal's *Mein Kampf*: History, Toys, and the Play of Memory," in *At Memory's Edge*, 42–61.

97. Stephanie Barish, interview by author, VHF, June 24, 1999.

98. Alan Mintz is also critical of the mediated nature of Holocaust videotestimonies and pessimistic about their usefulness. "We will necessarily always be beholden to a class of Holocaust educator-archivists . . . who, selecting and editing and splicing, will act as a kind of interface between the oceanic variety of the archive and our own wonderment" (*Popular Culture and the Shaping of Holocaust Memory in America*, 183). For another consideration of the role of computer media in shaping Holocaust memory, see Reading, "Clicking on Hitler." Speaking mostly about Holocaust Web sites, Reading argues that "we should recognize that these practices [accessing representations of the Holocaust via digital technologies] take place within a commercially framed context. In this way, rather than dismissing Holocaust sites as somehow contaminated or ruined by their commercial context, I would suggest a reading that places the tension between the two— between the Holocaust and the commercial software that tells its story, using a visual language of shared icons, flickering quicktime figures, and hot spots at its heart" (330).

99. *The Last Days*, exec. prod. Spielberg, videocassette. A companion book consisting of transcriptions of the testimonies, black-and-white archival footage,

and color stills and outtakes from the film is also available. See Survivors of the Shoah Visual History Foundation, *The Last Days*.

100. While the film includes testimony by Münch, the book version does not.

101. Rothberg, *Traumatic Realism*, 140, 156; Rothberg's emphasis.

102. Young, *Writing and Rewriting the Holocaust*, 163.

103. Hartman, "Holocaust Testimony, Art, and Trauma," 156.

104. Hartman, "Cinema Animal," 70.

FOUR. MEDIATING MEMORY

1. It is difficult to assess the extent to which the Hollerith machine can be implicated in Nazi activities. Edward Linenthal states that the device was "used by the Nazis to tabulate racial data from census forms and identify 'enemies of the state.'" See Linenthal, *Preserving Memory*, 150. Michael Berenbaum offers a more thorough assessment: "The work of identifying and locating Jews was done efficiently with the help of the German-made American-engineered Hollerith machine, one of the earliest card sorters. The Hollerith was developed by Herman Hollerith, a German American and an employee of the United States Census Office, who invented the first punch-card counting device. Its first major use was in the 1890 census. In 1896 Hollerith founded his own company, which he sold in 1911 to the Computing-Tabulating Recording Company (CTR), better known by its post-1924 name of International Business Machines (IBM). The Hollerith machines used by the Germans were developed by the Deutsche-Hollerith Maschinen Gesellschaft (Dehomag), a company of which IBM controlled a 90 percent share. The Hollerith made it possible to process vast quantities of data in a relatively short time. During the war, the Hollerith was used to identify and allocate conscript labor. Whether the machine was used to compile deportation lists of Jews in Germany cannot be determined. But in many concentration camps, the political section of the Gestapo used the Hollerith to process the records of those who entered. The IBM technology was neutral; its use by the Nazi regime was malevolent. Clearly, its potential use was understood by the German manufacturer." See Berenbaum, *The World Must Know*, 42. I thank Richard Hecht for providing me with the latter reference. Inspired by viewing the Hollerith, Edwin Black wrote *IBM and the Holocaust*.

2. Linenthal, "Locating Holocaust Memory," 243.

3. Michael Berenbaum, personal email communication, April 12, 2002. The accounting here is a revision by Berenbaum of figures provided by Judith Miller in *One, by One, by One*, 234, citing Berenbaum. Liliane Weissberg offers a view that complicates this reading of the building's design: "Its steel and glass construction of corridors not only tells the story of ghetto bridges and railroad tracks, but turns them into an object praised for its aesthetic satisfaction, even pleasure." See Liliane Weissberg, "In Plain Sight," in Zelizer, *Visual Culture and the Holocaust*, p. 20.

4. Linenthal, "Locating Holocaust Memory," 221, 252.

5. Lisus, "Misplacing Memory," 19. See also Lisus and Ericson, "Misplacing Memory."

6. Huyssen, "Monument and Memory in a Postmodern Age," 11.

7. Huyssen, *Twilight Memories*, 13.

8. Adorno, "Valéry Proust Museum," 175.

9. Huyssen, *Twilight Memories*, 255.

10. Ibid., 16, 15.

11. Rogoff, "From Ruins to Debris," 231.

12. Azoulay, "With Open Doors," 92.

13. Donato, "Museum's Furnace," 223.

14. Ibid., 221; as Douglas Crimp suggests, "the history of museology is a history of all the various attempts to deny the heterogeneity of the museum, to reduce it to a homogeneous system or series. The faith in the possibility of ordering the museum's 'bric-a-brac' . . . persists until today." See Crimp, "On the Museum's Ruins," 49.

15. MacDonald, "Change and Challenge," 160.

16. "As the objects in a public collection or a museum continue a cultural tradition, they are conceived as links between the spectators and the inhabitants of previous worlds and experiences, as connections between the tangible and intangible or visible and invisible worlds." See Richard I. Cohen, "Self-Image through Objects," 205.

17. Social ideas are the "set of beliefs, assumptions, and feelings in terms of which people judge one another and which they sometimes use to guide their actions." See Karp, "Introduction: Museums and Communities," 6.

18. Daniel Sherman and Irit Rogoff suggest that, "by presenting objects as signifiers within an artificially created institutional frame, museums underline their irretrievable otherness, their separation from the world of lived experience. In so doing, museums simultaneously construct a self, the viewer, or in collective terms a public." See Sherman and Rogoff, "Introduction: Frameworks for Critical Analysis," xii.

19. Lowenthal, *The Past Is a Foreign Country*, 248.

20. Ibid., 243.

21. Young, *Texture of Memory*, 127.

22. According to Eugenio Donato, "The museum can only display objects metonymically at least twice removed from that which they are originally supposed to represent or signify. The objects displayed as a series are of necessity only part of the totality to which they originally belonged. Spatially and temporally detached from their origin and function, they signify only by arbitrary and derived associations. The series in which the individual pieces and fragments are displayed is also arbitrary and incapable of investing the particular object with anything but irrelevant fabulations." Interestingly, as he continues he draws a distinction between linguistic representation, as in the classical image of the library, which "carries within itself . . . its own memory, its own origin, its own *arche*," and the museum, which "testifies to an archeological memory that cannot be recovered except through fabulation" (Donato, "Museum's Furnace," 224).

23. Rogoff, "From Ruins to Debris," 232, 233.

24. Linenthal, "Locating Holocaust Memory," 253.

25. But consider Walter Benjamin, who, in speaking about art, says that even "the most perfect reproduction of a work of art is lacking in one element: its presence in time and space, its unique existence at the place where it happens to be. . . .

The presence of the original is the prerequisite to the concept of authenticity." See Benjamin, "Work of Art," 220.

26. Quotations in Linenthal, "Locating Holocaust Memory," 241.

27. Linenthal, *Preserving Memory*, 54.

28. Lowenthal, *The Past Is a Foreign Country*, 246; MacDonald, "Change and Challenge," 165; Sherman and Rogoff, "Introduction: Frameworks for Critical Analysis," xvi.

29. Friedländer, in collaboration with Seligman, "Memory of the *Shoah* in Israel," 154.

30. Cole, *Selling the Holocaust*, 142. As Yad Vashem completes a series of major renovations to its museum-memorial complex, it will be interesting to see what shifts, if any, occur in its sacred function.

31. Linenthal, *Preserving Memory*, 122. This initiatory function was reflected in the trips made by museum staff members to visit the sites of destruction and comb the countryside for artifacts to be brought to the museum: "Traveling to these sites would come to be seen as a way to initiate those responsible for the creation of a memorial to an imported event. Eventually, the impact of these sites convinced members of the staff that museum visitors would have to experience such a trip *within* the space of the museum in order to confront the Holocaust viscerally" (ibid., 35).

32. I am borrowing this understanding of the mystery of the Holocaust from Linenthal's characterization of Elie Wiesel's approach. While Linenthal uses it to distinguish Wiesel's more abstract characterization of the Shoah from the task of housing and translating it, in concrete form, in a museum, I understand it as well-articulating the position of the museum itself. See ibid., 136.

33. Linenthal, *Preserving Memory*, 82.

34. Harold Kaplan, for example, writes, "We are inclined to say that, as in a religious mystery, the Holocaust should remain unexplained or should be declared holy in its transcendent meaning." Or, as Peter Novick adds, "In what might be called American 'folk Judaism'—less bound by tradition and less scrupulous about theological consistency—a de facto sacralization of the Holocaust has taken place." See Kaplan, *Conscience and Memory*, 20, and Novick, *Holocaust in American Life*, 200.

35. Weinberg and Elieli, *Holocaust Museum in Washington*, 18. See also chapter 5 in this book.

36. Weinberg and Elieli, 25–27.

37. Nutkiewicz, "Holocaust Museums," 18.

38. Linenthal, *Preserving Memory*, 94. Linenthal notes elsewhere in his book that the very trips museum staff made to gather soil for burial at the site of the museum functioned as pilgrimages: "The excavation of the physical landscape, and the highly publicized trips for the purpose of collecting soil from various sites to bury at the museum site, were designed to provide a spiritual transformation to those who entered the physical remnants of the world of the Holocaust" (35).

39. Nutkiewicz, "Holocaust Museums," 18.

40. Linenthal, *Preserving Memory*, 147.

41. Cole notes that the USHMM carefully stopped short of declaring their boxcar identical with one used for deportation, despite assurances from the Polish government as to the artifact's authenticity (*Selling the Holocaust*, 164–65).

42. Linenthal, *Preserving Memory*, 162–63. Linenthal recounts here his own personal encounters with artifacts, both "at home" in Holocaust space and displaced in museum space.

43. Cole, *Selling the Holocaust*, 151.

44. Linenthal, *Preserving Memory*, 164.

45. For Michael Rothberg, this transplantation of artifacts runs the risk of "simplifying the relationship between the extremity and everydayness of genocidal violence" (*Traumatic Realism*, 261).

46. All quotations from Linenthal, *Preserving Memory*, 212–13.

47. Rosenfeld quoted in Linenthal, *Preserving Memory*, 213. The Alvin Rosenfeld quoted here worked for the museum in the late eighties to early nineties and had once been a journalist, covering the Eichmann trial for NBC. He is not the Alvin Rosenfeld who is a professor and noted scholar of the Holocaust at Indiana University, as pointed out to me by Michael Berenbaum (personal email communication, April 11, 2002).

48. Linenthal, *Preserving Memory*, 212–16. This discussion also recalls Nutkiewicz's description of the dual role of the museum. In addition, Andrea Liss suggests, "Perhaps it would have been better to have shown no imagery at all and to have made the photographic caption visible in large type against a black background. In the absence of the palpable yet ethereal horror of the hair, the museum planners might have relinquished all desire to show and to use evidence so as to avoid the risk of the obscenity rebounding on the victims. To let it relay in our own minds. To allow the viewer intelligence. To allow the victims fitting yet impossible recompense." See Liss, *Trespassing through Shadows*, 83.

49. Young, *Texture of Memory*, 132.

50. Linenthal, *Preserving Memory*, 199.

51. See ibid., 192–216.

52. Liss, *Trespassing through Shadows*, 79–80.

53. Young, *Texture of Memory*, 133.

54. Shandler, "While America Watches," 560. The description that follows is based on visits to the museum in 1995–96. In 1997, much of the Tolerancenter portion of the museum was closed for extensive renovations. When I visited the museum in December 1997, this section had not yet reopened, and the tour moved from the entrance area directly to the display, "The Other America."

55. Recognizing that this "exhibit" had outlived its timeliness and relevance, museum organizers' main aim in their 1997 renovations was to create a new centerpiece for the Tolerancenter.

56. This film, while still available for viewing, was also replaced with a new, updated film charting more recent genocidal and hate-oriented incidents.

57. Simon Wiesenthal Center, *Beit Hashoah·Museum of Tolerance*, 24; bold face type in original.

58. Liebe Geft, museum director, interview by author, at the MOT's offices, June 24, 1999.

59. This latest installation at the MOT opened on January 15, 2001, to coincide with Martin Luther King Jr. Day. It is the product of years of ongoing research by the staff of the Simon Wiesenthal Center into hate on the Internet, and it features computer touch screens that display some of the Web sites discovered by the

researchers, a large wall display, and a video screen featuring examples of hate speech.

60. This exhibit opened in March 2001.

61. Patraka, *Spectacular Suffering*, 126.

62. Lisus, "Misplacing Memory," 16–17.

63. Quoted from "Press Information," available in the Simon Wiesenthal Center's Beit Hashoah-Museum of Tolerance Press Kit.

64. Quoting Lowenthal, *The Past Is a Foreign Country*. For an extended discussion of the USHMM's version of these photo passports, see Liss, *Trespassing through Shadows*, 13–26.

65. It would be wrong to suggest that there are no artifacts at the Wiesenthal Center's museum. Though none is featured in the permanent installation, a room upstairs highlights several pieces of the museum's wide-ranging archival collection, including an American flag sewn by inmates of Mauthausen and presented to U.S. troops at liberation, medical instruments from Auschwitz, musical instruments made from Torah scrolls by the Nazis, original bunk beds from Majdanek, and more. Shandler observes: "This section, named 'They Will Always Be Heard: Artifacts and Documents of the Holocaust,' displays its contents in a remarkably retrograde fashion, in glass cases with label captions, and—in an ironic twist, given the section's name—a complete absence of recorded sound or electronic display. The isolation of these materials in what amounts to a reliquary reflects the vestigial status of such displays of 'original' artifacts in contemporary museum practice" (Shandler, "While America Watches," 564 n. 112). The visitor eager to explore the museum in its entirety would surely spend time in this room, which is, however, not part of the narrative of the main exhibition. As for choice, one could argue that, over time, the Tolerancenter itself features less and less choice in its growing preference for preprogrammed "interactive" displays over its earlier free-flowing exploratory environment.

66. Shandler, *While America Watches*, 235.

67. According to Shandler, this setting "plac[es] visitors in the black and white world of the Holocaust" (ibid., 236).

68. Writing about the very different dioramas of African mammal habitat groups in the American Museum of Natural History, Donna Haraway presents a fascinating angle on the religious character of such displays as they represent a progression of history: "each diorama presents itself as a side altar, a stage . . . a hearth for home and family. As an altar, each diorama tells a part of the story of salvation history; each has its special emblems indicating particular virtues. Above all, inviting the visitor to share in its revelation, each tells the truth. Each offers a vision. Each is a window onto knowledge." See Haraway, "Teddy Bear Patriarchy," 29. While exposing a narrative diametrically opposed, in the moral sphere, to that of the Wiesenthal museum, Haraway's analysis remains relevant here in the way it highlights a museum's use of dioramas to tell a story. I am grateful to Roger Friedland for bringing this chapter to my attention.

69. Lisus argues that the "hyper-television experience is intensified further. Here the visitor does not just interact with the television format, she actually enters into it. Inside the docudrama/televised set, the visitor feels part of the staged

environment because it is so familiar, so 'readable' and so real" ("Misplacing Memory," 23).

70. Lisus, "Misplacing Memory," 29.

71. Simon Wiesenthal Center, *Beit Hashoah*, 33.

72. The gate, apparently modeled after the one at Auschwitz-Birkenau, is not inscribed with the famous "Arbeit Macht Frei," so that the resulting experience is of a less recognizable (and less iconic) threshold.

73. On a certain level, this powerful space becomes the peak point of mediation between the wholly other experience of the camp prisoner and the voyeuristic and vicarious journey of the museum-goer. Shandler expresses that mediation as a fusion of "a simulation of entering what is, for many, the quintessential and most inaccessible locus within the landscape of the Holocaust—the gas chamber—with what has become the most pervasive and accessible point of entry to this chapter of history—the television set" (Shandler, "While America Watches," 566). The display in the Hall of Testimony has also been updated; the photomontages used to appear on television monitors that are now closed up with concrete.

74. Kirshenblatt-Gimblett, *Destination Culture*, 173–74.

75. If one is fortunate, this printout tells the story of one of the thirty survivors whose testimonies, recorded by the VHF, are available for viewing upstairs at the museum.

76. Simon Wiesenthal Center, *Beit Hashoah*, 42. Young comments: "At the end, visitors return to the present day in the form of a 'situation room,' complete with wire-service monitors relaying minute-by-minute instances of anti-Semitism and other human rights violations. Whether this will bring the past forward or make the present moment seem already historical and archaic in its museum setting remains to be seen" (*Texture of Memory*, 308).

77. Turan, "Viewing the Unthinkable," L8–9; Kornblau, "Museum of Tolerance," 48.

78. Halevi, "Who Owns the Memory?" 31.

79. Telephone communication with Avra Shapiro, director of public relations, MOT, June 14, 2001.

80. Parr and Parr, "An Afterword: Beyond Lamentation," 138.

81. Enzensberger, "Constituents of a Theory of the Media," 104–5.

82. See Kaes, "History and Film," 112–13.

83. See also Enzensberger, "Constituents of a Theory of the Media," 116; Baudrillard, "Simulacra and Simulations."

84. See Huyssen, "Monument and Memory in a Postmodern Age," 12, and Lisus, "Misplacing Memory," 33, 41–42.

85. Lisus, "Misplacing Memory," 35; Kaes, "History and Film," 120.

86. Patraka, *Spectacular Suffering*, 122. She notes as well: "In a museum of the dead, the critical actors are gone, and it is up to us to perform acts of reinterpretation to make meaning and memory. To some degree, then, the usual museum situation (in which we look at objects) is exploited to underscore the absence to be read in the presence of objects that stand for the violent loss of which they are only the remains. To the degree that this historical, material, human loss is allowed to remain a tangible 'presence,' a Holocaust museum can constitute a particular

metonymic situation: inanimate material objects document and mark the loss instead of simply substituting for them through representation. In this case, the enormity of the absent referent is neither contained nor scaled down through a representation that claims its presence over the terrible absence produced by genocide" (122).

87. Young, *Texture of Memory*, 342–44. On the USHMM's proposed identity card program, see Linenthal, *Preserving Memory*, 187, and Liss, *Trespassing through Shadows*, 13–26. The USHMM's identity card program, in its fully computerized form, was scrapped because of unexpectedly high attendance rates. It is ironic that the passport/identity card display echoes the wartime use of the Hollerith machine. Patraka implies this analogy in *Spectacular Suffering*, 141 n. 6.

88. Patraka, "Situating History and Difference," 57. Patraka cites Michel de Certeau, *The Practice of Everyday Life*, trans. Steven Rendall (Berkeley: University of California Press, 1984), 117–18.

89. Patraka says that "place means a pre-scripted performance of interpretation, and space produces sites for multiple performances of interpretation that situate/produce the spectator as historical subject" (*Spectacular Suffering*, 122–23).

90. Patraka, "Situating History and Difference," 59, 60.

91. Patraka, "Situating History and Difference," 72.

92. Norden, "Yes and No to the Holocaust Museums," 32.

93. Young, *Texture of Memory*, 348.

94. Another not-so-subtle bit of code plays on the popular Jewish password "member of the tribe," or "MOT," also the initials for Museum of Tolerance. The museum's gift shop sells a variety of MOT mementos, "practical, everyday items that declare your support of the Museum of Tolerance's mission," such as T-shirts, tote bags, sports bottles, and coffee mugs, which also declare, to those in the know, Jewish identification. Quotation from the Museum's Gift Galleria catalogue. I thank Amy Kesselhaut for bringing this issue, as well as a number of references, to my attention.

95. Novick argues, coincidentally, that it "was during the Hitler years that American philo-Semites invented the 'Judeo-Christian tradition' to combat innocent, or not so innocent, language that spoke of a totalitarian assault on 'Christian civilization'" (*Holocaust in American Life*, 28). Novick cites here Mark Silk, "Notes on the Judeo-Christian Tradition in America," *American Quarterly* 36 (1984).

96. Bartov, *Murder in Our Midst*, 184.

97. Karp, "Introduction: Museums and Communities," 6; Patraka, *Spectacular Suffering*, 121.

98. Kaplan, *Conscience and Memory*, 8.

99. Patraka notes: "Unlike the D.C. museum, then, which presents its spectators with an accretion of detail, the Beit Hashoah museum provides its spectators with an accretion of information, thereby suggesting that technologies in the current historical moment can reenact the events of the Holocaust in a coherent, complete narrative of memory" (*Spectacular Suffering*, 129).

100. Rosen, "Trivialization of Tragedy," 82.

101. Ibid., 85.

102. Babylonian Talmud, *Shabbat*, 31a.

FIVE. PERFORMING MEMORY

1. See Gilbert, *Holocaust Journey*. See also the article in the *New York Times* travel section on visiting Holocaust sites in Eastern Europe: Gruber, "Remembering Poland's Jews."

2. Member of Knesset Avraham Hirchson, president and founder of the March of the Living, April 7, 1994, at the Birkenau ceremony at the end of the actual March of the Living (the silent walk on Holocaust Memorial Day; quotation from the official English translation read at the ceremony). In 2002 the March of the Living, responding to the situation in Israel, decided for the first time in its history not to go to Israel, which significantly changed the character of the march in that year. In its full international incarnation, the march took place every two years until 1994, but on "off years" a small contingent came from Israel and also had a ceremony at Birkenau. The march now takes place every year, with participants from all over the world.

3. Leibowitz, *Judaism, Human Values, and the Jewish State*, 217.

4. Segev, *Seventh Million*, 436–39. For a detailed discussion of the integration of Yom ha-Shoah into the rhythms of time and space of Zionist ideology, cosmology, and history, see Handelman and Katz, "State Ceremonies of Israel," as well as the references in Liebman and Don-Yehiya, *Civil Religion in Israel*. For a full description and analysis of this commemorative day, see Young, "When a Day Remembers: A Performative History of Yom Hashoah," in *Texture of Memory*, 263–81. For an excellent exploration, in a particular case, of themes such as those raised by Handelman and Katz, see Feldman, "'It Is My Brothers Whom I Am Seeking.'" For important critical perspectives on the assimilation of the Shoah into "historical consciousness," through commemorative strategies and otherwise, as well as for relevant discussions of the possible frameworks for meaning and interpretation of the Holocaust, especially in Israel, see the following essays by Saul Friedländer: "Die Shoah als Element in der Konstruktion israelischer Erinnerung"; "The Shoah in Present Historical Consciousness"; and "Memory of the *Shoah* in Israel: Symbols, Rituals, and Ideological Polarization."

5. I will use "March of the Living," in quotation marks, to indicate the actual mass walk on Holocaust Memorial Day, and March of the Living, without quotes, to refer to the entire two-week experience. The march was initiated in conversations between Jewish educators in Miami and Avraham Hirchson, an Israeli member of Knesset who had been running an international quiz competition for teenagers dealing with Holocaust heroism. The Miami organizers had no interest in the competition but had a keen desire for developing some event that would educate teens as to the experience of Jews during the Holocaust in Europe as well as in the significance of the founding of the State of Israel. The March of the Living was born of this interchange between the Israeli and American organizers (from discussions on June 18 and 27, 2001, respectively, with Miles Bunder, director of the South Florida March of the Living, and Gene Greenzweig, former executive vice president of the Central Agency for Jewish Education in Miami, both of whom were involved in the planning and organization of the march from its inception. All information in this chapter attributed to Bunder or Greenzweig comes from these conversations, unless otherwise noted). On the March of the Living as an ed-

ucational experience, see chapter 5, "From Auschwitz to Jerusalem: Reenacting Jewish History on the March of the Living," in Rona Sheramy, "Defining Lessons."

6. In 2000, according to Greenzweig, the march involved over seven thousand teenagers. According to Yosef Kedem, executive vice chairman of the March of the Living, the march has taken more than fifty thousand teens from sixty-plus countries since its inception (phone conversation on July 3, 2001).

7. The primary material for this chapter comes from my own experience accompanying the participants on the March of the Living both as a researcher and as a *madrikh* (guide). In the pre-march phase, I accompanied and observed students from Los Angeles as they studied and prepared for the trip. Following this period, I was one of several adults assigned to a busload of sixteen- to eighteen-year-olds from the San Francisco Bay Area. I documented the public activities of the march participants with an 8 mm videocamera, a 35 mm still camera, and a tape recorder. Supplementing this material is a wide variety of march media, including promotional literature, souvenir books from past marches (made up of students' own writing and photographs), documentary and promotional videotapes of past marches, and even an audiotape keepsake, *Songs for March of the Living* (produced by the United Israel Appeal of Canada), mailed out to the 1994 American participants upon their return to the United States.

8. Nora, "Between Memory and History." I am indebted to Jackie Feldman for his important discussion of a similar phenomenon. Feldman concentrates on the symbolic development of what he calls the Jewish memory "paradigm 'from exile to redemption'" ("'It Is My Brothers Whom I Am Seeking,'" 34), analyzing that development in the case of Israeli students' pilgrimages. My analysis, in contrast, is concerned more with specific symbolic details of *American* student pilgrims' experiences and the competing discourses established and developed through their engagement with Jewish history and Zionist ideology. I remain grateful to Feldman for sharing his analysis with me as I prepared my own for an earlier version of this chapter.

9. The current version of the study guide (available online at <http://www.motl.org/resource/curriculum.htm>) is largely unchanged from the version mailed out in 1994, though according to Miles Bunder the guide is continually updated and incorporates new sections on Germany during the war and Poland now. An example of the latter appears to be an extension of the existing "postscript" to unit 2—"The Persecution Years" (section 11 of the guide), which now includes, among other added readings, an excerpt on the postwar period cited as *A Chosen Few*, by Mark Kurlansky. It is introduced with the following: "Jews in Poland today? After the war, they were not welcome. Are they now? You must read this reading, then decide for yourself." The excerpt briefly reviews the postwar history of Polish pogroms and anti-Semitism. The conclusion to the excerpt reads, "How many Jews remain today in Poland remains unknown. Some estimate between 5,000 and 7,000. There is one operating synagogue in Warsaw, a small Jewish community in Wroclaw, another in Lodz, two synagogues in Cracow (only one 'works' at a time), a 'Hidden Children' society with 500 members, a Jewish Day School in Warsaw with 18 students in first grade, 30 Bris's in Warsaw in 1994, and Jewish youth clubs in Warsaw and Cracow" (see <http://www.motl.org/resource/

curriculum/curriculum_11.htm>). Another observable change between the 1994 version and the online version of the guide is the collapsing of the two sections on "Israel" and "Israel Today" into one.

10. I mailed two sets of questionnaires to U.S. western region march participants, one before and one after the trip, asking a variety of questions. Out of 93 mailed in each set, 21 and 16 responses were received, respectively, with 6 overlaps (students returning both questionnaires). Though the numbers are too small to be statistically useful, the responses are instructive inasmuch as they draw us closer to the thoughts of the participants themselves.

11. Kugelmass, "Rites of the Tribe," 419.

12. This analysis necessarily follows the path and experience of only one bus, part of a five-bus convoy (three buses from the western region of the United States and two from the Midwest, led by the bus from Chicago) on the march in 1994. It is fair to say, however, that this itinerary is representative of the March of the Living in general, especially as most of the other buses went (and continue to go) to the same sites, albeit in shuffled order.

13. For a fascinating, novelistic reflection on this site of memory, see Rymkiewicz, *The Final Station.*

14. See Young, *Texture of Memory,* 203–6.

15. For a detailed "biography" of Rapoport's "memorial icon," see ibid., 155–84.

16. For their reflection on this, as well as many other important facts related to the memorial and museological landscapes at the Auschwitz camps, see Dwork and van Pelt, "Reclaiming Auschwitz"; see also Young, *Texture of Memory,* 128–54.

17. See Dwork and van Pelt, "Reclaiming Auschwitz," for their detailed contextualization of this memorable structure. See also Marianne Hirsch's engaging reading of the gate as a trope for Holocaust memory in "Surviving Images," 225–31.

18. It might be useful here to point out, as an interesting counterweight to the march's educational agenda, that, according to Jonathan Webber, "unknown to most Jews . . . Auschwitz has been treated for the past forty-five years as a key symbol of the wartime Polish tragedy—so that for example the visit to Auschwitz became an indispensable part of the curriculum for Polish schoolchildren" (Webber, *Future of Auschwitz,* 10).

19. Hirsch, "Surviving Images," 227.

20. See Young, *Texture of Memory,* 185–92.

21. One of the more significant changes in the march experience has occurred here. Because of the resurgence in recent years of Jewish life in Poland, whose institutional growth has been largely facilitated by the Ronald S. Lauder Foundation, Shabbat at the Nozyck Synagogue now includes young Polish Jews interacting with march participants (interviews with Miles Bunder and Gene Greenzweig).

22. See Young, *Texture of Memory,* 121–26.

23. Indeed, Greenzweig repeatedly suggests that one of the most important aspects of the march experience is the forming of a "bond" between survivors and the teenagers in order to facilitate the teens' ability to adopt the "voice of the survivor."

24. Bunder maintains that problems with maintaining the Jewish dietary laws of *kashrut* are the main reasons for not offering prepared foods originating in Poland on that part of the tour, and he suggests that even Polish fruits and vegetables would

be "unsafe" in Poland because of health standards. Greenzweig offers a more logistical explanation, noting that now the march produces its own kosher bread in
Poland while still bringing the rest of the food in from Israel because it "keeps better" and travels better to the far-flung groups in Poland.

25. Sheramy argues that, here, "marchers again engage in a reenactment of the
saga of Holocaust survivors, this time in Palestine. Participants enter a memorial
space which invites comparison between the experiences of Jews in Nazi Europe
and in the British-run camps for illegal immigrants. According to the narrative presented by this route, the war against the Jews did not end in Europe, but continued
in Palestine, at the hands of the British and the Arabs" (Sheramy, "Defining
Lessons," 141).

26. This song is also used at the emotional closing scene of *Schindler's List* in
non-Israeli versions of the movie.

27. Handelman and Katz, "State Ceremonies of Israel," 193.

28. The parallel between the ruined memorial landscape in Poland and the
Western Wall, itself a remnant of destruction, is emphasized by Young in his discussion of the "veneration of ruins"; see Young, *Texture of Memory*, 126–28. For
an excellent ethnographic overview of Jewish activities at the wall, see Storper-
Perez and Goldberg, "Kotel."

29. As another parallel to the ritual of commemoration at the wall, I think of
the Israeli custom, one week earlier, of sounding a siren on the morning of Yom ha-
Shoah as well, during which all activity across the country stops (including traffic)
and the Holocaust is remembered. Young has documented this in a videotape that
was screened as part of the exhibition *The Art of Memory: Holocaust Memorials in
History* at the Jewish Museum in New York, March 13–July 31, 1994.

30. I should note that, rather than learn the important and quite relevant story
of the battles at Latrun (relevant because many of those who died at Latrun had
only recently come off boats that had brought them from the displaced persons
camps in Europe), we spent most of our time there watching what can only be described as a recruitment video (in English!) for the tank corps of the Israel Defense
Forces.

31. On the evolving memory of Masada, see Zerubavel, *Recovered Roots*.

32. Though I do not want to discount the time constraints under which we
were operating, I also want to note that there was little need for us to go inside the
museum at Yad Vashem; having already "seen with our own eyes" the landscape
of destruction, we had no need to explore its pale (and not terribly sophisticated)
reflection. For a brief reading of Yad Vashem's strategies of remembrance, see Bartov, *Murder in Our Midst*, 175–78.

33. The use of "Eli, Eli" in the context of Shoah commemoration deserves
serious attention. Originally written as "Halikhah l'Caesarea" ("A Walk to Caesarea") by a young Hannah Senesh *before* the war, the romantic, simple poem has
become an indispensable element of American Jewish youth group sing-alongs
and, because of its martyred author, captured, tortured, and killed after para-
trooping behind enemy lines as part of an ill-fated commando operation sponsored by the Yishuv, an essential element of Holocaust commemoration ceremonies as well. It also replaced "Yerushalayim shel Zahav" as the closing music
for *Schindler's List* in Israeli screenings of the film. About this replacement,

see Bartov, "Spielberg's Oskar," esp. 45, and Bresheeth, "Great Taboo Broken," esp. 205.

34. Victor Turner, "Center Out There," 221.

35. In 2000 a pilot program developed by the American Jewish Committee called "The Next Generation: Strengthening Ties between Polish Society and the American Jewish Community" ran in conjunction with the march. It allowed Polish high school students, along with young Polish Catholics involved in interreligious dialogue and representatives of Poland's small but growing Jewish community, to meet with members of the march's greater New York contingent. The groups were able to explore each other's views of World War II and Polish-Jewish relations through dialogue and travel on the march's Polish itinerary. Since then, the program has also begun to include other contingents on the march.

36. Liebman and Don-Yehiya, *Civil Religion in Israel,* 153.

37. Eliade, "Sacred Places," 368.

38. Kugelmass, "Rites of the Tribe," 417.

39. Ibid., 421.

40. Handelman and Katz, "State Ceremonies of Israel," 225.

41. He says, "We can characterise this feature negatively, by saying that it does not employ forms of communication which have propositional force. It does not consist in the reporting of events or the description of objects or the statement of experimental findings or the formulation of hypotheses. We can characterise this positively, by saying that liturgical language is a certain form of action and puts something into practice. It is not a verbal commentary on an action external to itself; in and of itself liturgical language is an action. And the nature of this action may be broken down into two distinctive properties, whose existence and effectiveness explains, at the same time, why it is that ritual language works so powerfully as a mnemonic device." Connerton, *How Societies Remember,* 57–58.

42. Moore and Myerhoff, "Introduction: Secular Ritual: Forms and Meanings," in *Secular Ritual,* ed. Moore and Myerhoff, 7.

43. Quoted from the 1994 March of the Living brochure.

44. Young, *Texture of Memory,* 269.

45. Handelman and Katz, "State Ceremonies of Israel," 198, 291 n. 12. There is some significant tension between, on the one hand, a logic that equates the cessation of mourning with the end of Diaspora living and, on the other, the real final destination of the march participants (the United States), which is outside that logic. I address this issue below.

46. Ibid., 226.

47. Ibid., 198–99.

48. Friedländer, "Memory of the *Shoah* in Israel," 152.

49. Greenberg, *Jewish Way,* 309.

50. Ibid., 329. Greenberg adds: "Far from coming to grips with the awesome emotional, historical, and theological weight of the Holocaust, the rabbinate still was operating under the sign of the destruction of the Temple. For it, that was the catastrophe of record. Far from considering that the Holocaust was a novum or at least was too massive to be subsumed within existing rubrics, far from confronting the Holocaust as a category-shattering event, the rabbinate sought to incorporate

this *churban* within an existing (minor) halachic pattern in order to strengthen that pattern" (330).

51. Ibid., 333.

52. Strassfeld, *Jewish Holidays*, 61.

53. Greenberg, *Jewish Way*, 333, 337.

54. Ibid., 339.

55. See Feldman, "'It Is My Brothers Whom I Am Seeking'"; see also Handelman and Katz, "State Ceremonies of Israel."

56. March of the Living, *To Know and to Remember*, 6. See also Michael Berenbaum's foreword to Shevelev, with Schomer, *Liberating the Ghosts.*

57. See, for example, Bilu, "Dreams and Wishes of the Saint"; Myerhoff, "Pilgrimage to Meron"; Sered, "Rachel's Tomb"; Edith Turner, "Bar Yohai, Mystic"; and Weingrod, *Saint of Beersheba.*

58. Victor Turner, "Center Out There," 213–14. See also Turner and Turner, *Image and Pilgrimage in Christian Culture*, esp. 34–35, and Graburn, "Tourism."

59. Turner, "Center Out There," 216; see also John Eade and Michael J. Sallnow's introduction to Eade and Sallnow, *Contesting the Sacred*, 4.

60. Young, *Texture of Memory*, 144. Feldman expresses this disjunction in an even more nuanced manner while comparing Israeli and North American trips: "The Israeli trip is bi-polar: the visit to the death-world of Poland reifies the centrality of their normal life-world Israel, and imbues it with added significance and devotion. The March of the Living trip is tri-polar: the constructed death-world of Poland is followed by a visit to a *constructed*, idealized life-world of Israel. After the gray deprivation, vulnerability and death of Poland, Israel is *constructed* as the land of milk and honey, sexy soldiers, military force, sun, beach, and abundant falafel and chocolate. Israel is an idealized 'future of the Jewish people' world. The students then return to their *present* world in Los Angeles or Montreal. . . . If, in the trip's construction of reality, the answer to Auschwitz is a strong Israel, how does the student living in L. A. account for his life elsewhere upon his return?" (Feldman, "'It Is My Brothers Whom I Am Seeking,'" 36).

61. Kugelmass, "Rites of the Tribe," 419.

62. Simon Herman, for example, maintains, "Jewishness of even nonreligious Jews cannot be completely divorced from its religious associations. Although the term is used as a matter of convenience, there is strictly speaking no 'secular' Jewishness." See Herman, *Jewish Identity*, 36.

63. Greenzweig bases his assumption on an estimate that in twenty years, one hundred thousand teens will have been on the march. For Bunder, the clearest indication of the success of the march is not so much in present or future Jewish communal involvement as it is in fighting intermarriage, assimilation, and the general ravages of contemporary American culture. The Miami office keeps statistics showing that 1,100 students have gone from South Florida; 475 have married, with no divorces and only two intermarriages.

64. Though I must point out that what they saw in Poland were generally ruins and reconstructions, memorials and museum displays, all requiring a fair amount of "filling in" through explanation or imagination and evocation so that what was seen and what was experienced complemented each other at each site of remembrance.

65. Woocher, "Sacred Survival," and *Sacred Survival.* See also Kugelmass, "Rites of the Tribe," 424–33.

66. They define the three as "(1) integration (uniting the society by involving its members in a set of common ceremonies and myths, which are themselves integrative and in turn express a sense of a common past, a common condition, and a common destiny on the part of the participants); (2) legitimation (transmitting the sense of an inherent justness or rightness in the nature of the social order and in the goals pursued by the society); and (3) mobilization (galvanizing the efforts and energies of society's members on behalf of socially approved tasks and responsibilities)" (Liebman and Don-Yehiya, *Civil Religion in Israel,* 5).

67. Woocher, *Sacred Survival,* 15–16.

68. Ibid., 131.

69. Ibid., 133. Speaking of using the Holocaust as an "antidote" to the challenges of contemporary Jewish education, Alan Mintz notes that "it is only the most hardened teenager who remains unaffected . . . by being taken to visit the extermination sites in Europe. Because these scenes of pathos and atrocity often have the power to trigger a strong visceral reaction, exposure to the Holocaust is prone to being mobilized as the last functioning weapon in the arsenal of Jewish education. The use of the Holocaust in this way thus represents not so much the success of Jewish historical memory as the failure to convey the real contents of Jewish literacy" (*Popular Culture and the Shaping of Holocaust Memory in America,* 162).

70. See Helmreich, "March of the Living." These tenets are "1. The unity of the Jewish people; 2. Mutual responsibility; 3. Jewish survival in a threatening world; 4. The centrality of the State of Israel; 5. The enduring value of Jewish tradition; 6. *Tzedakah:* philanthropy and social justice; 7. Americanness as a virtue." See Woocher, *Sacred Survival,* 67–68.

71. Woocher, *Sacred Survival,* 150; emphasis added.

72. Handelman, *Models and Mirrors,* 22–62.

73. Webber reminds us that these same fields were spread with the "cremated ashes" of those murdered at Birkenau, even though the site was never "consecrated as a cemetery as such, either during the war or after" (*Future of Auschwitz,* 7–8). He says later that "part of Auschwitz should be treated as a cemetery, at which people wishing to commemorate those individuals and communities murdered in Auschwitz could be invited to lay their tombstones, say their prayers, find their consolations, observe their silences. Apart from anything else, this would have the effect of sacralizing the ground, sacralizing part of the Auschwitz space, and thereby institutionalizing the link between the events of Auschwitz, the memorial ground of Auschwitz, and ourselves" (27). To my knowledge, the March of the Living, in organizing the planting of memorial plaques, goes furthest in such an institutionalization and sacralization of memory.

74. Elon, *Israelis,* 200. Interestingly, Elon's own language suggests a connection through the theme of planting to the law establishing Yad Vashem as well: "The law empowers and calls upon the memorial authority of Yad Vashem to . . . '*implant* in the country and throughout the Jewish people the day designated by the Knesset as Memorial Day for the holocaust and for the heroism [of the resisters] and foster an atmosphere of unanimity in memory'" (206; Elon's emphasis and brackets).

75. Horn, *March of the Living, 1992*, 42–43. March organizers have made Horn's reflections into a short video with the same title. The details of her own act of planting help reinforce my argument for the thematic unity of this genre of march activity, while such planting also effects a connection between the two landscapes, negative and positive, of the pilgrimage, as she plants her tree with soil from the camps: "I took out a plastic bag, and I poured its contents onto the earth around the little tree. Mud from Auschwitz, saturated with human blood. Earth from Treblinka, gray and dusty with human ashes. Soil from Majdanek, black with human ashes and with my own tears. Dirt from Birkenau, with its weird flecks of white ashes from human bones" (42). For another account of tree planting in Israel, see Goldman, "The March of the Living in Retrospect," 35. See also the discussion by Elon (*Israelis*, 189–221) and the development of such themes in the context of Holocaust literature in Ezrahi, "Revisioning the Past." Recall also the burial of soil underneath the Hall of Remembrance at the USHMM.

76. Quoted in Halevi, "Who Owns the Memory?" 28.

77. Kugelmass, "Rites of the Tribe," 437.

78. Feldman "'It Is My Brothers Whom I Am Seeking.'" See also Victor Turner, "Center Out There," esp. 214–15.

79. Security considerations have greatly curtailed the experiences of latter-day marchers. One could speculate that in 2002, when the march did not go to Israel at all, a serious rupture at the center of the experience had occurred, leaving the march essentially unfinished. The impact of this radical change in itinerary would be interesting to study.

80. On the issue of "managing" the Holocaust, see Patraka, *Spectacular Suffering*, 126–31.

81. Erik Cohen, "Phenomenology of Tourist Experiences," 190, 191.

82. Kugelmass, "Rites of the Tribe," 419–20, 428.

83. Eade and Sallnow, *Contesting the Sacred*, 4; Erik Cohen, "Phenomenology of Tourist Experiences," 196; Kugelmass, "Rites of the Tribe," 418.

84. Furthermore, what can we make of the report I received from Michael Berl, director of the March of the Living Center on Mount Scopus in Jerusalem, that, some time after the march has left Birkenau, the plaques marking it as a symbolic graveyard and a memorial text are regularly cleared by the Polish authority responsible for camp upkeep and, according to Berl, are then used as heating fuel for their homes? For more criticism of the hegemonic discourse of the march organizers, see Elaine Shizgal Cohen, "March of the Living: An Educator's Perspective." See also Novick, *Holocaust in American Life*, 160.

85. Eade and Sallnow, *Contesting the Sacred*, 10.

86. Myerhoff, "We Don't Wrap Herring," 199.

87. The quotation is from a previous version of the March of the Living Web site's homepage, last accessed in July 2002, that is no longer available. The site's description of the 2003 High School March says, "As one of the Marchers you will retrace the steps of the 'March of Death,' the actual route which countless numbers of our people were forced to take on their way to the gas chambers at Birkenau" (<http://www.motl.org/programs/highSchool.htm>). The "welcome" to participants (unchanged at least since 1994) opening the study guide further states, "You will be one of the chosen few who will walk in the footsteps of the 6,000,000.

The march from Auschwitz to Birkenau will be along the same path which once two million of our people marched to their death in the gas chambers and crematoria of hell." See <http://www.motl.org/resource/curriculum/curriculum_a.htm>. A description in section 11 of the march's study guide is more precise and offers some explanation of the genesis of this foundational concept. It puts the "March of the Living" in the context of the infamous "death marches," though it revises and expands the accepted meaning of the term. What Holocaust scholars and survivors generally agree is a term referring only to the forced marches west out of the camps, late in the war, ahead of advancing Russian armies, here includes a variety of "death marches," such as deportations from the ghettos, movements of prisoners, removals from railway transports, and camp evacuations. "The March of the Living will take you from the Auschwitz Concentration Camp to the Birkenau Death Camp. You will walk beneath the sign that says 'Arbeit Macht Frei' and then walk through the gate that took millions of Jews to their death inside the Birkenau Death Camp. *At this point you will be marching on the same path that millions of Jews marched before you, on the way to their death.* However, you will immediately recognize the difference—you are alive! Indeed, the March of the Living is your testimony to the survival of the Jewish people" (see <http://www. motl.org/resource/curriculum/curriculum_11.htm>; emphasis added). Greenzweig insists that the "march" is not so literal; the point is that "many marched into Auschwitz and didn't come out, [whereas] we march into Auschwitz and come out." Regarding the actual number of Jews marched to their deaths from Auschwitz to Birkenau, it is clear that only a very small percentage (1–4 percent) of all the Jews who arrived at the Auschwitz complex could have been transferred in this manner, and many of them would not have gone immediately to the gas. This is because only those Jews (no more than 11,000) who arrived in the first transports (March–April 1942) were initially housed in Auschwitz I, with those who survived later transferring to Birkenau, and only about 30,000 more (arriving May–June 1942) may have been incarcerated and transferred in the same way. It is likely that a much larger number of Jews (about 400,000, arriving July 1942–April 1944) did walk roughly the last portion of the route, from the first "Judenrampe" (off the railway spur) into the Birkenau camp, though not all those were immediately selected for gassing. The majority of Jewish Auschwitz victims did not walk the "March of the Living" path (based on an email exchange between the author and Robert Jan van Pelt, September 5, 2002).

88. Myerhoff, "We Don't Wrap Herring," 222.

89. Bell, *Ritual Theory, Ritual Practice*, 124.

90. Young, *Texture of Memory*, xii, xi–xii, 7.

91. Smith, *To Take Place*, 103, 104.

92. Eliade, "Sacred Places," 392.

93. See Halbwachs, *Collective Memory*, and *On Collective Memory*, esp. 46–51.

94. He suggests that "we may say that our experiences of the present largely depend upon our knowledge of the past, and that our images of the past commonly serve to legitimate a present social order. And yet these points, though true, are as they stand insufficient when thus put. For images of the past and recollected knowledge of the past, I want to argue, are conveyed and sustained by (more or less ritual) performances" (Connerton, *How Societies Remember*, 3–4).

95. Connerton, 4.

96. Connerton, 38, 70, 45. With regard to ritual enactments of the past, see also Zerubavel, *Recovered Roots*, and Gillis, "Memory and Identity."

97. Connerton says, "Incorporating practices depend for their particular mnemonic effect on two distinctive features: their mode of existence and their mode of acquisition. They do not exist 'objectively,' independently of their being performed. And they are acquired in such a way as not to require explicit reflection on their performance. . . . [C]ommemorative ceremonies also are preserved through their performance; and, because of their performativity and their formalisation, they too are not easily susceptible to critical scrutiny and evaluation by those habituated to their performance. Both commemorative ceremonies and bodily practices therefore contain a measure of insurance against the process of cumulative questioning entailed in all discursive practices. This is the source of their importance and persistence as mnemonic systems" (*How Societies Remember*, 102).

98. Fentress and Wickham, *Social Memory*, ix.

99. Fentress and Wickham, x, 201.

100. Yerushalmi, *Zakhor*, 44.

101. Casey, *Remembering*, 218, 250.

102. Ibid., 228.

103. Ibid., 256.

104. Kugelmass, "Rites of the Tribe," 433.

CONCLUSION. REMEMBER FORGETTING / FORGET REMEMBERING

1. The best overview of Holocaust literature remains Ezrahi's groundbreaking *By Words Alone*. See also, among others, Langer, *The Holocaust and the Literary Imagination*; Rosenfeld, *A Double Dying*; Mintz, *Hurban*; Young, *Writing and Rewriting the Holocaust*; and Horowitz, *Voicing the Void*.

2. Cited in Friedländer, "Preface to a Symposium," 201; ibid., 203.

3. Friedländer, *Reflections of Nazism*, 11–19.

4. Ibid., 39, 49.

5. Saul Friedländer, quoted in "On Kitsch," 227–28, 218.

6. Friedländer, *Reflections of Nazism*, 20.

7. All references to Wiesel's *The Forgotten* will be given parenthetically.

8. Wiesel offers here a vicarious acting out of "Jewish rage," in contrast to the suppressed rage Naomi Seidman has argued is present in Wiesel's seminal Holocaust memoir *Night*, in its translation from Yiddish to French. For example, note the difference Seidman perceives between Wiesel's accounts in the two versions of the activities of the survivors following liberation: "*Un die velt* [*hot geshvign* (And the World Kept Silent)] depicts a post-Holocaust landscape in which Jewish boys 'run off' to steal provisions and rape German girls; *Night* extracts from this scene of lawless retribution a far more innocent picture of the aftermath of the war, with young men going off to the nearest city to look for clothes and sex." See Seidman, "Elie Wiesel and the Scandal of Jewish Rage," 6. Note as well that in *The Forgotten* this acting out is itself accomplished through an "other"—Itzik, not Elhanan—and later recalled through translation, as I will discuss: setting up two filters for the very imagination of the acting out of Jewish rage.

9. Larry Nachman, quoted in "On Kitsch," 227.

10. The phrase is the title of a fine collection of essays published in honor of Saul Friedländer. See Arad, *Passing into History*.

11. All citations to Grossman's *See Under: Love* and Ozick's *Messiah of Stockholm* will be given parenthetically in the text.

12. Sokoloff, "Reinventing Bruno Schulz," 177–78.

13. Perhaps this is why Lars acts in such a proprietary manner with respect to this text (is that not how we all act with respect to our Jewish past?)—to the point of an almost sacred engagement. Adela even calls him a priest, adding: "A priest is just what's needed. You'd be on your knees, wouldn't you? On your knees to every word. You'd think you were anointed" (Ozick, *Messiah of Stockholm*, 79–80). Lars as priest is thus seen as both master of and slave to the text to which he finally gains access.

14. Recall Gershom Scholem's argument that "Jewish messianism is in its origins and by its nature . . . a theory of catastrophe." See Scholem, *Messianic Idea in Judaism*, 7.

15. The themes of doubling and duplicity, illegibility and intertextuality, here and in Grossman's novel, suggest that a thorough postmodern, poststructuralist reading of the imagined Schulzian *Messiah* remains to be investigated.

16. Could Ozick be suggesting that the Messiah is an idol of sorts or that the messianic idea is an idolatrous one? Sokoloff considers Ozick's "moral abhorrence of idolatry" ("Reinventing Bruno Schulz," 176) and refers to Ozick's own essay on Schulz (in Ozick's *Art and Ardor*, 224–28) as proof of the association in Ozick's mind of Schulz with idolatry. It is also interesting that Schulz himself prepared a portfolio of drawings (he was a graphic artist long before he became a writer) that he distributed among his friends, titled *The Book of Idolatry*.

17. Scholem, *Messianic Idea*, 18.

18. "It had receded, whatever it was—he retained nothing, nothing lingered: only the faintest tremor of some strenuous force. Mute imprint of noise—a city falling, crumbling, his own moans, relentless lamentation. Sound of shooting. Amnesia. Lost. Nothing remained. Lamentation remained. Elegy after great pain" (Ozick, *Messiah of Stockholm*, 115).

19. Sokoloff makes this point clearly: "Offering a view of art as just such a form of ersatz community, a weak substitute for shared social values and customs, the novel expresses dissatisfaction with a Jewishness that, after the Holocaust, depends on imagined or adopted affinities with Jewish ancestors rather than on a natural process of succession, the inheriting of traditions and a sense of self from previous generations." See Sokoloff, "Reinventing Bruno Schulz," 178. See also Yerushalmi, *Zakhor*, 109, 105–17, for further discussions of this issue.

20. Jewish mystical tradition considers fish "pure" animals and highly symbolic, as they were the only animals to survive the flood outside Noah's ark.

21. Here Grossman reads back into Schulz's genius the common post-Holocaust argument that language itself is diseased because of recent history. In this regard see Michael Rothberg's excellent reading of Theodor Adorno's famous statement, in *Traumatic Realism*, 19–58. Note also that, in this passage, "Messiah" is not italicized.

22. I am grateful to Jonathan Boyarin for pointing out that this image of forgetting is precisely the opposite of Walter Benjamin's idea that "only a redeemed mankind receives the fullness of its past—which is to say, only for a redeemed mankind has its past become citable in all its moments" ("Theses on the Philosophy of History," in *Illuminations*, 256). For a whole range of essays that take Benjamin as a point of departure, see Boyarin's *Storm from Paradise*.

23. Momik's knowledge of Bruno is, after all, a product of textuality and narrative.

24. See Sokoloff, "Reinventing Bruno Schulz," 189. Sokoloff notes, somewhat wryly, that Grossman's text "soberly recognizes and warns the reader that art, of necessity, accomplishes only more modest goals than salvation" (197).

25. Sokoloff counters: "Bruno tells [Momik] that Anshel's is a story everyone repeatedly learns and forgets. It is the most intimate, elusive of tales, recalcitrant to narrative formulation because it unravels itself as quickly as it can be intuited. Approaching the writing of this tale is where madness begins. In other words, to confront the Holocaust through art, to imagine the unimaginable, is impossible. Nevertheless, finding a way both to grasp and to cope with the horror is something each individual must discover for himself" (ibid., 195).

26. Hartman, "Book of the Destruction," 326; Ezrahi, *By Words Alone*, 217.

27. Yerushalmi, *Zakhor*, 99.

28. Ezrahi writes: "It is, therefore, not over the relative jurisdiction of referential and symbolic languages that the discussion of legitimacy takes place in Israel; rather, it is between innocent and subversive appropriations of the 'master narrative.' Whereas ironic appropriations of the philosophical and literary premises of Jewish survival are built in to the dialectics of the lamentation tradition, a few contemporary writers have so assaulted the iconic configurations as to challenge the narrative in its most strategic places. In fiction, Yoram Kaniuk was one of the earliest and David Grossman one of the most recent writers to have co-opted the consensual symbols of the Holocaust and the Zionist story of collective regeneration into a radical parody of the paradigm of secular redemption" ("'The Grave in the Air'": 274). She adds in a footnote to this passage: "Grossman . . . is rewriting not the history but the constitutive myth that underlies the social ethos" (392 n. 52). That Grossman tells an Israeli story and Ozick one of the Diaspora, with all the complexities of myth and memory this distinction inaugurates, deserves further scrutiny.

29. Schulz, *Sanatorium*, 21.

30. Amis, *Time's Arrow*, 80.

31. Ibid., 120. The author borrows the famous German phrase from Levi, *Survival in Auschwitz*, 29.

32. Amis, *Time's Arrow*, 122.

33. Zelizer, *Remembering to Forget*, 14, 141, 163.

34. Ibid., 171, 175 (Zelizer's emphasis).

35. Ibid., 202.

36. See ibid., 213–20.

37. Ibid., 227.

38. In addition to the *Critical Inquiry* article, see also Young, *At Memory's Edge*, esp. chaps. 4 and 5, "Memory, Countermemory, and the End of the Monument: Horst Hoheisel, Micha Ullman, Rachel Whiteread, and Renata Stih and Frieder Schnock," 90–119, and "Memory against Itself in Germany Today: Jochen

Gerz's Countermonuments," 120–51, respectively. Both chapters are elaborations and expansions on "The Counter-Monument."

39. Young, *At Memory's Edge*, 135.

40. Young, "Counter-Monument," 272.

41. Ibid., 295.

42. Huyssen, *Twilight Memories*, 250.

43. Zerubavel, *Recovered Roots*, 214.

44. Finkielkraut, *Imaginary Jew*, 15.

45. Bauman, "Hereditary Victimhood," 36.

46. Novick, *Holocaust in American Life*, 151, 164, citing Yehuda Elkana, "A Plea for Forgetting," *Ha'aretz*, March 2, 1988.

47. Novick, *Holocaust in American Life*, 261.

48. Deut. 25:17–19. *JPS Hebrew-English Tanakh*, 2d ed. Philadelphia: Jewish Publication Society, 1999.

Bibliography

Adorno, Theodor W. "Valéry Proust Museum." In *Prisms*. Translated by Samuel Weber and Shierry Weber. Cambridge: MIT Press, 1981.

Agamben, Giorgio. *Remnants of Auschwitz: The Witness and the Archive*. Translated by Daniel Heller-Roazen. New York: Zone Books, 1999.

Amis, Martin. *Time's Arrow, or The Memory of the Offense*. New York: Harmony Books, 1991.

Amishai-Maisels, Ziva. *Depiction and Interpretation: The Influence of the Holocaust on the Visual Arts*. Oxford: Pergamon, 1993.

Apel, Dora. "The Tattooed Jew." In *Visual Culture and the Holocaust*, edited by Barbie Zelizer, 300–320. New Brunswick: Rutgers University Press, 2001.

Arad, Gulie Ne'eman, ed. *Passing into History: Nazism and the Holocaust beyond Memory: In Honor of Saul Friedländer on His Sixty-Fifth Birthday*. Special issue of *History and Memory: Studies in Representation of the Past* 9, nos. 1/2 (1997).

Azoulay, Ariella. "With Open Doors: Museums and Historical Narratives in Israel's Public Space." In *Museum Culture: Histories, Discourses, Spectacles*, edited by Daniel J. Sherman and Irit Rogoff, 85–109. Minneapolis: University of Minnesota Press, 1994.

Bal, Mieke, Jonathan Crew, and Leo Spitzer, eds. *Acts of Memory: Cultural Recall in the Present*. Hanover: University Press of New England, 1999.

Bartov, Omer. *Murder in Our Midst: The Holocaust, Industrial Killing, and Representation*. New York: Oxford University Press, 1996.

———. "Spielberg's Oskar: Hollywood Tries Evil." In *Spielberg's Holocaust: Critical Perspectives on "Schindler's List,"* edited by Yosefa Loshitzky, 41–60. Bloomington: Indiana University Press, 1997.

Baudrillard, Jean. "Simulacra and Simulations." In *Jean Baudrillard: Selected Writings*, edited by Mark Poster, 166–84. Stanford: Stanford University Press, 1988.

Bauman, Zygmunt. "Hereditary Victimhood: The Holocaust's Life as a Ghost." *Tikkun* 13, no. 4 (1998): 33–38.

Bell, Catherine. *Ritual Theory, Ritual Practice*. New York: Oxford University Press, 1992.

Benjamin, Walter. *Illuminations*. Edited by Hannah Arendt. Translated by Harry Zohn. New York: Schocken, 1969.

———. "The Work of Art in the Age of Mechanical Reproduction." In *Illuminations*, edited by Hannah Arendt, translated by Harry Zohn, 217–51. New York: Schocken, 1969.

Berenbaum, Michael. *The World Must Know: The History of the Holocaust as Told in the United States Holocaust Memorial Museum*. Boston: Little, Brown and Company, 1993.

Bilu, Yoram. "Dreams and Wishes of the Saint." In *Judaism Viewed from Within and from Without: Anthropological Studies*, edited by Harvey E. Goldberg, 285–313. Albany: State University of New York Press, 1987.

Black, Edwin. *IBM and the Holocaust: The Strategic Alliance between Nazi Germany and America's Most Powerful Corporation.* New York: Crown, 2001.

Bland, Kalman P. *The Artless Jew: Medieval and Modern Affirmations and Denials of the Visual.* Princeton: Princeton University Press, 2000.

Bloch, Sara Kviat. "Redeeming the Holocaust: Survivors of the Shoah Visual History Foundation." Unpublished paper.

Blum-Dobkin, Toby. "Videotaping Holocaust Interviews: Questions and Answers from an Interviewer." *Jews and the Media.* Special issue of *Jewish Folklore and Ethnology Review* 16, no. 1 (1994): 46–50.

Boyarin, Jonathan. *Polish Jews in Paris: The Ethnography of Memory.* Bloomington: Indiana University Press, 1991.

———. *Storm from Paradise: The Politics of Jewish Memory.* Minneapolis: University of Minnesota Press, 1992.

Boym, Svetlana. *The Future of Nostalgia.* New York: Basic Books, 2001.

Braiterman, Zachary. *(God) after Auschwitz: Tradition and Change in Post-Holocaust Jewish Thought.* Princeton: Princeton University Press, 1998.

Brenner, Rachel Feldhay. "Teaching the Holocaust in Academia: Educational Mission(s) and Pedagogical Approaches." *Journal of Holocaust Education* 8, no. 2 (1999): 1–26.

Bresheeth, Haim. "The Great Taboo Broken: Reflections on the Israeli Reception of *Schindler's List.*" In *Spielberg's Holocaust: Critical Perspectives on "Schindler's List,"* edited by Yosefa Loshitzky, 193–212 Bloomington: Indiana University Press, 1997.

Browning, Christopher R. *Ordinary Men: Reserve Police Battalion 101 and the Final Solution in Poland.* New York: HarperCollins, 1992.

Cantor, Jay. "Kat and Maus." *Yale Review* 77, no. 1 (1987): 29–40.

Casey, Edward. *Remembering: A Phenomenological Study.* Bloomington: Indiana University Press, 1987.

Celan, Paul. "Death Fugue." Translated by John Felstiner. In *Against Forgetting: Twentieth-Century Poetry of Witness,* edited and with an introduction by Carolyn Forché, 380–82. New York: W. W. Norton, 1993.

Childs, Brevard S. *Memory and Tradition in Israel.* London: SCM Press, 1962.

Cohen, Elaine Shizgal. "The March of the Living: An Educator's Perspective." *Jewish Spectator* 56, no. 2 (fall 1991): 11–12.

Cohen, Erik. "A Phenomenology of Tourist Experiences." *Sociology* 13 (May 1979): 179–201.

Cohen, Richard I. "Self-Image through Objects: Toward a Social History of Jewish Art Collecting and Jewish Museums." In *The Uses of Tradition: Jewish Continuity in the Modern Era,* edited by Jack Wertheimer, 203–42. New York: Jewish Theological Seminary of America, 1992.

Cole, Tim. *Selling the Holocaust: From Auschwitz to Schindler: How History Is Bought, Packaged, and Sold.* New York: Routledge, 1999.

Connerton, Paul. *How Societies Remember.* Cambridge: Cambridge University Press, 1989.

Coser, Lewis A. Introduction to *On Collective Memory,* by Maurice Halbwachs. Edited and translated by Lewis A. Coser, 1–34. Chicago: University of Chicago Press, 1992.

Crimp, Douglas. "On the Museum's Ruins." In *The Anti-Aesthetic: Essays on Postmodern Culture*, edited by Hal Foster, 43–56. Seattle: Bay Press, 1983.

Culler, Jonathan. "Semiotics of Tourism." *American Journal of Semiotics* 1, nos. 1–2 (1981): 127–40.

Davis, Natalie Zemon, and Randolph Starn. Introduction. *Memory and Counter-Memory*, edited by Natalie Zemon Davis and Randolph Starn. Special issue of *Representations*, no. 26 (1989): 1–6.

Derrida, Jacques. *Archive Fever: A Freudian Impression*. Translated by Eric Prenowitz. Chicago: University of Chicago Press, 1995.

Donato, Eugenio. "The Museum's Furnace: Notes toward a Contextual Reading of *Bouvard and Pécuchet*." In *Textual Strategies: Perspectives in Post-Structuralist Criticism*, edited by Josué V. Harari, 213–38. Ithaca: Cornell University Press, 1979.

Doneson, Judith E. *The Holocaust in American Film*. 2d ed. Syracuse: Syracuse University Press, 2002.

Dubner, Stephen J. "Steven the Good." In *Steven Spielberg: Interviews*, edited by Lester D. Friedman and Brent Notbohm. Jackson: University Press of Mississippi, 2000.

Dwork, Debórah, and Robert Jan van Pelt. "Reclaiming Auschwitz." In *Holocaust Remembrance: The Shapes of Memory*, edited by Geoffrey H. Hartman, 232–51. Oxford, United Kingdom: Basil Blackwell, 1994.

Eade, John, and Michael J. Sallnow, eds. *Contesting the Sacred: The Anthropology of Christian Pilgrimage*. London: Routledge, 1991.

Eliade, Mircea. "Sacred Places: Temple, Palace, 'Center of the World.'" In *Patterns in Comparative Religion*, by Mircea Eliade, translated by Rosemary Sheed, 367–87. Cleveland: Meridian Books, 1963.

Elon, Amos. *The Israelis: Founders and Sons*. New York: Holt, Rinehart and Winston, 1971.

Enzensberger, Hans Magnus. "Constituents of a Theory of the Media." In *Video Culture: A Critical Investigation*, edited by John G. Hanhardt, 96–123. Rochester, N.Y.: Visual Studies Workshop Press, 1986.

Ezrahi, Sidra DeKoven. *Booking Passage: Exile and Homecoming in the Modern Jewish Imagination*. Berkeley: University of California Press, 2000.

———. *By Words Alone: The Holocaust in Literature*. Chicago: University of Chicago Press, 1980.

———. "Dan Pagis—Out of Line: A Poetics of Decomposition." *Prooftexts* 10, no. 2 (1990): 335–63.

———. "'The Grave in the Air': Unbound Metaphors in Holocaust Poetry." In *Probing the Limits of Representation: Nazism and the "Final Solution,"* edited by Saul Friedländer, 259–76. Cambridge: Harvard University Press, 1992.

———. "Representing Auschwitz." *History and Memory* 7, no. 2 (1996): 121–54.

———. "Revisioning the Past: The Changing Legacy of the Holocaust in Hebrew Literature." *Salmagundi*, nos. 68–69 (1986): 245–70.

Feldman, Jackie. "'It Is My Brothers Whom I Am Seeking': Israeli Youths' Pilgrimages to Poland of the Shoah." *Pilgrimage*, edited by Shifra Epstein. Special issue of *Jewish Folklore and Ethnology Review* 17, nos. 1–2 (1995): 33–37.

Felman, Shoshana. "Education and Crisis, or the Vicissitudes of Teaching." In *Testimony: Crises of Witnessing in Literature, Psychoanalysis, and History*, by Shoshana Felman and Dori Laub, M. D., 1–56. New York: Routledge, 1992.

Felman, Shoshana, and Dori Laub, M. D. *Testimony: Crises of Witnessing in Literature, Psychoanalysis, and History*. New York: Routledge, 1992.

Fentress, James, and Chris Wickham. *Social Memory*. Oxford, U.K.: Blackwell, 1992.

Finkielkraut, Alain. *The Imaginary Jew*. Translated by Kevin O'Neill and David Suchoff. Lincoln: University of Nebraska Press, 1994.

Flax, Jane. "Re-Membering the Selves: Is the Repressed Gendered?" *Women and Memory*, edited by Margaret A. Lourie, Domna C. Stanton, and Martha Vicinus. Special issue of *Michigan Quarterly Review* 26, no. 1 (1987): 92–110.

Frank, Anne. *Anne Frank: The Diary of a Young Girl*. New York: Simon and Schuster, 1953.

———. *The Diary of Anne Frank: The Critical Edition*. Edited by David Barnouw and Gerrold Van Der Stroom. Translated by Arnold Pomerans and B. M. Mooyaart-Doubleday. New York: Doubleday, 1986.

Friedländer, Saul. Introduction to *Probing the Limits of Representation: Nazism and the "Final Solution,"* edited by Saul Friedländer, 1–21. Cambridge: Harvard University Press, 1992.

———. "Preface to a Symposium: Kitsch and the Apocalyptic Imagination." *Salmagundi*, nos. 85–86 (1990): 201–6.

———. *Reflections of Nazism: An Essay on Kitsch and Death*. Translated by Thomas Weyr. New York: Harper and Row, 1984.

———. "Die Shoah als Element in der Konstruktion israelischer Erinnerung." *Babylon* (Frankfurt am Main) 2 (1987): 10–22.

———. "The Shoah in Present Historical Consciousness." In *Memory, History, and the Extermination of the Jews of Europe*, 42–63. Bloomington: Indiana University Press, 1993.

Friedländer, Saul, in collaboration with Adam Seligman. "Memory of the *Shoah* in Israel: Symbols, Rituals, and Ideological Polarization." In *The Art of Memory: Holocaust Memorials in History*, edited by James E. Young, 149–57. New York: Jewish Museum; Munich: Prestel-Verlag, 1994.

Friedman, Jeanette. "Steven Spielberg: Partner in History." *Lifestyles 5757*, summer 1997, 19–23.

Friedman, Michelle A. "The Labor of Remembrance." In *Mapping Jewish Identities*, ed. Laurence J. Silberstein, 97–121. New York: New York University Press, 2000.

———. "Reckoning with Ghosts: Second-Generation Holocaust Literature and the Labor of Remembrance." Ph.D. diss., Bryn Mawr, 2001.

Funkenstein, Amos. "Collective Memory and Historical Consciousness." *History and Memory* 1, no. 1 (1989): 5–26.

———. "Response from Amos Funkenstein [to David Myers]." *History and Memory* 4, no. 2 (1992): 147–48.

Gedi, Noa, and Yigal Elam. "Collective Memory—What Is It?" *History and Memory* 8, no. 1 (1996): 30–50.

Gilbert, Martin. *Holocaust Journey: Travelling in Search of the Past*. New York: Columbia University Press, 1997.

Gillis, John R. "Memory and Identity: The History of a Relationship." In *Commemorations: The Politics of National Identity*, edited by John R. Gillis, 3–24. Princeton: Princeton University Press, 1994.

Glassie, Henry. *Passing the Time in Ballymenone: Culture and History of an Ulster Community*. Philadelphia: University of Pennsylvania Press, 1982.

Goldhagen, Daniel Jonah. *Hitler's Willing Executioners: Ordinary Germans and the Holocaust*. New York: Knopf, 1996.

Goldman, Solomon. "The March of the Living in Retrospect." *Jewish Education* 59, no. 3 (1992): 33–36.

Gopnik, Adam. "Comics and Catastrophe." *New Republic*, June 22, 1987, 29–34.

Graburn, Nelson H. H. "Tourism: The Sacred Journey." In *Hosts and Guests: The Anthropology of Tourism*, edited by Valene L. Smith, 21–36. 2d ed. Philadelphia: University of Pennsylvania Press, 1989.

Graham-Dixon, Andrew. "Deliverance for Art's Sake." *Independent*, September 10, 1987.

Greenberg, Irving. *The Jewish Way: Living the Holidays*. New York: Simon and Schuster, 1988.

Greene, Joshua M., and Shiva Kumar, eds., in consultation with Joanne Weiner Rudof. *Witness: Voices from the Holocaust*. New York: Free Press, 2000.

Grossman, David. *See Under: Love*. Translated by Betsy Rosenberg. New York: Farrar Straus Giroux, 1989.

Gruber, Ruth Ellen. "Remembering Poland's Jews." *New York Times*, January 29, 1995, sec. 5, pp. 8–9, 19.

Halbertal, Moshe, and Avishai Margalit. *Idolatry*. Translated by Naomi Goldblum. Cambridge: Harvard University Press, 1992.

Halbwachs, Maurice. *Les cadres sociaux de la mémoire*. 1925. Reprint, Paris: Presses Universitaires de France, 1952.

———. *The Collective Memory*. Translated by Francis Ditter Jr. and Vida Ditter. New York: Harper-Colophon, 1980.

———. *La mémoire collective*. Paris: Presses Universitaires de France, 1950.

———. *On Collective Memory*. Edited, translated, and introduction by Lewis A. Coser. Chicago: University of Chicago Press, 1992.

———. *La topographie légendaire des évangiles en terre sainte: Etude de mémoire collective*. Paris: Presses Universitaires de France, 1941.

Halevi, Yossi Klein. "Who Owns the Memory?" *Jerusalem Report*, February 25, 1993, 28–33.

Handelman, Don. *Models and Mirrors: Towards an Anthropology of Public Events*. Cambridge: Cambridge University Press, 1990.

Handelman, Don, and Elihu Katz. "State Ceremonies of Israel—Remembrance Day and Independence Day." In *Models and Mirrors: Towards an Anthropology of Public Events*, by Don Handelman, 191–233. Cambridge: Cambridge University Press, 1990.

Haraway, Donna. "Teddy Bear Patriarchy: Taxidermy in the Garden of Eden, New York City, 1908–1936." In *Primate Visions: Gender, Race, and Nature in the World of Modern Science*. New York: Routledge, 1989.

Hartman, Geoffrey H. "The Book of the Destruction." In *Probing the Limits of Representation: Nazism and the "Final Solution,"* edited by Saul Friedländer, 318–34. Cambridge: Harvard University Press, 1992.

———. "The Cinema Animal." In *Spielberg's Holocaust: Critical Perspectives on "Schindler's List,"* edited by Yosefa Loshitzky, 61–76. Bloomington: Indiana University Press, 1997.

———. *The Longest Shadow: In the Aftermath of the Holocaust.* Bloomington: Indiana University Press, 1996.

———. "Public Memory and Modern Experience." *Yale Journal of Criticism* 6, no. 2 (1993): 239–47.

———. "Tele-Suffering and Testimony in the Dot Com Era." In *Visual Culture and the Holocaust,* edited by Barbie Zelizer, 111–24. New Brunswick: Rutgers University Press, 2001.

Helmreich, William. "The March of the Living: A Follow-Up Study of Its Long Range Impact and Effects." Departments of Sociology and Judaic Studies, City University of New York Graduate Center and City College of New York, n.d.

Herman, Simon. *Jewish Identity: A Social Psychological Perspective.* Beverly Hills: Sage, 1977.

Hertzberg, Arthur. "How Jews Use Antisemitism." In *Antisemitism in America Today: Outspoken Experts Explode the Myths,* edited by Jerome A. Chanes. Seacaucus, N.J.: Carol Publishing Group, 1995.

Hirsch, Marianne. *Family Frames: Photography, Narrative, and Postmemory.* Cambridge: Harvard University Press, 1997.

———. "Projected Memory: Holocaust Photographs in Personal and Public Fantasy." In *Acts of Memory: Cultural Recall in the Present,* edited by Mieke Bal, Jonathan Crewe, and Leo Spitzer, 3–23. Hanover: University Press of New England, 1999.

———. "Surviving Images: Holocaust Photographs and the Work of Postmemory." In *Visual Culture and the Holocaust,* edited by Barbie Zelizer, 215–46. New Brunswick: Rutgers University Press, 2001.

Horn, Dara. *March of the Living, 1992: Excerpts from My Journal.* Miami: Central Agency for Jewish Education, 1993.

Horowitz, Sara R. "Mengele, the Gynecologist, and Other Stories of Women's Survival." In *Judaism since Gender,* edited by Miriam Peskowitz and Laura Levitt, 200–212. New York: Routledge, 1997.

———. *Voicing the Void: Muteness and Memory in Holocaust Fiction.* Albany: State University of New York Press, 1997.

Hunter, Robert. *A Box of Rain: Lyrics, 1965–1993.* New York: Penguin, 1993.

Huyssen, Andreas. "Monument and Memory in a Postmodern Age." In *The Art of Memory: Holocaust Memorials in History,* edited by James E. Young, 9–17. New York: Jewish Museum, 1994.

———. "Of Mice and Mimesis: Rending Spiegelman with Adorno." In *Visual Culture and the Holocaust,* edited by Barbie Zelizer, 28–42. New Brunswick: Rutgers University Press, 2001.

———. *Twilight Memories: Marking Time in a Culture of Amnesia.* New York: Routledge, 1995.

Irwin-Zarecka, Iwona. *Frames of Remembrance: The Dynamics of Collective Memory.* New Brunswick, N.J.: Transaction, 1994.

Jabès, Edmond. *The Book of Questions.* Vols. 1 and 2. Translated by Rosmarie Waldrop. Hanover: Wesleyan University Press, published by University Press of New England, 1991.

Kaes, Anton. "History and Film: Public Memory in the Age of Electronic Dissemination." *History and Memory* 2, no. 1 (1990): 111–29.

Kammen, Michael. *Mystic Chords of Memory: The Transformation of Tradition in American Culture.* New York: Knopf, 1991; New York: Vintage Books, 1993.

Kaplan, Harold. *Conscience and Memory: Meditations in a Museum of the Holocaust.* Chicago: University of Chicago Press, 1994.

Karp, Ivan. "Introduction: Museums and Communities: The Politics of Public Culture." In *Museums and Communities: The Politics of Public Culture,* edited by Ivan Karp, Christine Mullen Kreamer, and Stephen D. Lavine, 1–17. Washington: Smithsonian Institution Press, 1992.

Kaveny, Roz. "Suffering in Style." *Times Literary Supplement,* January 24, 1991, 21.

Kirshenblatt-Gimblett, Barbara. *Destination Culture: Tourism, Museums, and Heritage.* Berkeley: University of California Press, 1998.

Kochan, Lionel. *Beyond the Graven Image: A Jewish View.* New York: New York University Press, 1997.

Koonz, Claudia. *Mothers in the Fatherland: Women, the Family, and Nazi Politics.* New York: St. Martin's, 1987.

Kornblau, Gary. "The Museum of Tolerance." *Art Issues,* May/June 1993, 48.

Kugelmass, Jack. "Jewish Icons: Envisioning the Self in Images of the Other." In *Jews and Other Differences: The New Jewish Cultural Studies,* edited by Jonathan Boyarin and Daniel Boyarin, 30–53. Minneapolis: University of Minnesota Press, 1997.

———. "The Rites of the Tribe: The Meaning of Poland for American Jewish Tourists." *Going Home: YIVO Annual* 21 (1993): 395–453.

LaCapra, Dominick. *Representing the Holocaust: History, Theory, Trauma.* Ithaca: Cornell University Press, 1994.

Laderman, Gary, Oren Stier, and Richard Hecht. "Art Spiegelman's *Maus* and the Crisis of Representing the Holocaust." Unpublished paper.

Langer, Lawrence L. *The Holocaust and the Literary Imagination.* New Haven: Yale University Press, 1975.

———. *Holocaust Testimonies: The Ruins of Memory.* New Haven: Yale University Press, 1991.

———. "Memory's Time: Chronology and Duration in Holocaust Testimonies." *Yale Journal of Criticism* 6, no. 2 (1993): 263–73.

The Last Days. Executive producer Steven Spielberg. Produced by June Beallor and Ken Lipper. Directed by James Moll. Presented by Steven Spielberg and the Survivors of the Shoah Visual History Foundation. Distributed by October Films. 1998. Videocassette.

Laub, Dori, M. D. "Bearing Witness, or the Vicissitudes of Listening." In *Testimony: Crises of Witnessing in Literature, Psychoanalysis, and History,* by Shoshana Felman and Dori Laub, M. D., 57–74. New York: Routledge, 1992.

———. "An Event without a Witness: Truth, Testimony, and Survival." In *Testimony: Crises of Witnessing in Literature, Psychoanalysis, and History,* by Shoshana Felman and Dori Laub, M. D., 75–92. New York: Routledge, 1992.

Leibowitz, Yeshayahu. *Judaism, Human Values, and the Jewish State.* Edited by Eliezer Goldman. Translated by Eliezer Goldman and Yoram Navon, and by Zvi Jacobson, Gershon Levi, and Raphael Levi. Cambridge: Harvard University Press, 1992.

Levi, Primo. "The Memory of Offense." In *Bitburg in Moral and Political Perspective,* edited by Geoffrey Hartman, 130–37. Bloomington: Indiana University Press, 1986.

———. *Survival in Auschwitz: The Nazi Assault on Humanity.* Translated by Stuart Woolf. New York: Touchstone, 1996.

Lewis, Bernard. *History: Remembered, Recovered, Invented.* Princeton: Princeton University Press, 1975.

Liebman, Charles S., and Eliezer Don-Yehiya. *Civil Religion in Israel: Traditional Religion and Political Culture in the Jewish State.* Berkeley: University of California Press, 1983.

Linenthal, Edward Tabor. "Locating Holocaust Memory: The United States Holocaust Memorial Museum." In *American Sacred Space,* edited by David Chidester and Edward T. Linenthal, 220–61. Bloomington: Indiana University Press, 1995.

———. *Preserving Memory: The Struggle to Create America's Holocaust Museum.* New York: Viking, 1995.

———. *Sacred Ground: Americans and Their Battlefields.* Urbana: University of Illinois Press, 1991.

Lipsitz, George. *Time Passages: Collective Memory and American Popular Culture.* Minneapolis: University of Minnesota Press, 1990.

Liss, Andrea. *Trespassing through Shadows: Memory, Photography, and the Holocaust.* Minneapolis: University of Minnesota Press, 1998.

Lisus, Nicola A. "Misplacing Memory: The Effect of Television Format on Holocaust Remembrance." Master's thesis, University of Toronto, 1993.

Lisus, Nicola A., and Richard V. Ericson. "Misplacing Memory: The Effect of Television Format on Holocaust Remembrance." *British Journal of Sociology* 46, no. 1 (1995): 1–19.

Long, Charles H. *Significations: Signs, Symbols, and Images in the Interpretation of Religion.* Philadelphia: Fortress Press, 1986.

Lowenthal, David. *The Past Is a Foreign Country.* Cambridge: Cambridge University Press, 1985.

MacDonald, George F. "Change and Challenge: Museums in the Information Society." In *Museums and Communities: The Politics of Public Culture,* edited by Ivan Karp, Christine Mullen Kreamer, and Stephen D. Lavine, 158–81. Washington, D.C.: Smithsonian Institution Press, 1992.

March of the Living. *To Know and to Remember.* Israel: March of the Living, n.d.

Marmur, Dow. "The Struggle between Text and Land in Contemporary Jewry: Reflections on George Steiner's *Our Homeland, the Text.*" *History of European Ideas* 20, nos. 4–6 (1995): 807–13.

Miller, Judith. *One, by One, by One: Facing the Holocaust.* New York: Simon and Schuster, 1990.

Mintz, Alan. *Hurban: Responses to Catastrophe in Hebrew Literature.* New York: Columbia University Press, 1984.

————. *Popular Culture and the Shaping of Holocaust Memory in America.* Seattle: University of Washington Press, 2001.

Mitchell, W. J. T. *Iconology: Image, Text, Ideology.* Chicago: University of Chicago Press, 1986.

Moore, Sally F., and Barbara G. Myerhoff, eds. *Secular Ritual.* Assen, Netherlands: Van Gorcum, 1977.

Morgan, Michael L. "Overcoming the Remoteness of the Past: Memory and Historiography in Modern Jewish Thought." *Judaism* 38, no. 2 (1989): 160–73.

Myerhoff, Barbara G. "Pilgrimage to Meron: Inner and Outer Peregrinations." In *Creativity/Anthropology,* edited by Smadar Lavie, Kirin Narayan, and Renato Rosaldo, 211–22. Ithaca: Cornell University Press, 1993.

————. "We Don't Wrap Herring in a Printed Page: Fusion, Fictions, and Continuity in Secular Ritual." In *Secular Ritual,* edited by Sally F. Moore and Barbara G. Myerhoff, 199–224. Assen, Netherlands: Van Gorcum, 1977.

Myers, David N. "Remembering *Zakhor:* A Super-Commentary." *History and Memory* 4, no. 2 (1992): 129–46.

Neusner, Jacob. "Map without Territory: Mishnah's System of Sacrifice and Sanctuary." In *Method and Meaning in Ancient Judaism.* Missoula, Mont.: Scholars Press, 1979.

Nora, Pierre. "Between Memory and History: *Les Lieux de mémoire.*" Translated by Marc Roudebush. *Memory and Counter-Memory,* edited by Natalie Zemon Davis and Randolph Starn. Special issue of *Representations,* no. 26 (1989): 7–25.

Norden, Edward. "Yes and No to the Holocaust Museums." *Commentary* 96, no. 2 (1993): 23–32.

Novick, Peter. *The Holocaust in American Life.* Boston: Houghton Mifflin, 1999.

Nutkiewicz, Michael. "Holocaust Museums: The Paradox of Sacred Spaces and Public Access." *Forum,* summer/autumn 1993, 18–20.

"On Kitsch: A Symposium." *Salmagundi,* nos. 85–86 (1990): 197–312.

Ophir, Adi. "On Sanctifying the Holocaust: An Anti-Theological Treatise." *Tikkun* 2, no. 1 (1987): 61–67.

O'Siadhail, Micheal. "Never." In *The Gossamer Wall: Poems in Witness to the Holocaust,* 120. St. Louis: Time Being Books, 2002.

Ozick, Cynthia. *The Messiah of Stockholm.* New York: Alfred A. Knopf, 1987.

Pagis, Dan. *Kol Hashirim: "Abba" (pirkei proza)* (Collected Poems and "Father" [prose passages]). Edited by Hanan Hever and T. Carmi. Jerusalem: Hakibbutz Hameuchad and the Bialik Institute, 1991.

————. *The Selected Poetry of Dan Pagis.* Translated by Stephen Mitchell. Berkeley: University of California Press, 1996.

Parr, Christopher, and Debra Parr. "An Afterword: Beyond Lamentation." In *Video Icons and Values,* edited by Alan M. Olson, Christopher Parr, and Debra Parr, 135–48. Albany: State University of New York Press, 1991.

Patraka, Vivian M. "Situating History and Difference: The Performance of the Term *Holocaust* in Public Discourse." In *Jews and Other Differences: The New Jewish Cultural Studies,* edited by Jonathan Boyarin and Daniel Boyarin, 54–78. Minneapolis: University of Minnesota Press, 1997.

————. *Spectacular Suffering: Theatre, Fascism, and the Holocaust.* Bloomington: Indiana University Press, 1999.

Prager, Emily. *Eve's Tattoo.* New York: Random House, 1991.

Reading, Anna. "Clicking on Hitler: The Virtual Holocaust @ Home." In *Visual Culture and the Holocaust,* edited by Barbie Zelizer, 323–39. New Brunswick: Rutgers University Press, 2001.

Reflections on the 1988/1990 March of the Living. Miami: Central Agency for Jewish Education and the National Operations Office of the March of the Living, 1991.

Rittner, Carol, and John K. Roth, eds. *Memory Offended: The Auschwitz Convent Controversy.* New York: Praeger, 1991.

Rogoff, Irit. "From Ruins to Debris: The Feminization of Fascism in German-History Museums." In *Museum Culture: Histories, Discourses, Spectacles,* edited by Daniel J. Sherman and Irit Rogoff, 223–49. Minneapolis: University of Minnesota Press, 1994.

Rosen, Jonathan. "The Trivialization of Tragedy." *Culturefront,* winter 1997, 80–85.

Rosenfeld, Alvin H. "The Americanization of the Holocaust." In *Thinking about the Holocaust: After Half a Century,* edited by Alvin H. Rosenfeld, 119–50. Bloomington: Indiana University Press, 1997.

———. *A Double Dying: Reflections on Holocaust Literature.* Bloomington: Indiana University Press, 1980.

Roskies, David G. *Against the Apocalypse: Responses to Catastrophe in Modern Jewish Culture.* Cambridge: Harvard University Press, 1984.

———. *The Jewish Search for a Usable Past.* Bloomington: Indiana University Press, 1999.

———. *Nightwords: A Midrash on the Holocaust.* Washington, D.C.: B'nai B'rith Hillel Foundation, 1971.

Rothberg, Michael. *Traumatic Realism: The Demands of Holocaust Representation.* Minneapolis: University of Minnesota Press, 2000.

Ryback, Timothy. "Evidence of Evil." *New Yorker,* November 15, 1993, 68–81.

Rymkiewicz, Jaroslaw M. *The Final Station: Umschlagplatz.* Translated by Nina Taylor. New York: Farrar, Straus and Giroux, 1994.

Scholem, Gershom. *The Messianic Idea in Judaism.* New York: Schocken, 1971.

Schulz, Bruno. *The Book of Idolatry.* Edited and introduction by Jerzy Ficowski. Translated by Bogna Piotrowska. Warsaw: Interpress, n.d.

———. *Sanatorium under the Sign of the Hourglass.* Translated by Celina Wieniewska. London: Penguin, 1979.

Segev, Tom. *The Seventh Million: The Israelis and the Holocaust.* Translated by Haim Watzman. New York: Hill and Wang, 1993.

Seidman, Naomi. "Elie Wiesel and the Scandal of Jewish Rage." *Jewish Social Studies* 3, no. 1 (1996): 1–19.

Sered, Susan Starr. "Rachel's Tomb and the Milk Grotto of the Virgin Mary: Two Women's Shrines in Bethlehem." *Journal of Feminist Studies in Religion* 2, no. 2 (1986): 7–22.

Shandler, Jeffrey. "'City of Jews, City of Gays': Amsterdam as an Impromptu Pilgrimage Site at the Tenth International Conference of Gay and Lesbian Jews (1987)." *Pilgrimage,* edited by Shifra Epstein. Special issue of *Jewish Folklore and Ethnology Review* 17, nos. 1–2 (1995): 47–52.

————. *While America Watches: Televising the Holocaust.* New York: Oxford University Press, 1999.

————. "While America Watches: Television and the Holocaust in the United States, from 1945 to the Present." Ph.D. diss., Columbia University, 1995.

Shavit, Yaakov. "Review of *Zakhor: Jewish History and Jewish Memory,*" *Studies in Zionism* 6, no. 1 (1985): 143–48.

Sheramy, Rona. "Defining Lessons: The Holocaust in American Jewish Education." Ph.D. diss., Brandeis University, 2001.

Sherman, Daniel J., and Irit Rogoff. "Introduction: Frameworks for Critical Analysis." In *Museum Culture: Histories, Discourses, Spectacles,* edited by Daniel J. Sherman and Irit Rogoff. Minneapolis: University of Minnesota Press, 1994.

————, eds. *Museum Culture: Histories, Discourses, Spectacles.* Minneapolis: University of Minnesota Press, 1994.

Shevelev, Raphael, with Karine Schomer. *Liberating the Ghosts: Photographs and Text from the March of the Living with Excerpts from the Writings of Participants.* Portland, Oreg.: LensWork Publishing, 1996.

"Shoah Foundation Embarks on New Mission." *Past Forward: The Newsletter of the Shoah Foundation,* winter 2001, 2–3.

Simon Wiesenthal Center. *Beit Hashoah·Museum of Tolerance* [exhibition catalogue]. Santa Barbara: Albion Publishing Group, 1993.

Smith, Jonathan Z. *To Take Place: Toward Theory in Ritual.* Chicago: University of Chicago Press, 1987.

Sokoloff, Naomi. "Reinventing Bruno Schulz: Cynthia Ozick's *The Messiah of Stockholm* and David Grossman's *See Under: Love.*" *AJS Review* 13, nos. 1–2 (1988): 171–99.

Spiegelman, Art. *Maus: A Survivor's Tale.* New York: Pantheon Books, 1986.

————. *Maus II: A Survivor's Tale: And Here My Troubles Began.* New York: Pantheon Books, 1991.

Spitzer, Leo. "Back through the Future: Nostalgic Memory and Critical Memory in a Refuge from Nazism." In *Acts of Memory: Cultural Recall in the Present,* edited by Mieke Bal, Jonathan Crewe, and Leo Spitzer, 87–104. Hanover: University Press of New England, 1999.

Steiner, George. "Our Homeland, the Text." *Salmagundi,* no. 66 (1985): 4–25.

Stier, Oren Baruch. "Framing the Witness: The Memorial Role of Holocaust Videotestimonies." In *Memory.* Vol. 3 of *Remembering for the Future: The Holocaust in an Age of Genocide,* edited by John K. Roth and Elisabeth Maxwell, 189–204. London: Palgrave, 2001.

————. "Lunch at Majdanek: The March of the Living as a Contemporary Pilgrimage of Memory." *Pilgrimage,* edited by Shifra Epstein. Special issue of *Jewish Folklore and Ethnology Review* 17, nos. 1–2 (1995): 57–66.

————. "Memory Matters: Reading Collective Memory in Contemporary Jewish Culture." *Prooftexts* 18, no. 1 (1998): 67–94.

————. "Virtual Memories: Mediating the Holocaust at the Simon Wiesenthal Center's Beit Hashoah-Museum of Tolerance." *Journal of the American Academy of Religion* 64, no. 4 (1996): 831–51.

Storper-Perez, Danielle, and Harvey Goldberg. "The Kotel: Toward an Ethnographic Portrait." *Religion* 24, no. 4 (1994): 309–32.

The Story of the Boxcar. Florida Holocaust Museum, St. Petersburg, n.d. Video-cassette.

Strassfeld, Michael. *The Jewish Holidays: A Guide and Commentary.* New York: Harper and Row, 1985.

Sturken, Marita. *Tangled Memories: The Vietnam War, the AIDS Epidemic, and the Politics of Remembering.* Berkeley: University of California Press, 1997.

Survivors of the Shoah Visual History Foundation. *The Last Days.* Introduction by David Cesarani. New York: St. Martin's Press, 1999.

Survivors: Testimonies of the Holocaust. Produced and directed by Stephanie Barish. Survivors of the Shoah Visual History Foundation, in association with Maxell-Corporation of America and Burda Media, 1998, CD-ROM.

Turan, Kenneth. "Viewing the Unthinkable." *Los Angeles Times,* December 12, 1993, L8–9.

Turner, Edith. "Bar Yohai, Mystic: The Creative Persona and His Pilgrimage." In *Creativity/Anthropology,* edited by Smadar Lavie, Kirin Narayan, and Renato Rosaldo. Ithaca: Cornell University Press, 1993.

Turner, Victor. "The Center Out There: Pilgrim's Goal." *History of Religions* 12, no. 3 (1973): 191–230.

Turner, Victor, and Edith Turner. *Image and Pilgrimage in Christian Culture: Anthropological Perspectives.* Oxford: Basil Blackwell, 1978.

van Alphen, Ernst. *Caught by History: Holocaust Effects in Contemporary Art, Literature, and Theory.* Stanford: Stanford University Press, 1997.

Webber, Jonathan. *The Future of Auschwitz: Some Personal Reflections.* Oxford: Oxford Centre for Postgraduate Hebrew Studies, 1992.

Weinberg, Jeshajahu, and Rina Elieli. *The Holocaust Museum in Washington.* New York: Rizzoli, 1995.

Weingrod, Alex. *The Saint of Beersheba.* Albany: State University of New York Press, 1990.

White, Hayden. *Tropics of Discourse: Essays in Cultural Criticism.* Baltimore: Johns Hopkins University Press, 1978.

Wiesel, Elie. *The Forgotten.* Translated by Stephen Becker. New York: Summit Books, 1992.

Witness: Voices from the Holocaust. Produced and directed by Joshua M. Greene and Shiva Kumar. Joshua M. Greene Productions, Inc. 1999. Videocassette.

Woocher, Jonathan S. "Sacred Survival: American Jewry's Civil Religion." *Judaism: A Quarterly Journal* 34, no. 2 (1985): 151–62.

———. *Sacred Survival: The Civil Religion of American Jews.* Bloomington: Indiana University Press, 1986.

Wyschogrod, Edith. "The Mind of a Critical Moralist—Steiner as a Jew." *New England Review* 15, no. 2 (1993): 168–88.

Yerushalmi, Yosef Hayim. *Zakhor: Jewish History and Jewish Memory.* Seattle: University of Washington Press, 1982; reprint, New York: Schocken, 1989.

Young, James E. *At Memory's Edge: After-Images of the Holocaust in Contemporary Art and Architecture.* New Haven: Yale University Press, 2000.

———. "The Counter-Monument: Memory against Itself in Germany Today." *Critical Inquiry* 18 (winter 1992): 267–96.

————. *The Texture of Memory: Holocaust Memorials and Meaning*. New Haven: Yale University Press, 1993.

————. *Writing and Rewriting the Holocaust: Narrative and the Consequences of Interpretation*. Bloomington: Indiana University Press, 1988.

————, ed. *The Art of Memory: Holocaust Memorials in History*. New York: Jewish Museum, 1994.

Zelizer, Barbie. *Remembering to Forget: Holocaust Memory through the Camera's Eye*. Chicago: University of Chicago Press, 1998.

————, ed. *Visual Culture and the Holocaust*. New Brunswick: Rutgers University Press, 2001.

Zerubavel, Yael. *Recovered Roots: Collective Memory and the Making of Israeli National Tradition*. Chicago: University of Chicago Press, 1995.

Index

OREN BARUCH STIER was born in Haifa, Israel, and grew up on Long Island, New York. He received his A.B. with honors from Princeton University in 1988 and his M.A. and Ph.D. from the University of California, Santa Barbara, in 1990 and 1996, respectively. Stier taught for three years at the University of Cape Town, South Africa, prior to his current position as assistant professor of religious studies at Florida International University, where he also serves as associate director of the university's Judaic Studies Program. Stier is a recipient of a Center for Advanced Holocaust Studies fellowship at the United States Holocaust Memorial Museum in Washington, D.C. He and his wife Danielle live in Miami Beach.

CPSIA information can be obtained at www.ICGtesting.com
Printed in the USA
LVOW132301150313

324549LV00001B/96/P